Created and Directed by Hans Höfer

P9-CKG-334

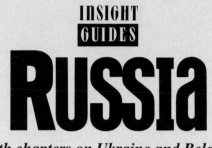

INSIGHT GUIDES
RUSSIA

with chapters on Ukraine and Belarus

Edited by Anna Benn
Managing Editor: Dorothy Stannard

Editorial Director: Brian Bell

HOUGHTON MIFFLIN COMPANY

APA PUBLICATIONS

Russia

First Edition
© **1994 APA PUBLICATIONS (HK) LTD**
All Rights Reserved
Printed In Singapore by Höfer Press Pte Ltd

Distributed in the United States by:	Distributed in Canada by:	Distributed in the UK & Ireland by:	Worldwide distribution enquiries:
Houghton Mifflin Company	**Thomas Allen & Son**	**GeoCenter International UK Ltd**	**Höfer Communications Pte Ltd**
222 Berkeley Street	390 Steelcase Road East	The Viables Center, Harrow Way	38 Joo Koon Road
Boston, Massachusetts 02116-3764	Markham, Ontario L3R 1G2	Basingstoke, Hampshire RG22 4BJ	Singapore 2262
ISBN: 0-395-66167-6	ISBN: 0-395-66167-6	ISBN: 9-62421-183-3	ISBN: 9-62421-183-3

ABOUT THIS BOOK

The dismantling of the Berlin Wall was the dramatic beginning of the break-up of the old Soviet Union. As Russia shed its republics and emerged reborn to face a vastly different future with a mixture of boldness and trepidation, Insight Guides set about replacing its mould-breaking *Insight Guide: USSR* with a brand-new title, *Insight Guide: Russia*.

The project was masterminded in Insight Guides' London editorial office by editorial director **Brian Bell** and managing editor **Dorothy Stannard**. They quickly enlisted as project editor **Anna Benn**, who had just written *Insight Pocket Guide: St Petersburg*. Benn, an English writer and editor, had made her first trip to Russia in 1982 as a student at the University of Leningrad; by the early 1990s she had become fluent in Russian and was dividing her time between England and the renamed St Petersburg, witnessing Russia's hesitant progress from Communism to democracy. Travelling extensively throughout the country, she continued to be bowled over by Russia's sheer size and by its unrealised potential for travel.

The Writing Team

Benn's first task was to decide how much of *Insight Guide: USSR* could be retained in the new book. That title, edited in 1990 by **Wilhelm Klein**, had broken new ground by using a team of local writers and photographers, under the guidance of the celebrated poet **Yevgeny Yevtushenko**, to convey the essence of their country to the outside world. The same team was behind *Insight Cityguide: Moscow* and *Insight Cityguide: St Petersburg*.

It quickly became apparent, however, that to capture the spirit of the new Russia, many new talents would need to be recruited. An early decision was to commission chapters on Ukraine and Belarus ("Little Russia" and "White Russia"), which are included on many visitors' itineraries.

Rowlinson Carter, author of *Insight Guide: Eastern Europe* and currently writing a history of the world, brought Russia's history and people vividly to life. Carter is a widely-travelled journalist, documentary-maker and historian who has the rare ability to turn the dates and events of history into stories about people. Carter also tackled features on Russian literature and religion, both experiencing a revival thanks to the new political climate.

Ann Imse, an American who had been an Associated Press correspondent in Moscow during the dramatic break-up of the Soviet Union, took up the story by charting the era of perestroika and glasnost, examining how Russians are adapting to the turbulent changes. "Before Gorbachev, many Russians were afraid to be seen with foreigners – and with good reason," she says. "But by 1988 they were willing to talk to reporters, giving not only their opinions but their names. It was an exhilarating time."

With her in Russia was her husband, photographer **Robert Tonsing**, whose pictures were printed all over the world – particularly at one point in 1988 when he was the only Western photographer in Moscow. Many of his best shots now enhance this book.

Ivan Samarine, an expert with Sotheby's Russian department in London, was signed up to write about the great artists and artworks, in particular icon painting. His specialist knowledge and enthusiasm for Russian art

Benn

Stannard

Carter

Imse

Samarine

stem from his extensive travels in the country. **Rosamund Bartlett**, a specialist on Russian literature and music who teaches Russian literature at the University of Michigan, tackled the equally rich subject of Russian music. In 1989 she helped set up Vladimir Ashkenazy's tour to Moscow with the Royal Philharmonic orchestra and was location manager for the televised broadcast of their concerts.

In Russia, the help of **Elena Zelinskaya** at the Severo Zapad agency was invaluable. Severo Zapad (North-West) was the first privately-run news agency in St Petersburg. During the abortive 1991 coup by the old guard, it was through this agency's sophisticated technological equipment that communications remained open and people knew what was happening in the city.

Another contributor is one of Russia's most important feminist leaders, **Olga Lipovskaya**. Lipovskaya has written articles on feminism for many journals in the West, and frequently travels and lectures outside Russia. Recently she set up the St Petersburg Women's Foundation.

Valera Katsuba, a freelance journalist, has his finger on the pulse of the popular culture of new Russia that has emerged from the Underground movements. He has written for Western publications and worked on many films and documentaries with Western film crews, including the film *Orlando*.

Catherine Phillips, who lives in St Petersburg, has taken extensive trips into the European North of Russia, a region she covered for this guide. **Vladislav Govorukhin**, a key contributor to *Insight Guide: USSR*, introduced the Russian journalists **Natalia Kardashenko** (author of "Along the Volga") and **Vladimir Brodetsky** (author of "The European South"). Three professional journalists at the *Moscow Times* took on the rest of the country. In between covering the dramatic political events for their newspaper, **Michael Hetzer** turned his attention as far afield as Siberia, **Adam Tanner** tackled the Urals, and **Joanne Levine** contributed to the chapter on the Ukraine, along with **Albert Lantuch**. The freelance journalist **Anne Lavelle**, a collaborator on *Insight Pocket Guide: Moscow*, wrote the chapter on Moscow, a city she has lived in for several years.

The Photographers

Like all Insight Guides, this book owes much to its superb photography. The images come from many sources, but most particularly from photographers **David Kampfner**, **Jimmy Holmes**, and **Tony Perrottet.** Britain's **Anglia Survival Series** travelled extensively throughout Russia for their television programmes and some of their incredible wildlife pictures – many taken by Russian photographers – are reproduced here.

The slides of **Anatoly Siyagin** and **Georgy Guryanov**, taken a week or so before the book went to press, reached Insight's offices in London by the kind hands of friends travelling to and from St Petersburg. The pictures of artists **Sergei (Africa) Bugayev** and **Andrei Khlobystin** are reproduced by courtesy of **Paul Judelson** in New York.

Special thanks go to **Katya Galitzine** and to **Xa Sturgis** who have helped with this book in all sorts of ways. **Karen Johnson**, who lives in Moscow, also provided helpful advice, as did the **Great-Britain Russia Association** in London. **John Goulding** completed the proof-reading and indexing.

Bartlett

Lipovskaya

Govorukhin

Lavelle

History

Features

Places

Maps

TRAVEL TIPS

**For detailed information
see page 313**

THE RIDDLE OF RUSSIA

Russia cannot be understood
With the mind,
Nor can she be measured
By a common yardstick
A special character she has:
In Russia one can only have faith.
　—Fedor Tiuchev, 19th-century poet

Such understanding has never come easily. "Russia is impenetrable," wrote the American historian Henry Adams in 1895, "and any intelligent man will deal with her better, the less closely he knows her." Sir Winston Churchill, trying to predict Russia's behaviour in 1939, coined the masterly description: "a riddle wrapped in a mystery inside an enigma." And one American ambassador to Moscow claimed there were no experts on the country, "only varying degrees of ignorance."

Such mystery always fascinates, of course, and, since the raising of the Iron Curtain at the end of the 1980s, plane-loads of curious tourists have poured into Russia, many of them venturing beyond the cities of St Petersburg and Moscow to find out what provincial and rural Russia is like. Just as Russians are discovering that foreigners are not, in the words of the poet Yevgeny Yevtushenko, "all spies with cameras in their buttons, radio transmitters in the heels of their shoes, and pockets full of Colorado beetles," so Westerners are having their own preconceived ideas overturned. Siberia, for example, is shedding its *Gulag Archipelago* image and revealing itself as a stunningly beautiful and diverse land so vast that a pocket of Old Believers stumbled upon in the 1980s were unaware of the fall of the tsar.

Meanwhile, Russia's pre-Revolution culture has been emerging from cold storage. Religion is resuming its central role in society, and art, music and literature are rediscovering their pre- and immediate post-Revolutionary vigour. Added to these is the explosive energy of Russia's "New Culture", in which young Muscovites and St Petersburgers are experimenting with brand-new modes of expression – and not all of them copied from the West.

This book divides into two parts: Russia (the lion's share) and, at the end, Belarus and the Ukraine. Although no longer part of the Commonwealth of Independent States, they are included because many tours to Russia still cross the political boundaries, and Kiev and Minsk, the capitals of the Ukraine and Belarus respectively, remain major tourist destinations.

Preceding pages: the Space Obelisk, Moscow; Russian girl; the Kuzma Minin and Dmitry Pozharsky monument in front of St Basil's, Moscow; ceiling panel from Moscow metro station; medals and memories; caviar is good for you. <u>Left</u>, resident of Kostroma, in Russia's Golden Ring.

The 9th-century Viking conquest of hitherto stateless Slavs scattered across modern Russia, Ukraine and Belarus was traditionally made to sound like an act of high-minded charity. "Our land is great and rich but there is no order in it," the Slavs are reputed to have cried. "Come and rule over us." Prince Rurik of South Jutland in Denmark was ready to oblige. He made himself master of Novgorod, the most northwesterly Slav settlement, and within three years of his death in 879 his successors, who came to be known as Varangians, had extended their rule to include Smolensk and Kiev.

The invitation – such as it was – fitted in perfectly with the Varangian desire to monopolise the lucrative trade route between the Baltic and the Black Sea, which happened to pass through the allegedly rich but disorderly land in question. The main artery of this largely river-borne trade was the Dnieper river, and of the settlements which the Varangians deigned to rule over, Kiev was the most valuable strategically. It was accordingly declared "the Mother of Russian cities".

Kiev was only one, but by far the grandest, in a network of embryonic city-states which various Varangian princes established and fought over among themselves. The estate of Yuri Dolgoruky of Suzdal was the beginning of Moscow while Prince of Polotsk's settlement farther west on the Dvina river was the nucleus of Belarus.

It was not until the Mongol invasions of the 13th century that the focus of Russia moved from Kiev to the north. Viewed from the forests, the depopulated area around Kiev was seen as "Ukraine", meaning the borderland. Ukraine was also referred to as "Black" land because of its dark rich soil, but it was common land on which the semi-nomadic population had the right to roam on payment of a kind of licence fee to the ruling prince, and "Black" became synonomous with these property rights. "White Russia", on the other hand – the translation of "Belarus" – drew

attention to the fact that the territory was not common land but subject to the feudal tenure which applied while it was, as we shall see, under Polish administration. The people living on it were tied serfs.

Three Russias therefore came about, even if the dividing lines were historically and geographically fluid: Great Russia, born of Muscovy and these days simply Russia; Ukraine, which picked up yet another name, Little Russia; and White Russia (Belarus).

Cultural melting pot: To begin with there

were no ethnic or cultural divisions. Migration across the northern plain from Central Asia into Europe had long been taking place before the founding of Kievan Rus by the Rurikid dynasty. The Slavs who supposedly invited the Vikings to come and rule over them were relatively recent arrivals, mostly 5th and 6th century, who spoke kindred Slavonic languages.

They followed in the wake of Finno-Ugrians who ended up in Finland and Estonia, Indo-Europeans who became Lithuanians and Latvians, and a whole host of Germanic tribes who, one way or another, became not only Germans but French and

Preceding pages: Moscow during the Time of Troubles. **Left**, ancient hero of Rus. **Right**, Rurik, the legendary Viking.

Anglo-Saxon English, which helps to explain why even into the 20th century Russians were inclined to dismiss all non-Slavic Europeans as "Germans".

There was undoubtedly a high degree of fusion between the newly arrived Slavs and earlier inhabitants. The Lithuanians were spread widely across the plains and the forests until, under pressure from the Slavs, they retreated to the marshy Baltic shores. The high cheekbones, darkish complexion and broad nose which are typical of the Great Russian are attributed to the Finno-Ugrians, obviously a far cry from notions of fair-haired, blue-eyed Scandinavians, a different group altogether.

The Varangians did fit the Scandinavian model, but they were only a military elite and it was a case common throughout history of conquerors being completely assimilated by the numerically superior conquered. It is unrealistic to think of the Varangians as being anything other than *bona fide* Slavs quite soon after their conquest.

Cultural comparisons between modern Russians and the tribes who roamed the northern plain long before the Slavs are irresistible. Russians cheerfully admit to being a trifle xenophobic and, according to Herodotus, the Scythians, who inhabited the steppes in the 5th century BC, had "an extreme hatred of all foreign customs". Herodotus was sceptical about Scythian descriptions of people living even farther north. According to them, they had goats' feet, could turn themselves into wolves if the occasion arose, and slept for six months at a time like hibernating animals. He did not doubt, however, that the northern winters were so cold that the inhabitants could drive wagons across frozen rivers and lakes and if necessary make war on them. "The ground is frozen iron-hard, so that to turn earth into mud requires not water but fire."

The Empire moves east: The Scythians eventually had to make room for new migrants arriving from Central Asia, and it was the overflow of these northern tribes – notably Huns, Goths, Visigoths and Vandals – across the Danube that spelt the end of the Roman Empire in the West. With repeated sackings of Rome, the Empire was moved from west to east, specifically to the ancient Greek colony of Byzantium nicely positioned at the narrow Bosphorus crossing to control what was becoming the greatest trade route in the world, the one between Europe and the East.

The Mediterranean provided the obvious connection between Byzantium and Western Europe, but it was plagued by pirates. In any case, Northern Europe had something special to offer the markets of Byzantium: amber from the Baltic shore, furs and honey from the Russian forests and fair-skinned slaves, in many cases males who were castrated by their suppliers in readiness for eunuch service in Eastern harems. It was this trade via the Dnieper and to some extent the Volga that attracted the Varangians. By the time the Slavs had settled along the Dnieper, the transplanted Roman Empire had made Constantinople, the Christianised capital of the East, the richest and most glamorous city on earth, Greek in flavour rather than Roman. Rome was degenerating into a run-down dump on a dirty river.

The Slavs arrived at the tail-end of the transition from Rome to Constantinople. They drifted in different directions on reaching Europe and later assumed regional characteristics on either side of considerable natural boundaries like the Carpathian mountains, or because they were split by alien invaders like the Finno-Ugrian Magyars, the founders of Hungary. The Slavs in the Balkans came to be recognised as Southern

Slavs, or "Yugoslavs", while those in the West took on the national identities of Poles, Czechs and Slovaks. The future Great, Little and White Russians were lumped together as Eastern Slavs. The first split in the homogeneity of the Eastern Slavs was between those who elected to remain on the steppes, which were reminiscent of the grasslands they had left behind in Central Asia, and those who ventured into the northern forests. The plain-dwellers grew rye and barley and kept a few cattle on the side.

The main drawback to living on the plain was exposure to new and invariably hostile migrants arriving from Asia. The forests, on the other hand, were relatively safe. What's

was so impressed that she defied powerful pagan traditions to be baptised as an Eastern Orthodox Christian. This was a most portentous development. The Christian world was then torn by a contest between the Eastern and Western Churches for converts among the still substantial heathen hordes of Europe, the forces of Rome being led by the German-dominated Holy Roman Empire founded by Charlemagne in 800. The Western Church was then doing well, having won over the the kings of Poland and Norway among others. The most notable Orthodox success had been with the formidable Bulgarian Empire.

Princess Olga tried to persuade her son

more, the natural products of the forest, notably furs, honey and wax, were so plentiful that the forest-dwellers generally had surpluses available for trade.

Sailing to Byzantium: It was their surplus wealth which the Vikings needed to trade with Constantinople. Every spring a flotilla would sail down the Dnieper with its cargo of furs, honey and luckless slaves in order to return with gold, silk, wines and spices. In 957 Princess Olga of Kiev joined the convoy to see the fabled sights of Constantinople and

Left, Finno-Ugrian tribeswoman. **Above**, Vladimir the Saint.

Svyatoslav to follow her example but he was more interested in a military campaign which in due course added the Volga region to Kievan Rus. The question of the religious allegiance of the Eastern Slavs was passed on to his successor, Prince Vladimir, and he was not to be rushed either. Vladimir wished to hear not only from advocates of Byzantium and Rome but also those of Islam and Judaism. They were invited to state their cases, the lead being given to the Jewish representatives. Both they and the Muslims who followed made a poor impression by mentioning circumcision and abstention from pork. The Muslims put themselves right out of contention by going on to say that their religion banned alcohol.

The Pope's emissaries were able to guarantee flexibility on the issues of circumcision, pork and alcohol, but they were obliged to add that a certain amount of fasting was required of the faithful to further the glory of God. Vladimir's response to the prospect of fasting was swift and unambiguous: "Depart hence!" Forewarned, the Byzantine Greeks launched into a history of the world from the beginning of time, saving till last a painting which showed in terrifying detail just what an infidel could expect come the Day of Judgement. Vladimir was unsettled by this revelation, but nevertheless reserved final

judgement until emissaries could visit Constantinople and confirm that joining the Eastern Church would bring material benefits. They returned to say that the city was so magnificent they had wondered whether they were in heaven.

Vladimir's alignment with Byzantium was formalised by his baptism at Kherson in 990 and cemented by marriage to Anna, the Byzantine Emperor's sister. This illustrious marriage brought up a point of principle which had so far been overlooked. Vladimir was already married several times over and had a harem packed with hundreds of women and he had no intention of giving up any of them.

The Orthodox authorities and his brother-in-law quietly conceded the point. Vladimir was truly, says the chronicle recounting these events, a "fornicator *immensus et crudelis*".

Kiev's rise and fall: Kiev acquired a cathedral, named after and modelled on St Sophia's in Constantinople, and numerous churches. It was more emphatically than ever the outstanding Russian city of the age, but not for long. The eastern Mediterranean, long closed to traders by pirates and the Arabs who had taken over the Levant, was reopened by the success of the early Crusades. The sea route to northern Europe through the Strait of Gibraltar was longer, but it could take ships of any size and eliminated porterage. The value of the Dnieper route dwindled and so did Kiev's profits from it.

The Varangian princes were inclined to move north. Prince Yuri Dolgoruky, founder of Moscow, managed to acquire Kiev as well only to be told it had become virtually worthless. "Here, father, we have nothing," his son said, "let us depart to Suzdal while it is still warm." The same son in due course inherited Sudzal, and in 1169 he proved his own point by sacking Kiev and casually tossing the princedom that went with it to a younger brother.

In both trade and religion, Russia's orientation had been towards Constantinople, but in 1204 the Fourth Crusade abandoned its avowed purpose of fighting the infidel Turk in the Holy Land in order to ransack Constantinople and put a hostile "Latin Emperor" on the throne of Byzantium. Baldwin, the emperor in question, was not long in office, but the reprieve became meaningless in the light of what was developing unseen thousands of miles away. While Alexander Nevsky ("of the Neva") defended Russia's western borders from attack from Sweden and the Teutonic Order of Knights, a very different threat was gathering force in the east, where Temuchin Bagatur, the chief of a Mongol tribe, had conquered China in the space of nine years, a victory which prompted him to assume the more imposing name of Genghis Khan, "Ruler of the World". He meant to make that boast good by finding out what lay west of the Ural mountains and conquering it as well.

Left, Prince Yuri Dolgoruky. Right, Alexander Nevsky defeats the Swedes.

THE MONGOL YOKE

Genghis Khan was frank about his ambition to conquer the world. "The greatest pleasure," he said, "is to vanquish your enemies and chase them before you, to rob them of their wealth and see those dear to them bathed in tears, to ride their horses and clasp to your bosom their wives and daughters."

Such sentiments no doubt assisted the Mongols (or Tartars) and everything about them towards their place in the blackest pages of European and especially Russian history; and the Russians were presumed to have been indelibly tainted by the 250 years they subsequently spent under the "Mongol yoke". Russian attempts to join the mainstream of Western civilisation in the centuries ahead were invariably rebuffed with taunts like "Scratch a Russian and you'll catch a Tartar", and even Stalin's 20th-century atrocities were blamed on atavistic Tartar tendencies.

In military respects, at least, the Tartars were more advanced than their European contemporaries, not excluding the Crusader knights. They were unfazed by the Russian winters and in fact preferred to campaign when the rivers were frozen and provided a relatively hard surface for their ponies, which were trained to dig through snow to find grass. Every Mongol was mounted and kept two or three ponies in tow, which gave them remarkable speed and endurance.

They never went into a prepared battle without first erecting dressing stations, and soldiers wore next to their skin a special undershirt of raw silk which sank in under the impact of an arrow, enabling the arrow to be drawn out without aggravating the wound. Their small, double-curved composite bows had a range far longer than the celebrated English long-bows used at Crécy, and could be fired from the saddle at a gallop.

Intelligence gathering: The death of three Russian princes and 80,000 of their men at the Kalka river notwithstanding, the Mongols' first invasion of Russia in 1223 was merely a reconnaissance in which they refrained from laying sieges or committing

Left, the Mongols acquired a reputation for being bloodthirsty. Right, Genghis Khan.

themselves to protracted actions. It was more important that the Chinese mandarins travelling with them were able to plot maps and gather intelligence for a subsequent invasion. If anyone wondered why on earth the Mongols collected scarce Bibles and religious tracts, the answer was given on their return visit, by which time printers had made hundreds of copies which were sold from the baggage train at bargain prices.

On Genghis Khan's death in 1227, his empire was divided among numerous heirs,

and it was his grandson Batu Khan who emerged as the strong-man in charge of the second invasion in 1236. The Volga Bulgars and their magnificent capital, called Bulgar, were the first to fall to a Mongol army of 120,000. Riazan, a small vassal state of Suzdal, was the next objective. Suspecting nothing untoward, the princes of Riazan were tickled pink when three strangers in exotic costume, one a woman, rode up to the city wall and demanded one-tenth of their wealth there and then. They were apparently still chuckling at the presumption when the army trotted into view. The population of Riazan, the princes and their families included, were flayed alive, although a few were allowed to escape specifically to broadcast the fact that the Mongols were back.

Moscow and Sudzal were razed before it was Vladimir's turn. The royal family were given just enough warning to hide in the choir loft of a cathedral packed with citizens trusting that consecrated walls would provide sanctuary. In the event, the cathedral was put to the torch, roasting the royals and bringing the roof down on the huddled refugees. Among the losses was a precious icon of the Madonna credited with numerous miracles. Novgorod was next on the Mongol list but it was saved because of an unseasonal thaw which deprived the Mongols of their

"roads". Rather than be stuck in a quagmire, Batu Khan turned on his heel and let Novgorod off the hook.

The main Mongol force spent the summer in western Ukraine. In November they resumed the offensive with a devastating attack on Kiev. Only St Sophia's Cathedral and 200 houses were left standing. A visitor to the scene five years later reported that the streets were still a sea of skulls and bones.

During the winter of 1240–41, the Mongols conquered most of Hungary, Romania and Poland and it seemed that nothing could stop them. But just as it looked as if the whole of Europe was in peril, Batu Khan learned that his Uncle Ogedei had died in Karakorum, the Mongol capital. He had been driven to drink by his wife Toregene's flagrant affair with a Persian slave-girl named Fatima. So besotted was she with Fatima that the girl had been able to pack the Imperial Household with her unsavoury friends. Batu Khan decided that in the circumstances he had better get back to Karakorum fast, thus bringing to a premature end a campaign which had already netted everything between the Ural and Carpathian mountains. He left his unfinished empire in the charge of officers and a modest force of Turkoman conscripts whose base, Sarai ("Encampment"), was near the site of Volgograd or, as it was in World War II, Stalingrad. This particular Mongol detachment was known as the Golden Horde.

The rise of Moscow: The "Mongol yoke" imposed on Russia for the next 250 years was concentrated on what is sometimes called the Russian mesopotamia, which is to say Moscow and the "Golden Ring" of cities between the Oka and Volga rivers. No one in the West had the faintest idea of what happened under the Mongol yoke. The European links had been with Kiev, notably the stream of nubile princesses, and for all practical purposes Kiev had ceased to exist. The only part of Russia of which there was any real knowledge was the northwest, where cities like Novgorod and Pskov, lying beyond the Mongol orbit, retained links with the Baltic region.

We now know that as long as the Russian principalities paid their annual tribute to the Golden Horde at Sarai they were left very largely to their own devices. There seems to have been a measure of mingling and even inter-marriage among members of the ruling classes, and indeed Boris Godunov, elected tsar more than a century after the lifting of the Mongol yoke, was of Tartar stock. Moscow, or Muscovy, seems to have enjoyed a special status, and in 1328 the Muscovite Prince Ivan Kalita was put in charge of collecting the tribute and delivering it to the Golden Horde, a responsibility which earned him the nickname "Moneybags". Curiously, Moscow's annual tribute was only 4,000 roubles compared with Vladimir's 85,000 roubles. Moscow was also made the seat of the Orthodox Metropolitan, an ecclesiastical rank comparable with cardinal in the Roman Church, and a clear indication that Eastern

Orthodoxy had made an unimpeded transition from Kievan Rus to the north.

Only once did a Prince of Moscow raise his hand against the Tartars, and that was Grand Prince Dmitri, grandson of "Moneybags", in 1380. His army was routed and Moscow sacked. "It was terrible and pitiful to see Christian corpses lying like stooks of hay by the banks of the great Don," wrote a chronicler. "And for three days the River Don flowed blood." This episode apart, the greatest threat to Moscow came from the West, where the Teutonic Order of Knights were expanding from their base in Prussia and the Lithuanians had emerged as a very considerable military force which skirted

also unwilling to pay, Khan Ahmed felt that sterner measures were called for. The Muscovite and Tartar armies squared up at the confluence of the Oka and Ugra rivers in 1480, but neither side was anxious to fire the first shot. Khan Ahmed intimated that he would listen to an offer to pay off the arrears in instalments, although it transpired that he was actually buying time because reinforcements promised by Poland, as alarmed as he was by Muscovy's growing strength, had not yet materialised. For his part, Ivan was worried at the news that two of his brothers had gone over to the Poles and Lithuanians with their armies.

The battle was never fought. When Khan

around the Mongol yoke in order to build an empire which stretched to the Black Sea. In 1370 the Lithuanians laid siege to Moscow but were unable to scale the recently improved walls of the Kremlin. The Mongols arrived from Sarai in time to teach the Lithuanians a salutory lesson.

Although Muscovy's annual tribute was trifling, Basil the Blind decided it was still too much and from 1452 refused to pay. When his son Ivan III indicated that he was

Ahmed decided that the Poles were not coming, he turned for Sarai. He never got there. Possibly tipped off by Ivan that Ahmed had a mountain of treasure in his luggage train, the rival Khan Ivak crept into Ahmed's tent during an overnight stop and strangled him. Ahmed's two sons and possible heirs were soon afterwards killed in battle with the Crimean Tartars and the Golden Horde simply petered out. It was at roughly this point, just as Christopher Columbus was planning his voyage across the Atlantic, that one or two Western ambassadors were despatched to find out what had been going on in Russia over the previous 250 years.

Left, a 16th-century miniature depicting combat between Russians and Tartars in 1238. **Above**, a Tartar encampment.

A wandering German knight ventured into Muscovy some six years after Khan Ahmed had meekly brought 250 years of Mongol overlordship to an end and he captivated the Holy Roman Emperor Frederick III with what he learned. The title which anyone addressing the Grand Prince of Muscovy was required to know by heart was a measure of recent military successes. He was "Ivan, by the grace of God, Sovereign of all Russ, and grand prince of Vladimir and of Moscow and of Novgorod and of Pskov and of Tver and of Yugria and of Viatka and of Perm and of Bolgary and of others".

Frederick was impressed and sent word that as Holy Roman Emperor he was prepared to bestow on Ivan the title of king. "We have been sovereign in our land from our earliest forefathers," came the reply, "and our sovereignty we hold from God." It seems that Ivan was not as disdainful of titles as this reply implied because soon afterwards he commissioned an investigation into his family tree and was gratified to be advised, albeit without a shred of truth, that he was descended from a certain Prus, an obscure but nevertheless blood brother of the Roman Emperor Augustus. This was more to Ivan's liking, and thereafter he signed himself "Tsar", a derivation of "Caesar".

Reports of Italian architects and engineers engaged in strengthening Moscow's defences and building a number of churches and cathedrals aroused more curiosity than did a proposal then being hawked around the courts of Western Europe by Christopher Columbus. In 1517 the Emperor sent Sigismund von Herberstein on the first of two fact-finding missions. His reports caused a sensation. A book based on them was published in 1549 and ran to 18 editions in several languages, although not in English.

Four years after the book's publication but unaware of its existence, Sir Richard Chancellor, an English seaman, was looking for a northern sea route to China when storms forced him to land near Archangel in the White Sea. Local fishermen, terrified at first

by the "strange greatness" of his ship, informed him that he had wandered into the realm of Ivan Vassilievtch. Chancellor made arrangements to travel inland with a view to meeting this king, a journey which he described as colder and more uncomfortable than anything he had ever experienced at sea. Russia, he observed, was "a very large and spacious country, every way bounded with divers nations". It was only after "much ado" tht he came to Moscow, "the chief city of the kingdom and the seat of the king".

The 12 days he spent waiting for an audience were an eye-opener. Moscow was larger than London, he decided, but "rude and without order". The nine churches in the Kremlin were "not altogether unhandsome" but he did not think the royal palace compared with "the beauty and elegance of the houses of the kings of England". The king, he learned, commanded an army of more than 200,000 mounted archers, and what he heard about the system of government sounded like tyranny. There was evidently nothing to prevent the king from seizing private property if he felt like it, and the legal system began and ended with extracting con-

Left, the crowning of Mikhail Romanov. **Right**, Ivan III.

fession of crimes through torture. In the circumstances, sentences were lenient. Convicted persons, whatever the offence, were hanged only for a third offence.

Chancellor was dazed by the splendour of the court when at last he got to see it. A hundred courtiers were dressed in gold down to their ankles. The king himself was not only dressed in gold but had a gold crown on his head and a gold sceptre inlaid with precious stones. All the tableware at the state banquet he attended was gold. He dined on roast swan and other dishes accompanied by copious quantities of mead which had to be drained to the last drop. Ivan, who turned out to be Ivan IV rather than Ivan III whom the

wandering German knight had met, was clearly impressed by what Chancellor told him of England, so much so that he decided there and then that he wished to marry the English queen, the redoubtable Elizabeth I. Chancellor secured a favourable trade agreement for English merchants and said he would forward the proposal.

Ivan the Terrible: Chancellor's suspicions of tyranny at work were well-founded because Ivan IV came to be known in his own lifetime as "Ivan the Terrible". Despotism was in the nature of the tsars from the start. While a European monarch was generally just one among many powerful nobles who,

if they got together, could easily depose him, the tsars ruled in the tradition of the Mongol Great Khans. They held all the reins, secular and religious, in their own hands, and their survival depended on it.

Ivan IV succeeded to the throne when he was only three, and he owed his early survival to the clever machinations of his mother and regent, the Polish Princess Helen Glinskaya. She was eventually poisoned by the lesser nobles, or boyars, when she could no longer keep them at bay. Instead of murdering the young tsar at the same time, it suited the boyars to let him be and in the meantime do as they pleased. Ivan continued to live in the palace, but the boyars used it as a kind of playground, brawling in what was supposed to be his private apartment and helping themselves to anything in the palace that caught their fancy, Ivan's toys included.

These experiences evidently planted in Ivan an implacable desire for revenge, but to begin with he joined lustily in the unbridled licence of palace life. He lost his virginity at 13 and is reputed to have rollicked in the company of several hundred women before his 16th birthday, when it was thought he ought to get married. He chose Anastasia, a member of the Romanov family.

Ivan's foreign policy was to mop up the remaining fragments of the Mongol Empire. He conquered the Kazan khanate on the Upper Volga, a victory he celebrated by building St Basil's cathedral in Moscow. The capture of Astrakhan four years later made him master of the whole Volga from Moscow to the Caspian. These victories opened the way to the conquest and colonisation of Siberia, a task entrusted to the Stroganov family of merchant-adventurers with protection provided by the Cossack hero Yermak and his men.

With the Stroganovs energetically at work, Ivan looked west towards the Baltic, especially as the Turkish conquest of Constantinople in 1453 had made the Varangian trade routes down the Dnieper and Volga redundant. Ivan's Baltic ambitions ran into stiff opposition. The Teutonic Order of Knights had dug themselves into Estonia and were in possession of Narva, the port which was Russia's most obvious Baltic outlet. Moreover, neither Denmark nor Sweden were inclined to sit back and let the Russians encroach, and farther south Poland and

Lithuania had united to become a powerful imperial force.

If military setbacks in the Baltic unsettled Ivan's mind, he seemed to lose it completely on the death of Anastasia, which he put down to boyars and poison, the same combination which had killed his mother. He immediately demanded of the government, such as it was, the right to ban, execute or dispossess his subjects, especially boyars, entirely at his own discretion. On the very day these powers were granted, he showed that he meant business by having one eminent boyar impaled on a stake and a further six beheaded. He decided that while he was at it he wanted a number of judges skinned alive. "If they

Ivan "nationalised" boyars' estates, he had his *pomeshchiki* standing by like apparatchiks to take over the running of them. He ensured that the *pomeshchiki* had the labour they needed by nailing the peasants to the land, the cornerstone of Russian serfdom. Peasants who risked the death penalty by running away often headed south to the steppes where they joined the growing number of footloose adventurers, outlaws and fugitive slaves who together constituted the Cossacks.

The worst single example of Ivan's terror was the result of his conviction that Novgorod was seething with treachery. In 1570 he sentenced the entire population to death and more than 60,000 inhabitants were killed in

grow new skins," he quipped, "their fault shall be forgiven them."

The mechanics of Ivan's mounting atrocities from then on set a precedent for many of his successors up to and including Stalin. The Oprichnina he established were the original intelligence-cum-enforcement agency answerable only to the tsar, although in Ivan's time its members were far from invisible. They wore black, rode black horses and used as their symbol a severed dog's head. When

Left, Ivan the Terrible. **Above left**, Tsar Boris Godunov, plagued by Russia's Time of Troubles. **Above right**, the fake Dmitry.

the space of five weeks. The terrified Archbishop of Novgorod invited Ivan to dinner hoping to negotiate a truce. During the meal, and while Ivan's men were carrying out orders to loot St Sophia's Church, Ivan broke the news to the archbishop that his ecclesiastical career was over. For a start, he was to be married at once – to a horse. He would then earn his living as a bagpiper with a dancing bear. "Since he had never learned to play," a sympathetic report notes, "it may well be imagined how the music sounded."

While Russia braced itself for Ivan's next brainwave, he dropped dead. Sir Jerome Horsey, the agent of the English-run Muscovy

Company, was on the spot to record the manner of his passing. "The Emperor began grievously to swell in his cods," he wrote, "with which he had most horribly offended above 50 years together, boasting of a thousand virgins he had deflowered and thousands of children of his begetting destroyed." He choked to death while playing chess according to his own set of rules. These eliminated the king from the board – so that the king could never be checked.

Sir Jerome was by no means confident that Ivan's death meant the problems were over. The heir was his second son Fyodor, an idiot. What followed was Russia's "Time of Troubles". Fyodor's regent and successor as tsar was Boris Godunov, and the final act of Moussorgsky's opera of that name, with the stage knee-deep in the dying and dead, is a fair representation of the flavour of the era. Godunov wasn't liked and an old rumour surfaced that he had murdered Fyodor's infant son Dmitry (who had, in fact, died in mysterious circumstances in 1591). When a young man turned up with a Polish army swelled with Russians and Cossacks and claiming to be Dmitry, the nobles believed him. Boris dropped down dead, and Dmitry was installed tsar. It was in part Poland's riposte to Russia's Baltic ambitions. The solution, as Poland saw it, was to annex Russia and convert the country to Roman Catholicism, the schism between Orthodoxy and Roman Catholicism then being as deep and contentious as that produced by the Iron Curtain in the 20th century

Peter the Great: The Time of Troubles receded with the election of Tsar Mikhail, chosen because he was innocuous but nevertheless the first of Russia's most famous dynasty, the Romanovs. Tsar Alexis, who followed, introduced an unprecedented note of piety into the Kremlin. However, he did not expect or require the same level of piety in a bustling cosmopolitan quarter which was developing on the River Yauza outside Moscow. It was full of foreign entrepreneurs, craftsmen and mercenaries. The libertine atmosphere in the colony enchanted the future Peter the Great who, as a boy, was whisked out of the Kremlin to escape murderous Streltsi ("Sharp-shooters") whom his aunt Sophia had employed to keep him off the throne. She was not the most attractive of women if a contemporary description is to be believed: "immensely fat, with a head as large as a bushel, hairs on her face and tumours on her legs."

Peter, who became tsar at 17, was an enormous youth who eventually grew to nearly 7ft and was proportionately well-built. He also had lofty ideals. He aimed to put his country in the first rank of European powers and thus remove lingering suspicions of Tartar despotism. His first priority was to acquire a navy to drive the Turks from the Sea of Azov. If he could do that, he hoped to go on to liberate Constantinople, opening Russia's "Window to the East" through the Black Sea. It followed that he could then open a "Window to the West" via the Baltic, although Ivan the Terrible's experience would have told him that a Baltic campaign was bound to provoke robust opposition.

Having decided that the defeat of Turkey could best be achieved by forming a Grand European Alliance, Peter organised in 1697 an ambassadorial mission to a round of European capitals which he accompanied under the implausible alias of "Corporal Peter Mikhailov" of the Preobrazhenski Guards.

He was the first tsar ever to have travelled outside Russia. On his return, he ordered the Russian nobility to affect a more European appearance by shaving off their beards, the first manifestation of what turned out to be a fixation about beards, including an attempt to tax them. Peter never got his European Grand Alliance, but he managed to squeeze sufficient concessions out of an independent war with Turkey to turn his attention to the Baltic. His campaign opened disastrously with a defeat at Narva by Charles XII of Sweden, who was just 18 years old. There then followed the Northern War which lasted 21 years and devasted huge tracts of Eastern Europe. Under the ultimate Peace of Nystad, Russia acquired a substantial Baltic coastline and most of what is now Estonia and Latvia. The founding of St Petersburg was Peter's way of showing that his "Window to the West" was open, and he capped his triumph by assuming the title "Emperor of All Russia".

Ivan III and Peter were both dubbed "the Great" because of their substantial additions to the Russian Empire, and the next to win this accolade was Catherine II.

Right, Peter the Great.

CATHERINE THE GREAT

Catherine the Great (1729–96), the towering woman in Russian history, was a German princess who transcended a sexless marriage to the mad and invariably drunk Tsar Peter III to become Empress in her own right and set about building a Russian Empire that surpassed those of Rome and Byzantium put together. She mixed lofty correspondence with the likes of Voltaire with an earthy quest to overcome the aching privations of her marriage.

She was the second Tsarina Catherine, born two years after the death of Catherine I (1684–1727), who had similarly succeeded to the throne

on the strength of a colourful marriage, in her case to Peter the Great. The two Catherines bracketed, if they are not themselves part of, what John Knox called a "monstrous regiment of women" who sat on the throne in the interim, including empresses Anna and Elizabeth, the latter the owner of a staggering 15,000 dresses.

Catherine II was born into the minor German aristocracy as Princess Sophia Augusta of Anhalt-Zerbst and changed her name to Catherine Alekseyevna on converting to Russian Orthodoxy in order to marry Peter III, Peter the Great's grandson. She was 14 and he was two years older, a small boy for his age with a long pale face and no shoulders to speak of. Playing with his toy

soldiers was one thing, but even at 14 Catherine wondered whether there might be more deep-seated problems when she found her husband conducting a court-martial on a rat, which he found guilty on all charges and hanged.

In the fifth year of the marriage, Peter had still not taken a bath, neither literally nor, as Russian custom required, as a signal that the marriage had been consummated. Her patience finally at an end, Catherine invited a succession of young army officers to her apartment, while a Frau Grooth, the imaginative widow of a Stuttgart artist, was engaged to see if anything could be done about Peter. Frau Grooth claimed success, but when Catherine gave birth to a son christened Paul no one believed that Peter could be the father, least of all him.

Catherine borrowed £10,000 from Sir Charles Hanbury-Williams, the British ambassador, so that in the event of her husband's death she could afford a few bribes to help ensure that the throne would pass to her. She requested an additional £100,000, but the money was neither available nor, as it turned out, necessary. Peter made it plain even in rare moments of sobriety that he was more loyal to Frederick of Prussia than Russia. Catherine won the backing of the Preobrazhensky Regiment, and in particular the brothers Alexis and Gregory Orlov and Gregory Potemkin, lovers all, to depose him. Forced to abdicate, he was then poisoned and for good measure strangled. The official autopsy put his death down to colic.

Private correspondence with Voltaire and other French intellectuals had introduced Catherine to the spirit of the Enlightenment, which she saw in the context of Russia as reducing the burden of serfdom. While she professed these principles loudly, the practicalities of her situation meant granting the nobility more independent powers than previous Russian rulers would or could have countenanced. Whatever Catherine might have said about serfdom, the nobles certainly had no intention of putting her theories into practice on their estates.

Thwarted in this respect, Catherine was remarkably industrious in others. She built new towns, overhauled the government, encouraged industrial development, expanded the navy and founded, among 25 major schools throughout Russia, the Smolny Institute for young ladies in St Petersburg.

The thrust of her foreign policy in the West was to capitalise on Peter the Great's victory over Sweden by tackling the remaining obstacle,

Poland, then in rapid decline but still in possession of Ukraine. A constitutional crisis which led to an unoccupied Polish throne provided the opportunity. One of her favourite lovers happened to be Polish, Stanislaus Poniatowski, whom she had met as Sir Charles Hanbury-Williams's private secretary. A Russian expeditionary force ensured that his election as King of Poland went smoothly. What Catherine had not counted on was that while he would always insist that he loved her deeply, his loyalties were with Poland. Catherine later joined forces with Frederick of Prussia to act against Poland's persecution of Russian Orthodox believers and Lutherans in its imperial territories. The outcome was the systematic dismemberment not only of the Polish empire but Poland itself so that by the end of the 18th century the country, and of course her gift to Stanislaus Poniatowski, ceased to exist.

At home, the failure of Catherine's high-minded thoughts on serfdom to produce any meaningful results led to a peasant uprising in 1771 which put Moscow at risk. Two years later, she was plunged into a repetition of the False Dmitri nightmare which had haunted Boris Godunov and driven Russia into its "Time of Troubles". The rebel leader in this instance was the Cossack Emilian Pugachev masquerading as, of all people, her late husband Peter III. To make matters worse, there was the daughter of a Prague publican claiming to be Princess Trakanova, the Empress Elizabeth's daughter and the rightful heiress to Catherine's throne. Like the False Dmitry, her claim had Polish support. All the military skills of Suvorov, Russia's greatest general, were needed to put down the rebellion. Pugachev was quartered alive in Red Square; "Princess Trakanova" died in the Peter and Paul Fortress in St Petersburg.

Throughout these crises, Catherine's stream of lovers continued unabated. She may secretly have married one of them, Alexander Potemkin. After running his course, he was shunted off as her "Commissioner and Protector of Tartars", although it seems that Catherine relied on his judgement concerning new lovers, who as she grew older became progressively younger. A Madame Protasow was employed in a similar capacity. "I usually first test the candidate for the favour in order to find out whether he combines prowess with his appearance of general merit. And

no one gets the position unless he has been beforehand tried and approved by me."

One of the lovers, Count Platon Zubov (22 when she was 61), expanded on Catherine's "Eastern Project", which was to conquer the Balkans, capture Constantinople, and reconstitute the Byzantine Empire as Russian. She had a grandson christened Constantine in readiness to occupy the throne. Zubov wished to emulate Alexander the Great by adding Persia and India to the Empire. At one point Catherine sent the Russian fleet through the Strait of Gibraltar to engage and defeat the Turkish navy at Çeşme. She had acquired control over the northern shore of the Black Sea from Turkey and looked likely to win Azerbaijan from Persia when she died in

1796, leaving Russia in the hands of her son Paul, who was bent on undoing her achievements.

Catherine left voluminous autobiographical writings and letters in which she repeatedly said she was content to let history judge her. As so much subsequently written about her dwelt on her love-life, perhaps she deserves the last word: "If I may venture to be frank, I would say about myself that I was every inch a gentleman with a mind much more male than female; but together with this I was anything but masculine... I have just said that I was attractive. Consequently, one-half of the road to temptation was already covered and it is only human in such situations that one should not stop half-way..." ∎

Left, Catherine the Great in her prime. **Right**, a homely-looking Catherine at Tsarskoe Selo.

Alexander I, who succeeded Paul in 1801, received a liberal education which predisposed him towards the abolition of serfdom and other democratic reforms; but his attention was soon distracted by events in France and in particular by Napoleon. He first joined Austria, Britain and Prussia in opposition to him, but French victories over Austria at Ulm and Austerlitz, and over Prussia at Jena and Auerstadt, made him reconsider. In the summer of 1807 he and Napoleon met to discuss a separate peace. One thing led to another, and they were soon deciding how to carve up half the world between them.

The venue for these negotiations was a raft in the middle of the River Niemen near Tilsit. Unknown to them, dangling under the raft and listening to every word was Count Simon Vorontsov, a former Russian ambassador to London. It was agreed between them that Napoleon would reconstitute as the Duchy of Warsaw a part of Poland which, as a country, had been dismembered out of existence by Catherine the Great and her Austrian and Prussian allies. Russia would expand throughout Eastern Europe generally and add Sweden to its Baltic possessions. Vorontsov reported the entire conversation to his friends in London.

As things turned out, Alexander made his move on Sweden through Finland and at the same time invaded Bessarabia (now Moldova), part of the Ottoman Empire. Everything seemed to be going according to the plan hatched on the raft when in June 1812 Napoleon sprang an invasion on Russia with 600,000 men without so much as a declaration of war. On 26 August the French Grand Army and the Russians met at Borodino, about 112km (70 miles) west of Moscow, and on that one day alone they lost 100,000 men between them.

For the Russians, the stand at Borodino was merely a holding action, because they then executed the classic Russian "defence in depth", which entailed drawing the invaders ever deeper into the interior and thus extending their supply line to perilous lengths.

Left, the liberally-inclined Alexander I. Right, Alexander I meets Napoleon in Tilsit in 1807.

Napoleon arrived at Moscow on 2 September to discover that most of the inhabitants had already left, but not before putting their city to the torch. Their sacrifice brought Napoleon down to earth. He realised that the blackened city would be unable to feed his troops during the approaching winter. He accordingly ordered a withdrawal to Smolensk and Vilna (as Vilnius, the capital of Lithuania, then was). The retreat began in October, the long column harassed all the way by Russian cavalry and Cossacks. Of

the 600,000 men who had crossed into Russia six months earlier, only 20,000 limped into Vilna. Napoleon abandoned them in order to hurry back to Paris.

Amazingly, Napoleon managed to raise a new army in time for the so-called Battle of the Nations at Leipzig a year later. After four days of heavy fighting he was forced to retreat across the Rhine and in December Alexander led the victorious Allied advance into France. Napoleon was forced to abdicate while Alexander was proclaimed Alexander the Blessed by the the Holy Synod in St Petersburg. The Congress of Vienna confirmed Russian sovereignty over the part of

Poland which Napoleon had earmarked for his Duchy of Warsaw.

Alexander cut a suave and heroic figure in Europe and looked likely to be the first tsar to put to rest the old suspicions about barbarous Tartar tendencies. But Nicholas, who stepped forward to assume the crown when Alexander died, was an outright reactionary. "Revolution stands on the threshold of Russia, but I swear it will never enter Russia while my breath lasts," he vowed.

His intolerance knew no bounds. He disliked the smell of tobacco, so he banned smoking not merely in his presence but throughout Russia; he could not stand the sight of moustaches on the men of the Impe-

offer, but Austria asked for help in dealing with the nationalist uprising in Hungary. In 1853 Nicholas ordered his army into Ottoman Romania, at which point Britain and France warily positioned their Mediterranean fleets in the Bosphorus. The Crimean War commenced the following year, creating the legendary tales of Florence Nightingale and the Charge of the Light Brigade into the "Valley of Death". Back in the Winter Palace in St Petersburg, Nicholas could not understand what was going wrong. He died in early 1855 shortly before the fall of Sevastopol, officially from an infection of the lungs but, according to other accounts, from a self-administered dose of poison.

rial Guard unless they were black (although he made what was for him a major concession by permitting moustaches of other colours to be painted black); he annulled a marriage of which he disapproved and officially reinstated the protesting bride as a virgin; and M. Rigaud, a professor of French at Moscow University, was committed to a lunatic asylum for failing to stand up at the appropriate time during a church service.

When the revolutions of 1848 broke, Nicholas relished the thought of being "Europe's gendarme" and had an army of 400,000 standing by for service wherever it might be needed. France and Germany declined the

His son Alexander II swept into office like a new broom. Like his earlier namesake, he was committed to the abolition of serfdom and prepared even to trim the powers of the secret police, a hint of perestroika and glasnost combined. But his liberal instincts were shattered when a student at St Petersburg University tried to assassinate him. "My attention is now turned to the education of the youth," he said as a prelude to a total clamp-down. As a result, thousands of students left for Geneva and Zurich to take up positions at the feet of revolutionaries preaching anarchy and the recently published opinions of Karl Marx. Russian intellectual life had come alive and could not be extinguished. The country was suddenly awash with writers of genius: Gogol, Turgenev, Herzen, Tolstoy, Dostoevsky, Chekhov, Pushkin and so on.

The flood of ideas took various channels, including Pan-Slavism and Nihilism. While the campaign against Turkey was conducted in the name of the former, Nihilism was having its day with repeated attempts on Alexander's life. It was not long before a bomb flew through the air and exploded near his carriage. Alexander was unhurt, but the explosion killed the horses and two of his Cossack bodyguards. "Thank God your Majesty is safe," said a policeman quickly on the scene. "Rather too early to thank God," came

On Sunday, 22 January 1905, huge crowds of workers carrying icons and singing hymns converged on the Winter Palace in St Petersburg to show their dissatisfaction with the status quo. The demonstration was proceeding in an orderly and unremarkable fashion when troops opened fire and the Cossacks staged one of their fearsome charges. Several hundred people were killed. Bloody Sunday, as it came to be called, led to a general strike in October and the formation in St Petersburg of a "Soviet" (i.e. workers' council), among whose members was Leon Trotsky. Peasants rose throughout Russia to evict their landlords and claim possession of the land they had worked. Even military

the reply from an unseen voice. A second bomb arced over and exploded at Alexander's feet. The injuries were appalling. The last words he managed to get out were: "Quickly, home to the palace to die."

His successor, Nicholas, struggled to adjust to the realities of an industrialisation process which had made steady progress throughout the 19th century. By 1900 some 3 million uprooted peasants had become factory workers and were fertile ground for Russia's first Marxist party, founded in 1898.

Left, Nicholas I at sea. <u>Above left</u>, Alexander II. <u>Above right</u>, the Bloody Sunday massacre.

units mutinied, the most famous example being the crew of the battleship *Potemkin*.

Although Nicholas's first instinct was to meet the uprising with brute force, he allowed a few concessions. The peasants' share of arable land in Russia rose to three-quarters, trades unions came into being, and conditions in industry improved. Lenin, for one, theorised that a war between Russia and Austria would turn the tide to the advantage of the Revolutionaries, but in 1913 he thought such a war was "not likely".

Lenin reckoned without the fact that in the interest of cementing Pan-Slavism in Serbia, it was necessary to frustrate Habsburg Austrian plans to move its own imperial expansion, blocked off by and under pressure from Prussia in the West, into the Slavic Balkans. When the Habsburg Archduke Franz Ferdinand travelled to Sarajevo in Bosnia to further these interests, he was assassinated by agents working for the Serbian secret service. An enraged Austria declared war on Serbia, and Russia hurried to Serbia's defence. It was, of course, the notorious snowball that resulted in World War I.

Apart from one victory in Galicia, the Russians suffered colossal casualties in battle after battle. The troops were as brave and uncomplaining as ever, but the army command was corrupt, incompetent and thought

nothing of sending men to the front without rifles. In the summer of 1915, the Austrians and Germans took possession of the whole of Poland, most of the Baltic provinces, and much of Ukraine and White Russia.

Rasputin: Not sure what to do next, Nicholas relied increasingly on the judgement of his German wife Alexandra. Her greatest inspiration in turn was Gregory Rasputin, a monk "from Siberia" who was treating their haemophilic son through hypnosis. Whether or not the hypnosis worked on the boy, it seemed to rivet Nicholas and Alexandra. "His gaze," said the French ambassador, "was at once piercing and caressing, naive and cunning, far off and concentrated. When he is in earnest conversation, his pupils seem to radiate magnetism. He carries with him a strong animal smell, like that of a goat."

People who were not under his gaze lent their voices to a general cry "to deliver Russia from this filthy, vicious and venal peasant". Prince Yusupov invited Rasputin home ostensibly to meet his wife. He was asked to wait in a room and was invited to help himself to an array of cakes and wine, all poisoned. Yusupov stayed away long enough to allow Rasputin to be tempted. When he put his head round the door, Rasputin was polishing off the last of the cake and wine with obvious relish. The exasperated prince drew his revolver and fired a shot which brought Rasputin down to all fours but did not prevent him from crawling up a flight of stairs and escaping into a courtyard.

The prince cornered Rasputin in the courtyard and put three more bullets into him. The second volley alerted police. Nothing to worry about, Yusupov cried, he was merely disposing of a dog. Incredibly, Rasputin was still alive, so Yusupov dragged him down to the frozen river, dumping him through a hole in the ice. Rasputin did then die, but not immediately. When his body was found the following morning, his frozen hands were clinging to the supports of a nearby bridge.

Some three months later, a shortage of bread in St Petersburg led to riots, demonstrations and strikes. The police who intervened were stoned but, unusually, the Cossacks did nothing. On 9 March 1917, Alexandra was able to say in a letter that she thought there was nothing to worry about. The very next day, two regiments of the Imperial Guard went over to the rioters, taking the contents of the arsenal with them and handing them out. A couple of days after that, workers' and soldiers' deputies took possession of one wing of the Tauride Palace, and on 14 March a provisional government was formed under Prince Lvov.

Under pressure from the army, Nicholas abdicated. The execution of Nicholas and his family – and the Bolshevik Revolution – still lay some months ahead, but when his brother Michael declined the offer of the throne, the history of Russia under the tsars ceased.

Left, the infamous Rasputin. **Right**, the Imperial family at Peterhof, 1901.

The first of the two Russian revolutions in 1917, the "February Revolution", had nothing to do with Communism. If anything, the overthrow of Nicholas II was an attempt to get rid of an incompetent war-time leader and save the monarchy for better things. All the seasoned troops were at the front, and the raw recruits in St Petersburg did not know what was expected of them.

Germany recognised an opportunity to sow utter confusion among the Russian ranks and accordingly arranged to have Lenin and other Revolutionaries injected into the mayhem from their exile in Switzerland. To ensure that he did not start stirring trouble too soon, Lenin was spirited from Switzerland and across Germany in a sealed train, "like a plague bacillus" as Sir Winston Churchill later put it.

The Bolsheviks: Russia's provisional leadership, with "Sasha" Kerensky taking over from Prince Lvov, had assumed that the greatest threat facing them was from the conservative military, but with food shortages and popular discontent worsening, it dawned on them that the Revolution was endangered by the Left, and in particular by the firebrand Leon Trotsky.

While Trotsky directed the almost bloodless seizure of undefended railway stations and post offices around St Petersburg, Lenin addressed the members of his central committee on 6 November: "If we seize power today, we seize it not against the Soviets (i.e. workers' councils) but for them. Seizure of power is the point of the uprising; its political goal will become clear after the seizure." Only a handful of military cadets and a women's battalion stood between the "Military Revolutionary Committee" and the Winter Palace, the seat of the Provisional Government. The rebels infiltrated the palace that night under the sympathetic guns of the cruiser *Aurora* moored on the Neva. Kerensky managed to get away in a borrowed American Legation car while his colleagues were led quietly to the Peter and Paul Fortress.

Left, poster of Lenin directing the Revolution. **Right**, a commander of the Red Army wears his heart on his sleeve.

The Bolsheviks established their revolutionary government in the Smolny Institute, until then a school for St Petersburg's fashionable young ladies, and worked out how to transport the Revolution to Moscow and points beyond. Lenin and Trotsky were the dominant figures. Among the lesser personnel was Josef Dzhugashvili who, because he was not a Russian but a Georgian and presumably knew a thing or two about the mentality of Russian minorities, was appointed Commissar of Nationalities. The

name he soon adopted was easier to pronounce: Stalin.

The number of fighting men engaged in the civil war was remarkably low. Although by 1920 the Red Army had 5 million troops on paper, it never had more than about 60,000 in the field against various factions, the most notable of which was the "White Russian" army of General Denikin, which got within 320 km (200 miles) of Moscow.

The Communists were ultimately triumphant, of course, but six years of war, revolution and civil war presented them with problems almost beyond belief, including the accusation, levelled by mutineers at the naval barracks at Kronstadt, that the Revolution had betrayed the peasants. Lenin decided that Communism's high-minded commitment to world revolution would have to wait while Russia's internal problems were attended to. His "New Economic Policy" allowed a measure of free enterprise which legitimised the black market, got production and exports up, and created a new albeit temporary breed of flashy capitalist.

There was no glasnost to accompany this short-lived perestroika. Lenin's Cheka, organised by Felix Dzerzhinksky and a direct descendant of Ivan the Terrible's *Oprichniki*, advocated "no other measures to fight counter-Revolutionaries, spies, speculators, ruf-

who had been rising rather too rapidly for Lenin's liking. Because of – not in spite of – his Georgian origins, Stalin was a pathological chauvinist by very narrow criteria. His vision of Soviet Man was specifically of a Great Russian who sprouted socialist wings, and that left no room for Little Russians or White Russians (Ukrainians and Belarussians) or any other deviation.

His intolerance was greatest when directed at his fellow Georgians and neighbouring Armenians and Azerbaijanis. Trotsky had a vision of Soviet Man, too, but it was broader. Stalin's narrow nationalism and his advancement of those who shared his views, or expediently said they did, made Trotsky a

fians, hooligans, saboteurs and other parasites than merciless annihilation on the spot of the offence." When the Patriarch of Moscow raised his voice against these measures, the clamp-down on religion and the clergy was accelerated. The Orthodox Church soon came to terms with the atheist Soviet regime, however, just as it had with the pagan Mongols in the 13th century. When Lenin died in 1924 and his mummified body went on show in the mausoleum in Red Square, he was looked upon as a Communist saint competing with the older variety in St Basil's.

Trotsky tumbles: Lenin's death led to a power struggle between Trotsky and Stalin,

pariah on the seven-member Politburo. He observed Stalin's purges of the opposition with growing alarm.

In order to justify the purges, a film was rushed out which depicted Ivan the Terrible as a national hero who was obliged to cut down the overweening boyars in the interest of the masses. The actor who played the villain of the piece bore an unmistakable resemblance to Trotsky. Trotsky in turn drew a comparison between Stalin and an earlier historical figure than Ivan the Terrible. "Imagine," he remarked, "Genghis Khan with a telephone." In December 1927, the wholesale expulsion of Trotskyists from the Fifteenth Congress saw their leader exiled first to Alma Ata and thence to Prinkipo in the Sea of Marmora. Trotsky made his way to Norway and eventually to Mexico where, in 1940, he was tracked down and murdered.

With Trotsky out of the way, Stalin in 1928 launched his "Revolution" with the first of his Five-Year Plans. The targets it set were monitored on an annual basis, but it was felt that a "One-Year Plan" was too ambitious to produce the theoretical benefits, and anything longer than five years would be dangling the carrot too far from the noses of those who were supposed to bend their backs to the task. Stalin, of course, needed his henchmen, and he kept them in line by making it plain through regular purges that but for his grace would they go the same way.

Soviet foreign policy in the midst of all this moved from the initial conviction that world revolution was about to wipe out all capitalist and imperialist governments to the cultivation of "socialism in a single land" and a *modus vivendi* with advanced capitalist countries, particularly Germany. When World War II was about to break out Hitler persuaded Stalin that his best hope was to stand well clear while Germany redressed the injustices of the Paris Peace Conference. These involved recovering parts of Poland and the German-speaking parts of Czechoslovakia. The pact signed by Ribbentrop and Molotov in 1939 was powerfully reminiscent of the agreement between Alexander I and Napoleon in 1807: a Russian autocrat giving a Western dictator a licence to attack Britain in exchange for territorial concessions. In this instance, Russia would be allowed to annex the Baltic states, the rest of Poland and Romania.

In a virtual repetition of Napoleon's surprise attack on Alexander, Hitler invaded Russia without formal warning on 22 June 1941. The German siege of Moscow and Leningrad, as it then was, did not break Russian resistance. Hitler could probably have taken both cities, but his primary goal was the industrial and agricultural capacity of Ukraine, beyond which lay the vital oil of Azerbaijan on the Caspian Sea and ultimately the Persian Gulf. Access to oil was

Left, Trotsky as Commissar of Defence. **Right**, Nikita Khrushchev extolling the virtues of collectivised agriculture.

for Hitler so critical that his insurance policy was to attempt to reach the supply in the Middle East by driving across North Africa. The turning points of the German advances on these two fronts were at El Alamein in October 1942, shortly before the American forces started closing in on the Afrika Korps from their beachhead in western North Africa, and at Stalingrad in early 1943.

With these defeats, the German *Drang nach Osten* went into reverse. This is not the place to trace the rolling back of the Nazi carpet: it need only be said that it was not achieved without colossal loss of Russian life, at least 10 million dead, millions more maimed, and the demolition of practically all

the achievements of the Five-Year Plans.

The last weeks of the war in Europe were characterised by a race between the Allies to stake their claims to the liberated territories over and above, certainly in Russia's case, what had been agreed in principle at the Yalta Conference by Stalin, Roosevelt and Churchill. The areas physically occupied by the Red Army, together with European states delivered into the Communist fold by strategically placed Russian Quislings, constituted the eastern sector of a continent divided for the next 40 years by the Iron Curtain.

With the German threat removed, Stalin was at liberty to resume his Five-Year Plans and vent his paranoia on those whom he regarded as traitors to the cause of Soviet Man. The worse offenders, in his opinion, were Ukrainians and Belarussians (the "Little" and "White Russians") who saw collaboration with the Nazis as an opportunity to throw off the Great Russian Yoke. The number of victims of Stalin's purges in this respect are only now being totted up. Estimates have already passed 30 million.

Expansionist dreams: Stalin died on 5 March 1953. Under his successor, Nikita Khrushchev, Russia seemed to make the bid for world leadership that Lenin in his time decided was premature. There were questions in the West about Russia's ability to pay for

the Aswan Dam in Egypt and a $90-million foreign aid programme for India. The answer, it transpired, was by selling gold reserves. Khrushchev was willing to gamble with very high stakes, never more so than when at the 20th Party Congress he denounced Stalin by name. He took the risk of shifting the Soviet economy slightly away from heavy industry to consumer goods. He was willing publicly to forgive Tito in Yugoslavia for deserting the Soviet camp. His personal triumph was to put the first sputnik into space on 4 October 1957, a considerable snub to American technology.

In 1961, however, he went a gamble too

far with his decision to put nuclear missiles on bases in Cuba, partly as a gesture of support for Communism's most promising convert, Fidel Castro, and partly to let Americans know, as he put it, what is was like to have missiles peering at them from just beyond their backyards. The reference was to American missile bases in Turkey, which Khrushchev claimed to be able to see from his Black Sea *dacha*. The world held its breath in fear of nuclear war until Khrushchev backed down to the young John Kennedy.

Khrushchev was deposed by his fellow Party leaders in 1964. His successor was Leonid Brezhnev, a Ukrainian. He made it plain that Ukrainians who mattered had buried past distinctions between Great and Little Russians. To reinforce the point, he packed the Politburo with fellow Ukrainians, leading to taunts about a Ukrainian mafia.

Brezhnev's proclamations on unbreakable bonds between not only the 15 Soviet Republics but also the Soviet Union and its East European satellite states were tested by Alexander Dubcek's gentle revolution in Czechoslovakia in 1968. The 400,000 Soviet troops who poured over Czechoslovakia's borders were the short answer to what was later spelled out as the Brezhnev Doctrine: "The weakening of any of the links in the world socialist system directly affects all the socialist countries, which cannot look on indifferently when this happens."

With that policy supposedly set in stone, Brezhnev set about expanding the world socialist system into Africa, Asia and Latin America, to which the United States responded in kind. When Americans counted the cost of Vietnam and similar undertakings and wondered how the Soviet Union was paying its way, the answer was oil.

The sudden wealth of the Arab oil sheikhs was legendary, but the Soviet Union was actually the world's largest oil producer and profited accordingly from the steep climb in oil prices. Part of the windfall went towards the cost of the invasion of Afghanistan. By 1982 it was apparent that intervention in Afghanistan was not going according to plan, Brezhnev was on his death bed – and the price of oil plummeted.

Left, Leonid Brezhnev. **Right**, despite the slogan of this poster – "Those who do not labour do not eat" – the sun began to set on Communism.

When Mikhail Gorbachev came to power in the Kremlin in 1985, following the sudden deaths of Brezhnev's two successors, Yury Andropov and Konstantin Chernenko, the Soviet economy was already a secret wreck. Production had been sliding for years. Shortages were endemic. Technology was stuck in the 1950s, while the West was forging into the age of computers and star wars.

Although Gorbachev wouldn't admit it, Communism simply wasn't working. It was physically impossible for central planners to allocate every item in the country from their offices in Moscow. Factories produced cars with one wheel missing for lack of parts, farmers shipped their potatoes rotting in mud because they were paid per kilogramme, regardless of the quality of their produce. No one owned the land or buildings, so no one took care of them. No one was ever fired, so few put much effort into their work.

Factories built in the 1930s and others trucked from Germany as war booty were wearing out. Tangled in bureaucracy and Communist prohibitions against normal Western business practices, the Soviets could not replace them. There was no incentive for workers to make anything better, faster or cheaper. Independent thinking was absent.

In fact, the whole house of cards had been kept afloat since the 1970s on Siberian oil. The Soviet Union had massive oil fields, and the 1973 oil embargo had been its salvation. The world price of oil rocketed from $3 a barrel to $11 in four months. Suddenly, the Soviet government was rich. As the price rose to $35 in the early 1980s, it grew fat.

Dependence on imports: With oil money, the Soviet government bought grain from America, canned fruit and vegetables from Eastern Europe, industrial machinery, technology and raw materials from Western Europe. By 1985, the country was completely dependent on imports to feed the people and keep the foreign-equipped factories running. Just as Gorbachev came to power, the price of oil halved. Key imports had to be cut, and

Left, Gorbachev supporters at the beginning of perestroika. Right, popularity cannot be achieved behind closed doors.

over the six years of Gorbachev's historic tenure, one industry after another was crippled. The Soviet people, kept ignorant of their nation's dependence on oil, blamed Gorbachev. He spoke of the need for a market economy, but left it to Boris Yeltsin, then the Moscow Communist Party boss, to start the painful reforms necessary to achieve that. It was through politics that he changed his country, and the world.

In fact, many Western observers believe Gorbachev began his reforms in an attempt

to save Communism and the totalitarian system. But his closest aides say they realised early that the Soviet Union could not have a modern economy without the free flow of accurate information – and that would logically lead to a demand for democracy.

Gorbachev started out as a popular leader – a healthy, energetic contrast to the three old men who had preceded him. He plunged into crowds on street corners and said it was time to speak openly of problems, so they could be solved. He backed up his words by freeing dissidents from prison.

It took Gorbachev three years to replace enough of the old, hard-line Communists to dare to begin his programme. In June 1988, he electrified the world by proposing elections, the transfer of power from the Communist Party to the government, and the creation of a real legislature that would debate and pass laws.

Breakaway moves: The Baltic republics of Estonia, Latvia and Lithuania quickly grabbed the opportunity offered by the reforms to agitate for the independence they lost in 1940 when occupied by the Red Army. Estonia struck the first blow in November 1988. Taking advantage of Gorbachev's promise to abide by the law, Estonia's previously compliant republic parliament passed a "declaration of sovereignty",

whole nationalities from their homelands and redrawn borders. Families remembered being hauled off in cattle cars to Siberia and fighting squatters to regain their homes.

Soviet minorities suddenly demanded justice. In many cases, it was impossible. Two generations had been born in others' homes and lands. Across the Soviet south, from Moldavia to Azerbaijan to Uzbekistan, the anger exploded into violence, and several thousand died over the next four years.

But while the danger grew at home, the Cold War thawed. Gorbachev told the United Nations he planned to cut half a million troops. When an earthquake killed more than 25,000 in Armenia, he allowed thousands of

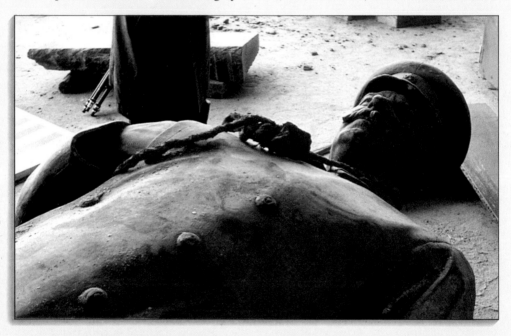

giving itself the right to overrule Soviet laws. Gorbachev denounced the move but took no other action. Gradually, the Estonians and the other Baltic peoples took control of government, schools and the criminal justice system – all the day-to-day aspects of life that had been under the thumb of the Communist Party. It was the beginning of the end of the Soviet Union. Eventually, every one of the 15 Soviet republics would follow Estonia's lead.

Meanwhile, the end of censorship opened another Pandora's box. Ethnic minorities began to speak out against decades of discrimination and horror. Stalin had deported

international relief workers and millions of dollars in aid to pour into the country, demolishing at a stroke the propaganda-fed image of a West poised to blast the USSR off the face of the earth.

Put to the vote: In the spring of 1989, the Soviet people voted in the first multi-candidate elections in their lives. The Communist Party was still the only political party but, for the first time, people could vote against it, and did. Across the nation, hundreds of Communist Party leaders lost. In Lithuania, the pro-democracy popular front won 39 of 42 Lithuanian seats in the Soviet Union's new Congress of People's Deputies.

At first, Russians found their new Congress enthralling. Work ground to a halt as millions tuned in to live broadcasts to hear the legislators break silence and detail the country's terrible past and disastrous present.

Over the next two years, the Congress and its working legislature, the Supreme Soviet, passed historic laws guaranteeing freedom of the press, travel and religion. But the Congress was masterfully manipulated by Gorbachev and took no serious action on economic reform. It permitted small private business cooperatives for the first time, but left all property in the hands of the state and all power in the hands of the bureaucrats.

But the first Congress freed citizens to speak out and act, not only in the Soviet Union. In September, Hungary took Gorbachev at his word about allowing self-determination in the fraternal nations of the Soviet bloc and threw open its border with the West. East Germans poured through it. Within two months, the Velvet Revolution was sweeping Czechoslovakia, and the Berlin Wall was down. The only Communist dictator who resisted the march of change, Romania's Nicolai Ceaucescu, died in front of a firing squad. The tape of his execution was shown repeatedly on Soviet television, sending chills through the old guard.

Meanwhile, Baltic activists raised their demands from democracy within the Soviet Union to full independence. Gorbachev flew to Vilnius to put a stop to the separatism and was greeted by signs saying: "Welcome to the leader of a neighbouring country."

Hoping to undermine the Lithuanian activists, Gorbachev dropped the biggest bombshell of his reforms at a meeting with Lithuanian Communists: "I see no tragedy in a multi-party system. We should not be afraid of it, the way the devil is afraid of incense."

It was no slip of the tongue. It was revolutionary, for everyone but Gorbachev realised that the Communist Party could not remain in power once the Soviet people had a choice. Gorbachev pushed the change through the Party leadership and Congress within two months. Finally free, millions of Party members quit, sapping the Party of its strength.

Simultaneously, Gorbachev asked Congress for new laws to prevent the break-up of the union. Lithuania decided not to wait, and declared independence. Gorbachev launched a war of nerves, with a 10-week economic blockade and threatening troop manoeuvres in Lithuanian cities. But the Lithuanians held fast. Other republics took note. Kremlin orders could be ignored.

Left, the fallen. **Above**, Azerbaijanians destroy their Communist Party membership cards.

Among the radical republic leaders emerging to challenge Gorbachev was Boris Yeltsin. At first, Yeltsin was no supporter of democracy. But unlike most old Communists, he was sincere in trying to improve people's lives. In 1987, when he complained about Party corruption, Gorbachev kicked his protégé Yeltsin out of the leadership.

Two years later, in 1989, Yeltsin stormed back into political life by winning the Moscow seat in the new Soviet congress by 89 per cent. He had a talent for the "sound bites" that work on television, and he discovered that democracy was good for him.

In 1990, he won a seat in the parliament of the Russian republic, which covered half the

in August of 1991. He said he figured he could not beat them, and the reforms would fare better if he remained at least nominally in charge.

On 13 January 1991, with the world's attention riveted on the Persian Gulf, where United Nations forces expected to explode into battle against Iraq within two days, the hardliners used the diversion to strike at Lithuania. Soviet troops and tanks attacked unarmed demonstrators guarding the television tower, and 16 people were killed. Later, it became clear that it was a dress rehearsal for the national coup. Gorbachev blamed the Lithuanians, destroying his tarnished reputation as a reformer.

Soviet population and three-quarters of its land mass. Then the Russian congress elected him its chairman. A year later, Yeltsin won the first popular election for president of Russia, again by a landslide.

Yeltsin and the Democratic Russia movement pushed hard for drastic political and economic reform, yet Gorbachev held back. In the autumn of 1990, he rolled back many of his reforms. He reimposed censorship on state-run television, and appointed hardliners to critical positions of power, and his progressive allies quit. Gorbachev said later he was forced into it by hardliners threatening a coup, nine months before they actually struck

But, without change, the economy was worsening. Production shrank 10 per cent in the first three months of the year. People stripped already sparsely stocked shops when the government announced plans to raise prices frozen for 30 years. Oil production plummeted because most petroleum equipment was manufactured in Azerbaijan, which was racked by ethnic violence. The government secretly sold off its gold reserves.

Finally, in April, Gorbachev realised the hard-line approach could not solve the country's problems, and he changed course again. He gave up his impossible dream of preserving the entire Soviet Union. He negotiated a new unifying treaty with nine of the 15 republics, leaving out the six small ones seeking independence: Lithuania, Latvia, Estonia, Georgia, Moldavia and Armenia.

The August 1991 coup: Two days before the signing of the treaty, in August 1991, the hardliners struck. Their coup imprisoned Gorbachev in his Black Sea *dacha* and sent troops and tanks into the streets of Moscow. No-one in the capital on that terrible Monday morning when the armour clanked into the city could have predicted that it would all backfire and within seven days the Soviet Union would be disintegrating and the Communist Party smashed.

The coup conspirators – nearly all mem-

Russia just two months earlier, and they might not appreciate being overruled by a few old Communists.

The plotters said later they expected Gorbachev to cave into their demands for a crackdown. When he refused, they figured a couple of tank divisions in the capital would be enough to scare everyone into obeying.

Instead, the KGB officers sent to arrest Yeltsin let him escape, and KGB troops refused orders to attack the democrats' headquarters in the Russian parliament building. The air force chief threatened to send his planes against any attack on the building, known as the Russian "White House". Yeltsin's people spread throughout the city,

bers of Gorbachev's own cabinet – were not the bumblers they were portrayed as in the international media. But they grossly underestimated the effect of Gorbachev's reforms. Unlike the Chinese democracy activists crushed at Tiananmen Square a year earlier, the Russian reformers were backed by a free press and elected democratic leaders. Somehow, the plotters forgot that 40 million people had voted for Yeltsin to be president of

Left, participants in a human chain from Tallinn to Vilnius agitating for independence. **Above**, Muscovites demonstrating against the August 1991 attempted coup.

persuading soldiers and officers not to fire on their own people. Journalists shut out of their newspapers wrote for photocopied sheets stuck to Metro station walls. In Leningrad, the elected mayor, Anatoly Sobchak, talked the local military commander out of sending troops into the city. That meant he could broadcast calls for resistance on St Petersburg television, which reached most of Russia. And it meant that for the coup to succeed, the conspirators would have had to mount a full-scale attack on the country's heavily fortified second-largest city.

In the end, several of the conspirators flew to see Gorbachev. When they arrived, Gorbachev's personal bodyguards sprang from the bushes, prepared for a fight. Instead, the plotters surrendered.

Gorbachev returned to a Moscow transformed. Thousands screamed "traitors!" at the KGB building, and Yeltsin and his people moved quickly to show Gorbachev how his own Communist Party had betrayed him. By Saturday night – less than a week after the coup attempt – Gorbachev moved against the Party, shutting down its headquarters and freezing its operations.

But the coup had also taught the republics' leaders that they could not trust anyone in the Kremlin government. The same night Gorbachev denounced the Party, the Ukraine

clared the Soviet Union finally dead, leaving Gorbachev president of a non-existent country. On 25 December 1991 he resigned.

Unfortunately for the people of the Soviet Union, that was not the happy ending. Instead, it merely freed the republics' leaders to pursue their own agendas. In Russia, Armenia and the Baltics, this meant aggressive moves toward free-market economies to go with their political freedom. In Azerbaijan and Uzbekistan, the old Communist dictators solidified their iron control without the Communist name. Ethnic clashes became far more dangerous as the combatants gained access to the heavy weaponry of the former Soviet army.

declared independence. With the heartland of the Soviet Union gone, it was only a matter of time before the Soviet Union formally dissolved. Within days, most other republics followed the Ukraine's example.

With the Party's power crushed, the dictatorial glue holding the Soviet Union together was dissolved. With all the economic benefits going to the privileged few, each republic saw itself as a pillaged colony. The empire no longer had a reason to exist.

It took another four months for the details to sort out and for Gorbachev to fail in his last-ditch attempts to hold the union together. Yeltsin and other republic presidents de-

Yeltsin's reforms: In Russia, Boris Yeltsin was finally free to undertake the radical reforms he had promised in his presidential campaign, and he swore to pursue them to the painful end, even at the cost of all his popularity. His prediction proved accurate. The reforms are excruciating, and his people don't understand them. Every reform begets new problems. In the first winter of independent Russia, the cities were in danger of starving because farms and warehouses were hoarding in anticipation of Yeltsin raising prices. Finally, he was forced to free prices, to put the market to work feeding people. But inflation soared to 1,000 percent, and suddenly most Russians realised they were poor.

Almost overnight, everyone and everything, from workers to factories, needed 10 times as much cash to operate, and the money did not exist. Workers went without pay, and cities even tried printing their own local currency to keep the economy moving.

Yeltsin ordered collective farms to start breaking up, but the few hundred thousand families brave enough to try private farming found they could not afford tractors and seed at the newly freed prices. Reformers argued over whether state-owned factories, shops and land should be sold or simply given away, and ended up doing neither in all but a few places.

But in the first stage, with goods still scarce and prices still outrageous, many Russians were furious.

A year after the coup, Yeltsin had achieved only a few of the many reforms he promised. The Communist Party was finished as a ruling, all-encompassing organisation of absolute power. But the people and ideas of the Communist Party were proving to be tenacious. Former Communist officials remained in power in many places, some profiting and others merely obstructing change. Communism was thoroughly discredited, but remained alive because its teachings are so deeply rooted in the minds of the people. They still looked to the government to tell

Yeltsin's most effective first reforms were *ukazes*, decrees signed without consulting his parliament – leading to charges that he was bypassing the democratic system. In one sweeping order, he repealed the web of laws barring ordinary wholesale and retail trade. Within months, stores had goods to offer, and thousands of Russians took to the streets to sell a pair of shoes or a bottle of vodka to passers-by. The black market came out into the open in the first step toward a real market with real competition to hold down prices.

Left, pro-Communist demonstrators, 1992. **Above**, Boris Yeltsin after a Congress meeting.

them what to do, and to provide for them. The government still owned all the land, and nearly all the buildings and businesses.

But, despite dire predictions, bitter ethnic disputes on the fringes of Russia remained local. Only a few districts tried to declare independence from Russia. The Cold War was over, and nuclear weapons were being dismantled on both sides of the vanished Iron Curtain. The West promised $24 billion in aid, and it was beginning to flow. More importantly, Western companies with the combined clout to invest many times that amount sent their agents scouting throughout Russia. Reform was under way at last.

Imagine that you are creating a fabric of human destiny with the object of making men happy in the end, giving them peace and rest at last, but that it was essential and inevitable to torture to death only one tiny creature... would you consent to be the architect under those conditions?
–Fyodor Dostoevsky, *The Brothers Karamazov*

Late into the night, educated Russians debate philosophical dilemmas like this one posed by Dostoevsky, worrying at each point and fuelling the furious discussion with copious amounts of vodka. They buttress their arguments with lengthy quotations from the world's great books. Western visitors are often surprised to find Russians more well-read than they are, even in their own language's literature.

But look again at the opening quote. Russians are not *only* fascinated by awful choices such as the one posed by Dostoevsky. They actually subscribed to this one for seven decades. They believed the Communist Party's promises of a nirvana tomorrow if they would suffer and sacrifice today – and ignore the murder of millions of their fellow citizens who allegedly stood in the way of progress.

Only today are Russians at last beginning to learn the extent of the horror of Stalinism. On the basis of the latest information from newly opened Soviet archives, historians estimate that as many as 47 million people may have died in purges, prison camps, civil war and forced famines – about one in four people. Virtually every family included victims, perpetrators or both. Yet enormous numbers of Russians claim they knew nothing of the atrocities.

Others, however, tell remarkable stories. In the Northern Caucasus, old men and women recount in chilling detail how they and their families were rounded up and tossed into trucks and cattle trains, and then dumped in the freezing winter in isolated fields in Siberia and Kazakhstan – along with every

Preceding pages: keeping in touch in Moscow; beauty contestants; busking on Moscow's Arbat. **Left,** young Russian. **Right,** souvenir seller.

other member of their ethnic group. They explain how on their return between 1958 and 1960 they had physically to fight to regain their homes from those who had moved in during their 10 to 15-year exile, and how they had to start again without furniture, farm implements or animals.

Experiences like these go a long way towards explaining the ethnic violence that erupted after the break-up of the former Soviet Union. Russia is composed of dozens of nationalities, from dark-complexioned

Muslims to Eskimo-like tribes in the Arctic, and many of them blame the Russian majority for the terrible oppression of the Communist regime.

In central Russia, the horror stories are individual. One man will tell of an uncle who disappeared one night in 1937. Others tell of being forced to bury bodies in the forest – truckloads full of them, each shot once in the back of the head. Others remain staunch supporters of Communism, either convinced that Stalin was a great leader or ashamed that they supported him for so long.

Unfortunately, today's reformers are forced to repeat the same line that the Communists used: "Suffer and sacrifice now, and life will improve in the long run." The problem is that Russians have been making sacrifices for 70 years – now they want immediate results from their leaders.

Changes for better and for worse: Until relatively recently, central Moscow was a scene of shoving shoppers, crowding into dusty, virtually empty stores to fight for the right to buy a piece of meat for the family dinner. Today, the crowds are still there, but they sport the bright colours and flashy fashions found in private shops instead of the frumpy darks that used to be favoured by clothing bureaucrats and they linger around makeshift tables where the new breed of entrepre-

and they no longer risk arrest when they spend it.

Even for the casual visitor, it is obvious that everyday life has been transformed by the Gorbachev and Yeltsin reforms. For Russians, the changes have washed away the foundations of society as they know it. Some have found new roots; some have not.

Since 1988 Russians have discovered elections, religion, newspapers with real news, street performers, political demonstrations, unemployment, stores full of goods, millionaires, legless street beggars, casinos and soup kitchens. Prices have skyrocketed for the Russian and plummeted for the tourist. As rich people emerged, so did criminals ready

neurs sell home-made jewellery, popular new independent newspapers, and foreign bubble-gum. The gum goes for three roubles per piece, a sum that would have bought a kilo of meat in 1988.

Two hundred people, mostly teenage boys, jam the line outside the Estée Lauder store to load up on chic Western cosmetics at the state-subsidised price, for later resale at enormous profit. The sparkling windows of this and other new Western stores glitter among the grimy Soviet-era shops on Tverskaya Street, formerly Gorky Street. Most of the Western franchises demand foreign currency, but now thousands of Russians have some –

to steal their wealth.

In May 1988, the Communist Party was still the undisputed dictator. Capitalism was unmentionable. *Pravda* was responding to US complaints about human rights violations by claiming that America had 11,000 political prisoners of its own. The Soviet president, Mikhail Gorbachev, was tentatively mentioning the possibility of tolerating a variety of viewpoints, providing they remained Communist. The Soviet Union was still a superpower.

No one dreamed that within four years both the country and Communism would be broken. No one fantasised about privately owned factories and land, non-Communist political parties or real parliaments. When a son went off to college in Kiev, no one dreamed it would be in a foreign country four years later.

In 1988, managers of military factories did not dare mention their facility's existence. Now, they give tours to Westerners, seeking investment and hard-currency sales. Then, too, the honoured Red Army was 5 million strong, and each young man served a mandatory two years despite the danger of dying in Afghanistan. Now, the vaunted Soviet Armed Forces are divided, resented as an occupying force in the Baltics, torn between two masters in the Ukraine, and half the young Russians are ignoring their draft calls.

Russians who worried about American nuclear bombs are now more concerned about their own nuclear weapons falling into the hands of madmen on the fringes of the former Soviet Union, or further nuclear power plant explosions, like Chernobyl or Tomsk. Security is no longer a question of mighty armed forces, but of solid metal apartment doors to keep out burglars and ethnic rioters.

Vladimir Lenin still lies in waxy state in his Red Square mausoleum, but the line is longer at the Moscow branch of McDonald's. Hundreds of monuments to the Soviet founder have been pulled down, and the city of Leningrad has returned to its old name of St Petersburg.

Meanwhile in a land where, under Communism, religion was vilified as the "opium of the people" and only elderly women dared attend services in the few remaining churches, millions of Russians are returning to worship. Some even send their youngsters to religious studies. Churches, mosques and synagogues that were turned into buildings for very different purposes – for example, a cabbage warehouse, an indoor swimming pool and a museum of atheism – are now being returned to their original uses.

The privileged classes: At one time Oil and Gas Ministry officials relaxed in their own sports club tucked behind the French embassy, enjoying private *banyas* (saunas), indoor tennis and a swimming pool with dozens of massaging water jets. It was part of a

network of special facilities, from resorts to daycare facilities, that provided a decent life for the Party's elite while the masses put up with much shoddier versions and shortages. Today, the Ministry's club has gone private, and it is open to any Russian who can afford membership.

In 1988, the US president, Ronald Reagan, backed off plans to visit a refusenik home after the Soviets signalled that the Jewish family would never be allowed to leave if he did so. Four years later, more than 250,000 Soviet Jews emigrated, mostly to Israel. It's now harder to gain an entry visa to the United States than an exit visa from Russia.

Millions of Russians and Westerners have

travelled to each others' countries, cementing friendships just as important to long-term peace as any number of treaties.

The Moscow McDonald's presented the first opportunity for ordinary Russians to see a piece of the West with their own eyes. It was not just the exotic, unknown food, "gambourgers", which they squashed flat in attempts to stuff them into their mouths. It was also the remarkable revelation that a restaurant could be clean, that service could be had in moments instead of hours and that employees could be polite and even welcoming to customers. Russians were accustomed to bribing their way into filthy restaurants

Left, newly-weds pay homage to Russia's past at the Tomb of the Unknown Soldier, Moscow. **Right**, McDonald's opens in Moscow.

staffed by rude, lazy waiters. They were willing to stand in line for 90 minutes to experience the difference. Most amazing of all was the fact that McDonald's managed to achieve the change not with foreigners but with 600 Russian employees. The company even taught them to smile – confounding the fear of one of the first employees who shook his head at the notion and said, "People will think we're idiots."

The pros and the cons: For ordinary people, the biggest change in the new Russia is the freedom to speak, and to starve. When Russia's president, Boris Yeltsin, freed prices which had been frozen for as long as 30 years, inflation went wild. Suddenly, milk

covered they were poor – and, naturally, they didn't like it.

For Sergei Borodin, it meant resigning a commission in the army and his job as a rocket engineer at the Baikonur Cosmodrome to start a sawmill to produce the lumber the country so desperately needs to rebuild. Borodin decided that the space programme and military had little future since they were both run by the deceased Soviet government. He decided to start a business "because it's a necessity. We have to feed ourselves."

For others it meant working in the new, small, private enterprises: manufacturing the expensive but dramatically more fashionable clothes now decorating Tverskaya Street,

that had cost 30 kopecks for a lifetime was selling for 2 roubles, if it could be found at all. A 5-kopeck bus ride rose to an extortionate 50 kopecks. Old women with 1,000 roubles stashed under their mattresses in readiness for their funerals suddenly found that their life savings would not even buy dinner for the wake.

A whole nation that had lost the incentive to work because there was nothing to buy with the salaries it earned suddenly found that it had better get moving and find some cash. The system where connections and favours were more important than money disappeared. Inevitably, people rapidly dis-

publishing the independent newspapers and selling Western luxuries like foreign beer for large sums of roubles.

Prices tumble for the tourist: For the foreign shopper, however, prices became extremely reasonable because exchange rates plummeted. In 1988, it was a criminal offence for a Russian to hold foreign currency, and exchange could be made legally only at government offices that paid 0.66 roubles to the dollar. Even the black market rate was only 3 roubles to the dollar. By 1992, the rouble had become effectively convertible, with private banks a few metres apart in Moscow's main post office offering competing rates. Those rates were near 200 roubles to the dollar and rising.

The result for tourists is that Russia has been transformed from a shopping wasteland to a bargain basement. Fur hats, formerly found only in the government dollar stores for hundreds of dollars, or from friends with connections, can be found for $30–$75 in private stores all over town. Handmade rugs from the Muslim mountain areas have dropped in price by hundreds of dollars. But for Russians, the rouble price tags now have two extra zeros on the end.

Fury over the price rises drives a rural grandmother named Nadia to rail away, openly calling for the return of a dictator.

for a Russian to sell anything he had not manufactured with his own hands. This law strangled wholesale and retail trade. Food rotted in the collective farm fields because no-one dared earn a profit by transporting it to the hungry cities. Only understaffed and inept government agencies were allowed to do that.

Yeltsin's decree wiping out restrictions on trade unleashed tens of thousands of would-be vendors. People started selling in the street, from a tiny table, a blanket spread on the sidewalk, or just by holding up a bottle of vodka and a pair of shoes to the buyers threading their way through crowds of sellers. Sometimes, sellers are pensioners des-

"Everything was normal under Stalin! The democrats are guilty! They brought chaos to the country. The Communists were great!" she insisted. But later, she proudly boasted that her daughter in Vladivostok can afford the new price of flying her mother across the continent for a visit because she is earning 40,000 roubles a month sewing her own fashionable clothing designs.

The new market economy: Most importantly for the future, a market is finally forming in Russia. Until February 1992, it was illegal

perate for a few roubles for food, selling off their valuables, one by one, but more often they are entrepreneurs, buying up scarce items in provincial cities where they are manufactured and transporting them to other cities, or even just other neighbourhoods. It is the black market gone public.

Car-owners in need of parts once had to go through a long round of contacts to find someone hoarding a spare windscreen. Now they can run out to the auto-parts flea market on the outer ring road. Hardware sellers congregate around the Kiev Station.

Stores have filled up too, because shoppers can no longer afford to snap up anything

Left, two sides to every story. **Above**, exchanging coupons for Western butter.

that appears on the shelves. In 1988, carpet stores sold their meagre shipments by lottery. Refrigerators were nowhere to be found. Within months after Yeltsin's decree, three stores in one block on Moscow's New Arbat Street had refrigerators – though there was only one refrigerator in each shop, and it would take a suitcase full of cash to buy it. One happy young Muscovite said she finally began to believe things were changing when she heard a store manager threaten to fire a clerk for being rude to a customer.

Although some Russians are thrilled with the new opportunities to buy, most are appalled at the high prices. After a lifetime of Communist condemnation of profit, many

looking for office and housing space, even decrepit flats in central Moscow have sky-rocketed in value from 10,000 roubles to hundreds of thousands and even millions.

So a Russian looking to move still starts by poring over the scraps of paper fluttering from walls all over town. "3 = 1 + 2" is the code for "Will change one 3-room apartment for a one-room and a two-room" – probably an advertisement from a divorcing couple. Irina Mikhailova rounded up fistfuls of such proposals and constructed an elaborate trade involving half a dozen families. The deal brought her a new apartment in a desirable neighbourhood of central Moscow, not far from Gorbachev's city apartment, and en-

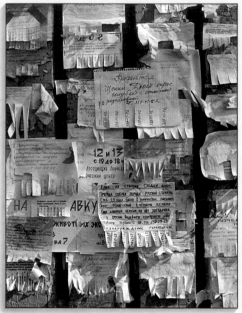

despise the new merchants. "You can buy anything now, but only for astronomical prices!" says Tamara Popova, a middle-aged Moscow mother. She was furious that milk, unavailable for months, had reappeared among the street vendors at 12 roubles instead of the state price of 1.90 roubles.

"Did they make that milk?" she complains. "Why should they make so much money? That's not trade, that's theft!" And she's warned her 18-year-old son he'd better not let her catch him selling on the street.

Most people are still paying token amounts for rent: 30-40 roubles a month. But with privatisation beginning, and foreign firms

sured that granny's flat would not revert to the state when she died. She even traded away a privately owned cooperative flat for the right to live in state-owned rooms, which she may be able to purchase when privatisation is approved. She did not dare simply sell her family's apartments and buy new ones with the cash because galloping inflation could leave her with a pile of useless roubles and no place to live.

The secret streets: But where perestroika has been rough, Gorbachev's policy of glasnost (openness) has wrought miracles. It's difficult to comprehend the extent to which Soviet censorship has effected every aspect of Russian life. Want a telephone number for a new friend? Forget it. There are no telephone directories. These and detailed city maps have started to appear only recently. Both were banned, allegedly to keep enemies from learning strategic details like population counts and the location of major bridges. Many maps were deliberately distorted: the tourist map of Odessa, for instance, was missing all side streets as well as an entire three-mile-wide industrial section of the city. Topographical maps were so secret that even field geologists searching for minerals could not retain one overnight.

Without accurate information, corruption became uncontrollable. Officials in Party was dependent on total censorship, for its hold on power would never last if the Soviet people figured out the allegedly enslaved workers of capitalism were earning salaries 10 times theirs. The final blow to censorship came when computers transformed the West, moving into every business and many homes, and advancing star wars. Leonid Brezhnev banned them for all but top-security purposes, because computers are effectively little printing presses.

Even history has changed. History examinations were cancelled one year because media accounts of Soviet history differed so dramatically from the textbooks used by students. Then the educators started a pro-

Uzbekistan ran a scam for years in which they lied to Moscow about cotton production, skimmed off the profits, and ran entire underground fiefdoms, complete with personal slaves and a silver statue of Lenin. Soviet citizens had to trade favours or bribes for everything from a taxi ride to a chunk of stewing meat.

In fact, the fierce secrecy and cavalier attitude toward accurate information was crippling the economy. But the Communist

Far left, a car bonnet sale. **Left**, are you looking for a bargain? **Above**, competing views in Moscow's underground.

gramme of rewriting. The result was a hybrid combining new truths and old lies. The 10th-grade text published in 1989 stated baldly: "Tentative estimates put the total number of deaths in the repressions at about 40 million people" – a statement that would have put the author in prison in the pre-Gorbachev era. But the text refrained from admitting that the Soviet Union had forcibly annexed the Baltics. And it insisted Japan's fate in the war "was decided not by the explosion of the atom bomb but by the reality of Soviet military forces," which attacked Japanese troops in China three days after Hiroshima.

Heaven and hell: The reformers are still

Curbing The Demon Drink

Nothing tempered the initial euphoria created by glasnost and perestroika like Mikhail Gorbachev's crackdown on drinking. Noting that a Russian population one-third larger than at the end of World War II was drinking 800 per cent more alcohol, and that 40 percent of the men were generally drunk, Gorbachev introduced rationing by reducing opening hours and decreeing, for example, that drinks would not be served with lunch until after 2pm.

While the rather sudden erosion of Gorbachev's popularity at home is usually put down to unfulfilled economic expectations, the curb on

drinking had a lot to do with it, and not just because the Russian thirst is notoriously unquenchable. The loss of government revenue from vodka sales was not in the same league as the previous drop in oil prices, but the vodka industry was the single shining light in an otherwise moribund economy. Instead, Russians retreated into basements and garden sheds to distill their own, and the country's consequent consumption of sugar soared beyond belief. The whole country became a bubbling cauldron of illicit brew.

The Russians evidently drank their cares away during the 250 years of Mongol subjugation; they were certainly hard at it when Westerners "discovered" the Moscow-based Russia of the 16th

and 17th centuries. Adam Olearius, a member of the Duke of Holstein's embassy to Muscovy, was forthright: "They are more addicted to drunkenness that any nation in the world. The vice of drunkenness is prevalent among this people in all classes, both secular and ecclesiastical, high and low, men and women, young and old."

At the turn of the 18th century, when Peter the Great wished to westernise Russia, an attempt was made along Gorbachev's lines to get the situation under control. Privately-owned taverns were closed down and towns were allowed only one liquor store. The thinking behind a law which required vodka to be sold by the jug or tankard, not less, was to put *vodichka* (literally, "darling little water") beyond the means of peasants who might otherwise be tempted to have a quick one. In practice, the result was *ad hoc* syndicates which bought a jug and shared it.

Gorbachev, himself a tea-drinker, could at least address the problem of alcohol abuse in Russia from high moral ground. In setting the precedent, however, Peter the Great was wholly disingenuous. He not only drank like a fish but smoked like a chimney, and his sanctimonious stance on tobacco was equally implausible. The official objections to smoking were not based on health considerations so much as practicality – cities were made almost exclusively of wood – and, curiously, aesthetics. If the story can be believed, Russian smokers puffed away furiously even in church, and the ensuing fog was said to discomfort icons more accustomed to the pleasant waft of incense and "pleasant-scented things". Those who violated the ban on smoking ran the risk of having their nostrils slit, a potentially fatal knouting, or even the death penalty.

If the Russian taste for tobacco is merely an unremarkable addiction to nicotine, vodka is written into the national psyche, the *sine qua non* of manliness, courage and camaraderie. It is also an anaesthetic, a point acknowledged by the post-Gorbachev decision to freeze the price of vodka while everything else, including bread, was allowed to float on the inflationary tidal wave. While drink is the third most common cause of death in Russia, and industrial productivity plummets on Mondays and pay-day, a populist leader like Boris Yeltsin is unlikely to go teetotal. If, as legend has it, over-refreshment tipped him into the Moscow river during a public function one night, most Russians would be comforted to know that human fallibility just like theirs was stalking the corridors of the Kremlin. ∎

battling against a Russian character formed during 70 years in which anyone who stuck out from the crowd – even to excel – was struck down. "They pretend to pay us, and we pretend to work" was how many workers summed up their relationship with their employer in 1988. Employees who bothered to show up for work quickly left to go and stand in line for a soup bone or a bottle of milk. Would-be diners virtually had to drag waiters out of the kitchen for service in state-owned restaurants. The staff knew they would never be fired. It was a worker's paradise, but a consumer's hell.

Ten years ago, kowtowing was so much part of life that a burly lifeguard could be

did not understand what it really meant to be free until I lived in the West," marvelled one émigrée when she returned to Moscow for a visit and saw through new eyes the behaviour she had once thought normal.

Meanwhile, factory workers are wondering whether their bankrupt companies will have enough roubles to meet the next payroll. Everyone fears the consequences of mass unemployment when hopelessly inefficient, pollution-belching industrial plants are shut down.

But ambitious, entrepreneurial Russians are thriving. Serge, a Moscow State University student and until 1988 a conscientious member of the Young Communist League,

reduced to snivelling by a grandmotherly guard barring him from a foreigners' campground. Servility was even an essential part of day-to-day shopping. Empty stores did not compete for customers; customers competed with each other for a tiny supply of goods. Russians were reduced to pleading with clerks or bribing them to obtain a hunk of meat for dinner. Attitudes of servility and passivity are only now being shaken off.

However, when a Russian takes a tentative step into the unknown opened up by the reforms and succeeds the joy is boundless. "I

<u>**Above**</u>, **art offered for sale to foreign visitors.**

has been chosen by a major Western company to earn $31,000 a year while on a two-year training programme to become a Moscow representative for the firm. Sieva, a one-time *dvortsovchik* (black marketeer) who hung around the palace or *dvorets* in St Petersburg to sell trinkets to tourists, is now running his own export operation and travelling to the United States on business. Thousands of families have opened small private restaurants, and ex-KGB officers are forming private security guard companies to defend the fledgling entrepreneurs against extortion rings.

In the countryside, most villagers still toil

on huge collective farms to grow potatoes, cabbage and wheat, which spoil before they reach the city. They still congregate in the grocery store to gossip, but now the latest news is the fate of the few brave souls in town struggling to make it as some of Russia's first private farmers in 60 years.

The knowledge that Russia's last private farmers were killed off by Stalin when he collectivised the farms is not exactly encouraging. A pioneer private farmer is so alien a concept that the Russians had to adopt an English word to describe one – *fermer* is never used in relation to those who work on collective farms.

These pioneers, like Misha Pashchenko in

the village of Nedelnoe 120 km (75 miles) from Moscow, finally won the right to obtain full-sized fields in 1992. But by then tractor prices had jumped from 2,500 to 250,000 roubles. Pashchenko has no hope of ever earning that kind of money. So he waits and hopes the government will give it to him. Meanwhile, he struggles to survive on barely an acre (half a hectare), with a few sheep, goats and beehives.

With no legal access to the collective farms' distribution system, few hardware stores and no agricultural stores anywhere in Russia, finding even hand tools is a major difficulty for the new farmers. When Pashchenko

needed a pair of sheep shears, for example, he had to track down a factory which made them – in a country with no directories listing such things, where it is likely that one company has the monopoly on their manufacture, and when it might be located in what is now another country. Even if he was successful in his search for such a company he would then have to work out a barter deal, trading food for the shears, since nobody wants worthless roubles anymore.

Pashchenko did not find an electric shears before spring. He ended up using a pair of pre-Revolutionary scissors belonging to a neighbour. His wife had to hold each squirming sheep for more than an hour while he snipped by hand.

Meanwhile, villages near major cities are quickly turning into suburbs. All over the country, salmon-brick houses are sprouting up, transforming sleepy hamlets into construction sites overnight. Authorities are dividing up plots of land, and new private construction companies are rushing into the virgin housing market. With most Russian families currently living at least two to a flat, demand for private houses is limitless. Four years ago, most Russians would look at a small private house outside the city and think: "I can never have one of those." Only families actually working the land or the Communist elite could obtain permission to own a single-family home. Other families had to settle for sharing, or for a summer shack elegantly termed a *dacha*. Now, with restrictions slipping away, everyone is trying to build.

Doting parents: Crowded into tiny apartments, the Russians have extremely close family ties. They dote on their children (as they do their pets), keeping toddlers close to parents or grandparents and rarely sending them off to play. In winter, they bundle children into balls of snow clothes. Each outfit is topped off with a woollen scarf around the neck, tied at the back so that the mother can grab it when the child tries to wander off.

But with a typical family of mother, father and grandparents living in two rooms, few ethnic Russians have more than one or two children. With birth control rarely available, the average Russian woman winds up undergoing six abortions in her lifetime, with the accompanying problems for her long-term health. The cramped living conditions exacerbate marital difficulties, and the divorce rate is high. Alcoholism doesn't help.

Many families deal with the cramped living conditions by escaping to a *dacha*, typically translated as summer home. Gorbachev's *dacha* was a three-storey mansion with an escalator down to a private beach on the Black Sea, with an indoor swimming pool and a compound full of guards, and outbuildings. For most Russians, however, a *dacha* is an unheated wooden hut, a summer home because they could not possibly live in it during the severe Russian winter.

But they are delightful nonetheless. They are places where residents of polluted, con-

ers. Even at the height of the Cold War, ordinary Russians were intensely curious about foreigners rather than hostile. Officialdom went to great effort to keep tourists so busy at palaces, monuments and ballet performances that they had no opportunity to mingle with ordinary people on the street and in the shops. Still, travellers sitting down in a restaurant would often be invited to join a table of locals for a wild night of drinking, dancing and eating. The first toast was always, *Za mir* (to peace), and at some point in the evening, a Russian would enquire why the West wanted to blow his or her country off the face of the earth.

Russia's history of unforgivable horrors,

crete Soviet-built cities can bask in fresh air and sunshine, and raise a garden that will feed the family for months. Typically, grandparents and grandchildren move from the family flat to the *dacha* for the summer, and working couples join them on the weekend. This system gives younger couples much-needed privacy in the city flat.

Getting to know them: For the traveller, the most wonderful part of the recent reforms is that Russians no longer have to worry about the KGB if they are seen talking to foreign-

official anti-Semitism, the crushing of religion and its morals, discrimination against various minorities, as well as an entire way of life based on privileges for the few and corruption for the many, has left the country with a basketful of prejudices. Many Russians are bigoted against black foreigners, Jews, homosexuals, entrepreneurs, and *chornie* – literally "blacks" but referring to olive-skinned Caucasians from the southern regions of the former Soviet Union. Chukchi, an Eskimo-type people from the northeast corner of Siberia, near Alaska, bear the brunt of rude ethnic jokes.

But put these same people in a living room,

Left, **puppy for sale. Above**, a pampered pet, evidence that Russians are great animal-lovers.

or in any one-to-one situation, and the rude street fighters become generous and welcoming. Friendship means something very special in Russia – a tight bond, daily visits, drop-ins at midnight. When goods were scarce it meant buying shoes and toilet paper for one another when they appeared in a store. No favour is too great, and this is a land where everything is accomplished through trading favours.

Guests in a Russian home warrant a feast, even in times of shortages. There is always a spare bed, even when a family of four lives in a single room. After decades of hearing nothing about the rest of the world but propaganda, Russians are thrilled to meet foreign-

ers and eager to hear of life outside. In the provinces, where a Russian may never have seen a foreigner, the first round of questions is often detailed and personal. Do you have children? How much is your salary? Your rent? Later, the questions become more sophisticated. How did you get your house? You mean, your employer did not give it to you after 10 years on a waiting list?

Today, meeting Russians is getting easier all the time. Keep clear of the tourist hotels and seek out co-op (private) restaurants, local bars (rare and therefore packed with drunks, all male) and trains. Call a foreign language school and offer to be a guest speaker; you will find dozens of them listed on scraps of paper pasted to walls of Metro stations and buildings. Most would be delighted to hear from you. Professional associations are also terrific matchmakers – whether you're a bricklayer or a stockbroker, there is a Russian who would be thrilled to compare notes on or off the job. Many major organisations, such as the Academy of Sciences, large factories and trade unions, have foreign affairs departments which handle these contacts. But don't be afraid to show up at the botanical garden, hospital or kindergarten and simply say hello.

Once you've made the initial contact, you may get yourself invited home to dinner or out to the family *dacha*, the only places to enjoy a good meal and to see the generous, friendly nature of a people who can seem like angry football players when encountered on the street.

For the most incredible, warm outpourings of curiosity and hospitality, get out beyond the tourist centres of Moscow and St Petersburg. These days, it is possible to swerve off the main highways without being halted by police, who are stationed at virtually every major intersection in the country.

Driving up a dirt road into the farms of the Caucasus Mountains, foreigners may find themselves transported to a time and place where the village elders smoke in the evenings on benches in front of their homes and watch the world pass by. Young boys will surround a stranger's vehicle, chattering and pointing, sometimes even daring to sneak a look at the engine. Soon, someone is racing off to catch a sheep to slaughter for a feast in the visitor's honour. This sounds romantic until one is faced with the prospect of the freshly roasted sheep's head and boiled entrails on the dining table.

Don't be surprised, however, when nearly everyone you meet tries to enlist your expertise and imagined vaults full of cash to help their fledgling business. Entrepreneurial instincts are blossoming across the country, fuelled by unlimited demand for any product someone can manage to produce. The Russians' imaginations are limited only by lack of funds and utter ignorance of the basics of a market economy and making a profit.

Above, enjoying a heat wave in July. **Right**, a lace-maker sells her wares.

The name "Russia" has a feminine gender in the Russian language and according to Russian tradition the country itself has a feminine soul. The myth of "mother Russia", deriving from the divinity of "mother earth" is central to the history of Russian culture from pre-Christian times to the present day. This is reflected in Russian fairytales, folklore, art and social structures.

Although the concept of motherhood was and still is very important in Russian culture, there are other images of feminine strength, such as *Russalki*, virgin mermaids with powers of witchcraft and self-transformation, and *Baba Yaga,* an unmarried old witch with a wooden leg, and *Vassilisa Premudraya* (Vassilisa the Wisest), a woman who is far wiser and cleverer than any of the men in pagan myths and fairytales.

Until the 13th century many Russian women had a certain status, power and even equality in some spheres of life, including military affairs. The situation changed when the central government moved from Kiev to Moscow. With the introduction and growing influence of Byzantine religion and the militarisation of Muscovite society, particularly during the Tartar invasion, the status of women diminished and the Christian doctrine of "female impurity" spread to Russia. From then on women from the upper classes were confined to the realm of domestic life and their status there was the lowest.

In rural areas, in peasant communities, women continued to have some freedom and power. They worked in the fields with the men, and they often ruled the roost at home, particularly if their husbands were serving in the army. They could even become the head of a rural community – *starosta*.

Female achievers: Russian history is full of outstanding women who played key roles in the political, cultural and social life of the country. Catherine the Great, who ruled Russia from 1762 to 1796, extended the territories of the country, introduced new liberal laws and improved educational institutions.

Her foreign policy made Russia one of the greatest European countries. Her friend and companion Catherine Dashkov (born Vorontsova) was the first woman in the world to become the head of an Academy of Sciences, an institution which she herself founded, together with the Russian Academy of Arts. Other outstanding figures include Vassilisa Kozhina, who led the peasant army during the Napoleonic War, and Sofia Kovalevskaya, a mathematician, astronomer, physicist and writer. The first fe-

male astronaut, Valentina Tereshkova, was also Russian.

In the 19th century, Russian women were more prominent as instigators of social and political change than women anywhere else in Europe. They campaigned for equal education of the sexes, organised charity fairs for women from a lower social background and worked as nurses in the Crimean War. They fought for social justice and equality on the barricades of the Paris Commune and in the underground terrorist groups in St Petersburg.

Many of them were educated in Europe where organisations were established to raise

Left, *Traktoristka* **(the Tractor Driver) by Georgy Gurianov. Right, political poster: "Emancipated Women Build Socialism".**

the level of education. Thousands of women belonging to a movement called *Narodniki* (Going to the People) walked down miles and miles of muddy country tracks to take literacy and social consciousness to the peasants. Equality of the sexes was a very popular concept, particularly among sections of the urban intelligentsia. The women who actively supported the cause were known as *Ravnopravki* (women for equal rights). They organised small ventures, providing jobs for other women, published newsletters and journals and founded publishing houses where they worked as editors and administrators.

Opportunities open: In 1917 feminist ideas were swallowed up by Socialist ideology.

women to produce more soldiers and workers for the Motherland. A special tax for childless families was introduced and abortion became illegal in 1936. Divorce procedure in court became far more complicated. As well as fulfilling the role of mother, Soviet women were also expected to perform state duties, such as working in factories and collective farms, as well as in professional spheres.

During World War II women fought side by side with men on the battlefields, serving as doctors, surgeons and nurses. There were also women pilots and women snipers in both the artillery and among the marine troops. Women formed the overall majority

However a decade later, Russian women again achieved a certain equality and social status. Beside the right to vote which was guaranteed by the new Soviet Constitution, the state provided a child daycare system, as well as other domestic services, free abortion and a new marital law which made husbands provide child support in cases of divorce. Marriage and divorce themselves became very easy and the ideas of free love were expressed and supported by a prominent Bolshevik and feminist leader called Alexandra Kollontai.

Stalinist industrialisation and militarisation of the Soviet state put a new demand on

of the workforce in the plants and factories producing arms and military equipment, and constituted the bulk of labour in the collective farms growing crops and raising livestock to feed the fighting country.

During the Soviet period Russian women enjoyed increased success in professional spheres. In 1988, 52 per cent of the labour force were women, and the same percentage applied to those who possessed higher education, such as university teachers, doctors and lawyers. But since the family tradition was and still is very patriarchal, women were also supposed to carry the double burden of domestic chores and childcare. Equality was harder to achieve in reality than on paper. The Soviet period, marked by the declining economy of the state, has been especially hard on Russian women. Poor household equipment (lack of washing machines, vacuum cleaners and the nonexistence of dishwashers), a poor (though cheap) system of childcare, and a deteriorating medical service – made Soviet women resent the achievements of "emancipation".

Perestroika ushered in new aspirations for social and political change. However, it didn't improve the position of women. If anything, their situation has become worse than before. In the preceding period women were guaranteed 33–34 per cent of parliamentary seats. The first election in the democratic period left women with 5–6 per cent of seats in the Russian parliament and in all local governing bodies.

Growing unemployment in the early 1990s hit women particularly badly. Statistics for Moscow and St Petersburg estimated that up to 75 or 80 per cent of the unemployed are women, most of them professionals with higher education.

The return of the sex-object: The social and cultural climate is even more conservative than before. The growing power of the Orthodox Church, overwhelmingly dominated by men, and a popular obsession with the mythological past have produced a new concept of womanhood in Russian society. The idea of equality is illogically associated with the rejected ideas of Communism, and therefore considered misguided and wrong. The former concept of woman-comrade, and woman friend, is being replaced by woman-wife and woman-mother. A new phenomenon, prompted by the Westernisation of Russian society through advertisements and films, is the image of woman as a beautiful sex-object.

Women's response to this new development is not so simple. Some believe that their only place is in the home as wives, mothers and caretakers. Others are struggling for the economic survival of their children and themselves in a difficult economic reality. Those who are active socially and politically are operating in a changed society.

The experience of building a civil society

is new to Russia, but women are actively bringing it about. They have formed various political, social, environmental and cultural groups, associations of women in business, single mothers and widows. There are also professional unions of women writers, women journalists and women with university education. Freedom of the press has produced many new women's journals and newspapers. Despite their differences in content and purpose, these publications indicate a growing desire of women to express themselves. Like their 19th-century predecessors, they are striving to maintain and improve their social and political status and are reluctant to give in to conservatism.

Despite the hardship of everyday life, Russian women still form the majority among the producers and consumers of cultural values. In museums and theatres, in libraries and exhibitions you will see far more women than men. In cities and villages it is the women who do the shopping and take care of the children, it is the women who help the poor, and it is the women who perform the duties of social workers.

The battle to achieve real equality and status for women in Russian society might be long, but the evidence of Russian history, the strength and great abilities of the women themselves, are proof that it will be won.

Left, women labourers. **Right**, an unconventional view of Russian women.

For many decades generations of Soviet people were trained to believe that in the "society of developed socialism" there was no organised crime. Nevertheless, a mafia in Russia undoubtedly existed under Communism, feeding off the capital controlled by state authorities, and continues to exist today, in spite of perestroika and glasnost.

The main difference between the mafia in Russia and mafia organisations elsewhere lies in the structure. If Western criminal organisations need to launder money, they bribe officials and politicians. In Russia the mafia operates at the top; crimes are hatched in the studies of the secretaries of the Party district committees, in the corridors of the Central Committee and Council of Ministers, and then delegated.

The mafia post-perestroika: The mafia operates in a variety of spheres. Firstly, it is active in the fertile field of privatisation, a process governed by a narrow circle of state functionaries who have the right to decide who, and at what price, is given property for businesses and housing. The volume of bribery has spiralled.

Secondly, through bribery and blackmail, the mafia attempts to channel state money into the black economy. The example of a recent well-known case connected with the Ministry of Agriculture is typical. When the work of this Ministry was examined, it became clear that in 38 out of 110 trade deals in a year agricultural products had been bought at twice the going world rate. The republic suffered multi-million losses. According to experts, every seventh criminal group in Russia has backers in the government.

Thirdly, the Russian mafia has become a key player in the international drug trade. At a recent conference on the drug trade held in St Petersburg it was reported that the amount of drugs seized in Russia has increased tenfold in the past decade. The number of drug addicts in the republic was given as 1½ million. Moreover, it is through Russia, with the help of the mafia, that drugs are shipped from Asian countries. Russian drug dealers are now behind drug shipments to Scandinavia, Germany, France, Greece and Poland.

Fourthly, there are the huge sums of money – about 5 billion roubles – that the Communist Party spirited into Western banks during the Soviet era. When privatisation began, they made their way back to the inner markets of Russia, usually through joint ventures, but not to the benefit of the State.

Lastly, there are the racketeering, prostitution and weapons trades. The mafia benefited from the national conflicts, and the withdrawal of Soviet troops from the former Soviet republics. Some sources even claim the conflicts were engineered by the mafia. In an interview with *Pravda,* Evgeny Oleinik, a KGB colonel, claimed: "Three months before the bloody events in Dushanbe, I was approached by one of the leading members of a mafia group. A press conference was organised in the Union of Journalists in the presence of 12 people well known in this country. The man told us about impending troubles in Dushanbe and the fact that his clan had been solicited as *agents provocateurs* by high party officials. Hearing this, a famous economist proclaimed it rubbish. Three months later, however, the tragedy happened just as we'd been told it would."

Mafiosi from all republics converge on Moscow. The godfathers of the Russian mafia work out their multi-billion deals in the city's deluxe hard currency restaurants. According to Mr Yuri Boldyrev, the corruption of Moscow authorities is so complex that special measures are needed to deter state officials from accepting bribes, in particular guaranteed high salaries and social status.

Explosions in St Petersburg: But organised crime is almost as prevalent in St Petersburg. In 1992 the chief of the Krasnoselskii city region authority, his assistant, the department chief of the Northwest Procurator Office, the department chief and lawyer of the Mayor's Office Committee for the Management of the City Property, and the lawyer of the Mayor's Office Committee for Foreign Economic Relations were all arrested for accepting bribes.

Meanwhile different mafia groups are engaged in an armed struggle for control of key zones In the summer the Chechen mafia removed its competitors by planting a bomb at the Moscow railway station: one person was killed and a few people were wounded. But the real battles started when the law arrested Aleksandr Malyshev, a top member of the city's mafia, and one of the leaders of the Tambov city mafia operating in St Petersburg. In both cases the police seized weapons and valuables worth several million roubles. The mafia responded by killing Evgeny Oleinik, the former chief of the service charged with the struggle against economic crimes.

Do business with caution: The growing number of foreign businessmen in Russia also encounter problems with the mafia, as the St Petersburg Commercial Centre "Baltika", an official representative of the firm Philip Morris, discovered when it set up dozens of kiosks selling Marlboro cigarettes. When the local trade mafia put up prices on the American cigarettes, Baltika went on selling them at the price they had agreed with the American firm. At first there were phone threats to the director of the commercial centre, but when these had no effect 10 kiosks owned by Baltika were blown up. The

criminals have not yet been found, but Baltika stuck to their guns and prices on cigarettes were increased only after the dollar rate rose.

Big joint ventures with foreign participation have set up their own security services, not even hoping for help from the local police. Smaller firms hire local policemen or private security agents. In big cities there are also special firms which collect information about the financial solvency of business clients in the Russian market (there have been cases of foreign businessmen being conned

by people passing themselves off as owners of enterprises and stock companies). Another phenomenon are the "night butterflies" – prostitutes who rob their clients. Prostitutes in Russia work under strict mafia control and are well equipped for robbery.

In a conference on crime convened in 1993, Boris Yeltsin cited crime as the number one problem facing Russia. Though some claimed the pronouncement was scare-mongering, and made merely to deflect attention from the multiplicity of other problems besetting Russia, statistics appear to bear it out. The previous year, 2.7 million crimes were reported and 4,000 mafia gangs smashed.

Above, violent crime on the streets.

Looking at the rotund physique of the average Russian, it is easy to assume that Russian cuisine must be irresistibly delicious. In fact the Russian tendency to add a layer each year, like trees, is the result of a terribly fattening diet – 69 per cent grain, potatoes, fats, oils and sugar, according to one estimate – and a very human reaction to a history of repeated famines.

As a result, Russian teenagers begin to bloat as soon as they hit their twenties and can no longer burn off 3,400 calories a day –

Because the Soviet government tried to prevent future famine by planting all cropland with wheat and potatoes, fresh fruits and vegetables are expensive luxuries in Russia. At least 30 per cent of fruits and vegetables rot before reaching the market or canneries.

The good news is that the new market economy is dramatically changing the choice of food. Fresh fruits and vegetables are already much more plentiful, although at prices the average Russian cannot afford. And the freed media are broadcasting exercise shows

a calorie intake 70 per cent higher than in America, which has a weight problem of its own. In the pre-Gorbachev days, *Moscow News* boasted: "In terms of calorie value of food consumed, the USSR is among the world's most affluent countries."

Most Russians weigh themselves by paying a few kopecks to an old woman with a scale standing on a street corner. The accompanying weight charts are eye openers. While an American woman of 5' 8" might be told 135 lbs is a healthy weight, Russian women are told that 152 lbs. is a suitable weight when they are in their twenties and 174 lbs is normal once they hit 40.

and foreign films that show Russians what exercise and a decent diet do.

Influences: Russian food was always bland, like that of most northern cultures. Spices are nearly unknown in traditional Russian cuisine, in spite of the Mongol hordes that overran ancient Rus. Strong flavours are found in dishes from the southern republics of the former Soviet Union, such as Georgia, Armenia and Uzbekistan, where herbs and spices grow naturally.

Years of Soviet government homogenised a cuisine that was not particularly sparkling in the first place. Russians will wax poetic about the way their bread used to taste, before farmers started growing hard wheat. Ordered by the Communist bureaucrats to produce more tons of wheat, they logically opted for the heaviest varieties.

Shortages also sapped the flavours of Russian cuisine. Even the famous Russian beetroot soup, *borscht*, appeared in restaurants as cabbage soup without a single beet.

Consequently, some of the worst food in the world is found in Russian restaurants. Menus are often lengthy lists of dishes which the restaurant has never even considered

of foreign currency. Only a few years ago, St Petersburg had about 25 restaurants for a city of 5 million. All were state-owned and awful. Now, hundreds of people have opened up private restaurants, also called co-ops, and the quality of food and service is 10 times better than in the filthy state-owned cafés. Most have dropped the loud dance band music common in state-owned restaurants in favour of a few minstrels wandering between the tables.

The private restaurants are also daring to

offering. Add a system where no one was ever fired, and where the staff could make more money selling food at inflated black market prices out the back door than at state-controlled prices on a diner's plate and where customers were forced to drag reluctant waiters out of the kitchen to get service and you have a recipe for disaster.

But Russian restaurants are being transformed by a market economy and the power

experiment. They use mushrooms (*gribi*) and Siberian cranberries (*klukvi*), for example, to make interesting sauces. Others specialise in the tastier foods of the former Soviet republics, such as spicy Georgian cuisine at U Peresmani in Moscow. Former client states are well-represented too – private restaurants feature the food of North Korea, Vietnam and China.

Foreign firms are opening joint-venture restaurants offering the cleanliness, comfort, food and service of the West. The difference in price is just as dramatic – a few dollars in a Russian state restaurant, a few more in a private rouble restaurant, and $30

Preceding pages: window of a seafood restaurant in St Petersburg. **Left,** inside the Elyseev's food store in St Petersburg. **Above,** cabbage, a perennially popular vegetable.

to $100 a person in the hard currency cafés.

The one truly gourmet food is genuine black caviar (*ikra* in Russian). With traders now selling openly on the streets, a 4-oz. (113-gram) glass jar of Beluga sturgeon eggs can be found for less than $10. (Be sure it's viscous, wet and black, not brown or dried up.) In rouble restaurants, caviar is also inexpensive, and especially delicious served on thin pancakes known as *blini*. Red caviar (*krasnaya ikra* instead of *chornaya ikra* or black caviar) is also good. Restaurants occasionally offer canned crab (*krabi*) or shrimp (*krevetki*) from the Soviet Far East.

Russians also do wonderful things with their immense variety of mushrooms. Fami-

lies go mushrooming in the woods for weekend outings. One popular dish is *julienne* (in Russian, *zhulienn*), a tiny casserole of mushrooms and sour cream served in individual metal dishes.

All of these are found on the *zakuski* or *hors d'oeuvre* section of the menu, and the most expensive private restaurants will have them waiting on the table when clients arrive. Other *zakuski* include slices of sturgeon or fatty sausage. *Salat* might be a dish of tomatoes or cucumbers but for greens, there's *travi* (literally, "grass") and in reality fresh basil, dill and green onions. Lettuce is unknown.

Main courses are likely to be *kotleti* (ground meat patties) or *bif-shtek* (beef), *svinina* (pork), or just plain *myaso* (meat of indeterminate origin). Chicken can be either *tsiplyonok* or *kuritsa* but beware: foreigners joke that the Russian method of slaughtering poultry is starvation.

More than a drop: Russians put up with shortages and poor food in restaurants because the main point of going to a restaurant in the first place is not eating but getting falling-down drunk. Among Russians, drinking is a major form of social bonding, especially among men.

One Western businessman tells of waking up in his hotel room covered with round bruises under his wet, muddy clothes, with a roaring hangover headache and no memory of how he wound up that way. A telephone call to a colleague revealed that he, too, was covered with mud and bruises, but at least he remembered how they got there. It seemed that on the return bus trip from a factory with their prospective Russian business partners, the Russians had cracked open an entire case of *konyak* and passed one bottle out to each man. Then they stopped for a roadside picnic, and the Westerner ended up falling down a hillside into a muddy river. His partner, trying to help, leaned over the embankment to look and tipped over too, rolling down the rock-covered hillside to join him. Hence, the round bruises, wet clothes and hangover.

The Russians fished them out, and now consider the pair of Westerners fast friends. For a Russian, a good restaurant is one where the white table-cloths are covered in bottles in preparation. Top-quality Stolichnaya vodka is widely available (locals always check to make sure the cap is still factory-sealed in case they end up with an expensive bottle of rubbing alcohol). Russian champagne (*shampanskoye*) is also excellent, as long as the drinker is not expecting the subtlety of the French variety. *Konyak* is the Russian word for brandy, and the ones from the former Soviet republics of Armenia or Georgia which have been aged for 10 years or more have a fine smooth flavour.

Good home cooking: For a good meal, get invited to someone's home. Despite food shortages and high prices, Russian generosity blossoms when there is a guest for dinner. Be prepared to stuff yourself, and then discover that there are three or more courses yet to come. The names of the dishes may be the same as on a restaurant menu – ravioli-like *pelmeni* (stuffed cabbage leaves), *pirozhki* (deep-fried parcels of meat, rice or potato) and pots of meat-and-potato stew – but there is no comparison. Russian housewives know all the tricks for plucking a feast out of a bare pantry, and they always have something set aside for a special occasion.

Be sure you go to dinner bearing flowers for the hostess, but never an even number of blooms – an omen for a death in the family. Hosts also appreciate a gift of Western food or drink – these items are still exotic in spite of their increased visibility in shops. Try a bottle of whisky, Swiss chocolates or some-

you might find someone on the street selling *pirozhki*. Recently, street kiosks have popped up all over the place, offering pizza, sausage sandwiches, and Georgian *khatchapuri* (a delicious hot cheese bread).

The enticing smell of grilled meat at roadside stands and in packed parks emanates from *shashlik*, chunks of spicy lamb grilled on a skewer. The quality of the meat varies markedly; the best *shashlik* is found in the southern Caucasus mountains. Good, fast food can also be found in the farmers' markets. Fresh or dried fruit, a chunk of cheese and a loaf of bread are heavenly when the hotel restaurant seems permanently closed. The prices in farmers' markets are stun-

thing really practical like a canned ham.

Fast food is such an alien concept in Russia that even McDonald's could not pull it off. The line at the sparkling clean McDonald's restaurant in Moscow often holds more than 1,000 people, as hordes of Russians wait for a glimpse of life in the West. The alternative is a *stolovaya*, a dirty Russian workers' cafeteria, where the proletariat is served cheap slop like a plate of rice topped with a few bits of fat and a ladle of grease. If you're lucky,

Left, red caviar served in a Moscow restaurant. Caucasians enjoy the produce of their favourable climate.

ningly high for Russians, but still reasonably cheap for foreigners.

Those desperate for Western food will find that Moscow and St Petersburg now have foreign-currency stores that sell all kinds of imported food at exorbitant prices – for example, $4 for a head of imported lettuce in the winter. With growing numbers of Russians earning foreign currency from the flood of new international businesses, many of these stores now have queues outside their doors at all hours. But Stockmann, near Paveletsky Railroad Station, accepts credit cards only, keeping most Russians away and the crowds down.

St Basil's Cathedral, whose cluster of twirling towers above Red Square makes it one of the most familiar landmarks in Moscow, is once again functioning as a church after a long spell under Communism as an anti-God museum, the fate of many if not most of the 77,000 churches which existed in pre-Revolutionary Russia. The gradual rehabilitation of churches since the late 1980s, together with the congregations they attract and the growing number of novices entering the priesthood, constitutes something of a religious revival in Russia.

This revival is open to a number of interpretations. Some see it as a triumphant repudiation of all the propaganda drummed into Russians over four generations by State organs like the Society of the Militant Godless. Others draw comparisons with the rise of Islamic fundamentalism in the Asian republics of the former Soviet Union and elsewhere, a manifestation of confused societies dredging through their past for some kind of cultural anchor. In these circumstances, the thesis continues, "the opium of the masses" (as the Communists called religious faith) might be just what the doctor ordered.

Religion in Russia should not in any case be equated with, say, Roman Catholicism in Poland, itself undergoing a renaissance. The latter is a more political and intellectual force fundamentally at loggerheads with everything atheistic Communism represented. Russian Orthodoxy, on the other hand, was never intellectualised as Christianity in the West was by the likes of Thomas Aquinas in the 13th century and subsequent Protestant theologians. The Russian faith was and is rooted in ritual, not theology, and it is not inconceivable that it could have contrived a *modus vivendi* with Communism as it did with tsarist absolutism.

Visitors who drop in on a Russian Orthodox service will be struck by the meticulous orchestration of ritual. There are hardly any prayer books in evidence, but everyone knows the procedure. The air is thick with incense, the richly coloured icons hold pride of place, and there is close interaction between clergy and congregation, communicating with one another through the medium of splendidly sonorous chant. Anyone familiar with the Greek Orthodox service will see parallels reflecting their common Byzantine origins.

Preserve of the elderly: The congregations these days are predominantly elderly, and that raises other questions about the nature of the present religious revival. The older gen-

eration, bewildered by the speed of change and acutely nostalgic, are inclined to look backwards beyond Communism with a view to reliving the past, whereas younger Russians give the impression of indiscriminately rejecting the whole lot. This naturally concerns those who would prefer to see the country's cultural heritage back on its pedestal, where the Church has a place next to the literature and art banished by Stalin. The younger generation, brought up with a vague and generally distorted idea of their cultural bloodline, are mesmerised by what amounts to a parody of Western values, an ephemeral mix of fashion, pop music and fast food.

Preceding pages: Orthodox iconostasis. **Left**, St Petersburg's Spas no Krovi, where Alexander II was assassinated. **Right**, *A Russian Baptism*, by Jean-Baptist le Prince.

Because the Russian Church never went through the process which eventually separated Church and State to varying degrees in the West, it had a peculiar role in society. So inalienably integrated were Church and State in tsarist times that, with the single exception in the 17th century previously mentioned, there was never any question of the Russian patriarch challenging the joint spiritual and secular supremacy of the crown. For their part, the tsars surrendered not an iota of autonomy to Church leaders. When their time came, the Russian Communists regarded themselves as the ultimate spiritual authority in exactly the same way as they assumed command of the armed forces.

only to counter the hostility of Western Christianity to the Eastern rites as a whole.

The fall of Constantinople to the Turks in 1453, just as Russia was emerging from the Mongol yoke, was therefore a devastating blow to the Russian Church, and Ivan III decided it was Moscow's sacred duty to become the "Third Rome", the beacon of the True Faith. This mission ultimately led to what were in large part religious wars with Roman Catholic Poland in which the latter was no less determined to win Russia for the Pope and Rome.

"Old Believers": In the mid-17th century Russia was plunged into a religious dispute which was its closest approximation to a

The messianic manner in which the Bolsheviks presumed to convert the whole world to Communism was uncannily reminiscent of the phenomenon of Moscow as the "Third Rome". Constantinople became the "Second Rome" after Rome proper was overrun by "German" barbarians in the 4th century. Although the Russian Church had progressively distanced itself from its Greek origins by adopting Old Slavonic for liturgical purposes (the Cyrillic alphabet was invented specifically to facilitate the transliteration of Greek religious tracts into Slavonic languages) and replacing its Greek clergy with native Russians, the bonds remained close, if

Reformation. Nikon, a peasant monk appointed Patriarch of Moscow in 1652 by Tsar Alexis, was determined to restore liturgical ritual to its Byzantine origins. It was a case of people crossing themselves with three fingers rather than two and omitting an extra word which had crept into the recitation of the Creed. He also insisted that churches would again be built with five domes.

These proposals were opposed by conservative elements within the Russian Church who came to be known, somewhat paradoxically, as "Old Believers". The opposition was led by a young archpriest named Avvakum, and the punishment he received for his pains, including 15 years of detention in an underground cell (he was ultimately burnt at the stake), inspired him to write the first prose work in the Russian language, a case study in ecstatic masochism. The monks at the Solovyetsky Monastery near the Arctic Circle withstood an eight-year siege by the army rather than agree to the changes, while thousands of ordinary Old Believers had their tongues cut out and their hands chopped off if they were not actually hanged.

The persecution of Old Believers carried over into the reign of Peter the Great when they, especially, refused to surrender their beards in the interest of bringing Russian society into line with Western Europe, where

When official persecution ceased, many Old Believers chose to remain in their remote colonies. They became famous for their hospitality when strangers dropped in, albeit with certain quirks. If the visitors were not themselves Old Believers, any plates or glasses they happened to use had to be smashed when they were finished with them. Such guests were expected to leave money for replacements on departure.

More conventional monastic orders could claim much of the credit for opening up vast tracts of the Russian interior. Rather like Irish monks who sailed away in tiny coracles to find solitary spots for contemplation, Russian monks went deep into virgin forests to

men were in the habit of shaving. Old Believers fled to remote areas rather than shave; those who were not quick enough and had their beards forcibly removed were careful to save the shorn whiskers in case of sudden death, the theory being that they could be brandished as proof of piety when applying for permission to enter heaven.

Colonies of Old Believers exist to this day. Two secret monasteries and four secret convents, still in use, were uncovered deep in the Siberian forests as recently as the 1950s.

Far left, a nun (1908). **Left**, a priest and a deacon (1907). **Above**, Orthodox ceremony.

find sites for secluded monasteries. The tireless energy with which they made these remote areas habitable was their undoing because they were trailed by peasants pleased to exchange their labour for the right to settle on the monastic lands as tenants. These arrangements were preferable to ordinary serfdom, and they were the recipe which made monasteries collectively the biggest and richest landowners in Russia. Many monks were content to capitalise on their enterprise and become landlords, but others preferred to push the frontiers ever outwards and start all over again. There were more peasants ready to follow them so the cycle repeated itself until monasteries ringed the White Sea and encroached on the fringes of Siberia.

St Sergius of Radonezh was the foremost of the monks who simultaneously Christianised and colonised Russia, and his memory is revered at the Zdorsk monastery complex about 50km (30 miles) outside Moscow, probably the holiest shrine in the country. It is a veritable fortress containing no fewer than seven monasteries, the Russian equivalent of the Vatican. At the opposite end of the scale, the most reviled monk in Russian history was Gregory Rasputin, a member of a Khlysty flagellant sect in Siberia before entering the service of Nicholas and Alexandra, the last of the Russian royals. His

Tikhon issued an appeal to resist the theft of Church property, and the result was some 1,500 "bloody conflicts" followed by exile to Siberia or execution for the culprits. Tikhon was also arrested, making room for ecclesiastical Communist sympathisers to usurp his position. They declared the Patriarchate void and called on "every faithful Churchman…to fight with all his might together with the Soviet authority for the realisation of the Kingdom of God upon earth…and to use all means to realise in life that grand principle of the October Revolution."

The faithful proved to be singularly unmoved by the call and stayed loyal to the Patriarchate rather than the alternative "Liv-

success in treating their haemophiliac son through hypnosis was eclipsed when he applied his hypnotic powers to the tsar and tsarina with such appalling results that he discredited the Church as a whole in the estimation of the 1917 Revolutionaries.

The Church under Communism: The Bolsheviks did not at once ban religion outright. They nationalised all Church property, but most of the gold and silver plate and other valuables remained in the churches and monasteries. The terrible famine of 1921–22 persuaded the Patriarch Tikhon to pledge some of the Church's valuables as collateral for a foreign loan to buy food.

ing Church" offered to them. As the "Living Church" was clearly not going to stir, Tikhon was urged to repent in order to secure his release and resume duties. "I was filled with hostility against the Soviet authorities," he duly announced on his release in 1923. "I repent of all my actions directed against the government. I hereby declare that I am no more an enemy to the Soviet government." Tikhon's confession reaffirmed the traditional solidarity of Church and State, albeit a Communist state.

Assuming that Tikhon's confession had been made under duress, elements of the Church went underground. Taking their cue from the Communist cell system, they used passwords to make themselves known to one another. Priests in plain clothes would pop up unannounced in villages, administer to the faithful, and as suddenly disappear. In 1927, the year in which the first Five-Year Plan commenced, intellectuals and Christians were denounced as enemies of the revolution. Tax collectors swooped on churches and, if the sum demanded was not immediately forthcoming, they were summarily boarded up. Teaching religion to children under the age of 18 was forbidden except in private houses and to groups of no more than three children at a time.

Stalin relaxed the ban on Church activities

Christ Our Saviour. In that year Stalin ordered it to be blown up to make way for a new Palace of Congresses, designed to be taller than any building in America. It is said that monks living in cells beneath the church refused to leave before the fuses were lit and were buried alive in the rubble.

The project was postponed until after World War II, but as soon as construction did begin there was a curious development which many interpreted as the hand of divine retribution. On reaching a modest height, the building keeled over. Engineers decided that the river bank was too soft to support a building anywhere near the size of the proposed Palace and recommended that the

during World War II in an attempt to lift morale. As soon as the war was over, however, controls were reimposed in the form of intense anti-religion propaganda in schools and general intimidation of anyone who aired religious convictions. The Moscow Open-Air Swimming Pool on the banks of the Moscow river opposite the Fine Arts Museum is perhaps the most graphic example of the plight of religion under Stalin. It is on the site of what was until 1939 the Temple of

Left, 12th-century angel and 20th-century monk. **Above**, an invitation from Billy Graham: "A man who speaks with the people… entrance free."

project be abandoned.

As a face-saving exercise, the site was excavated to provide a genuinely popular amenity, the said Moscow Open-Air Swimming Pool. Water in the pool thus created was kept at a constant 27°C (80°F) all year round, warm enough to generate a dense cloud of vapour in winter. The belief persisted that the site was home to the souls of the monks who had perished, and under the cover of the cloud, the Moscow Open-Air Swimming Pool became a popular venue for clandestine baptisms. The talk these days is that the swimming pool may yet be filled in and a new church built on the site.

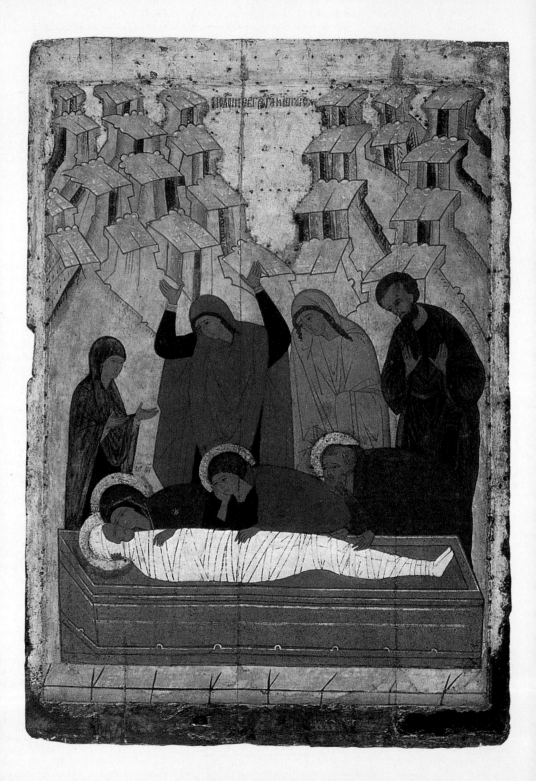

Russia derived its art and culture from Constantinople. When the Roman Emperor Constantine, the first Christian emperor, moved the capital of the Empire from Rome to the shores of the Bosphorus in 323, civilisation and Christianity prospered there for just over a millennium.

By the time the Turks captured Constantinople in 1453, Russia had been converted; Moscow was the "Third Rome", the legitimate heir to Rome and Byzantium. Until the time of Peter the Great, 700 years later, all art produced in Russia served the one ideal of a Christian, theocentric view of the universe. There was no Renaissance in Russia, and although it is possible to apply Western humanistic criticism to icon painting, in doing so we are seeing things that were not necessarily intended and not seeing other things that were. However, the austere spiritual power that radiates from icons is a reflection of a universe with God at its centre, and it is eloquent where words are difficult. And if this is not enough, their painterly language and use of colour and line are powerfully expressive; so much so that icon painting formed the basis on which a generation of Russian painters at the beginning of this century modelled their work, which in turn had a vital effect on 20th-century painting in general.

Revelations: The art-historical study of icons is a recent phenomenon; the first exhibition was held in 1913, during the celebrations of the tercentenary of the Romanov dynasty. At the turn of the 20th century, amidst a general revival of interest in indigenous Russian art forms, icons were cleaned for the first time. The public was amazed. The educated classes in Russia had received an artistic education that held Raphael to be the summit of achievement in painting; they were secretly ashamed of what they considered to be clumsily painted, primitive icons.

In general, people had assumed that the older an icon was, the gloomier and darker it would be; no one was prepared for the bright colours which emerged from centuries of over-paint. Research was begun, manuscripts were studied; but unlike Western paintings, icons are not signed, and positive evidence is hard to come by. In addition, icons were for much of the Soviet period systematically destroyed, left to rot in closed churches to which no one was allowed access, or even, in a typical act of Soviet cynicism, sold abroad to raise hard currency.

The two most important collections of icons in Russia are in the Tretyakov Gallery in Moscow and in the Russian Museum in St Petersburg.

Miraculous powers: *The Mother of God of Vladimir*, which originated in Jerusalem and was taken to Constantinople in the 12th century, is the greatest miracle-working icon of Russia. According to Orthodox tradition, it is one of the three likenesses of the Virgin Mary painted by Saint Luke during her lifetime. In the 5th century, it was taken from Jerusalem to Constantinople, where it remained until the middle of the 12th century. From there it was sent to Prince Yuri Vladimirovich Dolguruky in Kiev, who put it in the Devichy convent in Vyshgorod.

In 1155, the Prince of Vyshgorod took the icon on a military campaign in the north. As the Prince and his train were crossing the river Kliasma, the horses carrying the icon were unable to go forward. Taking this as a sign, the Prince built a church on the spot, which he named Bogoliubovo (loved by God), and placed the icon in it. It went on to play an important role in Russian history; tsars were crowned in its presence; it accompanied Prince Andrei Bogoliubsky to victory against the Volga Bulgars (it supposedly sent out fiery rays to protect Prince Andrei's soldiers); and it is credited with saving Moscow from the Tartars on two occasions, and from the Poles once.

It now occupies a new, slightly forlorn position in the Tretyakov Gallery, where pilgrims bring it offerings.

Pre-15th century: It is difficult to talk about Russian icon painting much before the 15th century; works do survive, but most icon painters at this time were either Greek masters invited to Russia, or their Russian pupils

Preceding pages: *The Apparition of Christ to the People* by Alexander Ivanov. **Left,** *The Entombment* by an anonymous master.

working so closely in the Byzantine tradition that it is impossible to see the difference. The most famous, and probably one of the last of these Greek painters to make his career in Russia was Theofan, called "the Greek", who arrived in Novgorod around 1380. Very few works have survived which can be positively attributed to him. The Tretyakov Gallery has a panel of the Transfiguration which is probably by him or a close pupil.

In 1240 the fire-worshipping Tartars reached and took Kiev, and there followed a humiliating period of Mongol occupation which lasted until the Muscovite victory at the battle of Kulikovo in 1380.

Only the merchant city state of Novgorod

remained relatively unaffected by the Tartars, mainly due to its isolated, northerly position. For the same reasons, Byzantine tradition here evolved into something new, something unmistakably native. Cut off from Constantinople until the late 14th century, the icon painting of Novgorod was for a time forced to fall back on its own resources. It is a provincial city, and the icons it produced are marked by their vivid colours and unsubtle, folkloric designs. They are best seen in Novgorod's Cathedral of the Holy Wisdom, where there is also one of the few intact iconastases left in Russia.

One of the best known panels contained in the Museum of Architecture and Ancient Monuments is the mid-15th century *Battle of the Novgorodians with the Suzdalians*. It is unusual in that it is not based on a biblical event, but commemorates a battle that took place in 1169.

The subject matter and its treatment reveal much about its Novgorodian creators; they were very down-to-earth people, interested in concrete facts and simple story-telling set out in a decorative and easily comprehensible manner. This has as much to do with their contact with the West as with their mercantile turn of mind. Although the painterly language derives from Byzantine painting, there is nothing particularly spiritual about the bold and rhythmic use of reds and whites. This is as Italian as Russian icon painting got until the beginning of the 17th century. And the Novgorodians were not "helped" by this icon; Moscow defeated Novgorod in 1471, and a century later the city fell completely under the dominance of Moscow.

Theofan, Rubliov and Dionisiy: After the defeat of the Tartars at Kulikovo in 1380, Moscow began to recover from Mongol domination, and to re-emerge as the torchbearer of Byzantium, not only in its Imperial aspirations but also in its painterly style. Theofan, who moved from Novgorod to Moscow some time before 1400, worked on the iconostasis of the Annunciation Cathedral in the Kremlin together with a young Russian monk by the name of Andrei Rubliov. The only reason his name is known is because he is referred to in contemporary manuscripts. It was not until 1904, when his famous *Holy Trinity* was cleaned for the first time, that scholars were able to get an idea of his style. The panel was painted for the Trinity-St Sergius monastery outside Moscow, in memory of its founder, St Sergius of Radonezh (*circa* 1319–42). Rubliov, who had entered the monastery as a monk before leaving to pursue his career as a painter, was asked to return in 1422 in order to decorate the new stone church, and it was at this time that he painted the *Holy Trinity*.

It is difficult to imagine a greater contrast in styles between the nervous, expressionistic Theofan, and his supposed pupil Rubliov. But it was Rubliov who had the greater influence in establishing a style for the next half century. *The Entombment* of the late 15th century (also in the Tretyakov Gallery) is the work of an anonymous master. It too uses a combination of mathematics, music and rhythm to achieve a devastating harmony. The theme of the icon is grief, but whereas a Western painter would have expressed the grief through the facial expressions of the assembled characters, the Orthodox painter does not concern himself with this kind of private feeling. The grief in this icon is the grief of the loss of Christ, the son of God, and in this icon even the mountains grieve. Christ's body, bound in white, is laid out, a horizontal, long note, against which a small rhythm of hands and faces is constructed, slowly fading as it moves towards His feet; behind is a rhythm of colour and rhetorical gesture, immediately reaching a high point with the scarlet-robed Mary Magdalene's outstretched arms. Even nature submits itself and inclines towards the dead King; the mountains are torn apart by the events unfolding at their feet, and like electricity cables allow the tension to be conducted out and away.

The last major figure in classical icon painting is Dionisius (1450–1508). Again, there is not much left that can be firmly attributed to him, and the main basis for an evaluation of his style is a cycle of frescoes in the Ferapont Monastery, 570 km (350 miles) north of Moscow. He deployed a delicate colour scheme, applying pale, translucent washes of paint over fine, precise drawing, to achieve an elegant solemnity. In the Tretyakov Gallery, one can see biographical icons of the sainted Metropolitans of Moscow, Peter and Alexei, which exude a cool and dignified mysticism.

When Ivan the Terrible killed his son in 1598, he put an end to the dynasty that had ruled Muscovy since its beginnings. The early 17th century brought with it military defeat and, for the first time, ideological confrontation with the Catholics to the west. The Poles overran Moscow in 1605 and 1610, and despite the murder of the Polish-supported false Dmitry by a Russian mob, and the coronation of Mikhail Romanov in 1613, Polish influence and Catholic claims in Russia continued well into the century.

From this time onwards, Russia could no longer live behind closed borders, protected by distance from the pervasive culture of the Germano-Latin West. Forced to seek help first from Sweden, and then from England and Holland in order to overcome the military threat posed by Poland, Russia opened itself up to Western trade; it was not long before Dutch engravings, and Piscator's Bible in particular, found their way to Russia, and this inevitably had an effect on icon painting. The best icons were produced in the tsar's workshops in the Armoury Palace of the Moscow Kremlin.

The 17th century was a period of transition; as so often happens when a culture begins to lose its way, ornament and decoration preoccupied the new generation of paint-

ers. Elaborate, jewel-encrusted silver covers that obscured the image, miniature painting to rival those of Persia, fine gold decoration; and, to the horror of those who upheld tradition, naturalism. According to Avvakum, the champion of the Old Believers, Christ was portrayed in the new icons "with a plump face, red lips, curly hair, fat arms and muscles… which altogether make him look like a German, big bellied and fat." Whatever the theological arguments, the golden age of icon painting was dead.

Secular themes: Painting as a purely secular art took time to develop, despite the push-start given by Peter the Great and his regime

Left, detail from *The last Day of Pompeii* by Karl Briullov. **Right**, *Harvesting: Summer* by Alexi Venetsianov.

of enforced Westernisation on an unwilling population. By the end of the 18th century there were a number of good portrait painters (Levitsky, Rokotov, Borivikovsky), but there is little to differentiate them from the French and German painters they imitated. Afterwards came the Romantic Orest Kiprensky (1782–1826), who spent most of his unhappy life in Italy, and is best remembered for his now classic portrait of Pushkin, in the Tretyakov Gallery.

Painting did not recapture its Russian voice again until the beginning of the 19th century, with Alexei Gavrilovich Venetsianov (1780–1847). Active at a time when the prevailing fashion, in Russia and elsewhere, was for

neoclassicism, Venetsianov turned his attention away from Ancient Greece and Rome, and focused on Russian peasant life. *Harvest Time: Summer* in the Tretyakov Gallery shows a peasant girl, in the traditional, colourful costume, breast-feeding her child while work continues in the hot sunshine. It is a simplified, rather than an idealised, vision of peasant life, for the idealisation is only in the deliberate beauty of the scene, and the bright, calm colours of the Russian countryside.

Venetsianov was the first Russian artist to devote himself to the countryside. While in his thirties, he bought an estate in the district of Tver, and spent the rest of his life there.

The second quarter of the 19th century was dominated by two figures: Karl Briullov (1799–1852), and Alexander Ivanov (1806–58). Each is well known for one monumental work (Briullov's *Last Day of Pompeii* and Ivanov's *Christ's Appearance before the People*, both in the Russian Museum), and they were both instrumental in raising the social standing of the artist, who had hitherto served, but not been part of, *le beau monde*.

Briullov, who is alleged to have refused to paint Nicholas I's portrait because the latter turned up late for the first sitting, lived in Italy for many years, and it was there that he painted his masterpiece. Its allegorical allusion to the collapse of antiquity and, by extension, the old regime has perhaps been overplayed by Soviet critics (Alexander Herzen claimed that the painting reflected the atmosphere in St Petersburg, alluding to the Decembrist uprising of 1825), but the canvas, for its sheer size and drama alone, made Briullov famous all over Europe, causing one critic to claim: "*The Last Day of Pompeii* is the first day of Russian art."

Throughout the reign of Alexander II Russian artists increasingly reflected the discussions and political life of the time; classicism and romanticism were rejected and gave way to genre painting and realism. Nicholas I, whose military, conservative character dominated his reign, was succeeded by Alexander II, whose reign witnessed a softening on the side of the autocracy which was mirrored by a hardening of the forces of opposition and Western-style "progressivism", leading finally to his assassination in 1881.

Spotlight on the bourgeoisie: During the 1840s and early 1850s, Pavel Fedotov (1815–52) painted canvases depicting dramatic moments in the lives of the bourgeoisie: the gestures and expressions are often so exaggerated as to be funny, and social criticism is never far from the surface. During the next decade Vasili Perov (1834–82) produced more serious, but less well painted works; humour was now more bitter, and during the Soviet period, anyone who idealised the pre-Revolutionary past too much was shown Perov's paintings; drunkenness, poverty, peasant backwardness and the corruption of the Church were some of his favourite themes.

By the 1870s, painting and campaigning for social reform had become so intertwined that the Society for Travelling Art Exhibitions was formed. This group, who came to be known as The Wanderers, took it upon themselves to tour the Empire with their exhibitions, which were intended to educate the population and press for social reform.

It is best represented by Russia's greatest realist, Ilia Repin (1844–1930). Repin lived a long, productive life, and worked in a number of styles, but his reputation was made with large-scale canvases such as *The Volga Bargehaulers*, *The Zaporozhie Cossacks Writing a Mocking Letter to the Turkish Sultan* and *Religious Procession in the Province of Kursk*. These monumental paintings, each of which took Repin many years of work, have a photographic quality that makes

also enjoyed a renewal in the second half of the 19th century. Ivan Aivazovsky (1817–1900), an extremely prolific painter of seascapes, achieved enormous fame in Russia and abroad for his dramatic, but very well-painted canvases. You either love them or you hate them, but they are undeniably impressive. Among the best is *The Wave* in the Russian Museum. For the convinced, there is an entire museum devoted to him in Theodosia, his birthplace in the Crimea.

The next 40 years, from about 1885–1925, saw the most extraordinary explosion of cultural life in Russia, during which Russian art – not only in the sphere of painting, but in that of music and literature – was

a direct appeal. They made a big impression on simple people who had never come into contact with painting before. The historical paintings of Vasili Surikov (1848–1916), Vasily Vereshchagin (1842–1904) and Viktor Vasnetsov (1848–1926), also executed on a huge scale, were similarly didactic.

Working at the same time as the Wanderers, but by their nature not politically engaged, were landscape painters, whose art

Left, *Portrait of Chaliapin* by **Boris Kustodiev**. **Above**, *The Zaporozhie Cossacks Writing a Mocking Letter to the Turkish Sultan* by **Ilia Repin**.

among the most exciting in the world. Instrumental in bringing about this frenzy of activity was the railway tycoon Savva Mamontov. He gathered young talent about him at his estate of Abramtsevo. Many of the most gifted artists spent time there, and the estate became a hothouse of activity in many media, sculpture, ceramics, architecture and art history, with a particular inclination for the study and revival of Russian folk art.

Mikhail Vrubel (1856–1910), a painter whose genius was so extraordinary that he does not fit comfortably in any movement, came to the colony in 1890; he became obsessed with visions of demons, which he painted in great quantity, and died in an asylum. He was perhaps the first to break the mould of the Wanderers' legacy, and to return to painting as an end in itself, rather than as a vehicle for social comment. His genius lay in the twin powers of draughtsmanship and imagination.

Vrubel's break with tradition encouraged others to follow his example. One who did so was Valentin Serov (1865–1911). Again, Serov's outstanding characteristic is his sure draughtsmanship; he had the ability to render a face, a figure or an expression in just a few fluid lines, and naturally this ability led him to portrait painting. His portrait of the dancer Ida Rubinstein (Russian Museum) is one of

critical acclaim in the 1910s with Diaghilev's Ballets Russes, but he is second only to Serov in his abilities as a portraitist. Another member, Nikolai Roerich, explored the theme of ancient Rus in his brightly coloured work, and later settled in the Himalayas where he became a guru figure to American pilgrims. Konstantin Somov, the most "decadent" of all, was fascinated by harlequins, fireworks and ladies in 18th-century costume, which he meticulously rendered on canvas. There is an underlying current of eroticism which runs through his painting.

Boris Kustodiev, who joined the group in 1911, differed from the others; his work, which sometimes borders on caricature, cel-

the outstanding Russian portraits.

Art for art's sake: The year 1898 saw the founding in St Petersburg of the *World of Art* magazine by a group of intellectual artists who shared an idealisation of the past and an interest in "art for art's sake". They were very metropolitan, typically St Petersburg painters, whose worldly outlook, influenced also by Russian art nouveau, seems both decadent and prophetic now. This was the pictorial accompaniment to Alexander Blok and the "Silver Age" of Russian poetry. Leon Bakst, one of the founders of the group, became famous in the West as a costume designer when he toured Europe to huge

ebrates the larger-than-life world of the provincial Russian merchant class; enormous ladies at tables straining under the weight of samovars, pots of jam, and pies stuffed with sturgeon's cheeks, buckwheat, boiled eggs and rice. It is a world familiar to readers of Gogol, and one that was shortly to disappear forever, liquidated in Stalin's camps. Among his best paintings are pictures of fairs, but he was also a fine portraitist, and enjoys the distinction of having painted the best portrait of the singer Chaliapin (Theatre Museum, St Petersburg), who was painted by everybody.

The early years of the century saw the appearance of a number of collectors of art, none more important than Sergei Schukin. His collection of more than 200 French Impressionist and Post-Impressionistic paintings, which is now mostly in the Hermitage, had an enormous effect on young painters. Schukin's house was open to the public once a week, and allowed Muscovites to become acquainted with important works by Cezanne, Matisse and Picasso.

The years 1906–11 witnessed the formation of dozens of groups, splinter groups and exhibitions. Two of the most active figures were Mikhail Larionov (1881–1964) and his wife Natalia Goncharova (1881–1962). Together with Pavel Kuznetsov (1878–1968), they formed the Blue Rose Group in 1906. Kuznetsov's main preoccupation was with colour, and from Symbolist beginnings, influenced by Puvis de Chavannes, he reached his artistic peak in the 1910s and '20s, when he painted a series of mystical landscapes of the Caucasian steppes. Goncharova drew her inspiration from folk art and icon painting, and her best work, with its strong linear rhythms and striking colour scheme, is a reworking of Byzantine draughtsmanship.

Larionov, whose early work was close to French Impressionism, delighted in the unexpected and the shocking. Close in spirit to his contemporaries, the Futurist poets, he was the first Russian neo-primitivist, and painted a series of paintings of soldiers, in which anatomy is deliberately distorted; in 1913 he turned to abstract painting, having devised a system known as rayonism by which he painted not objects but the rays emanating from objects, which by their intersection could define space.

Moscow's avant-garde: In 1910, Larionov helped to organise the first exhibition of the Knave of Diamonds group, which included works by foreign artists, and four compositions by Vasili Kandinsky. It was an important event in the history of the avant-garde, for it generated an independent, Moscow-based group.

Kandinsky, who spent much of his career with the Blaue Reiter group in Munich, can be considered the world's first abstract painter; his brand of expressionism was concerned primarily with spirituality and to achieve it he used explosions of colour and

Left, *The Bathing of the Red Horse* **by Kuzma Petrov-Vodkin.**

line, often including traces of figurative elements. Kazimir Malevich received little academic training. He began his career with Symbolist paintings, moved on to Neo-primitivist works inspired by Larionov, but towards 1912 was beginning to develop a style of his own, which he called Suprematism. This was an attempt to break away from representation of the visible world, to concentrate on space and through painting to forge a link with absolutes of everything and nothing. The supreme symbol of this period is his painting *Black Square* (circa 1914), which is everything its name suggests.

This uncompromising attitude towards art and the public is also found in Tatlin's work. His legacy is Constructivism; a type of semi-abstraction by which he sought, often with the help of relief, to penetrate the essence of objects, and then of material itself. Among his greatest works, however, is a self-portrait of 1911, housed in the Russian museum. Painted in tempera, it recalls icon painting in its use of curved lines and highlights.

Chagall's dream-like world is on view in early paintings contained in both the Tretyakov and the Russian Museums. He was the youngest of the avant-garde painters, spent most of his life abroad, and other than a penchant for neo-primitivism, had little in common with his contemporaries.

Kuzma Petrov-Vodkin (1878–1939) is another painter of this period who sought to use the language of icon painting to express the atmosphere of the time. His large canvases are built of areas of strongly contrasting colours, usually including a brilliant, almost luminous red. He deliberately manipulated space, to give an impression of flatness, and played with shadow and highlight, in such a way that his figures seem, as in icon painting, to be illuminated from within. The Russian Museum contains several outstanding examples of his work, including *The Bathing of the Red Horse* (1912).

This frenzy of artistic activity took place against a background of political intrigue, World War I, the Revolution and finally the Civil war. Many artists chose exile, and continued their work abroad; others decided to stay, but soon found that they could not remain above politics. In the 1930s, all art was by decree subjugated to the Party, and this situation remained, with a few underground exceptions, until the era of perestroika.

Communism suppressed but failed to kill off the Russian muse, which in the 19th century had produced literary immortals like Pushkin, Turgenev, Dostoevsky, Tolstoy, Gogol, Chekhov and so on. However, there were spells under Stalin, notably the years immediately before and after World War II, when writers were terrorised into total silence. A few voices were raised from the late 1950s onwards, but it was Mikhail Gorbachev's declaration of glasnost in 1986 that properly got things moving again.

The subsequent collapse of Communism delivered the *coup de grâce* to a system which had insisted that writers were servants of the state – membership of the Soviet Writers' Union stood at 15,000 – and one which rewarded loyalty with fat salaries and perks, notably *dachas* and cars. Censorship went down with Communism and, all in all, it was tempting to think that a Russian literary renaissance, not to say Second Coming, was just around the corner. The real world, alas, proved to be rather more complicated.

Some 3,000 independent publishing houses, some of them survivors of the former *samizdat* Underground press, opened for business in the ashes of the old state system. They joined existing literary journals which, depending on the editors' nerve and the political climate of the day, had slipped more and more dissenting voices between the covers of their so-called "thick" issues.

So far so good, but there was another side to the story of free enterprise. Unlike the retail trade, co-operative restaurants and so forth, publishing was not the kind of business that could grow organically from some humble acorn. Independent publishers did not have the financial backing to buy the paper on which to print books, let alone pay royalties capable of keeping a writer alive. The 15,000 writers previously employed full-time by the state had to find other jobs to subsidise their creative activities. Of the 3,000 hopeful independent publishers, barely a dozen could be taken seriously.

To make matters worse, there were doubts that a popular market existed for serious books. Russians had been so lobotomised by the Communist Party's list of approved reading that they were interested only in translations of imported pulp fiction.

The besieged writers had more to worry about than making ends meet in a market that did not want their wares. The demise of Communism deprived them of the ideological enemy which had fired them. There was still plenty to get angry about in post-Communist Russia, but tirades against black-marketeers in sharp suits did not carry the same noble indignation. Writers reared on acute moral issues could not easily turn their pens to love and laughter.

That is not to say, however, that agony in a writer's nursery is necessarily unproductive. The writers who produced the great Russian classics – the aforementioned Pushkin, Turgenev, Dostoevsky, Tolstoy, Gogol, Chekhov *et al* – were in their own time a chain reaction against an ideological enemy, in their case tsarist tyranny. What made this explosion of talent all the more remarkable was not only the speed – it happened in the space of a century – but the fact that it occurred in what had been a literary desert.

Emerging from a literary backwater: Isolated from Western culture during two centuries of Mongol rule and subsequently untouched by the Renaissance, Russia was a literary backwater when Catherine II (later "the Great") came to the throne in 1762. Whereas Martin Luther had standardised German for literary purposes in the early 16th century with his translation of the Bible, literary Russian, as distinct from Old Church Slavonic, had only just been formulated by Mikhail Lomonosov.

Catherine set about filling the vacuum with Russian translations of the Greek and Latin classics, Voltaire (with whom she conducted a lengthy private correspondence), Montesquieu, Defoe, Milton, Goethe, Rousseau and others. *All Sorts and Sundries* was launched as a weekly magazine modelled on *The Spectator* in London, and the imperial archives were opened to Prince Michel Shcherbatov for what became a seven-volume history of Russia. By 1778 translations of some 175 foreign works were on sale, an increasing number of Russians were sharpening their quills, and Catherine was optimistic. "Our Russian language," she remarked, "uniting as it does the strength, richness and energy of German and the sweetness of Italian, will one day become the language of the world."

The full impact of Catherine's patronage was not felt until nearly 30 years after her death. It was then that intellectuals and writers in particular had all their energies focused on a particular ideological target. The reign of Alexander I, Catherine's grandson, had been reasonably benign, at least to begin with, but his successor, Nicholas I, immediately made it plain that he would not tolerate in Russia the liberal reforms then fermenting elsewhere in Europe. As recounted in the history section of this book, a silly misunderstanding over the legitimacy of his succession turned sour when Nicholas notoriously ordered a "whiff of grapeshot" to be fired at peaceful demonstrators who had gathered in St Petersburg's Senate Square on 14 December 1825. The result was a massacre.

A witchhunt for the supposed ringleaders followed and more than 100 of the capital's intellectual lights were arrested. Five of them were sentenced to be quartered. On re-consideration, Nicholas commuted these sentences to hanging and packed the lesser culprits off to Siberia. It was still too much. "Out of the spark," someone predicted, "will come a conflagration." In the event, a name was coined in Russian for the intellectuals who declared themselves against Nicholas: the "intelligentsia".

The Russian Shakespeare: The most illustrious of these rebels was not actually present in St Petersburg on the ill-fated day, but only because he had previously been banished to his mother's estate at Pskov for a flippant declaration of atheism. Alexander Pushkin was already a published poet in 1825, when he was 26, but the execution of the five Decembrists, especially his friend Ryleiev, gave his later work a harder edge.

Pushkin had a curious family background: on his father's side it was patrician, while his mother was the granddaughter of an Ethopian slave named Ibrahim who had been sent to Peter the Great as a present. Pushkin's physical features reflected his African blood and this, he believed, was the secret of his precocious success with women. His first attempt at a novel made the most of family history and was called *The Negro of Peter the Great*. The fact that he never finished it was put down to the dissolute opportunities all too readily available to young aristocrats of the age, whether or not they were blessed with African endowments.

Pushkin had started *Eugene Onegin*, his poetic masterpiece, before the Decembrist uprising, and it seemed he might never finish it when he, too, was caught in the tsar's dragnet. Summoned before Nicholas personally, he did not deny his sympathy for the

dissenters and was therefore taken aback when the tsar not only forgave him but also exempted him from the scrutiny of the hastily inaugurated "Third Section", the inspiration for George Orwell's Thought Police. Count Uvarov, the Minister of Education, said frankly that he would only get a good night's sleep when literature ceased to be written, but the tsar's indulgence put Pushkin beyond such threats. He was answerable only to Nicholas, a kind of protective custody, but custody nevertheless.

Under these trying conditions, Pushkin turned his hand from poetry to drama with *Boris Godunov* and then to prose with *The*

Captain's Daughter, whose plot concerned the Pugachev peasant uprising in Catherine's reign. Under the "leaden eyes" of the tsar, Pushkin would have lived more easily had he stuck to romantic writing, but he was drawn into the perilous waters of history, returning to the topic of Peter the Great with his poem *The Bronze Horseman* in 1833.

Pushkin married Natalia Goncharova and her beauty, which far outshone her brains, transfixed Nicholas. In order to keep her at court, he allowed Pushkin a greater degree of literary licence than might otherwise have been the case. Her looks, however, were also Pushkin's eventual downfall. Baron Georges D'Anthès, a French officer serving in the Russian forces, was besotted with her, and Pushkin felt obliged to throw down a challenge. He walked from the Wolff and Beranger Café, now the Literary Café, in St Petersburg to the appointed rendezvous – and had to be carried back, fatally wounded. Pushkin died at the age of 37, probably short of the peak of his powers but having achieved enough to win later recognition as the Russian Shakespeare.

Pushkin's heir: Pushkin's greatest admirer and, as things turned out, his direct literary heir was Mikhail Lermontov, whose Russianised name concealed Scottish descent, the original being Learmont. As a combined scholar, cavalry officer and libertine, he drew comparisons with his contemporary Byron. Lermontov's first published poem was a lament on Pushkin's death and resulted in his arrest and exile to the Caucasus, a fate which became almost a routine apprenticeship for much of Russia's literary talent. In Lermontov's case, the fruit was *A Hero of Our Time* (1840), a short novel which, like Pushkin's *Eugene Onegin*, was one of Russia's first psychological novels. It rehabilitated Lermontov's reputation and allowed him to rejoin his regiment, but the reprieve was short-lived. A duel with the son of the French ambassador resulted in another term of banishment followed by a second reprieve. In 1841 he was involved in another duel, and this one cost him his life.

The hounding of Lermontov was typical not merely of the Third Section but of the monstrous bureaucracy designed under the slogan "Orthodoxy, Autocracy and Nationality" to stifle revolutionary tendencies at all levels of Russian society. Nikolai Gogol

(1809–1852), an upper-class Cossack, turned the heavy hand of bureaucracy into the plot of *The Government Inspector*, at which point he decamped to Rome to finish what many regard as his greatest work, *Dead Souls*. Ironically, Tsar Nicholas enjoyed *The Government Inspector*, although the young Ivan Turgenev was later arrested for presuming to praise it and Gogol's work in general in an obituary he wrote when Gogol died in 1852.

Turgenev's *A Sportsman's Sketches*, published a year before Gogol's death, was a robust indictment of serfdom and probably had as much to do with his exile as the controversial obituary. He spent his exile wandering around Europe while writing about

hero Bazarov as a "nihilist", a term later employed by bomb-toting revolutionaries.

Widespread revolution in Europe in 1848 prompted Nicholas to turn the screws ever tighter on Russian intellectual dissent and another group of writers was led to the scaffold. Once again the tsar relented at the last moment and reduced the severity of the sentences to exile with hard labour. One of the reprieved writers was Fyodor Dostoevsky. Somewhat morbid by nature, Dostoevsky's frame of mind was hardly improved by the ordeal of a mock execution and the four years he served afterwards in a Siberian prison. *Memoirs from the House of the Dead* was an autobiographical nightmare, a lesson

Russia (in *Rudin*, *Nest of the Gentlefolk*, *On the Eve*, etc), thereby setting an example for not a few 20th-century émigré successors.

Like Pushkin, whom as a student he knew, Turgenev wrote sensitively about women. Too sensitively, some said, with the implication that he was ill-equipped to deal with men. The criticism stung Turgenev into writing what is probably his best novel, *Fathers and Sons*, an account of rebellion against tradition and authority in favour of pragmatic materialism. Turgenev described his

for Freud and an obvious pointer to Solzhenitsyn's harrowing accounts of conditions in Stalin's labour camps.

Literary convention traces the line of the writers so far mentioned back to the Decembrist revolution, and the "revolutionary" tag gave them an aura of acceptability when the Bolsheviks took over. They were certainly critical of the status quo, but it was disingenuous of the Communists not to recognise that this was subversion from the top by disillusioned aristocrats rather than the proletariat rattling their chains.

With the exception of Leo Tolstoy, the pre-Revolutionary novelists were not in the

Left, Mikhail Lermontov. **Above**, Gogol reading from his work *The Government Inspector*.

business of advocating a socialist (or any other kind of) solution to the conditions they deplored. The aristocratic Tolstoy did offer idealistic alternatives, but over the years these degenerated into almost incomprehensible eccentricity. He established a school for peasant children, only to realise that he did not know what or how to teach them. He echoed Rousseau in denouncing materialism in favour of simple rustic virtues, and his conception of true Christianity eventually dispensed with Jesus as "blasphemy". Tolstoy's great strength as a writer, the basis of his colossal stature, lay in psychological analysis, the effect of *force majeure* on individuals. *War and Peace* traces the fortunes

Chekhov, the grandson of a serf, was a qualified and practising doctor as well as a versatile writer. He wrote his most famous plays towards the end of his life. *The Seagull* (1898) staged at the Moscow Arts Theatre, was followed by *Uncle Vanya* (1900), *The Three Sisters* (1901) and *The Cherry Orchard* (1903). The Moscow Arts Theatre was founded by Konstantin Stanislavsky and Vladimir Nemirovich-Danchenko and the plays were staged using a new realist style of acting which was radical for its time.

Maxim Gorky, like Chekhov of working-class origin, was the one writer who, as distinct from the Decembrist school, can be seen as a proletarian revolutionary. Impris-

of a huge cast of characters through Napoleon's traumatic war with Russia, all of it in prose which exploits Russian's rich idiom to the hilt, the perfect realisation of Catherine the Great's expectations.

Tolstoy expressed the opinion that "an economic revolution not only may, but must come". At the turn of the century, Baron Tusenbach in Chekhov's *The Three Sisters* says: "The time has come. An avalanche is moving down on us. A mighty, health-giving storm is brewing, is approaching, is already near and will soon sweep away from our society its idleness, its indifference, its prejudice against work, its foul *ennui*."

oned in 1905 for inciting strikes, he went abroad on his release and continued his revolutionary activities in exile. He returned to celebrate with the victorious Bolsheviks in 1917 but was not blind to their defects, criticising them from, as it were, the left: "This government which calls itself a Soviet of Workers and Peasants has done everything to oppose the will of the workers..." This sort of talk soon had him back in exile. Gorky's difficulties were symptomatic of the fact that the Bolsheviks were not sure about literature's role in the new order, and writers could not make up their minds either about where they stood in relation to the

Revolution. Many writers emigrated at the first opportunity; others, like Boris Pasternak, adopted a policy of wait and see. Lenin's personal taste ran to Pushkin, and under his influence the Party tolerated literary objectivity, if not rigorous criticism, as represented by Sholokhov's *And Quiet Flows the Don*. Writers did not have to be hide-bound Marxists as long as they were at least, in Trotsky's phrase, "fellow travellers".

These fellow travellers differed from the so-called "proletarian" writers who insisted on fanatical adherence to the party line. The latter were given their head in 1929: the "bolshevisation" of literature and the arts coincided with the collectivisation of the

of Soviet Writers set specific tasks, like commissioning hack historians to portray Ivan the Terrible as a patriotic saint. The aim was "Socialist Realism" by the "culture-creative class organisation of the proletariat". The result was unreadable rubbish, tedious subjects written in a style which stripped the language of its rich idiomatic vein. Many writers suffered for failing to meet the tenets of Socialist Realism, for example the poets Vladimir Mayakovsky and Sergei Esenin, who both committed suicide, and Anna Akhmatova and Mikhail Bulgakov. The likes of Pasternak and Babel could not debase themselves and turned instead to translating foreign works; in Pasternak's case, for ex-

peasants under the first of the Five-Year Plans. Fellow travellers were terrorised into submission or silence. Literature became the exclusive preserve of "Soviet" writers, a definition of their political allegiance rather than place of abode. This was a situation which Gorky felt he could live with, and he returned to Russia to become Stalin's personal adviser in literary matters, a much cosier relationship than had existed between Pushkin and Nicholas I.

Under Gorky's chairmanship, the Union

Far left, Anton Chekhov. **Left**, Fyodor Dostoevsky. **Above**, Maxim Gorky and his literary circle.

ample, *Hamlet*. Ironically, Gorky somehow fell foul of the system he had largely created, and poison was probably the cause of his mysterious death in 1936.

World War II gave writers something real to write about, and for the duration Stalin tolerated deviations from the strict Party line in much the same way, and for the same reasons, as he partially lifted the ban on religion. These small concessions were clawed back with a vengeance after the war, and it would be no exaggeration to say that between 1945 and Stalin's death in 1953, literature and the arts in Russia ceased to exist. In denouncing Stalin in 1956, Nikita

Khrushchev lifted the lid slightly, enough anyway to tolerate the appearance of new literary journals which provided writers with a more accessible outlet for their work. The state publishing machine printed approved works by the million while rejecting any manuscript likely to rock the boat. This followed the persecution of Boris Pasternak during the Khrushchev period for his novel *Dr Zhivago*. To this day, many Russians prefer his quite brilliant poetry.

On the whole, however, control over the arts eased over the late 1950s and 1960s, when Russian poets usch as Yevgeny Yevtushenko and Andrei Voznesensky became known in the West. Solzhenitsyn then

stuck his neck out with *One Day in the Life of Ivan Denisovich*, the first account in print of conditions in Stalin's camps, and followed it up with *Cancer Ward* and *The First Circle*. The Soviet authorities allowed him to accept the Nobel prize in 1970, but the appearance three years later of *The Gulag Archipelago* ended the fragile *modus vivendi* and he was exiled to join, among others, Vladimir Nabokov, whose saucy creation *Lolita* had titillated the West in 1959. Other Russian émigré wtriters include Joseph

Above, Vladimir Mayakovsky. **Right**, Tolstoy on his estate at Yasnaya Polyana.

Brodsky, winner of the 1986 Nobel prize.

A new freedom: Glasnost in 1986 removed the sword that for 70 years had been poised to cut off any head that rose too high above the parapet. Any number of heads immediately popped up to survey an unfamiliar landscape, but at the outset the more important gain (for Russian if not foreign readers) was to bring previously banned works out of hiding, such as Yevgeny Zamyatin's *We*, written in the early 1920s, a book whose brilliant protrayal of a totalitarian state was a precursor to Orwell's *Nineteen Eighty-Four*.

With the formal constraints disappearing by the day under Gorbachev, the problems facing Russian writers became, as we have seen, a matter of practicality. With hardly any of the 3,000 independent publishers able to realise their hopes, the "thick" journals remained the platform for writers old and new. The magazine *Ogonyok* was a huge success story. Founded in Moscow in 1923, it had mixed fortunes until it took off in the 1990s, reaching a circulation of 3 million.

The inauguration in 1992 of a Russian version of the Booker Prize, Britain's most prestigious literary award, neatly encapsulated the birthpains of the new wave. For a start, the prize of £10,000 was infinitely more money than even the most talented Russian writer could expect to earn from domestic sales. A deluge of entries was whittled down to a shortlist of six. These had been published in the thick journals, but surviving copies were so scarce that in some cases there were not enough around to give a copy to each of the five judges. The winner was Mark Kharitonov for his novel *Lines of Fate*, singled out because the author in an interview with the newspaper *Pravda* had managed to fasten his gaze on something other than the old ideological enemy. "His prose is intelligent, calm and sophisticated," a critic observed. "He is not over-excited, he does not denounce anyone: he is just himself."

One of the finalists, the black humorist Vladimir Sorokin, spoke for all of them when he lamented the absence of readers for even this distinguished company. "The new reader has not appeared yet," he said, "and it will take a long time for the present generation to tire of Stock Exchange news and James Bond novels, and start to want literature. At the moment, the writer just looks silly. It is not his time, no one needs him."

Russian music has come a long way since the middle of the 19th century when concerts could only be held during five weeks of the year, reviews were almost unheard of and composers had to be sent to Italy for their basic training. At a time when the content and language of music was undergoing radical change in the West under the powerful influence of Romanticism, Russian composers had yet to find their feet. Indeed, Mozart had been dead for almost 50 years before Russia's first real musical genius, Mikhail

Glinka, produced *A Life for the Tsar*, the opera traditionally regarded as the foundation stone of Russian music. Yet soon Russia was producing world-class composers.

Russia's long musical isolation from the rest of Europe was due to its religion. The Orthodox liturgy, which Vladimir adopted from Byzantium in 988, dictated that only the human voice could be used in divine worship. For a long time secular performers were regarded by the Church as "messengers of the devil who turn people's minds from God with songs and trumpets and games". Yet towards the end of the 16th century, as contacts with the West increased (Elizabeth

I, for example, sent an organ and virginals to Ivan the Terrible), even church music began to move with the times and five-line notation, polyphony and major and minor keys were gradually introduced to the liturgy. With the foundation of a court theatre during the reign of the enlightened Alexis Mikhailovich (1645–76), a secular musical tradition also emerged, but it was under Peter I that the greatest innovations in this sphere occurred.

By moving the capital from Moscow to his new city of St Petersburg in 1703, Peter transformed conservative, pious Muscovy into the modern state of Russia at a stroke. Along with all the architects and craftsmen imported to modernise his backward country came foreign musicians to play in the new military bands and sing in the new State choir. Music soon became an intrinsic part of everyday court life. Yet Peter was not very musical himself, so music-making remained entirely foreign in origin. For the vast majority of the population, hearing music meant either going to church or listening to traditional folk songs.

Opera performed by serfs: By the middle of the 18th century the Russian court had its own orchestra, and a special theatre was built for the performance of opera, which soon became the rage among the aristocracy, thanks largely to the patronage of the Imperial family. Indeed, opera became so popular in the 18th century that wealthy landowners like Count Sheremetev (whose enchanting miniature theatre can be visited at Ostankino) were soon setting up their own companies and orchestras on their estates, using serfs as well as foreign artists as performers. Horn bands also became very fashionable at this time; the horns came in different shapes and sizes but each only played one note.

For the most part, Russian music-making was dominated by enthusiastic amateurs from the nobility whose levels of expertise left much to be desired, yet there was nevertheless a great deal of talent around, particularly in the field of composition. It is customary to view Glinka as the first genuinely Russian composer, but the achievements of 18th-century composers like Bortnyansky, Berezovsky and Fomin (who was originally a serf musician) and their successors Alyabev and Verstovsky should not be overlooked, even if their Italian training meant that their music did not sound very Russian. They were among the first Russian musicians to compete with foreign counterparts on their own level, and they did much to raise musical standards in a country where performing musicians had no professional status and were therefore accorded little respect.

Peter the Great's relentless Westernising

(1836) and *Ruslan and Ludmila* (1842), combined Western techniques of composition with music that was clearly inspired by native folk sources. They were unashamedly Russian works.

Since opera was government-controlled in tsarist Russia, the conservative tastes of the St Petersburg aristocracy continued to determine what music was performed. While Nicholas I was tsar, for example, thousands of roubles continued to be spent in support of the resident Italian opera troupe, whilst the

encouraged the Russian nobility to regard Russian culture with contempt, but the great upsurge of patriotism which followed Napoleon's defeat in 1812 swelled Russian hearts with national pride for the first time. A new generation of artists, musicians and writers appeared on the scene who were anxious to create a genuinely Russian culture. Among them was Glinka (1804–57), whose two operas marked a turning point in the history of Russian music. Both *A Life for the Tsar*

Preceding pages: Rostropovich at work. **Left**, travelling musicians. **Above left**, Pyotr Tchaikovsky. **Above right**, Modest Mussorgsky.

neglected and under-funded Russian Opera had to struggle to make ends meet. Public concerts, meanwhile, which were held on a regular basis from the end of the 18th century, were allowed only during the five-week Lent period at the end of the season, when the Imperial theatres were closed.

There was still no professional training for budding Russian musicians. Strangely, Anton Rubinstein (1829–94), the virtuoso pianist and composer who did the most to change this situation during the more liberal years of Alexander II, was more concerned with raising general standards of musicianship than with promoting specifically Russian music.

Though cosmopolitan and conservative by nature, Rubinstein revolutionised Russian musical life by founding the Russian Musical Society in 1859 (the first organisation that was allowed to hold concerts throughout the winter season) and the St Petersburg Conservatoire in 1862. Similar institutions were founded a few years later in Moscow by Rubinstein's brother Nikolai (1835–81).

Not all Russian musicians favoured Rubinstein's reforms, however. In particular, the group of five Slavophile composers which gathered round Mily Balakirev (1837–1910) in the 1860s vigorously opposed the professionalism of the Conservatoire training and its classical Western orientation. In an attempt to keep Russian music free from foreign contamination and preserve its amateur status, Balakirev started up a rival Free School of Music. Together with Alexander Borodin (1834–87), who earned his living as a well-respected chemist, Nikolai Rimsky-Korsakov (1844–1908), who forged a career in the navy, Modest Mussorgsky (1839–81) and César Cui (1835–1918), Balakirev set about promoting a native musical tradition, believing that art belonged to the people and should be realistic in style.

It is to these composers that Russian music owes much of its distinctive sound. Drawing on the rich melodies of native folk song and Eastern music, they sought inspiration in the legends of Russian history and literature. Borodin based his opera *Prince Igor* (1874) on a 12th-century epic poem, Mussorgsky turned to Pushkin for his masterpiece *Boris Godunov* (1874), and Rimsky-Korsakov created a series of magical operas that had their source in Russian fairytales. Of the five, Mussorgsky, who drank his way to an early death, was unquestionably the most talented of the group and Cui the weakest and most anomalous. Cui's Lithuanian and French parentage may have had something to do with the fact that his own compositions sound anything but Russian in idiom.

A contemporary of the "Five" was Pyotr Tchaikovsky (1840–93), one of the first students at the St Petersburg Conservatoire. Despite his tuition by foreign professors, the Russian element in his music is unmistakable. Besides the six major symphonies, the piano concertos and the ever popular ballets, Tchaikovsky is also best remembered for the operas he wrote, which drew on the works of Pushkin and Gogol. *Eugene Onegin* is perhaps his greatest work in this genre.

By the end of the 19th century, Russian music was being performed regularly, both in the concert hall and in the opera house, and the by now well-established conservatoires of St Petersburg and Moscow were producing composers, conductors and performers of great talent. With the exception of the Imperial theatres, the government now had very little control over musical life in the two capitals, as more private opera companies and concert series were set up.

The brightest stars at the turn of the century were the great singer Fyodor Chaliapin and the composers Sergei Rachmaninov (1873–1943) and Alexander Scriabin (1872–1915), the most famous graduates of the Moscow Conservatoire. Rachmaninov, best known for his major contributions to the piano repertoire (but also a composer of some magnificent symphonic works), was himself a highly accomplished pianist, and was able to earn a good living on the concert platform during his long years of exile after the Revolution. Scriabin, in whose works the influence of Wagner, Liszt and Chopin can be clearly heard, formed close links with the mystical Russian Symbolists who emerged in the early years of the 20th century. At the time of his premature death Scriabin was in the midst of a grandiose orchestral work which would transport listeners and performers alike into a state of ecstasy and transform the universe.

It fell to Igor Stravinsky (1882–1971) and Sergei Prokofiev (1891–1953) to be the real innovators in the field of composition at this time. Stravinsky, one of the great musical giants of the 20th century, came to world prominence when Diaghilev staged his ballets *The Firebird* (1910) and *Petrushka* (1911) in Europe as part of his famous "Ballets Russes" seasons. His *Rite of Spring* (1913) was considered so modern when it was first performed that it caused an uproar all over Europe. Stravinsky continued to blaze new paths in music for the rest of his long career, his eclectic works transcending narrow national boundaries. Like Rachmaninov, he lived in exile after 1917, returning to his homeland only in 1962.

The precocious Prokofiev completed his studies, as Stravinsky had, at the Petersburg Conservatoire with Rimsky-Korsakov, but he too left the country in the aftermath of the Revolution, leaving Russia bereft of its greatest talents.

The Soviet muse: Whilst the 1917 Revolution had a cataclysmic effect on musical life in Russia, with theatres, concert series and publications changing names or, more often, closing down, it also injected it with energy. The years just after the Revolution were a time of chaos, but also a time of great freedom and experimentation. Opera performances were attended by people who had never been to the theatre before and vast musical and dramatic spectacles involving casts of thousands were organised to commemorate the events of 1917 which had

and *Sickle* and *Tosca* became *Battle for the Commune*.

The greatest period of artistic tolerance came during the 1920s. Two rival musical organisations formed in 1923 were most important at this time: the avant-garde and openly modernist "Association of Contemporary Music", which favoured experimentation, and the "Russian Association of Proletarian Musicians", which was by far the more militant of the two, and dismissed all previous music as bourgeois and alien. Among the more talented composers to appear during the 1920s were Nikolai Roslavets (1881–1944), later to be a victim of the purges but whose major contribution to the

already become a myth.

Music became an important weapon for propaganda purposes, as did all the arts during this time, in the effort to instil the population with the ideals of the new government. But until new composers appeared on the scene who could write morally uplifting Socialist music, the Bolsheviks were content for the old repertoire to be performed, but innocuous opera titles were often changed for ones that were more politically charged. Hence *A Life for the Tsar* became *Hammer*

Above, Dmitry Shostakovich working on his Seventh Symphony in besieged Leningrad.

development of atonal music is now beginning to be recognised, and Alexander Mossolov (1900–71), whose most famous piece, an orchestral work full of mechanical sound effects called *The Iron Foundry* (1926), is a testament to the early years of Soviet industrialisation.

By far the most gifted composer to emerge during the early years of Soviet power was Dmitry Shostakovich (1906–75), whose First Symphony was first performed in 1926 when he was just 20 years old, and followed by another masterpiece: his opera *The Nose* (1928), based on Gogol's short story.

For a time, Leningrad (as St Petersburg

became in 1924) vied with Berlin to be the centre of musical experimentation, but towards the end of the 1920s, as ideology came to play a bigger role in artistic life, the freedoms enjoyed by Soviet artists gradually disappeared. In 1932, the Union of Soviet Composers was formed and music was placed under direct government control. Composers were now told that they had to write music according to the doctrine of Socialist Realism. In other words, music had to be understandable to the masses and nationalistic in character. It was to depict, moreover, "reality in its revolutionary development".

It was not until 1936, however, that composers really came under pressure to con-

form. Prokofiev returned to Russia in 1933, and many of his best known works – *Lieutenant Kijé* (1934), *Romeo and Juliet* (1935), and *Alexander Nevsky* (1939) – were written during this time. Shostakovich's great operatic masterpiece *Lady Macbeth of Mtsensk* was first performed to great acclaim in 1934, but things started to go badly wrong after a Moscow performance in January 1936 was attended by Stalin. The next day an unsigned editorial entitled "Chaos Instead of Music" appeared in *Pravda*.

Shostakovich's opera, and avant-garde music in general, was subjected to a merciless and withering attack. Shostakovich re-

sponded with his Fifth Symphony, a darkly ambiguous work subtitled "A Soviet Artist's Reply to Just Criticism". His relationship with the authorities was ever after to be tortuous and complicated. It determined the content of the music he was to write over the next four decades.

Accusations of decadence: The attack on Shostakovich in 1936 signalled the beginning of a systematic decimation of the Soviet musical intelligentsia. After the temporary hiatus caused by World War II, the purges actually intensified. During the first Congress of Composers held in 1948, Shostakovich, together with Prokofiev, Khachaturian and several others, was found guilty of "formalism". By refusing to write music filled with bright, optimistic melodies, these composers were accused of following the "cult of atonality, dissonance and disharmony" which reflected the "decay of bourgeois culture".

Until Stalin's death in 1953, Russian musicians, together with all Soviet artists, lived in an atmosphere of unrelieved oppression and isolation. Khrushchev's accession to power heralded the thaw in cultural life, symbolised by the success of Shostakovich's Tenth Symphony in 1954. Restrictions began to be relaxed and contacts with the West were cautiously resumed. Stravinsky was allowed to return to Russia in 1962 and visits made by Western musicians such as Glenn Gould and Aaron Copland made a huge impact on the new generation of musicians studying at the conservatoires. Up to that point, Western music had been mostly banned from the concert platform and in the classroom was habitually denounced as "decadent" and "reactionary". It therefore came as something of a shock for these young Russian musicians to hear the music of Schoenberg and Webern for the first time.

Another bleak period of isolation and repression followed Khruschchev's removal from power in 1964. In the musical sphere it was spearheaded by Tikhon Khrennikov, who presided as head of the Union of Composers from 1948 until its collapse in the aftermath of the 1991 coup. The Soviet conservatoires had produced an array of outstanding talents, among them the pianist Svyatoslav Richter, the conductor Gennady Rozhdestvensky and the violinists Igor and David Oistrakh. Yet many gifted artists, including the cellist Mstislav Rostropovich, the violinist Gidon Kremer and the pianist Vladimir Ashkenazy, were forced to emigrate or defect.

Meanwhile, "official" composers continued to churn out leaden operas and orchestral works, and were rewarded for their efforts with trips abroad and privileged lifestyles, while avant-garde composers like Alfred Schnittke, Sofia Gubaidulina, Nikolai Karetnikov and Edison Denisov made a living as best they could, knowing their works could never be performed. Their music, which represented a defiant and triumphant statement of the values they steadfastly continued to believe in, also faithfully reflected the

temporaries started to receive the recognition they deserved, both in Russia and in the rest of the world, and the new generation of composers which had arrived on the scene also received attention. The most talented of these are Alexander Knaifel, Vladimir Tarnopolsky, and the husband and wife team of Dmitry Smirnov and Elena Firsova.

Russian music now finds itself in a state of chaos. Like their colleagues in the field of literature, composers are unsure what their next step will be now they no longer have the traditional moral values to uphold. Scores of composers and performers have left to find better living conditions in the West, while back in Russia orchestras and musical insti-

troubled times in which they lived.

A new flowering: All this changed when Mikhail Gorbachev came to power. With *glasnost* came an explosion of Soviet cultural life, as artists and writers were allowed to travel freely to the West for the first time, and previously forbidden works were published and performed. Rostropovich and Ashkenazy both made much-publicised visits back to Russia, concert repertoires widened and Russian music started to become popular in the West. Schnittke and his con-

Left, **Sergei Rachmaninov with his wife. Above**, **Vladimir Ashkenazy returns to Russia in 1989.**

tutions struggle to survive. Despite these problems, musical life in Russia continues to thrive, and the traditional venues will no doubt continue to offer concerts of a high calibre. In Moscow these are the Bolshoi Theatre, the Chamber Opera, the Tchaikovsky Hall and the concert halls of the Conservatoire, and in St Petersburg the Mariinsky and Maly theatres, the former State Chapel and the halls of the Philharmonia. But concerts are increasingly held in churches, whose warm acoustics and rich decor, together with the glorious sounds of Russian sacred music, contribute to a thrilling experience.

"The new, young self-styled artistic elite of Russia are mere parasites living off the money of the Russian mafia, attending parties with tickets paid for by the new and criminal rich." This is an accusation often voiced by the old school of formally trained artists when discussing the success of younger artists emerging from the Underground.

The Russian myth of the painter as a poor, unshaven, misunderstood genius is fading. Nonetheless it was used by some of the earliest Underground groups in their bid to enter mainstream culture in the 1980s. Mitki was one of the first groups to abandon the idea of artists as victims and fighters. They marked the birth of the first non-idealistic generation in Russia. Adopting a witty and ironical stance towards the old Russian myths, they stopped shaving, became fat, threw back glasses of vodka and smoked cheap cigarettes. Although such gestures now appear out of date, Mitki continue to throw back the vodka and puff on their cheap cigarettes – in spite of having amassed a considerable fortune.

The beginning of perestroika, in 1985, was a time of change and experiment. The forbidden was read and listened to, punks and rockers emerged out of nowhere, and artists painted on the streets. Art became a metaphor for truth. The painters were loved for their daring and spontaneity. Underground exhibitions caused a stir. At Underground rock concerts, teenagers who couldn't get tickets scaled the concert hall's walls.

However, the uncritical embracing of all things Underground did not last. Once-popular bands such as Alisa and DDT were abandoned by the intellectual youth and they now find their audiences among disaffected teenagers who spend their free time loafing about and sniffing glue.

St Petersburg versus Moscow: At the end of the 1980s the alternative music scene in St Petersburg focused on a handful of popular bands that had emerged from the Underground. Chief among these were Kino, led by Victor Tsoy (later killed in a car crash),

and Boris Gribenchikov's group Aquarium. The artists who associated with these groups adopted a satirical view of officialdom (they were often the children of former party officials) and organised acts of social provocation. Ivan Movsesyan, for example, organised an exhibition of huge avant-garde canvases hung from the Dvortsovy Most – the bridge that leads to the Hermitage. Another St Petersburg artist, Sergei "Africa" Bugayev, travelled to Moscow's statue of *The Worker and the Collective Farm Worker* by Vera

ПОБЕДИТ ЗЛО

Mukhinoi, and cut a door between the female figure's legs. He then climbed inside and invited his friends to join him.

The New Painters also attended the concerts of Sergei Kuryokhin and his group Pop Mechanics. Grandiose, entirely Russian in scope and inspiration, the Pop Mechanics distilled all that was best about the Underground. It was at one of their concerts that Russia's first drag artist "Marilyn Monroe", alias the painter and performer Vladik Mamishev, made his debut. It symbolised the end of Russia's conflict between American and Western Culture, the end of the battle between ideas and values it was neces-

Left, *What is That?* (Rebus Series) by Africa. **Right**, *Bad will Win* by Andrei Khlobystin.

sary to defend. Russians were inspired by the idea of revanchism, eager to prove themselves on the world stage.

Those pursuing this aim most vigorously in Moscow are the Moscow Conceptualists. They include Ilya Kabakov (nearly 60 years old) and Andrei Monasterski, as well as a younger new wave of artists such as Sergei Volkov, Sergei Anufriev, Sasha Mariev, Vadim Fishkin and Kostya Zvezdochetov. There is not the great age division that prevails in St Petersburg, for members of the Moscow Underground had access to the Socialist artistic elite prior to perestroika (the leaders of the Moscow avant garde, for example, have been members of the Union of Artists for a number of years) and collaboration with the West had been going on for some time. It was Moscow that produced the bravely experimental "Soz Art". Under the Soviets, Moscow was altogether superior to St Petersburg in its range of artistic activity.

Cultural rivals: Moscow and St Petersburg are the most important cultural centres of Russia, continually absorbing talented young people from the Russian provinces and former Soviet republics. The intellectual battle that has traditionally existed between them has lost its edge now that attention has turned to working with New York, London and Paris. The differences remain, however. Moscow the Imperial Capital concentrates on capital: it is alive, confident, philistine, monstrous, and has its own attractions. The relationships between people in Moscow are very similar to relationships in bigger Western capitals: here, for example, friends arrange to meet each other one or two weeks in advance, a social practice almost unheard of in the Soviet period. In St Petersburg, on the other hand, the informal and impromptu visit survives. Here an artist's studio in the centre of town is also a *salon*, where 10 or more people pass through each day and the life of a painter is an exhibition in itself.

But such informality has its commercial disadvantages. In Moscow there are 10 or more respectable galleries such as Shkola, L. Gallery, Volodia Levashov's gallery, Region Art and others, and a museum of modern art in Tsaritsino. In St Petersburg there are none; the galleries here are full of kitsch, *matreshkas*, Gorby dolls, Yeltsin dolls and, at one time, even Saddam dolls.

One reason for this is money. Moscow galleries could not survive without the help of Western money. In addition, Russian art is increasingly judged by Western criteria. Russians often only recognise the talent of their own people after the West has recognised it first. In the words of the Moscow art critic Victor Miziyano: "The Russian environment has not produced the criteria for understanding and dialogue with modern Russian art. And it is understandable why this art looks to the West, where the appreciation of modern art exists."

More serious perhaps – particularly in St Petersburg – is the lack of interest and support for modern art. The State Russian Museum is not spending money, and other cultural bodies in the city are filled by the "vestiges of the old Soviet Glory". They possess all the necessary office equipment as well as connections and money – but little of this is going into art funding. Those Russians who do have money, the new millionaires, lack the imagination and style of serious arts patrons. One can only expect funding from them at a later date – probably not for several generations.

The State has responded to the cultural links formed with the West by putting heavy taxes on exported art. Even if export is arranged through Western galleries, art dealers and patrons, as much as 600 per cent tax is sometimes levied. To help counteract such exploitation a new society called A-Ya (A–Z), based in St Petersburg, gives members of the ex-Underground a formal backing.

The party begins: Artists such as Africa, Timur Novikov, Georgy Guryanov and Monroe have encouraged another new phenomenon to Russia – rave parties. On 14 December 1991 about 4,000 painters, businessmen, prostitutes, diplomats of respected Western powers, foreign journalists and cosmonauts congregated at Cosmos in Moscow's Museum of Economic Achievements to enjoy themselves at the first Russian rave party. Party-goers danced among sputniks and works by Petersburg artists to music provided by DJs imported from London clubs. Not until the following evening did the last cars bearing diplomatic numberplates finally drive away.

In the wake of this party, companies were set up to organise night raves, among them Blokk, MX and Tanzpol. In St Petersburg rave venues included palaces and swimming pools. Many of the artists entered for free (hence the criticism "parasites of the rich") because of their name, charm or stealth. Black marketeers and foreigners paid a dollar fee (extortionate for most Russians).

The Saturday night clubs are now growing as fast as the magic mushrooms grown in the suburbs of St Petersburg, which along with marijuana from Central Asia are the most accessible drugs (magic mushrooms are to the Russian clubs what ecstasy was to the first acid-house parties in the West). Russian gays have also come out of the closet, even though the law prosecuting homosexuality is still in force. They too organise their own discos on Saturday nights, though at present

business (the Company LIC'C) began to put on their own discotheques, aimed at the young newly-rich. But although similar in scale – held in sports complexes of Olympic size – there was nothing new and alternative on offer, only the already familiar sounds of Madonna and competitions to find who can eat a banana in the most erotic way.

Unable to compete, they tried to muscle in on what already existed. "After the third party that I organised in St Petersburg's Planetarium," says Misha Vorontsov (23), the director of the company MX, "racketeers from the Tambov Group approached me and demanded documents showing the firm's profit." Deciding that Vorontsov's reactions

these remain unsophisticated events, reminiscent of village clubs, where everyone gets drunk – probably to overcome their embarrassment at demonstrating their sexual orientation.

The mafia muscles in: The success of the young rave organisers is all the more surprising given that they had no government backing in a country where nearly all private business is under mafia control. Impressed, envious and wishing to capitalise on this success, the former mafiosi of Soviet show-

were too slow, they broke his arm with a metal crowbar.

After that, Vorontsov began to pay 10 per cent of his profit to the racketeers. But the story was not over: "There is an association called 'Zashita' [Protection] formed by former KGB officers and they are pushing me to turn to them for help. This will cost us not 10 per cent but 30. Zashita and the racketeers are probably one and the same people," he says.

The music scene: In spite of all the new developments, Russian music cannot compete with that of England and America. Most modern music is still on a small regional

Above, Russia's first drag artist: Vladik Mamishev, also known as "Marilyn Monroe".

scale, though some groups such as The New Composers and Liuki are beginning to record abroad and a few groups such as Mamonov's Zvukiy Moo played in the West as early as 1989. The best places to hear Underground groups – psycho punk and rock groups – are the Tam Tam Club in St Petersburg and Sextone in Moscow.

One of the biggest difficulties faced by bands is the monopoly over sound recording (dominated by the company Melodiya). On top of this is the lack of funding and necessary technology needed to produce modern sound and video clips, although in St Petersburg a group of young artists called Engineers of Art produce their own video

graphics with great professionalism. Television is still showing "the vestiges of Soviet glory" although a few new and radical youth culture programmes have emerged, such as Artem Troitsky's *Exotica* and, in St Petersburg, the radical *Subcultura*, the brainchild of Oleg Povarov.

Although Western youth movements are copied, they often take on a comic character – and time scale – of their own on Russian soil. Thus skinheads and punks befriend one another. The Russian version of the Hell's Angels – Night Wolves – who were at the forefront of the struggle for democracy during the August 1991 coup, have only just

emerged. Fortunately, another violent gang, the Luberi, which beat up anyone who stood out from the crowd, has fallen silent.

The Russian cinema: After so many years of restricted viewing, Russians can watch sex and foreign films to their heart's content. The cinema critic Sergei Scholokhov says, "Everything is beginning to follow the normal bourgeois tracks – viewers now vote with their roubles." The eclipse of Communism meant that, due to lack of funding, the number of films made in Russia fell from 800 a year to around 60. Luckily, traditional "Soviet pathos" has disappeared, although its vacuum has been filled by soft porn. In the cinema, mainstream culture has come from Underground directors such as the brothers Aleinikov and the directors of "Nekrokino" (a branch of the Necrorealist movement.) The director Yufit is currently fashionable.

Realising that they could never be technically ahead of the West, other directors have begun to shoot very simple, yet brilliant silent films and the experiment continues. But as with all art forms in Russia, foreign backing is continually sought.

One area that is thriving is fashion. "The Russians are coming" was the motto of a fashion show in Latvia, Jurmala, in 1992. This event attracted around 100 fashion designers from Russia and the Baltic states as well as spectators from Western fashion houses and organisations. Russian models sported traditional costumes combining Slavonic irony with Western chic.

The changes currently taking place in Russia are as fantastical as the events in Russian folklore. The traditional power of darkness in folklore is the three-headed snake. The snake has now lost his three heads – the KGB, the CPSU and the BPK (War Industrial Complex) but another dark personality from Russian folklore – Koschei Bessmertniy (the skeleton of immortality) can still be found on Red Square.

Russian fairytales usually end happily ever after, even though much sorrow and grief befalls their citizens on the way. Let us hope that the situation in Russia will also have the familiar happy ending. "They began to live well and forget evil. Here the story ends and we'll all drink a toast."

Left, St Petersburg rave-goer. **Right**, Alexander Nevsorov, presenter of *600 Seconds*.

600 SECONDS

When the television programme *600 Seconds* was unleashed upon Russian viewers in the wake of perestroika, its approach and content were so earth-shattering that cynics half-wondered whether it might be the brainchild of the KGB. After all, with sudden freedom of speech abounding, what better way of controlling public opinion than having a short, hard-hitting news programme after the central news? It was aimed at the radicals in the St Petersburg region but could also be watched in Moscow.

What's more, to ensure that everybody sat glued to the 10-minute programme, it was fronted by Alexander Nevsorov, a persuasive presenter whom the housewives adored for his steely blue eyes and the husbands admired for his ability to walk out of any situation unharmed. Nevsorov, reputed to be a trained stuntman, was seen as bloodthirsty to the point of vampirism and fearless in the face of controversy.

Before *600 Seconds* the USSR appeared to be a country with hardly any street crime, few vices and no religion. Nevsorov showed the public that all these things existed. He interviewed self-confessed criminals on camera, appeared at the scenes of violent crimes (and showed the bloody corpses to the viewers), and he openly wore a crucifix. As the reputation of the KGB was savaged by the international press, the reality of Russian streetlife was laid bare by *600 Seconds*. People would rather stay at home to watch Nevsorov reveal yet another gruesome crime than be out on the streets and possibly confronting the real thing.

The programme goes out five days a week at a machine-gun pace, with computer graphics flashing, making the whole thing all the more exciting. It started on 4 December 1987 and shot Nevsorov to superstardom within weeks. His audience includes some 60 million viewers, spreading as far as Moscow and Murmansk. But fame has had its price. Since the programme went on the air Nevsorov's film-star wife has left him, he has been shot and wounded, and his reputation as a stuntman has been discovered to be fake. To cap it all, it is now known that his grandfather was head of the KGB, which may explain why he has never been afraid to break down people's doors on television.

The programme is divided into sections – Criminal Chronicle, Culture, Prominent People, Courts of Law – each with its own theme music and announced by a robotic voice. Nevzorov's approach is one of gleeful irreverence, especially when covering anything he regards as pretentious or pompous. Art exhibitions, plays and "events" are frequently targeted. Input from the public is welcomed: at the end of each programme a series of phone numbers appears on the screen for anyone keen to reveal a juicy news item to the leather-clad *600 Seconds* team.

But in spite of the show's revolutionary delivery and packaging, its political stance is reactionary. In the past year or two, Nevsorov has made no bones about his support for the old right-wing regime and, rather like some tabloid journalists in the West, he frequently champions

his viewers' worst impulses and instincts. He takes great pleasure in reporting crimes by Muslims and other racial groups. His dangerous personal opinion has entered every household and he now has a reputation for being a warmonger, an alarmist, and even a fascist. Some think it significant that the programme's symbol has been changed to an eagle (not the tsarist double-headed eagle) with its wings outspread.

As this book goes to press, Nevsorov is no longer on the screen, although *600 Seconds,* with new presenters, continues. His absence appears to have nothing to do with his controversial style and personality and he claims he is planning to return to front the programme in the future. ■

Travel to Russia becomes more exciting each year because of the greater freedom to explore. Even now that many former republics such as the Baltics (Estonia, Lithuania and Latvia) Uzbekistan, Kirghizstan and Armenia, have gained their independence, the Commonwealth of Independent States (CIS) remains a vast, enigmatic and diverse territory.

The European North, which stretches into the Arctic Circle, is one of Russia's wildest and most beautiful regions. One of the main attractions of St Petersburg and the palaces which surround it is the splendour, principally reflected in the architecture, of the Imperial past. A tour to St Petersburg often takes in the country's capital, Moscow, as well. The question as to which city is superior has been hotly debated for more than two centuries and continues to this day amongst both Russians and foreigners.

Even though much of Moscow was burnt, the city gives us a feel for the age of the country, and, with its myriad mushroom church domes, for holy Russia. Equally, with some of its many monuments to Communism intact, we are made aware of the more recent past. The city's Russianness attracts some people as much as St Petersburg's Europeanness attracts others.

The theme of holy Russia continues as one explores the golden ring of churches which surrounds Moscow, and a trip up the Volga takes in rural Russia as well as the towns on the way.

We have decided to include the Ukraine and Belarus in this book because, given their geographical position and their fascinating culture, many tours to Russia still cross over the political boundaries. The Crimea, with its hot climate and beaches, is still one of the most popular holiday areas for many Russians. The nearby mountainous region of the Caucasus, with its spa towns and hot springs, also attracts walkers and climbers.

The Ural mountains divide the European North with the huge steppe and expanse that makes up Siberia, whose furthest shores look towards Japan. And cutting through the whole expanse of Russia, from Moscow to Vladivostok, is the famous Trans-Siberian railway.

The dramatic differences between the lands that make up Russia add to its great appeal. You can tailor a visit there to suit your own interests and, for the first time in years, wander freely without an accompanying guide.

Preceding pages: Siberian reindeer; summer on the Volga; driving over Lake Baikal in winter; the Trans-Siberian Railway; the domes of the Church of St Nicholas of the Weavers, Komomolsky Prospekt, Moscow.

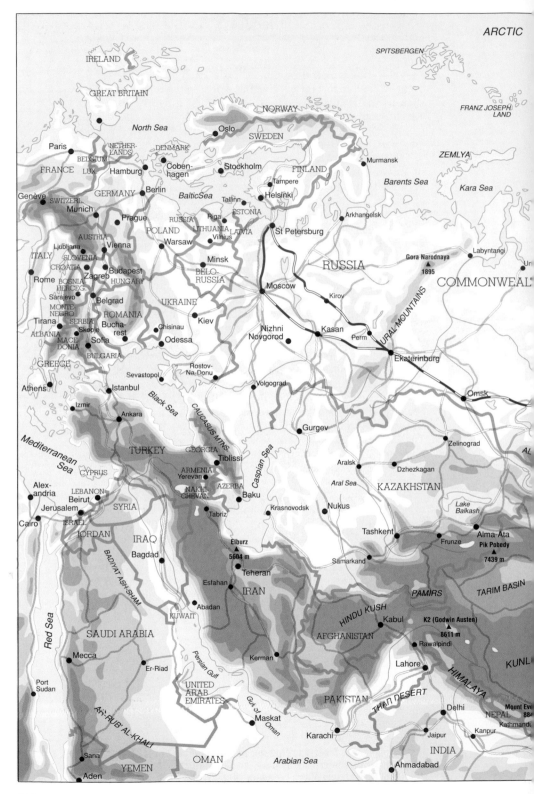

750 miles / 1200 km

OCEAN

NORTH LAND

NEW SIBERIAN ISLANDS

Ambartschik

Anadyr

Bering Sea

Laptev Sea

POLUOSTROV TAYMYR

KHREBET CHERSKOVO

ALEUTIAN ISLANDS

Verkhoyansk

VERKHOYANSKY KHREBET

Magadan

Klyuchevskaya Sopka
▲
4750 m

Petropoavlovsk-Kamchatsky

...arka

Yakutsk

Sea of Okhotsk

KURILE ISLANDS

OF INDEPENDENT STATES

Tura

STANOVOY KHREBET

SAKHALIN ISLAND

Ust-Ilimsk

Komsomolsk

Yuzhno-Sakhalinsk

...aoyarsk

Bratск

Lake Baikal

YABLONOVY KHREBET

GREATER KHINGAN

Khabarovsk

Sapporo

HOKKAIDO

Irkutsk

Nakhodka

Vladivostok

JAPAN

Harbin

Changchun

Sea of Japan

...mchi

CHANGA.IN NURUU

MONGOLIA

Shenyang

NORTH KOREA

HONSHU

Tokyo

Fuji-san 3776 m
▲

Pyangyang

Osaka

NAN SHAN

Beijing

Tianjin

Yellow Sea

Seoul

SOUTH KOREA

Pusan

Kitakyushu

KYUSHU

GOBI DESERT

Quingdao

Goldmud

Lanzhou

Zhengzhou

East China Sea

PACIFIC OCEAN

Xian

Shanghai

CHINA

Wuhan

Minya Konka 7556 m
▲

Chongqing

Taipei

Lhasa

Sadiya

TAIWAN

HUTAN

...HAN

...NGLA-...ESH
...ka

...cutta

BURMA

VIETNAM

Hongkong
Macao

RYUKYU ISLANDS

━━━━━ Trans-Siberian Railway

Moscow City Centre

0.5 miles / 800 m

BELORUSSKAYA

Belorussky Station

Leningradsky Prosp.

Gruzinsky Per.

Ul. Lesnaya

Ul. Fadeeva

Ul. Kalyaevskaya

Ul. Sadovaya-Karaetr

Ul. Pen

VAGAN'KOVSKOYE KLADB.

Ul. Gruzinsky Val

Bolshoi Tishinsky Per.

Ul. 1905 Goda

Ul. Presnenky

Zoologichesky Per.

Ul. Grasheka

MAYAKOV-SKAYA

Ul. Tverskaya

Ul. Medvedeva

Ul. Chekhova

Zvenigorodskoe Shosse

Ul. Krasina

Ul. Zoologicheskaya

Ul. Bolsaya Sado

Ul. Malaya Bronnaya

Ploshchad Pushkinskaya

Strastnoy Bulv.

Ul. Po

Ul. Sergeya Makeeva

Ul. 1905 Goda

Ul. Krasnaya Presnya

Ul. Malaya Gruzinskaya

ZOO · PARK

Ul. Kachalova

Tverskoy Bulv.

Ul. Stanislavskogo

Ul. Tversk.

Ul. Zamorenova

Ul. Barrikadnaya

Ul. Gertsena

Ul. Gertsena

Ul. Ogareva

OKH

Smitovsky Prosp.

Ul. Rochedelskaya

Ploshchad Vostannya

Suvorov Bulv.

Semashko

VOZDVIZ-HENKA

Okht

Ul. Mantulinskaya

Povarskaya

Ploshchad Arbat

Ul. Vozdvizhenka

PKiO KRASNAYA PRESNAYA

Krasnopresnenskaya Nab.

Noviy Arbat

ARBATS-KAYA

BORO-VITSKAYA

Krasnopresnenskaya Nab.

Moskva

Tarasa Shevchenko

Kalininsky Most

Novinsky Bulv.

Ul. Chajkovskogo

Ul. Arbat

Ul. Znamenka

Grand Krem Pala

Tarasa Shevchenko Nab.

Ukrainsky Bulv.

Smolenskaya Nab.

Nikitsky Bulv.

B. Kamen Mc

Kutuzovsky Prospekt

Ul. B. Dorogomilovskaya

Pichnikov

Pushkin Museum

Ul. Volkhonka

Ul. Studencheskaya

Ul. Kievskaya

Ul. Smolenskaya

Ul. Ryleeva

Gogolevsky Bulv.

Kievsky Station

Rostovskaya Nab.

Smolensky Bulv.

Ul. Vesnina

Ul. Prechistenka

Kropotkinskaya Nab.

Ul. Plushchiha

Ul. Burdenko

Ul. Ostozhenka

Ul. Plushchiha

Ul. Timura Frunze

Krymsky Most

Krymskaya Nab.

Berezhkovskaya Nab.

Bolshoi Savvinsky Per.

Savvinskaya Nab.

Ul. Pogodinskaya

Ul. Bolshaya Porogovskaya

Ul. Rossolimo

Hol'zunova Per.

Usacheva St.

Frunzenskaya Nab.

Ul. Krymsky Val

GORKY PARK

Plost Oktjab

Park Kultury

Ul. Malaya Pirogovskaya

Ul. Efremova

Komsomolsky Prosp.

Moskva

Pushkinskaya Nab.

Leninsky Prospekt

Ul. Sabolovka

MOSCOW

Moscow's first mention in historic chronicles is a brief note in an annal written in 1147 indicating that there was a small settlement surrounded by small hills on the banks of the Moskva River. Such limited mention is not surprising: Moscow lay on the extreme borders of the Suzdal Knyazhestvo (principality), the centre of which was far to the south-west in Kiev.

When Prince Yuri Dolgoruky arrived in 1156, Moscow must have been no more than a cluster of wooden huts. However, he saw its potential as an outpost against the Tartar Golden Horde and ordered a *kremlin* (fortification) to be built. Historians believe the name Moskva derives from an old Slavonic word meaning "wet", probably an allusion to the marshy countryside that surrounded the site.

The broad Moskva river winds through the city and used to be swelled by a number of smaller streams and rivers, so the site was ideal for a fortress. However, the Tartars still torched it at regular intervals, even after Grand Prince Ivan Kalita (nicknamed "Moneybags") built stonewalls around the settlement in the early 14th century. The walls were white-washed and earned Moscow the name Byelokamenaya (literally "white-walled").

As Ivan Kalita's power and prestige grew, so did Moscow. But his real coup was managing to persuade the Russian Orthodox Metropolitan to move the Holy See from Kiev to Moscow. As chief centre of both religious and secular power, Moscow was on the map.

The city blossomed during the reign of Ivan III (the Great), in the mid-15th century. Ivan dealt with the Tartars effectively and was the first prince to take the title "tsar", the Russianised form of Caesar. To match his new status, he imported Italian architects to create a new Kremlin. Many of the cathedrals and the walls they built still stand.

The Kremlin: When the Italian architects Fioravanti, Ruffo and Solari had finished their job in 1495, praise was effusive and another "eighth wonder of the world" was added to that already lengthy list. But the accolade was not entirely undeserved. The imposing red-brick walls running around the **Kremlin** are 2,230 metres (7,316 ft) long, 20 metres (65 ft) high and 6 metres (20 ft) wide in some places. It has four gates and 19 towers. Inside, the Italians created three stone cathedrals to replace the humble wooden structures that had existed. These came to symbolise tsarist power: the Uspensky was used for coronations, the Blagoveshchensky for baptisms and weddings, and the Arkhangelsky for funerals.

The main entrance for visitors is the **Troitsky (Trinity) Bridge** that crosses the Alexandrovsky Gardens and the Neglinka River (which was channelled into a large stone underground pipe on the orders of Catherine II in the 18th century). In pre-Revolutionary times this gate was used for regal entrances. Napoleon, in 1812, obviously didn't know this – although his army entered the

Preceding pages: Red Square. **Left,** marching past Lenin's tomb. **Right,** tourist transport.

Kremlin this way, he used the Spassky Gate. He is supposed to have lost his famous tricorn hat in the process, making it unlucky, according to popular lore, to pass through the Spassky Gate wearing a hat.

At one time the Kremlin was considered almost impregnable. Its southeastern side is protected by the Moskva, and a deep moat, which once linked the Moskva and Neglinka rivers, takes care of the remaining walls. The Arsenal Tower had its own well which fed a secret reservoir and an underground passage to the Neglinka River. During long sieges, the garrison could thus come and go as they pleased.

Although the Russian tricolour now flutters above the Kremlin, the symbols of Soviet power are still apparent in the red stars topping five of the towers. These have been there so long (since 1937) that most Muscovites don't feel strongly about their removal. But there is one Soviet eyesore that still makes Muscovite blood boil – the crass steel and glass Palace of Congresses that was planted in the middle of the Kremlin in 1961. (The architect, Mikhail Posokhin, is also responsible for the soulless Novyi Arbat, formerly Kalininsky Prospect.)

In spite of the Soviet-style "palace", the Kremlin has managed to retain most of its historic beauty. The former Arsenal buildings were built by Peter the Great between 1701 and 1736 and its facades are hung with Napoleonic military trophies.

The **Armoury** at the foot of the Borovitsky Gate houses the oldest Kremlin museum. It has armour, of course, but pride of place is taken by the valuables accumulated by the Russian aristocracy, in particular the diamonds and jewellery (Russia has one of the biggest diamond fields in the world).

The three original cathedrals still dominate the heart of the Kremlin, with the grandiose **Uspensky (Dormition)**, built by Fioravanti, as centrepiece. This is a prime example of European Renaissance building combined with Byzantine traditions. Inside is an amazing collection of frescoes devoted mainly to

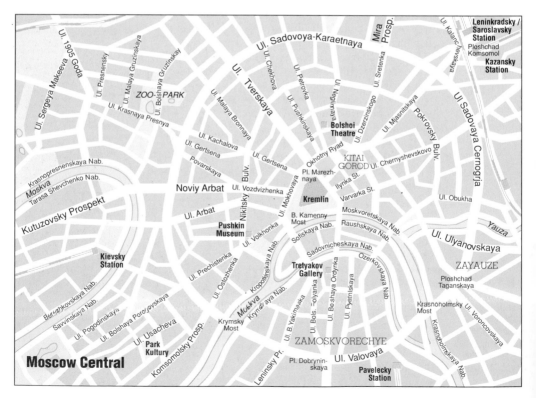

154

the Virgin, but the cathedral also houses the famous 14th-century Trinity icon and it is here the city's bishops and Patriarchs were interred.

To the south is the contemporary **Blagoveshchensky (Annunciation) Cathedral** which was built as a private church for Moscow's Grand Princes. The cathedral started life as a three-domed, galleried building in the Pskov style (Ivan III had opted for Russian rather than foreign stonemasons for this particular project).

As this was essentially a private church, the builders set it on a very high foundation so that its entrance would be accessible from the second floor of the royal palace. Ivan the Terrible thought the cathedral should be more imposing, so he ordered the addition of four small chapels surmounted by a cross and cupola. The result matched Ivan's nickname, so two more domes were added to restore the building's balance.

However, the Annunciation is generally regarded as superior to the other early cathedrals. Built on the site of a wooden structure of the same name, it inherited the original church's iconostasis, painted by two of the greatest names in Russian iconography: Theofan the Greek and Andrei Rubliov. Its floor is tiled with agate and jasper, a gift from the Shah of Persia. Portraits of the Grand Princes hang alongside biblical fathers and the Greek philosophers Aristotle, Plutarch and Virgil: doubtless an attempt by the princes to portray themselves as enlightened rulers.

Next to the Annunciation is the **Arkhangelsky (Archangel) Cathedral**, built in the early years of 16th century by Venetian architect Alevisio, nicknamed Novi (the new), because an Italian of the same name had worked in Moscow before him. It was here that the princes and tsars were buried until Peter the Great built his new capital in 1712. Portraits of dead aristocrats watch over the bronze sarcophagi containing their remains.

The Kremlin's focal point is the **Bell Tower of Ivan the Great**. Started by Ivan, it was augmented by Boris Godunov. Some said he undertook the

In the Palace of Facets.

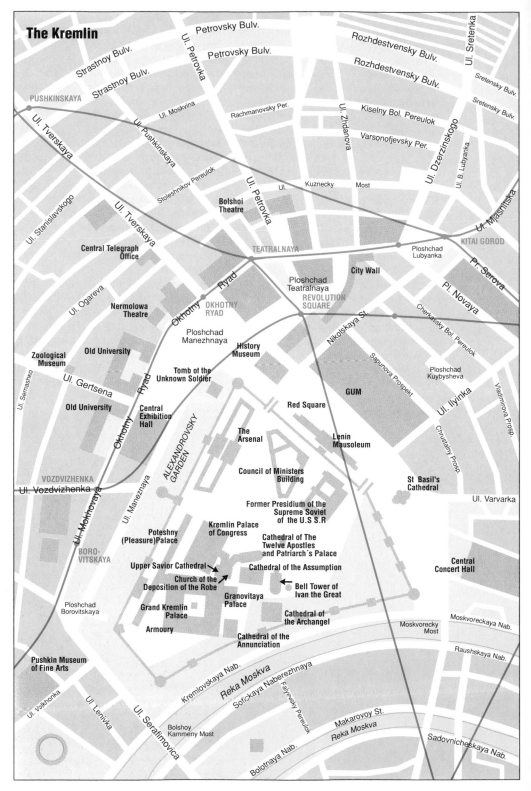

The Kremlin

PUSHKINSKAYA

Strastnoy Bulv.
Strastnoy Bulv.

Petrovsky Bulv.
Petrovsky Bulv.

Rozhdestvensky Bulv.
Rozhdestvensky Bulv.

Ul. Sretenka
Sretensky Bulv.
Sretensky Bulv.

Ul. Tverskaya

Ul. Pushkinskaya

Ul. Moskvina

Rachmanovsky Per.

Ul. Zhdanova

Kiselny Bol. Pereulok

Varsonofjevsky Per.

Ul. Dzerzinskogo

Ul. B. Lubyanka

Ul. Stanislavskogo

Ul. Tverskaya

Stoleshnikov Pereulok

Ul. Petrovka

Ul. Kuznecky Most

Ul. Mjasnitska

KITAI GOROD

Bolshoi
Theatre

TEATRALNAYA

Ploshchad
Lubyanka

Pr. Serova

Central Telegraph
Office

City Wall

Pl. Novaya

Ul. Ogareva

Nermolowa
Theatre

Ryad

Okhotny

OKHOTNY
RYAD

Ploshchad
Teatralnaya

REVOLUTION
SQUARE

Nikolskaya St.

Cherkassky Bol. Pereulok

Zoological
Museum

Old University

Ul. Gertsena

Ploshchad
Manezhnaya

History
Museum

Sapunova Prospekt

GUM

Ploshchad
Kuybysheva

Vladimirova Prosp.

Ul. Semashko

Ryad

Okhotny

Tomb of the
Unknown Soldier

Ul. Ilyinka

Old University

Central
Exhibition
Hall

Red Square

Chrustalny Prosp.

VOZDVIZHENKA
Ul. Vozdvizhenka

ALEXANDROVSKY
GARDEN

The
Arsenal

Lenin
Mausoleum

St Basil's
Cathedral

Ul. Mokhovaya

Ul. Manezhnaya

Council of Ministers
Building

Ul. Varvarka

BORO-
VITSKAYA

Poteshny
(Pleasure)Palace

Kremlin Palace
of Congress

Former Presidium of the
Supreme Soviet
of the U.S.S.R

Cathedral of The
Twelve Apostles
and Patriarch´s Palace

Central
Concert Hall

Upper Savior Cathedral

Church of the
Deposition of the Robe

Ploshchad
Borovitskaya

Grand Kremlin
Palace

Granovitaya
Palace

Cathedral of the Assumption

Bell Tower of
Ivan the Great

Cathedral of
the Archangel

Moskvoreckaya Nab.

Moskvorecky
Most

Armoury

Cathedral of the
Annunciation

Raushskaya Nab.

Pushkin Museum
of Fine Arts

Kremlovskaya Nab.

Reka Moskva

Sofickaya Naberezhnaya

Falyevsky Pereulok

Ul. Volkhonka

Ul. Lenivka

Ul. Serafimovica

Bolshoy
Kammeny Most

Bolotnaya Nab.

Makarovoy St.

Reka Moskva

Sadovnicheskaya Nab.

building work as a penance for murdering Prince Dmitry, the legitimate heir to the throne. Although Boris had been elected tsar, many people continued to see him as an upstart: they must have been delighted to see the bell tower grow shakier the taller it rose – rather like the tsar's hold on power. But it survived and is still the tallest structure in the Kremlin and still carries the inscription: "By the grace of the Holy Trinity and by order of the Tsar and Grand Prince Boris Fedorovich, Autocrat of all Russia, this temple was finished and gilded in the second year of their reign."

Ivan III was a prolific builder. The **Palace of the Facets** is perhaps the most fabulous of the secular buildings he initiated. Unlike any other structure in Moscow, the palace is a pure example of Italian Renaissance architecture, designed by Ruffo and Solari. It was here that the tsars received foreign ambassadors and other dignitaries and the whole place was decorated as a showpiece. The frescoes are painted on backgrounds of gold, and you'll even find a portrait of Ivan the Terrible in the guise of the "Just Knight" in the Hall of Facets.

These are the oldest buildings in the Kremlin, but over the centuries myriad others have been erected between them. Until the modern Palace of Congresses was built, the most recent was the **Great Kremlin Palace** built by Konstantin Thon to commemorate victory over Napoleon. Today, it houses the Russian parliament. Just in front is the spectacular **Terem** (Belvedere) **Palace** (now only accessible through the Great Kremlin Palace). Built along the lines of traditional wooden houses, it was first occupied by Mikhail Romanov's family. The first of his line, Mikhail (1613–45), and later his son Alexis, used this palace to conduct state affairs. It was meant to convey the power and unity of the Russian state so the interiors are lavish to say the least.

Before becoming tsars of Russia, the Romanovs were just one of many noble families. Young Mikhail was elected tsar by a council of all the Russias following a long period of popular unrest

and occupation by the Poles. The Poles were finally driven out in 1612 by a patriotic army that rallied to Russia's banner at the religious settlement founded by St Sergius just outside Moscow. Led by Prince Pozharsky and organised by a patriotic butcher called Minin from Nizhni Novgorod, the national army advanced on the capital and forced the Poles and the pretender they had put on the throne to flee. Pozharsky and Minin were immortalised in bronze in 1818; their statue stands outside the entrance to St Basil's on Red Square.

When Mikhail was elected tsar, his family's main claim to fame was the fact that Ivan the Terrible had taken a Romanov as his first wife. The new tsar entered the Kremlin with the country in tatters. For a generation, almost half the villages in central Russia were deserted; for much of the countryside had been laid waste during the years of unrest. The devastation was such that, as one historian remarked, "The rulers of Russia never recovered their old security."

But back to the Kremlin. Tucked be-

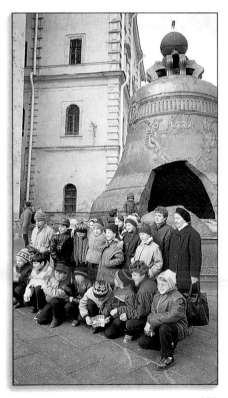

The Tsar Bell on display at the foot of the Bell Tower of Ivan the Great.

tween the Uspensky and Palace of the Facets is the tiny **Deposition of the Robe church**, commissioned by Patriarch Geronty in 1480 to commemorate an argument with Ivan III about whether a church procession should follow the course of the sun or vice versa. The religious leader threatened to resign if Ivan didn't admit he was wrong. The Grand Prince finally gave in and the church was built by masons from Pskov (Geronty wasn't having any of the new-fangled Italian-style architecture in vogue in Moscow at that time). Initially, the church served as a private chapel for the Russian Patriarchs, but was requisitioned by the Romanovs for their own use in 1653.

The eastern side of the Kremlin is reserved for government buildings. The main structure is late 18th-century and was designed by Matvei Kazakov for the Moscow department of the Senate, which was then located in St Petersburg. After the Revolution, Moscow became the capital once again and the top floor of this building was used by Lenin. It is still open as his Apartment Museum, but don't be surprised if that changes in the near future.

Although the buildings inside the Kremlin are the main attractions, some of the 20 towers that line the walls are worth mentioning. The oldest, the **Tower of Secrets** in the southern wall, has fascinated scholars for centuries. It has an underground passage to the river, but it is also thought to have been the site of Ivan the Terrible's famous library. The collection was started by his grandmother, Sofia Paleologue, who brought a wealth of manuscripts to Moscow as part of her dowry. Some believe the library is still hidden beneath the Kremlin walls, probably under the Arsenal Tower overlooking the Alexandrovsky Gardens. A Russian scholar thought he had found it in 1934 but Stalin ordered him to stop searching.

Another of the towers that shouldn't be missed is the **Saviour's Tower**. Built in 1625, its Gothic and Renaissance splendour served as a fitting background for the state entrances of the tsars. In the **War heroes.**

20th century, the guard of honour for Lenin's mausoleum passed through here on the choreographed march to the Revolutionary's tomb.

Red Square: Touching the wall as you leave the Kremlin is supposed to bring you luck and ensure your return. Red Square adjoins the eastern side of the Kremlin, but to get there you'll have to exit through the Trinity Gate and walk round as only top brass is allowed to use the Saviour's Gate on the square itself. Walk through the **Alexandrovsky Gardens**, with its old lime trees and remarkable 19th-century grotto in the Kremlin's wall, past the Tomb of the Unknown Soldier – still a popular spot for wedding pictures – and turn right. The ketchup-coloured building on your left is the city's **Historical Museum** which houses a rare collection of artefacts and traces Russian history right up to the present day.

The name **Red Square** was a happy coincidence when the Bolsheviks took power after the revolution. It had started life as the eastern moat protecting the Kremlin, but this was eventually filled in and the resulting square was cobbled in the 15th century. In old Russian, the word "red" also means beautiful and this is the source of its name. Whether it was deserved at the time is debatable. For much of its history Red Square was crammed to bursting point with wooden galleries of market stalls where merchants from all over the world set up shop. The whole place formed a major fire hazard and the Great Fire of Moscow that destroyed much of the old city in 1737 started here.

But today, as you cross Red Square towards St Basil's, there is definitely something beautiful about the red Kremlin wall and the elegant, stuccoed buildings on the east side. The **Lenin Mausoleum**, which partially obscures the walls, still houses the great man's embalmed body, but people no longer queue for hours to see the waxen features. The building itself was designed by Shchusev in 1930 and replaced a wooden structure built just after Lenin's death. Although the architectural merits

Lenin's Mausoleum.

are dubious, Shchusev did strive to keep the structure low so that it wouldn't disturb the essential elegance of Red Square – most Soviet builders were not so considerate.

The area of the Kremlin wall between the Nikolskaya and Senatskaya Towers is the burial place of top Soviet statesmen, public figures and military leaders. Here lie such names as Maxim Gorky, Lenin's wife, Nadezhda Krupskaya, spaceman Yuri Gagarin, nuclear physicist Igor Kurchatov, and John Reed, the American journalist whose book on the birth and early years of the Russian revolution, *Ten Days That Shook the World*, was a revelation to subsequent generations of Marxists throughout the Western world. It describes Western governments' attempts to undermine and destroy the Revolution, and until the 1960s seemed to explain and even justify the burgeoning paranoia and suspicion of the young Soviet state.

St Basil's is to Moscow what the Eiffel Tower is to Paris, or Big Ben is to London. It is essentially Muscovite.

There is a story that Ivan the Terrible had the architects blinded so they could not build anything like it again. Ivan shaped Red Square and much of old Moscow. He built St Basil's (originally called the Pokrovsky Sobor: Cathedral of the Veil) to commemorate major victories over the Tartars. Every victory (nine in all) added a new chapel to the structure, each one dedicated to the saint on whose day the victory was won. The whole golden-domed complex became known popularly as St Basil's when one of the chapels was dedicated to Basil the Blessed, a holy man who predicted that Ivan would murder his first-born.

In the 17th century Red Square became a centre of political debate and was the venue for many popular uprisings. The **Lobnoye Mesto** (a raised circular platform in front of the cathedral) was used as a place of execution (it is said that as a child Ivan the Terrible had a small wooden tower built on top of the Spasskaya Tower so he could watch beheadings in private).

Later the leader of the 1671 peasant

Easter on Red Square.

revolt, Stepan Razin, was executed here and in 1648 the Strelet mutineers and supporters of Tsarina Sofia, Peter the Great's half-sister, also met their deaths on this spot. When punishment moved indoors, the elevation was used for reading tsarist decrees.

It's hard to judge just how the wooden city of Moscow looked because Muscovites put it to the torch in order to frustrate the imminent arrival of Napoleon and his troops in 1812. By the time Napoeon arrived he found the buildings in flames and anybody who was anybody, and a lot who weren't, gone.

In retrospect, you could say Moscow should be grateful to Napoleon. The reconstruction transformed the city from a medieval warren of small alleys and streets into an elegant capital whose main streets and quarters were dominated by stylish mansions and buildings. In charge of the massive project was an architect called Osip Bovet. He restored the Kremlin Wall and rebuilt the shopping galleries that lined the eastern side of Red Square. These were later replaced by the still magnificent GUM building, with its pastel interiors and ornate fountain. GUM opened its doors in 1893, was nationalised in 1921 and celebrated its centenary by returning to the private sector following a public auction of the retail units that make up what was once, and could be again, the most up-market shopping mall in Russia.

In the late 19th century another red-brick building was added to the northern end of Red Square, just opposite the Historical Museum. It housed the city's Duma or council until the Revolution. After Lenin's death in 1924, it became a museum devoted to the father of the country. Little has changed on Red Square since then.

A street by any other name: The Kremlin and Red Square may have been the heart of the original city, but its arteries were the old quarters that clustered around them. Basically, the city was built in rings, with main roads to important towns, such as Smolensk, Tver and Kaluga, radiating in a wagon-wheel

GUM department store.

pattern that still exists today. Not surprisingly, these roads became major thoroughfares and until the revolution were simply named after the places they led to. Since 1917 they have had different names – Kalininsky Prospekt, Ulitsa Gorkovo and Leninsky Prospekt respectively – and these will probably still feature on your map. However, in day to day speech and on street signs they have reverted back to their original names.

Other street names are clues to the trades and businesses once conducted there, eg. Meshchanskaya (petty bourgeois street), Yamskaya (coachman's street), Zhivoderka (abattoir road), or are derived from a monastery or church.

The Kremlin formed the central ring, followed by the former Kitai-Gorod Wall which bordered the Kremlin to the northeast. The wall was 2.5 km (4 miles) long and had 12 towers and several gates. Built in the mid-16th century around the original market-place, its name derives from the Mongolian word for "middle", i.e. middle fortress. It is thought that Ivan the Terrible's mother,

Elena Glinskaya, first coined the name – she came from a place called Kitai-Gorod in Poland. These walls have not survived, but remains can be seen on Teatralnaya Ploschad, close to the Metropol Hotel, and on Kitaisky Prospekt in Zaryadye.

The third ring accounts for Moscow's reputation as the "White city". These walls ran 9 km (5 miles) along what is now the **Boulevard Ring**, had 10 gates and 17 blind towers, and were built of white stone. They were constructed in the early 16th century and served as a sturdy defence for the outskirts of Moscow until they were demolished in the late 18th century. The final ring, **Zemlyanoi Val**, was constructed at the end of the 16th century and was really a rampart. Two hundred years later it was replaced by gardens which gave their name to a whole area: the Garden Ring (**Sadovoye Koltso**) follows the course of the original ramparts.

Merchants of Moscow: Many of the old streets of **Kitai-Gorod** lost a lot of their original charm at the same time. This was one of Moscow's liveliest quarters and runs due east from the north end of Red Square. **Nikolskaya** (formerly Ulitsa October 25) was known as the "street of enlightenment" as the city's first higher education facility, the Slavonic-Greek-Latin Academy, was located at Nos 7–9. Further up the street on the same side is a magnificent Russian Gothic building with a sundial adorning its facade. Built in 1814 as the Orthodox Synod's printing house, it printed the first books in Russian. Today, it houses the **History and Archives Institute**.

On a less elevated note, check out No 17. This is the gloriously tacky **Slavyansky Bazaar** restaurant. Reputed to be the oldest surviving eatery in the city, it manages to combine what's left of Russian cuisine with a "traditional" floor show of Cossack dancing, sword fighting and other bits of pre-Revolutionary popular culture. Although the food is no better than average, the vodka flows and the place is certainly fun.

Turning right onto Ilyinka (formerly Kuibyshevskiy) Ulitsa you'll see the magnificent **Bogoyavensky Sobor** (the

Slavyansky Bazaar.

God-sent church) on your right, parts of which are 13th-century, but whose main facade is a typical example of 17th-century Moscow baroque. It was founded in 1290 by Prince Daniel Nevsky, the same man who built a string of fortified monasteries, including the Danilov, around the city.

Ilyinka Ulitsa used to be the Moscow equivalent of Wall Street, but during the Soviet era the bank buildings and the Mercantile Exchange (at No 6) were confiscated and turned into public offices – the Exchange became the Soviet Chamber of Commerce and Industry. Contemporary photographs show a lively commercial street cluttered with bright advertisements. Today, it's all rather grey.

If you turn down Rybnyy Pereulok at the exchange corner you'll see the old **Gostiny Dvor**, or Old Merchant Arcade, another of the city's famous shopping arcades. When it was completed in 1805 by the Italian-born architect Quarenghi it was considered a major accomplishment. Its elegant, white Cor-

inthian pillars still retain their original magic. If you can gain entrance, check out the magnificent open arcade, now warehouse space, and imagine how it must have looked when it was home to the most exclusive and chic boutiques in town.

At the south end of Rybnyy turn into Varvarka (formerly Razin) **Ulitsa**. Ironically the Revolutionary name given to this once exclusive street of nobles and wealthy merchants' homes was that of the Cossack rebel Stepan Razin. Little remains of the old street. Around 20 tiny churches and a number of houses were demolished to make way for the staggering **Rossiya Hotel** complex, reputed to be the biggest in the world with over 5,000 rooms. But a stretch of the old Kitai-Gorod walls is still extant, along with the small church of the Conception of St Ann, which was built at the time of Columbus's voyage to America.

To the right you'll see the **Vassilievsky Slope** running down to the Moskvoretsky Bridge, which German teenager Matthias Rust used as a land-

Roses in a Moscow market.

ing strip on his extraordinary flight to Moscow in the mid-1980s. The world held its breath when it was revealed that a teenager in a light plane had managed to dodge Soviet radar. As detente was well established and the Cold War beginning to thaw, most people thought Rust would be sent home with a slapped wrist. In the event, the Soviets imprisoned him for a short period before quietly letting him go home – on a scheduled flight, of course.

The humble-looking white-stone, wooden-roofed building (No 6) was once the English embassy. It was presented to English merchants by Ivan the Terrible in the mid-16th century when the tsar was considering marriage to Queen Elizabeth I of England. The building was restored in the 1970s. Next door is the **Znamensky** (Omen) **monastery** with its five domes. Started in 1684, the belfry was added in 1789 and today the second floor is used as a venue for classical and religious music concerts. The building beside it (No 10) was the home of Mikhail Romanov, the first tsar

of the dynasty which ruled Russia for over three centuries. The house had fallen into disrepair, but in the late 19th century it was restored; only the ground floor is original. Now a museum showing how the Russian nobility lived, the interiors are stunning.

If you follow Varvarka down to the square of the same name (formerly Nogina) and turn left, you'll see the squat grey buildings of the Central and Moscow Committees of the Communist Party of the Soviet Union. What will happen to them is still unknown.

Varvarkaya Ploschad runs northwest and if you cross it at its southern end you turn right onto **Solyanka** (salt) Street. For centuries, this eastern quarter was the centre of the artisans' guilds and became notorious in the 19th century for prostitutes, brothels and the criminal population that lived in its dreadful slums. The central marketplace at the top of Podkolokolnyy Pereulok was known as the Khitrovo and the pickpockets who thrived there were said to be so clever that they once stole a

At the pet market.

bronze cannon from the grounds of the Kremlin. To escape public disgrace, the Governor-General of Moscow ordered his men to find the cannon at all costs. As usual, the local police set up a meeting with the criminal bosses and the cannon was back in its place next day.

But there's a twist to the tale. It was soon discovered that the returned cannon had itself been stolen from the opposite side of the Kremlin Wall; the first cannon was never recovered. You can easily spend a couple of hours in this picturesque quarter which is bordered by the Yauza River whose embankment makes a pleasant walk up to the Yauza Boulevard, the starting point of the Boulevard Ring.

Solyanka and the main thoroughfares in the vicinity were popular residential streets for the nobility. Most of their mansion homes have either disappeared or have been turned into an institute or academy. The former home of the Naryshkin family at 14a is now the Obstetrics Institute. Peter the Great's mother was a Naryshkin and the family liked to remind everyone of its royal connections, so the palace they built (all gone now, of course) had more than its share of pomp and circumstance. The Court of Wards erected in the 1820s and the 18th-century Foundling Hospital at Nos 14 and 16 are now the buildings of the **Academy of Medical Science**. Solyanka runs into Yauzskaya then Taganskaya (formerly Internatsionalnaya) Street. Worth seeing is the former **Batashev Palace** (number 1), another aristocratic legacy. Now the 23rd City Hospital, the palatial building set back off the street in its own landscaped gardens is a real jewel.

On **Varvarskaya Ploshad**, you could opt to walk up Prospekt Serov and turn right onto **Maroseika Ulitsa** (formerly Bogdan Khmel'nitskogo Street). To your left in the central garden you'll see the **monument to the Grenadiers** who were killed at the battle of Plevna during the Russo-Turkish War in 1887. Also at the top of the square is the **Polytechnic Museum**, which was built between 1874 and 1907. It houses more than 40,000

Matreshka dolls.

exhibits tracing the development of Russian technology and science. On Novaya Ploschad to the left of the museum is a former Baptist church (No 12) which is now the **Museum of the History and Reconstruction of Moscow**.

The old embassy quarter: A walk along Maroseika Ulitsa, which runs into Pokvovka (formerly Chernishevsky), takes you into the old embassy quarter. A lot of embassies can still be found here and in the area around **Chistye Prudi** (the Clear Ponds). Like most old cities, certain quarters of Moscow came to be associated with particular nationalities. In Ivan the Terrible's day, much of the land behind the Clear Ponds was owned by German merchants. To the northwest, the French set up shops in the streets around Markhlevskogo and Lubyanka Malaya; the English and Poles gravitated to Myasnitzkaya (formerly Kirov) Street in between Markhlevskogo and Chistye Prudi.

By the end of the 17th century, Moscow's wealthy boyars had bought up much of the land and built superb palaces. A cluster of noble dynasties dominated the area – the Dolgorukiy family lived on Kolpachny Pereulok 1, the Lopoukhins at Starosdasky 5, and the Botkins at Pertoverigsky Pereulok 4 – all to the southwest of Chistye Prudi. But their grand palaces are overshadowed by the splendid **Archangel Gabriel church** on Telegrafnyy Lane. Grand Prince Menshikov had the church built in the early 18th century and the tower still bears his name. Menshikov's aim was to top the Kremlin Bell Tower. It was the tallest building in Moscow and an old tsarist decree prevented the erection of anything higher. His architect, Ivan Zarudnyi, managed to beat the record by 1.7 metres (5.6 ft).

The Grand Prince was something of a favourite with Peter the Great, but when the tower was struck by lightning in 1722 no one lifted a finger to put out the ensuing fire which consumed the giant bronze statue of Gabriel mounted on top. The disaster was seen as a sign of God's displeasure with the tsar's favourite. Muscovites had good reason to be angry with the tsar – he had moved the capital to St Petersburg some years earlier, relegating Moscow to provincial status.

Another church worth seeing is **St Ludovic's** (Lubyanka Malaya 12). It's a working Catholic church founded by the French in the early 19th century.

Myasnitzkaya (formerly Kirov) Street: The corner of Myasnitzkaya and the newly named Chistye Prudi (formerly Kirov) Square is dominated by what remains of the grand Yushkov Palace, built in the late 18th century by architect Vasily Bazhenov, when most of the boyars had become interested in philanthropy and art collections. The Yushkov family were flamboyant and most famous for their balls and parties. It is said that one Yushkov scion held a soirée that lasted three days – it ended only when the whole district had become disrupted by the crowds that had come to gape at the firework displays, the music and the gorgeously dressed guests.

From 1844 until recently the Yushkov Palace housed the Academy of Art and Sculpture. Next door is an amazing look-

A bouquet from the lady.

ing building that was constructed in the late 19th century for the tea-merchant Perlov. He was hoping to entertain the Chinese emperor's ambassador during Nicholas II's coronation celebrations so the classical three-storey house-cum-tea-shop was topped by a Chinese pagoda. The envoy never turned up, but the pagoda still graces the roof. Today, the shop sells tea from Georgia.

Lubyanka Ploschad: The pedestal from which the statue of Felix Dzerzhinsky, Lenin's closest associate and founder of the KGB, cast a stony stare over Moscow's citizens is now empty. The grim statue was one of the first to go following the unsuccessful coup against Boris Yeltsin and his reformers in 1991. The busy square now has its old name back, although it also has some creepy connotations. **Lubyanka prison** in the notorious KGB headquarters on the northeast side of the square can still send shivers up spines. It seems an odd location for the city's biggest children's store, but **Detsky Mir** is almost next door. It was built on the site of the Moscow foundry which in the 1580s produced the bronze Tsar Cannon now on display in the Kremlin.

If you walk westwards down Okhotny Ryad (formerly Marx Prospekt) you'll come to **Neglinnaya**, the first street of the city's main shopping centre. Neglinnaya takes its name from the river which used to flow down to the Moskva on this site but has long since been channelled deep underground. The area became a mecca for shoppers in the last century when it was noted for its French fashion stores. Russia's first department store (now TsUm)) was built in the late 19th century on Petrovka Ulitsa right behind the Maly Drama Theatre.

Nearby, on 1st Neglinnyi Pereulok, are the oldest **public baths** in the city. Built initially for a wealthy boyar's courtesans, they are elaborate and luxurious. Taking a bath in Russia is a social event (although they don't go in for mixed bathing) and traditionally you would drink *kvas*, a home-brewed low-alcohol beer, or even something a little stronger while steaming yourself clean.

KGB Headquarters.

Neglinnaya runs into **Tsvetnoy** (Flower) **Boulevard**, now famous for its excellent, though expensive, Tsentralny farmers' market. In the old days, its park was best known as a shelter for the homeless and the so-called Lilies of the Street. The Boulevard terminates at Sukharevskaya Ploschad which was named after the tower that stood here until the 1930s. Sukharev was the only officer who remained loyal to Peter the Great during the Strelet rebellion and the grateful tsar erected the tower in Sukharev's honour.

Later on the square's associations were less lofty: it hosted an officially recognised weekly market for stolen goods. Permission for the market was given by Governor Rostopchin following the great fire of 1812. When the wealthy Muscovites returned home, they found their homes stripped bare and scoured the market in the hope of retrieving their valuables. This is also the location of the Doctor Sklifasovsky Hospital which was founded by the noble Sheremetyev family of airport fame:

the land it is built on what was once one of their country estates.

Teatralnaya Ploschad: Two main thoroughfares come together on Teatralnaya – **Neglinnaya** and **Petrovka** (named after the Vysoko-Petrovsky monastery built by Prince Ivan Kalita). The world-famous **Bolshoi Theatre** (literally "big" theatre) dominates the northern side of the square. Formerly known as the Grand Imperial Theatre, it was built in 1825 and restored and remodelled following a fire some years later. Although internationally acclaimed as perhaps the greatest ballet company in the world, nowadays the Bolshoi is feeling the pinch. Founded by the tsars, it became a Soviet flagship and as such enjoyed hefty state subsidies.

However, decades of neglect of the building's structure and internal unrest (the younger dancers rebelled against the omnipotent theatre leadership in the late 1980s causing a serious rift) have left the Bolshoi in a shaky state. In 1992 and 1993 the company set off on a major world tour in an effort to raise the cash

Vodka and salad at the *banya*.

it needs to restore both the buildings and morale among the dancers. The new Russian state and Moscow's city council may want to assist, but both have more pressing problems at present. The Bolshoi's near neighbours are the **Maly Theatre**, the oldest drama hall in the city, and the **Central Children's Theatre**, opened in 1921 and Moscow's first ever professional theatre for children.

Underground Moscow: The fountain behind the statue of Karl Marx opposite the Bolshoi theatre is an improbable clue to a secret which, glasnost notwithstanding, the Kremlin says nothing about: a complete **underground city** with one section in particular, beneath the suburb of **Ramenki** about 4 km (6 miles) southwest of Red Square, designed to accommodate as many as 30,000 bigwigs in some splendour for as long as 30 years in the event of a catastrophe like nuclear war.

Vladimir Gonik, a Moscow writer, got an inkling of the existence of the secret city while employed in the Ministry of Defence and took it upon himself to explore the city's sewers for possible connections with the clandestine network of underground passages. Having gained access to part of it and then got thoroughly lost, it was through the fountain opposite the Bolshoi that he eventually and gratefully re-surfaced. Other entrances subsequently came to light.

Ivan the Terrible laid the foundations of subterranean Moscow, so to speak, to give his *oprichniki* militia secret access from his palace to various parts of the city. The KGB, successor to the *oprichniki,* built a tunnel to ferry prisoners from the former Ivanovsky nunnery, which they used as a prison, to their headquarters, but these efforts were nothing next to grandiose refinements incorporated in the 1960s and 1970s, largely at the direction of Leonid Brezhnev. The Ramenki complex was built at several levels over 500 acres with streets wide enough to take cars and its own Metro system with links to central Moscow and Vnukovo airport. It has cinemas and even swimming pools, to say nothing of warehouses filled with food and provisions, to keep the party elite and their families in comfort while waiting for the radiation from any nuclear war to disperse.

The filtered ventilation system required for an extended troglodyte existence adds an ironic twist to the old jest about Moscow's massive "wedding-cake" ministry buildings being perilously close to the breaking strain of the earth's crust. It seems that they are almost as deep underground as they are tall, and each has its own stop on the private "Metro 2" and other concealed links with the underground warren. Secret tunnels and lift shafts are also said to descend from the plush apartment block which used to house government apparatchiks.

Famous hotels: The eastern side of the square is home to the glamorous *fin-de-siècle* **Metropol Hotel**, designed by a Scottish-Russian team, William Valkot and Leo Kekushev. Recently restored to its original glory, it is once again the best and most exclusive hotel in town. It's worth popping in for a coffee in one

At the ballet.

of the ornate lounges if the room prices are beyond your reach.

Opposite is the **Moskva Hotel**, one of the grotesque Stalinist edifices that now dot the city's skyline. The story goes that Stalin insisted on approving every construction plan made in the city. Two architects worked on designs for the new hotel to house Soviet dignitaries and both were presented to Stalin. He initialled both, so both were built – after a fashion. Check the west facade and you'll see two very different towers at either end.

The north side of the hotel is on Okhotny Ryad (Hunter's Row) which was known as Marx Prospekt during the Soviet era. It runs from Neglinnaya to Tverskaya (formerly Gorky) Street. Okhotny Ryad was once a big covered market place where hunters would trade game, rabbits and such. The small stalls selling meat, fish and fruit and vegetables made it one of the dirtiest places in Moscow. All the booths were dismantled after the Revolution, but following the 1991 coup people remembered the

old tradition and set up their own stalls to sell all kinds of goods. The city authorities had to designate special areas in the suburbs as flea markets so people could practice "market economy".

On the corner of Okhotny Ryad and Pushkinskaya Ulitsa is a green-painted, white-colonnaded former mansion. Once the Nobles' Club, it is currently the **House of Trade Unions**. The mansion originally belonged to Prince Vasily Dolgorukov, the city's military commander in the early 1780s. In 1783, the house was sold to the newly-established Assembly of the Nobles, who started a very exclusive club in the building. Said to be the most beautiful house in Moscow, the interior is stunning, but the building is only open to the public when the white and gold Hall of the Columns is used as a concert venue. Keep your eyes open for these concerts, because in the old days the Hall saw the likes of Pushkin, Lermontov and even Leo Tolstoy tripping the light fantastic under the crystal chandeliers.

Moscow had a number of clubs for different social classes. The Tradesmen's Club was located in what is now the Stanislavsky Theatre on the street of the same name. The English Club has become the Museum of the Revolution while the Central House of Artists now occupies the former German or Schuster Club.

Walk west down Okhotny Ryad and can turn right into Tverskaya (formerly Gorky) Street. On the opposite corner is the **Nasional Hotel** (currently closed for renovation which could take years). Next door on Tverskaya is the first US embassy to the USSR – the Americans have moved twice since they left this building in 1954 and are now located on the Moskva River at the west end of the Novyi Arbat. Their former embassy on Tverskaya is now the Intourist office.

Okhotny Ryad runs all the way down to the river and if you follow its route, you'll pass **Moscow University**'s oldest building. Set slightly back from the street and fronted by a small garden, the classical yellow mansion was constructed between 1776 and 1793 by Matvei Kasakov and restored after the **Old and new juxtaposed.**

1812 fire by Domenico Gilardi. Just opposite on your left across the four-lane highway is the **Manege**, whose construction commemorated Russia's victory over Napoleon in the 1812 Patriotic War. The spacious hall was used for equine displays, military parades, exhibitions and concerts. There are no horses today, but expositions are still held here.

If you follow Okhotny Ryad down to the Moskva River, past the white marble Lenin Library on your right, you'll see an astounding palace. Built in the time of Peter the Great by the son of one of his administrators, Peter Pashkov, it was designed to vye with the Kremlin in magnificence and style. The money to build this gloriously baroque mansion had come from Pashkov's father Ygor, who had made a fortune by investigating the bookkeeping of the Siberian Governor, Prince Matvei Gagarin. Pashkov claimed the Prince was lining his own pockets on the proceeds of lucrative diamond and grain deals. Although well-liked by the Siberians, Matvei was hanged and a great deal of his wealth and estates along with a few thousand serfs passed to the punctilious Pashkov and his family. The last of the Pashkovs died in 1839 and the palace was presented to Moscow University which, in its turn, gave it to Count Rumiantsev to house his collection of art and manuscripts. After the Revolution, the art works were removed to the Pushkin, but the books remained and the mansion is still a library today.

Tverskaya Ulitsa: Moscow's best-known street is Tverskaya, the main thoroughfare since the early 19th century when, following the city's reinstatement as capital, wealthy nobles began building new palaces and mansions. Tverskaya was the main road to St Petersburg so members of the tsar's entourage were constantly shuttling between the two cities. Tverskaya also boasted two triumphal arches in Tver Gate (now Pushkinskaya) Ploschad and at the Byelorussky (White-Russia) Station. When this square was extended in the 1930s, the arch was dismantled and

Peddling icons.

relocated in Kutuzovsky Prospekt across the river.

The most incredible things were done to Tverskaya in the 1930s as part of Stalin's master plan to create a Communist capital of awe-inspiring proportions. It was straightened, evened out and widened. Several major buildings were moved deeper into the existing blocks of houses, including the former Governor General's residence which housed the Moscow Council of Deputies after the Revolution; it also gained two storeys in the process. The **Pushkin Monument**, about a third of the way up the street, was moved from one side of the boulevard to the other and into the small square in front of the grubby-looking Rossiya Cinema; the majestic Strastnoi Monastery was knocked down to accommodate the movie theatre. The building at No 14 Tverskaya housed one of Moscow's biggest food stores. It was bought in 1898 by an entrepreneur called Yeliseev who owned a chain of grocers. The "supermarket" on the ground floor even amazed sophisticated Muscovites;

the only people it amazes today are the Westerners who gather to stare through the empty shop windows. However, all that's in the process of changing now.

By turning left half-way up Tverskaya, you come to **Ploschad Mayakovskovo**, but on the way check out the new buildings at the beginning of the street. The striking thing about them is that they become increasingly pompous and grim as you proceed. But Mayakovsky itself has a batch of memorable places. The **Tchaikovsky Concert Hall** (official address is Sadovaya Bolshaya Street 20) was built in 1940 to celebrate the centenary of the composer's birth. It has a wonderful giant pipe organ with 7,800 pipes and weighing 20 tonnes. It is the venue for the prestigious Tchaikovsky music competitions.

Next door, in what used to be a circus, is the **Satire Theatre** – always a great favourite with Muscovites. Across the square you'll find the old **Pekin Hotel**. It was done up not long ago and is a lunch and dinner hot-spot for Moscow's growing population of yuppies.

Statue of Tchaikovsky.

Tverskaya terminates at the **Byelorussky Station**, which is also the terminus for trains from Western Europe and the start of the highway that will take you to Sheremetyevo international airport. (A few statistics might be useful here: Moscow has seven railway stations and five airports linking the city to all the regions of the CIS as well as countries abroad; 132 Metro stations linking a network of lines stretching 213 km/132 miles; and two river ports, the North and the South, accessible from any world seaport through the Volga and the Moscow Canal.)

Gertsena Ulitsa: Running parallel to Tverskaya is **Gertsena Ulitsa**. In the 16th century, this was the old road to Tver (now Kalinin, but this may change soon). Ivan the Terrible stationed a garrison on this stretch of the road and it was later a coveted site for boyar mansions. The **Orlov Palace**, at No. 5, is typical of 18th-century classical architecture. At No 11, the former home of the Kolychev boyars is now the voice department of the Moscow Conservatory and was recently returned to its original elegance.

The majestic Metro.

The **Palace of Ekaterina Romanovna Vorontsova** (1744–1810), one of the first patrons of the arts in Russia, is at No 12. A great friend of Catherine the Great, Voltaire and Diderot, she developed into a true philanthropist and spent her not inconsiderable fortune on sponsoring students, lectures and literary publications. Ekaterina was head of the Russian Academy of Sciences from 1783 until 1796. After her death, the palace was bought for the Moscow Conservatory of Music. Tchaikovsky, Glier and Neuhaus taught Rachmaninov, Scriabin and Oistrakh here and the Great Hall is the venue for the International Tchaikovsky Competition held every four years. The Lesser Hall presents chamber music and recitals.

Not all the best palaces are on the left side of the street. The **Menshikov Palace**, for example, is a classic piece of Moscow Empire style, incorporating six Corinthian columns in the front facade. Unfortunately it is partly obscured by

the hospital building, so you have to reach it from Ogarova Ulitsa.

The small, rather ungainly **church of the Little Ascension** on the corners of Gertsena and Stankevich (named after the poet who founded the Arbat literary circle in the early years of the 19th century) was built in 1584 and restored by Zakhary Chernyshev, the first Governor General of the city, in 1739.

Theatre buffs should head for the **Stanislavsky Museum**, just up the street and round the corner to the right (No 7) named after the famous Method actor/director who transformed theatre both in Russia and elsewhere. The one-time textile baron hated the artificiality of stage performances, which at that time tended to be no more than vehicles for big stars. He believed that every player had something important to contribute. It may all seem fairly self-evident today, but what Stanislavsky was propagating changed the way theatre is perceived as an art and medium.

At the same corner, Gertsena is crossed by Nikitsky (fomerly Suvorov-sky) Boulevard – the square building on your right belongs to the TASS **news agency**. If you cross Nikitsky here you'll see Gertsena continues on the opposite side of the boulevard but twists off to the left. The street directly ahead is Kachalova and the church on your left is the **Great Ascension**. Besides having the best choir in the city, it is also one of the centres of monarchist activity.

Turn right onto Ulitsa Alekseya Tolstovo to find the side entrance to the fabulous art-nouveau **Gorky Museum**, which fronts Kachalova. The house was commissioned at the turn of the century by the merchant Stepan Riabushinsky. Its architect, Fedor Shekhtel, was the most exciting of the day and he finished the lyrically imposing building in 1902. Be sure to go inside this one; and don't miss the ceilings. When Gorky returned to the young Soviet Union in the early 1930s, he was presented with the house although he liked neither it or its architect. Follow Alekseya Tolstovo to the next corner on the right and turn down Spiridonievsky. This will bring you to

On Patriarch's Pond in winter.

Malaya Bronnaya. Turn left and the street leads to **Patriarch's (formerly Pioneer's) Pond** where Mikhail Bulgakov set his famous *Master and Margarita*. On the corner is **Margarita**, a great restaurant. In the 19th century, this was Moscow's student quarter.

The Novodevichi Convent: The tsars had a love-hate relationship with the Orthodox Church. Some tsars used the Church for their own purposes, installing relatives as patriarchs, but others were suspicious of its power over the people. In the Soviet era, most of the Church's wealth and real estate were confiscated by the new authorities. But the Church and its members struggled on and, when liberalisation took place, it made the come-back of the millennium. In the meantime Muscovites who wanted to be baptised sneaked off to Sergyev Posad (formerly Zagorsk), one of the few surviving Orthodox enclaves, 65 km/40 miles) from Moscow. You only have to look around you in Moscow to see just how powerful the Church was, and can become again. Some of the city's most famous and most remarkable landmarks are religious, in spite of Stalin's efforts to dominate the skyline with pompous "wedding cake" structures.

Perhaps one of the most beautiful religious complexes is the **Novodevichi Convent**. To the southwest of the Kremlin, strategically placed on a bend in the river, the convent was founded by Vasily III in 1524. From a distance the white walls topped by red roofs and 16 golden domes look picturesque. But the convent's history is chequered. The strong walls and fortified towers were ultimately used as a prison for trouble-making female nobles. A whole string of well-born women ended up here, including Peter the Great's half-sister Sofia and his first wife Evdokia.

Check out the **cemeteries**: Chekhov and Scriabin lie buried in the old one, while Khrushchev and other Soviet bigwigs can be found in the new.

When Prince Daniel Nevsky built his string of fortified monasteries in the 13th century, he dedicated the best and most beautiful to his patron saint. The **Danilov Monastery** still stands today,

Window of Novodevichi Convent.

enclosed by its white walls. Recently, it was restored to its former gold-domed splendour and returned to the Orthodox Church. The Patriarch now has his residence here.

On the art's trail: Following Peter the Great's lead, the nobles of the 18th century began taking the kind of Grand Tour that created the fabulous aristocratic art collections of Europe. The great Russian collectors, the Rumiantsevs, Golenishchevs, Shchukins and Morozovs, were both catholic and discerning in taste.

Their collections were "nationalised" by Lenin in the early 1920s and brought together in the **Pushkin Fine Arts Museum** (Volkhonka Ulitsa 12), founded at the end of the 19th century as a school of art and incorporating copies of all major sculptural works from around the world (the notion being that then Russian artists could study the greats without leaving home). The reproductions are still there, but the Pushkin also has a wealth of original works, from ancient Egyptian art to a

collection of Impressionists and Post-Impressionists, including Cézanne, Gauguin, Matisse and Van Gogh. It is housed in a purpose-built, turn-of-the-century neoclassical style building to the southwest of the Kremlin.

There's only one problem: the outdoor swimming pool across the street. Of all Stalin's cultural barbarities, this is perhaps the worst. Until the 1930s, the great Christ the Saviour Cathedral occupied the pool's site. Built to commemorate Napoleon's defeat, the cathedral was a city landmark and vied with St Basil's as the most beautiful church in Moscow. It took a lengthy 46 years to complete, and the architects of the Palace of the Soviets which Stalin wanted to build in its place soon understood why. The marshy ground swallowed up their foundations with maddening regularity. Finally World War II put an end to Stalin's grandiose plans and the site was turned into an outdoor pool (not recommended). Unfortunately, the vapours it emits are gradually destroying the Pushkin's collection.

The **Tretyakov Gallery** (Lavrushinskiy Pereulok 10) across the river has different problems. The core of its art collection was accumulated by the Tretyakov brothers in the late 19th century. The two men, who had made their fortunes in textiles, later donated the collection and their palace to the state. Spanning 1,000 years of Russian art, the collection includes all the great iconographers' work, including the famous *Trinity* icon by Andrei Rubliov. But you'll also find Kandinsky and Malevich here. Unfortunately most of it is currently closed. Its renovation has become one of the scandals of Moscow: the remodelling has already taken years, and completion seems no nearer than it was in 1991 when Boris Yeltsin promised action to speed up the work. At present, only a part of the gallery is open to the public, so you're limited to the selection on show at the time of your visit. Nonetheless it is still worth going.

The whole area around the Tretyakov comes as something of a surprise after the appalling 20th-century urban plan- **Performing on the Arbat.**

ning generally apparent in the old heart of the city. **Zamoskvorechye** (literally "beyond the Moskva River") was the artisan centre in the 17th century, hence street names such as Kadashevskaya (barrel-maker) and Novokuznetskaya (blacksmith). The nobility moved in in the 19th century and built palaces and mansions. Today, it is embassy country and the classical 19th-century buildings, with their chantilly stucco, give you a taste of what Moscow must have been like before the Revolution. The **Tropinin Museum** (Shchetininskiy Lane 10) of 18th and 19th-century portraiture is not far from the Tretyakov and shouldn't be missed.

Gorky Park: You've read the book, seen the movie, unfortunately you probably won't be able to get a T-shirt. But don't miss **Gorky Park**. It surrounds the landscaped **Neskuchny Garden** (literally "never dull") created by the millionaire industrialist Demidov on the banks of the Moskva in the mid-18th century. Its name derives from the fantastic collection of plants that lined the pathways. Today, Demidov's main mansion is home to the Academy of Sciences. Leninsky Prospekt, which runs along the south side of the park, is known as the Avenue of Soviet Science because over 30 research centres are located there.

Novyi Arbat (formerly Kalininsky Prospekt): This broad eyesore begins at the Manege on Okhotny Ryad and runs due west, all the way to the Russian Parliament Building overlooking the Moskva River. If you start at the Manege end, the left corner is dominated by the **Lenin Library** which holds over 30 million books in 247 languages. The collection was started long before the Revolution in the Pashkov Mansion high on Vagankovo Hill; the new library was purpose-built in 1941. The opposite corner used to contain the reception building of the Presidium of the Supreme Soviet. In the 18th century, the Romanov, Naryshkin and Sheremetyev families all had houses on this part of the street. They no longer exist, but the Morozovs' rather eccentric Moorish

An ice-house in Gorky Park.

home remains and is now the Union of Friendship Societies.

Old Arbat: Novyi Arbat is dissected by Nikitsky Boulevard at Arbatskaya Ploschad and to your left is the beginning of the Old Arbat. The name derives from the Arabic word for suburb – *rabat*. Over five centuries old, the Arbat was the starting point of the road to Smolensk. In the 18th century it was popular with the aristocracy, who held soirées and literary salons in their homes. The Russian writer and revolutionary Alexander Herzen called it Moscow's St Germain, and true to its reputation the Arbat again became a mecca for artists when glasnost began. Satirical and political cartoonists, painters and sculptors, who couldn't get access to official art galleries began exhibiting their work on the pedestrian-only street. It has subsequently become a tourist trap, but in spite of that, the cafés, buskers and souvenir sellers make it lively and fun.

One building you shouldn't miss is the **Melnikov house**, tucked down a side-street off the Arbat. Krivoarbatskiy Pereulok is about half way down the pedestrian street on the left-hand side. It doesn't look particularly promising, which is why people rarely find the constructivist jewel built by one of the most innovative and creative architects ever. Constantin Melnikov was a founder member of the avant-garde arts movement that flourished in the first decade after the Revolution. Along with artists like Kandinsky and El Lizitsky, he formulated a new and iconoclastic approach to the arts.

But the movement which influenced the European Bauhaus and De Stijl schools was short-lived in Russia. Only a few of the buildings remain. Melnikov's house is one of them. When Stalin decided that the proletariat should have colonnades and neoclassical facades on their mass apartment blocks, Melnikov built himself a family home. The pure white cylindrical structure with its light-enhancing windows is currently hidden by scaffolding, but if you can speak at least a few words of Russian and you're lucky enough to see his son Viktor in the garden, you may be treated to a tour.

The Arbat ends on **Smolenskaya Square**, an enormous intersection which is dwarfed by the hideous Foreign Ministry. There are seven of these Stalinist "wedding cakes" in the city: all were built in the late 1940s and '50s, at the height of Stalin's despotism. But in a sense, they are part of Moscow's heritage and have added their own specific contribution to the city's skyline.

The ordinary Muscovite takes them for granted and is more concerned with repairing the decay to old and new buildings that have suffered decades of neglect. Such work is a respite from the every-day problem of survival in the city. Inflation and complex political issues, uncertainty about the future, and a host of related problems make life tough in the Russian capital, as elsewhere in the country. But Muscovites have survived Tartar hordes, Polish occupation, Napoleon and even Stalin, so there's hope they can ride out this one, and eventually see their city take its rightful place among the great metropolises of the world.

<u>Left</u>, artist on the Arbat. <u>Right</u>, the International Friendship Fountain at the Exhibition of Economic Achievements (VDNKH).

THE GOLDEN RING OF RUSSIA

Under the Communist regime **Sergiyev Posad** – Sergiy's town – was known as Zagorsk ("place beyond the mountains"). But, as usual, things are not what they seem, and it would be highly naive to think that the town's old name had something to do with mountains.

No, the town which bears the name of the venerable Sergius of Radonezh – the man who founded the Troitse-Sergiyevsky (Trinity-St Sergius) Monastery here in the middle of the 14th century, the man who blessed Prince Dmitry Donskoi on the eve of the battle at Kulikovo (1380), the man who, according to Dmitry Likhachev, was admired as "the spiritual leader of the Russian people" – was renamed out of the blue in 1930, in honour of an obscure secretary of the Moscow Party Committee, Vladimir Zagorsky, who had probably never even set foot there. The municipal authorities restored the original name after considerable public pressure.

That same year, the lavra (an honorary title which means, in Greek, "main monastery", bestowed upon the Trinity-St Sergius in 1744) lost two of its greatest treasures: the *Trinity*, Andrei Rubliov's masterpiece, painted by Russia's greatest artist of the Middle Ages "in honor of Sergiy" (transferred to Moscow's Tretyakov Art Gallery), and the world's largest bells from the Trinity Belfry (which was destroyed).

Of course, there is a reason for starting a tour of the Golden Ring – one of the most popular routes among Russian and foreign lovers of old Russian architecture – with Sergiyev Posad. The town demonstrates how the Russian people are discovering a spiritual yearning for the nation's cultural roots and origins. The Russian people are only now beginning to realise that without respect for the history and the roots of their culture, there is, figuratively speaking, neither present nor future. Hence the rejection of that which has been foisted upon them, place names included; hence the desire to get past the superficial and back to the origins.

In fact, a ring is what the zig-zags of the route resemble least of all. But whatever it is geometrically, the northeastern territory of ancient Muscovy, where whole towns are museums, is certainly solid gold as far as history and culture are concerned.

The 719 km-long (447-mile) route starts and ends in Moscow, passing through several towns of Ancient Rus – Pereyaslavl-Zalessky, Rostov Veliky, Yaroslavl, Kostroma, Suzdal, Vladimir and Sergiyev Posad, which we have already mentioned. Sergiyev Posad is the most convenient place to start: it lies a mere 70 km (44 miles) to the north of Moscow along the Yaroslavl Highway. However, by starting with Sergiyev Posad we disrupt the order of historical succession – there are older towns. Take, for example, the town of Pereyaslavl-Zalessky, the birthplace of the famed Russian prince Alexander Nevsky, who defeated an army of German knights on Lake Chudskoye in 1242. But we will return to Pereyaslavl later.

Sergiyev Posad: The matchless architecture of the **Trinity-St Sergius**, one of the oldest seats of the Orthodox church, and the vast collections of ancient Russian painting and precious-metal articles are an unfailing tourist attraction. The monastery is a mecca for Orthodox pilgrims, who come here, to the white stone Trinity Cathedral, to honour the remains of the venerable Sergiy of Radonezh, exalted as "protector of the Russian land" early in the 15th century. The monastery is a formidable fortress known for its heroic resistance (it was under siege for 16 months) during the Polish-Lithuanian invasion 370 years ago.

The monastery also played an important cultural role. The Trinity School of book writing and colour miniatures dates from the 15th century and is a museum of national importance; as such, it is protected by the state. The monastery is also a major religious centre: the faithful flock to its churches by the thousand. The monastery runs a clerical school (seminary); would-be students have to beat stiff competition to be accepted.

The architectural highlights of the Trinity-St Sergius include the dome and roof of the Trinity Cathedral, their gold plates and, inside the cathedral, a lovely iconostasis adorned by the works of Andrei Rubliov.

The five-domed **Assumption Cathedral** (formally the main church in the monastery) is the architectural centre of the ensemble. It was founded by Ivan the Terrible in 1559. The simple rectangular tomb near the northwestern corner of the cathedral contains the remains of Tsar Boris Godunov and his family. Along the south wall of the fortress is the refectory and the **Sergius Church** (late 17th-century). The former boasts a remarkable vaulted ceiling that has no internal supports – a testimony to the technical accomplishments of Russian builders.

Until recently, the handsome **Metropolitan's Quarters** housed the residence of the Patriarch of the Orthodox Church. The building has a two-storey main facade, but from the northern side, you see an extra ground floor; cut into the slope in the 16th century, it is the oldest part of the building.

The jewel of the architectural ensemble is the tall, five-level **steeple**, easily the most beautiful in Russia. It was built by Dmitry Ukhtomsky in the middle of the 18th century. Sergiyev Posad cannot be imagined without it (a fact acknowledged by movie people, both in Russia and abroad, who regularly use it in sets). Its remarkable silhouette is visible for some distance.

Pereyaslavl-Zalessky: An hour's drive to the northeast, on the banks of Lake Plescheevo, which resembles a giant crystal dish, stands the town of Pereyaslavl-Zalessky, also known as "town-on-the-waters". It was founded, together with Moscow, by Prince Yuri Dolgoruky (the Long-Armed) in the 12th century. Pereyaslavl is the birthplace of the Russian navy. It was here that Peter the Great built his *poteshnaya* (mock flotilla) at the end of the 1600s, thus laying the foundations of Russian shipbuilding and seafaring. The episode is

Domes of Trinity-St Sergius.

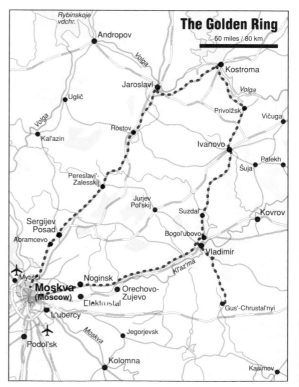

commemorated in the Botik ("Little Boat") Museum.

Start a tour of the town at the heart of Pereyaslavl, the Red Square and the white stone **Spaso Preobrazhensky Cathedral**, the oldest in the whole of northeastern Russia, Moscow included (1152–57). To the south of the cathedral stands the **church of Peter the Metropolitan** with its faceted, hipped roof (1585). Finally, there's the pride of Pereyaslavl, the **Goritsky Monastery**, founded between 1337 and 1340 during the reign of Ivan Kalita and two more monasteries – **Danilov** and **Nikitsky**. The gate of the Goritsky Monastery, voluptuously decorated with a whimsical ornament, is certainly something for the museum-goer. The monastery, by the way, has been a museum since 1919.

The road leads on to **Rostov Veliky** (Rostov the Great), an hour's drive away. Various admirers have dubbed the town "a symphony in stone", "Russia's Eternal City" and "the earthly wonder worthy of the next world". Standing behind Lake Nero and backed by the mid-Russia landscape, it has an undeniable fairy-tale quality.

Rostov, like its ancient rival, Novgorod, has been called "the Great" for centuries. At the end of the first millennium, it was the oldest, wealthiest and most populous centre in Russia.

Today, Rostov is famous for its **Kremlin** (18th-century), the former residence of the metropolitan, resplendent with gleaming gold and silver towers, cupolas, cornices and lace crosses. In August 1953, a tornado tore the churches of Rostov apart. It is thanks to the restorers' skills that we can enjoy their magnificence today.

It is utterly impossible to describe the treasures of the Kremlin in a few short lines. There is the **Spasna-Senyakh Church** (1675), the **Assumption Cathedral** (16th-century), the **Odigitry Church** (1693), the famous icons (15th to 18th centuries) the collection of portraits as well as china (18th to 19th centuries), and the Rostov enamels.

Enamels are the trademark of Rostov the Great and, as such, deserve special

A winter sunset in Suzdal.

attention. This ancient art was developed in Rostov at the end of the 18th century. It is based on the unique properties of an enamel surface, to which flammable paints are applied. The works of the Rostov enamel masters are known all over the world. For Russians they are nearly impossible to come by, except in the hard-currency Beriozka stores.

Yaroslavl: Moving on to Yaroslavl (60 km/37 miles away from Moscow), you reach one of Russia's largest regional centres (over 600,000 inhabitants). Yaroslavl is some 10 centuries old. In 1010 Yaroslav the Wise founded a fort on the bank of the Volga. Legend has it that the prince came upon a bear in those deserted parts and killed it with an axe. The bear then became the local totem and was included in the region's coat of arms. Today, the mascot greets visitors entering Yaroslavl. From time immemorial, Yaroslavl was considered one of the most beautiful towns in Russia. The abundance of frescoes and ceramic ornaments in its churches earned it the title "Florence of Russia". Most churches were built with the money donated by rich merchants.

A breathtaking vista of white (the walls and towers of the **Spassky Monastery**) and gold (the domes of its 16th-century cathedral) welcomes the traveller coming from Moscow. It is literally impossible to tear your gaze away from the tall **Bogoyavlenskaya church**, whose ceramic-tiled walls give it the appearance of being studded with jewels. In the central square of the city, there is one of the masterpieces of local architecture – the **Cathedral of Elijah the Prophet**, which was built under orders from the town's merchants between 1647 and 1650. Its walls and vaults contain a vast museum of old Russian paintings.

It was Yaroslavl that preserved for Russia its greatest literary treasure – *Slovo o polku Igoreve*, written in the 12th century. The only surviving copy of the work was found in the Spaso-Preobrazhensky Monastery.

Yaroslavl is also the birthplace of the Russian national theatre. Fyodor Vol-

Outdoor museum in Suzdal.

186

kov, the father of the Russian theatre, began his career in the town in the 18th century; the local theatre bears his name to this day.

Here the circle around the Golden Ring has to be interrupted to go, via Moscow, to Vladimir and Suzdal, thereby passing through the beautiful mid-Russian landscape. It's an enjoyable journey and travellers may want to linger – unlike those who live in the ancient Russian towns along the way who are forced to embark on weekly bus or electric-train voyages to Moscow to shop. The grandeur of nature and the magnificence of ancient towns are just as much a part of daily life as the provincial bleakness.

Vladimir: The city lies 166 km (103 miles) to the east of Moscow. It is another pearl of ancient Russian culture. Founded on the banks of the Kliazma by Prince Vladimir Monomakh in 1208, it played a key role in the formation of the Russian state. In the middle of the 12th century, the city became the capital of the Vladimir-Suzdal Principate. In 1288

Vladimir was besieged and looted by the Mongol hordes. Early in the 17th century, it fell to the invading Poles and Lithuanians.

Vladimir's white stone structures (12th-century) are known all over the world. Of these, the foremost is the **Assumption Cathedral**, with its striking decor, perfect architectural forms, and frescoes by Andrei Rubliov and Daniil Chyorny. But the most beautiful church in the city is the **Dmitrievsky Cathedral** with splendid carvings of plants, birds, animals and hunting scenes on its facade. The third architectural marvel in Vladimir, the **Golden Gate**, is a rare specimen of military architecture, a symbolic blend of impregnability and hospitality, it was built as a replica of the Golden Gate in Kiev.

Another place to see is the Assumption Cathedral in the **Knyaginin Monastery** (16th-century), located in the northwestern part of the city. Frescoes by 17th-century painters are the pride of the cathedral. It is these masterpieces of ancient Russian architecture that are the

Suzdal: built of stone as well as wood.

image of Vladimir. The historical centre of the city has over 700 less valuable buildings dating to the 19th and the early 20th centuries.

Suzdal: The last town left in the Golden Ring is **Suzdal**, the capital of Yuri Dolgoruky's Rostov-Suzdal Principate. It suddenly comes into view 30 km (18 miles) from Vladimir, standing on the Poklonnaya (Bowing) Hill, lost among the never-ending fields. First impressions are of jagged cornices, hipped roofs and cupolas. The town suffered many destructive assaults, yet rose from the ashes every time. Wood and stone houses were built by the dozen, and several monasteries were founded.

In the 19th century, when a railway was built between Moscow and Nizhni Novgorod, it passed Suzdal by. The town avoided becoming an industrial centre and kept its original image intact. There are over 100 architectural monuments of the 13th to 19th centuries crowded into a small area (only 9 sq km/ 3½ sq miles).

It is almost a sin to hurry along its streets because there are so few of them. Take a rest on the steep bank of the Kamenka River, and submit to the spell of its quiet beauty.

The town's most memorable sights include the orange-red walls of the **Spaso-Yefimiev Monastery** (founded in 1352), the foam-white walls of the **Pokrovsky**, the lacework of the gates leading to the **Monastery of the Deposition of the Virgin's Robe**, the architectural finesse of the churches, and the indented silhouettes of the belfries.

When Kiev fell to Lithuania, Suzdal was elevated as the Orthodox capital of medieval Rus. The Grand Princes and the Tsars spared no expense when it came to building "the sacred cloisters".

The townsfolk built their churches outside the city walls; there are so many for such a small town that it's difficult to name them all. Among the most important is the white stone **Cathedral of the Nativity of the Virgin** (1225) with its dark-blue, gold-spotted cupolas.

The **Golden Gates** stand without equal among the creations of medieval Rus. And, of course, there is the **Museum of Russian Carpentry** with its two magnificent wooden churches, built with nothing but an axe and a chisel – the **Preobrazhenskaya** and the **Nikolskaya** – brought to the museum from faraway corners of the Suzdal region.

Suzdal is one of the more comfortable tourist centres in Russia. Facilities and service are better developed. There is a good choice of restaurants (unlike in Yaroslavl and Vladimir), where you will find traditional Suzdal dishes – meat as the merchants traditionally cook it, fresh mushroom soup, and *medovukha*, the traditional Russian beverage made of honey. It is well served by hotels, including the wooden *izbas* (peasant cottages) in the territory of the Pokrovsky Monastery, complete with wooden furniture in the style of ancient Rus. A well-equipped beach, boating, troika and horse riding make it a suitable base in which to wind down.

Suzdal is the ideal place to end a tour of the Golden Ring, Russian history's "chronicle in stone".

Left, coat of arms of Yaroslavl and the coat of arms of Vladimir. **Right**, Mother of God icon from Yaroslavl.

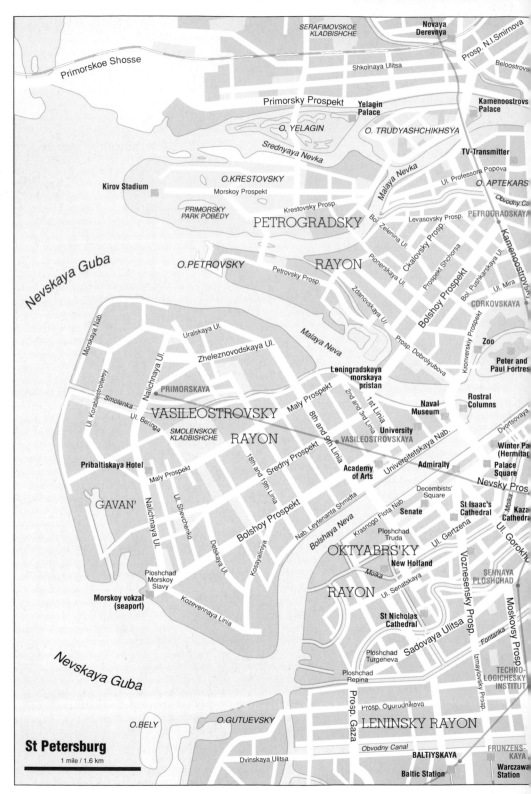

St Petersburg

1 mile / 1.6 km

192

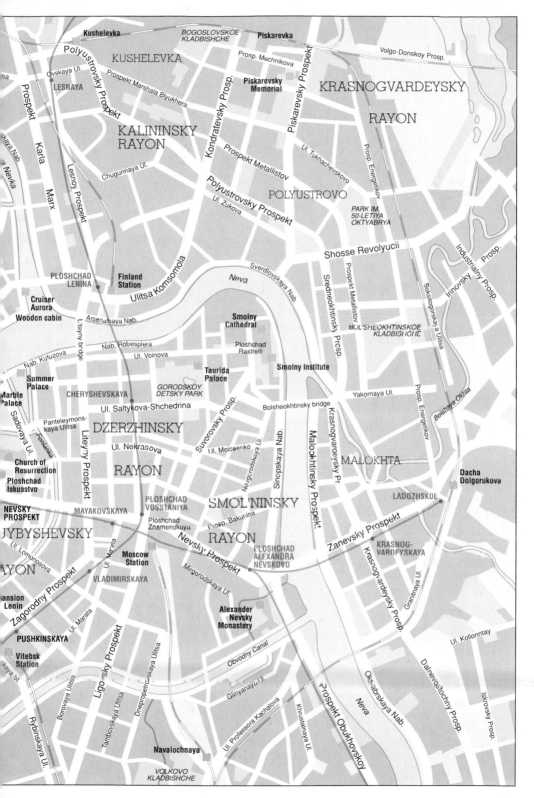

ST PETERSBURG

St Petersburg (1703), Petrograd (1914), Leningrad (1924), St Petersburg (1991): for two centuries St Petersburg bore the name of its tsar-founder, and for less than a century that of Lenin. The name changed to the more Slavic "Petrograd" at the beginning of World War I because of anti-German sentiment. It became Leningrad in 1924, not just because it had been the cradle of the 1917 Revolution, but also as a tribute to Lenin, who died that year (it was deemed the city most worthy of his god-like name). Nonetheless Lenin had never felt entirely at home here; in fact, he moved the capital back to Moscow in 1918.

Mad and foolhardy: From the beginning, St Petersburg has been something of an anomaly, a beautiful misfit, a new showpiece city in an old country. Peter the Great's vision of building a capital to rival the great cities of Europe was mad and foolhardy. He chose just about the worst terrain on which to build a city, a swampy mosquito-ridden marsh with an extremely harsh climate, scorned by its previous inhabitants, Finnish fishermen. However, in doing so he claimed from the Swedes a strategic Baltic port, which no enemy fleet has yet been able to penetrate.

Peter's foreign "imported" architects had a huge amount of space to play with, hence the city's layout of massive perspectives and ensembles, of straight and boldly symmetrical lines. The streets and buildings, although low, dwarf pedestrians. To appreciate the exterior of a building fully you have to view it from a distance, preferably from another island. This is particularly true when looking at the Hermitage.

The city was without bridges until 1727, when the first floating bridge was built (it had to be dismantled in the winter months when the river froze).

Tsarist tastes: Obviously, Peter the Great is not wholly responsible for the St Petersburg that we see today, although some fine examples of the buildings of his era remain. His taste was simple and sparse, some would argue better than that of his successors. The preferences of Empress Elizabeth (1741–61), for example, were much more over-the-top and fanciful; her favourite architect, Bartolomeo Rastrelli, liked colours and tended to decorate buildings as one would a cake for a great occasion, with piping and swirls. Catherine the Great (1762–96) was less frivolous in her tastes, but buildings were nevertheless grand in scope, and became even more so in the reign of Alexander I (1801–25) when they were designed to reflect the glory of Russia's victory over Napoleon and increasing foreign expansion.

Commerce and industrialisation before the Revolution brought some fine examples of art nouveau to the city, together with the first railways and the line linking Moscow and St Petersburg (1851). The architecture of Lenin and Stalin, much of it housing, was kept to the outskirts of the city. One outstanding feature of Stalin's time was the construction of the Leningrad Metro,

Preceding pages: the Peter and Paul Fortress. **Left,** the Alexander Column marking Russia's victory over Napoleon. **Right,** window of the house confiscated for use as Party headquarters in 1917.

which started running in 1955. Except for the Metro decorations (particularly impressive on the Kirov–Vyborg line) there is little, if any, art of the Soviet period – such as statues or busts of Lenin – in the centre of the city, although you will find a statue of Lenin outside the Finland Station and the famous Monument to the Defenders of Leningrad on Moskovsky Prospekt, one of the major routes to and from the airport. Despite extensive damage to older buildings during World War II, most of them have been rebuilt and faithfully restored to their original state. At the present time, lack of funding gives the city a shabby look where buildings that have been restored stand out in marked and unnatural contrast to their faded neighbours.

Literary connections: Architecture tells us much about a city, but equally revealing, particularly in St Petersburg, are the impressions of many famous writers. Pushkin, who put Russian literature on the international map, depicted St Petersburg's forbidding aspect in his poem *The Bronze Horseman*. The Statue of Peter the Great comes to life and bears down on an enfeebled and terrified clerk called Evgeny. Pushkin also describes St Petersburg high life in *Eugene Onegin*. The hero, one of literature's great dandies, becomes bored and disillusioned by an endless round of balls, restaurants and women.

Tolstoy takes up the same theme in his novels *War and Peace* and *Anna Karenina,* contrasting the spontaneity and simplicity of Moscow life with that of St Petersburg which he saw as false, artificial and corrupt. Dostoevsky, in marked contrast, wrote of low life and the poor. Later on, in the poem *The Twelve*, Alexander Blok found in the Revolution a vision of the city's rebirth and the Second Coming of Christ. Evgeny Zamyatin, in his short story *The Cavemen,* compared post-Revolutionary St Petersburg to a society of cave-dwellers, whose civilised values are subverted when the protagonist is forced to beg and then steal firewood in order to exist for just one more day.

The Bronze Horseman.

196

Hard times: But records of the city's suffering are not found only in literature – they also exist in living memory. The older generation remembers the Siege of Leningrad during World War II when the city was completely cut off from the outside world for more than 500 days. The Germans invaded Russia in July 1941 and reached Leningrad in August of that year. The town was encircled and cut off from September, when mass bombing began.

Only a tiny tract of land on the shores of Lake Ladoga remained unoccupied by the enemy. When the narrower part of the lake froze, a 37-km (23-mile) ice road – the Road of Life – was laid. But this did not supply enough food for an entire city. By November, the threat of mass famine was real. The bread ration at that time was 250 grams a day for a worker, 125 for anyone else. There was no electricity, and in December no water supply or public transport.

Soviet troops broke through the blockade in January 1943 and provisions reached the city through the Finland Station. The Germans were finally defeated in the Leningrad region in January 1944. In 1945 Leningrad received the Order of Lenin for the outstanding services of its people to their country.

During this time, some 16,000 civilians were killed from the air raids and shelling, and over 33,000 were wounded. Considerably more lives were lost through hunger. Some 470,000 victims of the blockade are buried at the **Piskarovskoe Memorial Cemetery** situated on the northern outskirts of the city. The sheer size of this cemetery, with the dead buried in mass graves, gives a more chilling impression of the loss of life than any statistic.

Facts and figures: St Petersburg is Russia's largest seaport and second largest city with a population of around 6 million. It lies on a parallel 60° North – the same latitude as Alaska, Hudson Bay, the Southern tip of Greenland and Oslo. It is 30° East of Greenwich. Finland lies 160 km (100 miles) to the north.

The city straddles 101 islands at the mouth of the great river Neva, which

St Petersburg from the air.

sweeps majestically through its centre, emptying Lake Ladoga, 74 km (46 miles) to the east, into the Gulf of Finland to the west. Here, where it branches into three arms, separating Petrograd side and Vasilievsky island from the mainland, the main channel is 400 metres (437 yards) wide. Today granite embankments (built in the time of Catherine the Great) contain the 65 rivers, canals, channels and streams which separate the islands but flooding occurs when gales drive in from the Baltic. These waterways, Lake Ladoga and the sea freeze over in winter but icebreakers keep the port open all year. There are 365 bridges joining the islands.

From the Admiralty on the south embankment, the main streets radiate like spokes of a wheel; the canals and other streets cross these spokes running parallel to the main channel of the Neva. On Vasilievsky island the streets are divided up into numbered Liniya (lines).

In the months after the renaming of Leningrad to St Petersburg streets began to revert to their original, pre-Revolutionary names, a process which continues. Everyone – taxi drivers, local residents and foreigners alike – finds this extremely confusing, expecially as there is a shortage of up-to-date maps. Two examples of street name changes are Prospekt Mayorova becoming Vosnesenski Prospekt and Ulitsa Dzherzhinskovo becoming Ulitsa Gorokhovaya. Mayorov was a Petrograd worker serving in the Red Army who was killed in 1919, while Vosneseniya means "Ascension". Before the days of Mayorov a church bearing that name stood here. Dzherzhinsky was the organiser of the Cheka (Secret Police) and Gorokhov was a Russian nobleman.

The climate in St Petersburg is harsh, with strong winds airing the streets and snow from November until late March. In the summer, between the end of May and the beginning of July, there is an air of festivity due to the extraordinary White Nights, when the sun doesn't set.

Touring the sights: The most appropriate place to begin a tour of St Petersburg is the **Peter and Paul Fortress**, built

Chess on Ploschad Ostrovskovo.

during the time of the Great Northern War (1700–21). The first stone was laid on 16 May 1703 Old Style (unlike Europe and America who by this date had switched to the new Gregorian Calendar, Russia still used the calendar of Julius Caesar, which was 13 days behind the Gregorian).

The fortress, built on Zayachy (Hare Island) according to plans drawn ·by Peter himself, was designed to stave off the enemy, occupying as it did a strategic position at the dividing point of the Neva into the Malaya (Small) and Bolshaya (Big) Neva. Though never really used for this purpose, the fortress became one of the most terrifying prisons – the Bastille – of tsarist Russia. In 1917 the **Commandant's House** was one of the Bolshevik command posts for the storming of the Winter Palace.

There are various buildings for the visitor to see within the fortress, as well as temporary exhibitions. The major features are the **Peter Gate**, built by Domenico Trezzini, who also designed the Cathedral. The gate, originally built

The soaring spire of the Peter and Paul Fortress.

in wood and later (1717–18) in stone, has hardly changed since it was built. The bas-relief above the tsarist emblem of the double-headed eagle depicts the Apostle Peter overthrowing Simon the Magus, an allegory of Russia's victory over the Swedes. The **Cathedral** – rectangular in layout – is quite unlike a traditional Russian place of worship. It bears a tall spire standing at 122 metres (400ft), which until the Television Tower (316 metres/1,036ft) was built was the tallest building in the city. On the top is an angel carrying a cross. In 1830, Pyotr Telushkin, a roofer, climbed to the very top, with the aid of just a rope, to repair the cross which had been struck by lightning.

Inside the church are the white marble tombs of most of the Romanov family as well as various grand dukes. Peter the Great's tomb lies in the far right-hand corner. Vladimir Kirilovich, one of the last surviving relatives of Nicholas II, who lived as an emigré in Paris, was recently buried here. The tombs of Alexander II and his wife, who were blown up by terrorists, are made out of Altai jasper and Urals rhodonite. The baroque iconostasis, carved by Moscow craftsmen in the 1720s, bears the figures of the archangels Gabriel and Michael. To the left is the pulpit, and to the right the tsar's throne.

The grounds of the fortress contain a strange and controversial statue of Peter the Great which was recently given to the city by Michael Chamyakin, a Russian New York-based sculptor. Peter is depicted as a seated, human figure, not as the customary terrifying giant.

In 1717 the fortress became a prison for political prisoners and the cells are now open as a museum in the **Trubetskoy Bastion**. One of its first prisoners, who was later beaten to death, was Peter the Great's son Alexei, who was involved in a plot against his father. Other distinguished inmates were Fyodor Dostoevsky; Alexander Radischev, author of *A Journey from St Petersburg to Moscow*, in which he criticised autocracy and serfdom; Nikolai Chernyshevsky, a Revolutionary democrat and author of *What is to be*

Done?; Lenin's elder brother, Alexander Ulyanov, who took part in the plot to murder Alexander III, and Maxim Gorky, who wrote a Revolutionary proclamation calling for the overthrow of the monarchy. Its last political prisoners were sentenced in 1921.

Dostoevsky was marched out of his cell and taken to Semyonovsky Square where, together with fellow members of a group of radical liberals known as the Petrashevsky Circle, he was condemned to immediate death by firing squad for conspiring to set up a printing press. They were lined up three at a time and covered in white shrouds. However, as the guard detachments took aim, the proceedings were halted by a man on horseback. Their sentence had changed to banishment to Siberia: the preparations for execution had been deliberately and callously staged.

The fortress has six bastions, one named after Peter, the rest after his generals. A cannon shot is fired every day at noon from the Naryshkin Bastion and can be heard all over the city.

The **Commandant's Pier** offers one of the best views over the Neva. In the summer the shores of the fortress are packed with sunbathers. In the winter too, swimmers break through the ice – a sight which has to be seen to be fully believed. On the river banks near the fortress, stands Peter the Great's **Wooden Cabin,** now a museum. Although protected by stone on the outside, inside there is a perfectly preserved, two-roomed hut. It was made out of rough pine over a period of three days in 1703. Peter lived here for six years while overseeing the building of the city.

Moored in front of the blue baroque **Nakhimov Naval Academy** (though designed in the style of Petrine baroque, the Academy was completed in 1912), where the Neva divides, is the battleship *Aurora*, famous for its part in the 1917 Revolution. At 9.45pm on 25 September 1917, the *Aurora* fired a blank round, the signal for the insurgent forces to storm the Winter Palace, the seat of the Provisional Government. Prior to this, between 1904 and 1905, it served the

Sailor on the battleship *Aurora*.

tsarist government at the Battle of Tsu-Shima. It now flies the tsarist flag again.

On the opposite side of the river is the tsar's modest **Summer Palace** (1710–11), also built by Domenico Trezzini and open to the public during the summer months. It has retained most of its original features, occupying two floors of identical layout, one for the tsar and one for the tsarina. Its simple exterior was later decorated by terracotta panels depicting scenes from mythology – allegorical portrayals of the Northern War.

The **Summer Gardens** in which the palace stands are the oldest gardens in the city. Much of the work was done by the architect Jean Baptiste Leblond. It was originally a formal garden, with many rare plants and trees, an aviary and a grotto, but its appearance has changed over the years as Venetian statues were commissioned and buildings such as the **Tea House** and a statue of Ivan Kryllov, famous author of children's fables, have been added. It still remains one of the most peaceful and shady places in the city. The path through

the centre of the gardens leads as far as the Fontanka Canal and the red **Engineer's Castle,** built by Catherine the Great's son Paul. The castle's strong walls and moat did not deter his assassins, who murdered him only 40 days after he had taken up residence. The building became a school for Engineers in 1819. Dostoevsky studied here.

The garden is enclosed on the Neva Embankment side by amazing **cast iron gates** with 36 pink granite columns, considered to be the finest in Russia. They were erected between 1770 and 1784 by Jegor Veldten.

Palace Embankment is occupied by the **The State Hermitage Museum**, the number one draw for Russian and foreign visitors alike. Unfortunately, many are daunted by scare stories of the museum's sheer size and paralysed by the limited amount of time they have to "do it" in. An idea of the museum's layout is therefore essential, so get hold of a good floor plan. A short visit will be less frustrating if you pinpoint what you want to see.

The Hermitage.

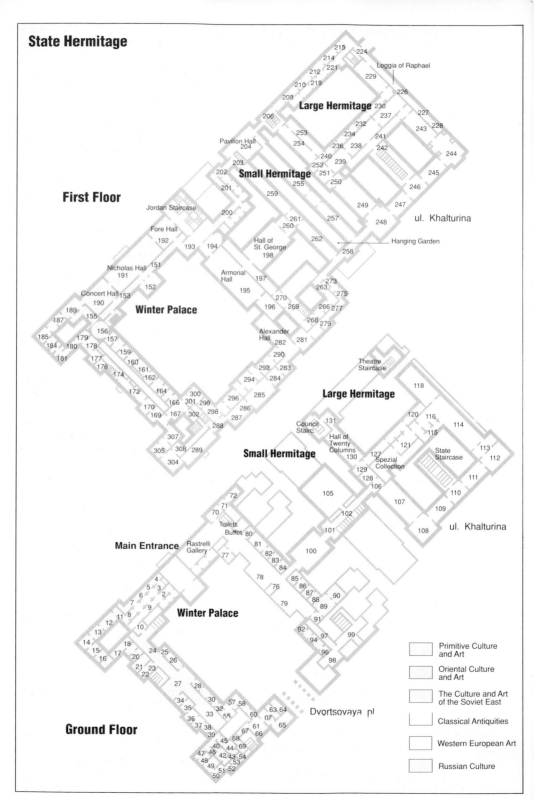

State Hermitage

First Floor

Large Hermitage

215 224
214 221
212 219
210 219
208
Loggia of Raphael
229
226

Large Hermitage
230 237 227
228
243
232
253 234 241
254 236 238 242 244
Pavilion Hall 240 239 245
204 252
203 250 246
202 **Small Hermitage** 251
201 255 250
259 249 247
Jordan Staircase 200
261 257 **ul. Khalturina**
260 248
Fore Hall 262
192 Hall of Hanging Garden
193 194 St. George 258
198

Nicholas Hall 151
191 Armorial 273
152 Hall 197 263 275
Concert Hall 153 195 270 266 277
190 196 269 268 279
189 155 **Winter Palace**
187
185 179 156 Alexander
184 180 178 157 Hall 282 281
181 177 159 290
176 160 292 283
174 161 294 284
172 164 162 296 285
170 166 301 300 299 286
169 167 302 298 287
288
307
305 308 289
304

Large Hermitage

118
Theatre
Staircase
120 116
131 115 114
121 113
Council 127 112
Stairc. Hall of Spezial State
Twenty 130 Collection Staircase
Columns 129 106
Small Hermitage 128 110
105 107 111
72 102 109
71 101 108 **ul. Khalturina**
70
Toilets
Buffet 80
81
Main Entrance Rastrelli 100
Gallery 82
77 83
84
78 85
76 86
79 87 90
88
89
91
92 97 99
94 96
98

4
5 3
6 2
7
8
9
Winter Palace
11 8
12 10
13
14 18
15 17 24 25
16 20 26
21 23
22
27 28
34 30 57 58
35 32 60
36 33 55 62 63 64
37 38 61 65
39 45 66
Ground Floor 40 68
47 46 42 44 69
48 43 54
49 51 52 53
50

Dvortsovaya pl

	Primitive Culture and Art
	Oriental Culture and Art
	The Culture and Art of the Soviet East
	Classical Antiquities
	Western European Art
	Russian Culture

The Hermitage is made up of three buildings, the large, avocado-green Winter Palace, the Small Hermitage and the Large Hermitage. The present **Winter Palace** (the fourth) was designed by Rastrelli, who started work on it in 1754, during Elizabeth's reign. He built it, to use his own words "solely for the glory of all Russia". It was the home of the Imperial family, with the exception of Paul I, until 1917, when it became the seat of the provisional government.

The **State Collection** was originally the private collection of Catherine the Great. She started collecting later than other European monarchs, but she did so in earnest, instructing her ambassadors in Europe to buy not just individual pictures, but whole collections. She housed them in her retreat, or Hermitage, and only a select few were permitted to see them. The museum was not open to the public until 1852. During the Siege, most of the artworks were successfully evacuated, although one Van Dyke was lost. There was another casualty in 1985 when a visitor to the museum sprayed Rembrant's *Danae* with sulphuric acid.

To discuss the Hermitage collection in only a few words is impossible. Although renowned for its collections of Western European art from early 13th-century Italian to the French Impressionists to modern, it has other important departments, notably Primitive Culture and the Art of the former USSR, Oriental and Classical Antiquities. Of equal interest is the architecture of the interiors: the Jordan Staircase, the Great Hall, the Large Throne Room and the Gallery of the 1812 War, to name a few.

In 1792 some distinguished visitors from England complained that "the apartments as well as the galleries are crowded with paintings, good and bad placed promiscuously together". It is true that many pictures are badly hung, and the implied criticism of quantity rather than quality has some weight: However, the collection houses some of the finest art treasures in the world.

Behind the Hermitage is the impressive **Palace Square**, with its huge **Alexander Column** erected to the design of August de Montferrand to commemorate the victory of Russian armies in the Napoleonic War during the reign of Alexander I. It is made from a granite monolith brought from the northern shore of the Gulf of Finland. This 47.5-metre (156-ft) high column is held up entirely by its own weight.

On the south side of the square is the curved, yellow **General Staff Building**, with its arch decorated with a chariot of victory and statues of warriors, designed by Carlo Rossi. Rossi designed many buildings in St Petersburg, most of which are painted pale yellow as opposed to the pale greens and blues preferred by Rastrelli. Before the Revolution many of the government buildings – with the exception of the Admiralty – were painted dark red (for example, the General Staff Building, the Winter Palace and the Senate and Synod), contributing to the city's gloomy and forbidding air.

In August 1991, Palace Square filled with some 100,000 people protesting against the attempted coup against Gorbachev in Moscow. During the White Nights Festival in July it provides the setting for rock concerts. On winter evenings it is deserted save for the occasional skate-boarder.

At the corner of Palace Square is **Millionnaya Ulitsa** (Millionaires' Row), which runs behind the Hermitage Buildings to **Marsovoe Polc** (The Field of Mars). The street was previously named Ulitsa Khalturina after Stepan Khalturin who planted a bomb inside the Winter Palace in 1880. At the beginning of the street the porch of the New Hermitage building is supported by figures of Atlas, designed by a German architect, Leo von Klenze (1784–1864).

At the end of the street is the **Marble Palace**, built by Catherine the Great for one of her favourites, Grigory Orlov, and designed by the architect Antonio Rinaldi. Before the Revolution it was the home of various grand dukes, but in 1937 it became a Lenin Museum. Now it houses exhibitions from the Russian Museum. **The Field of Mars**, a former marsh, then parade ground, was redesigned after the Revolution by the architect Rudnev (who was later to build the famous skyscraper of Moscow University.) Many who died in the Revolution and Civil War are buried here and an Eternal Flame burns in the centre.

Along the embankment from the Hermitage is the city's most famous statue: *The Bronze Horseman* – Peter the Great on a rearing horse. The statue has been immortalised by Alexander Pushkin's poem of that name, a poem which every Russian knows by heart. The statue was cast from the model of the French sculptor Etienne Falconet and completed in 1782. The head of Peter the Great was designed by Falconet's pupil, Marie Collot, who never earned the recognition she deserved for this particular work.

The square in which the statue stands, **Ploschad Dekabristov** (Decembrists' Square) is where, in 1825, tsarist troops fired on some 3,000 soldiers and spectators, many of whom were innocently driven into action by revolutionary-minded young officers protesting against Nicholas I's nomination as tsar. The yellow buildings of **The Senate and the Synod** were designed by Carlo Rossi between 1829 and 1832.

Nearby stands the golden spire of the **Admiralty.** This was one of the first buildings of the city, built in 1705, then replaced between 1806 and 1823 by the present neoclassical structure designed by A.D. Sakharov. It was used as a naval headquarters and as a shipyard. At the top of the spire is a weather-vane in the form of a ship, the emblem of the city. From the Admiralty the main streets – Nevsky, Gorokhovaya and Vosnesenski – stretch out like an open fan. The fountains in front of the Admiralty are surrounded by statues of Nikolai Gogol, Mikhail Lermontov, the composer Mikhail Glinka and the poet Vasily Zhukovsky.

St Isaac's Cathedral stands in the square behind. It was built during the reign of Alexander I by the French architect Auguste de Montferrand. It took some 40 years to build and is said to be standing on the bones of its builders. The dome is covered with 100 kg (220 lb) of pure gold. Forty-three types of

The Admiralty spire.

stone and marble were used to decorate the lavish interior, including the lapis lazuli and malachite columns of the iconostasis. Among the general surfeit of visual splendour is a statue of the architect carrying a model of the cathedral in his hand. Montferrand very much wanted to be buried here, but his wish was denied by Alexander II.

In the middle of St Isaac's Square stands a statue of Nicholas I on a prancing horse, by Pyotr Clodt. According to a Russian saying commenting on the obvious parallel with *The Bronze Horseman:* "The fool [Nicholas I] chases the wise man [Peter I] but St Isaac's stands in between."

The **Astoria** hotel has been redecorated and redesigned and is now one of the city's most luxurious hotels. It was built in the Style Moderne by the architect Fyodr Lidval between 1910 and 1912. Alas, its beautiful interior has been savagely gutted and replaced by the tasteless but expensive modern look you see today. (Another example of Lidval's Style Moderne can be seen at 1/3 Kamenoostrovsky Prospekt, on the Petrograd side.)

The Mariinsky Palace, on the south side of the square, was built between 1839 and 1844 by Andrei Stakenschneider, and presented by Nicholas I to his daughter Maria. It is now used as the city hall, the office of the mayor. The building was heavily defended by barricades and crowds during the August 1991 coup. The bridge in front crossing the River Moika is **The Blue Bridge** (its original colour when it was made of wood) and is the widest in the city.

Further along the Moika in the direction of **Novaya Gollandia** is the **Yusupov Palace** (No 94), home of Rasputin's chief assassin. Rasputin was murdered here in 1916 (*see page 46*). The rooms – part of the museum – have been restored to evoke the eerie atmosphere of the night of the murder; there is even a creepy wax figure of Rasputin.

Novaya Gollandia means New Holland and here, behind the red brickwork, Peter the Great stored his shipbuilding timber. The Moika turns a bend

Winter in the Field of Mars.

up the Kriukov Canal. Behind the canal is **Teatralnaya Ploschad** or Theatre Square, home of the **Mariinsky** (formerly Kirov) **Theatre** and, opposite, **the Conservatoire.** Maria, from whom the theatre took its original name, was the mother of Alexander II. Kirov, on the other hand, was the Secretary of the Leningrad Party organisation from 1926 until 1934. His murder at the Smolny triggered Stalin's purges of the 1930s.

The Mariinsky Theatre is where some of the first Russian operas and ballets were performed including Mussorgsky's *Boris Godunov* (1874) and Tchaikovsky's *Sleeping Beauty* (1890) and where many famous ballet dancers such as Kschessinska, Pavlova and Nijinsky made their debut. The present company is often on tour and tickets are expensive and difficult to obtain, but the theatre alone is worth seeing for its beautifully decorated auditorium. During the interval spectators promenade around a room specially built for the purpose.

Further up the Kriukov Canal is the blue and gold **Cathedral of St Nicholas**, otherwise know as the "Sailor's Church", built between 1753 and 1762 by Savva Chevakinsky. This working cathedral is often compared with Rastrelli's Smolny Cathedral. It's a fine example of Russian baroque.

Vasilevsky Island: On the other side of the Neva, facing *The Bronze Horseman* is one of the oldest parts of the city, **Vasilievsky Island.** One of its more "modern" buildings is the **Academy of Arts** built by Catherine the Great in 1757 as a training ground for professional painters, architects, sculptors and engravers. In front of it, on a granite pier, stand two sphinxes which date from 13 BC. They were brought to St Petersburg from Thebes in 1832.

The **Obelisk** standing next to the Academy commemorates Russia's victory over the Turks under Field-Marshal Rumyantsev in the 18th century. The next building is the **Menshikov Palace**. Alexander Menshikov was a friend, enemy and rival of Peter the Great. As Menshikov's palace was finished before Peter's, it was used for

Interior of the Menshikov Palace.

large-scale entertainment. Peter staged an extraordinary event for his niece here: a wedding feast attended by dwarfs brought from all over Russia. A look inside is recommended – it is now a museum – as this is one of the few buildings whose early interior is still intact. Note the beautiful broad oak staircase, walnut panels and an amazing collection of painted tiles.

The terracotta-coloured building further along the embankment is called the **Twelve Colleges**. It dates from the time of Peter the Great and is now part of **St Petersburg University**. The building's construction, in which a number of architects, including Rastrelli, participated, was set as a competition – Russia's first. Peter housed his "Kollegia" or ministeries here. The next building, **the Academy of Sciences**, was built to house the expanding collection of the **Kunstkamera (Chamber of Curiosities)**, a museum of anthropology and ethnography next door. Inside, under the dome, is a weird collection of genetic freaks, embryos and human organs, all of which held a particular fascination for Peter the Great.

Vasilievsky island has a famous "spit" from where you have one of the best views of the city. Newly-weds all come here to be photographed. The magnificent building which dominates the spit is now the **Central Naval Museum**. Before the Revolution it was the Stock Exchange. Until the 1880s this point of Vasilievsky island was St Petersburg's main port. The red columns were the lighthouses. They are decorated with the prows of boats representing four Russian rivers: the Volga, Dnieper, Neva and Volkhov.

Famous thoroughfare: The Nevsky Prospekt is the most famous street in St Petersburg. After the Admiralty was built, a path had to be cleared through the forest to link the shipbuilding yard with the town of Novgorod. Houses and palaces were built along the route, which later came to be known as "The Nevsky Perspective". Although narrow and nondescript to begin with, it soon widens out and stretches some 2 km (1 mile) to

The Kunstkamera on Vasilievsky Island.

Ploschad Vosstaniya (Square of the Uprising). It then continues another 2.5 km to the Neva.

Apart from the splendid architecture of the Nevsky Prospekt, there is much to see on street level as folk go about their everyday business. No-one walks gracefully or poses as in days gone by, for everyone is too busy shopping, going to work or struggling home at rush hour, and the street is not as clean as in Nikolai Gogol's time ("how spotlessly clean are its pavements swept and, good gracious, how many feet leave their marks on them!"), but it remains a good place to take the city's pulse.

The first important street which crosses the Nevsky is named after Gogol who lived at No 17. Here he wrote the first chapters of *Dead Souls*. Pyotr Tchaikovsky died at No 8 from drinking unboiled St Petersburg water. The next street which crosses the Nevsky is the once fashionable **Ulitsa Gertsena**, home of the famous Fabergé shop (No 24). It is still a jeweller's shop, but has lost its former glory.

The first river to cross the Nevsky is the **Moika** and on the right-hand side stands the green and white **Stroganov Palace**, home of one of Russia's leading families. It was designed by Rastrelli, architect of the Winter Palace. The next street on the left, **Ulitsa Bolshaya Konushennaya**, leads up to the former stables. The residents of No 13, Bolshaya Konushennaya, included the Russian writer Ivan Turgenev and, later on, the ballet dancer Nijinsky. The musician Rimsky-Korsakov lived at No 11.

Further up Nevsky Prospekt, on the right, stands the majestic **Kazan Cathedral** with its 96 columns, designed by the architect Andrei Voronikhin during and after the reign of Paul I. In the square in front are statues of the heroes of the 1812 war, M.I. Kutuzov (who is also buried here) and M.B. Barklay de Tolly. Once the museum of the History of Religion and Atheism, it is now just the **Museum of Religion**. Religious services have been restored and its cross has been replaced.

Opposite, at No 28, Nevsky Prospekt,

The Stroganov Palace.

is the art nouveau **Dom Knigi** (House of Books), once the Singer sewing machine factory. You can't miss the huge globe on the roof. As you cross the next canal, the **Griboedov** or Ekaterinsky canal, the multi-coloured domes of the **Church of the Resurrection**, built on the blood of the assassinated Alexander II, are visible to the left. This church has been under restoration for some 25 years and has recently re-emerged from a cocoon of scaffolding.

Two interesting bridges by the same architect, W. Traitteur (1825–26), cross the Griboedov canal as it flows away from Nevsky Prospekt to the right. The first is **Bankovsky Most** (Bankers' Bridge) on which sit two golden-winged griffins. Further down is **Lvinny Most** (Lion Bridge) where two lions hold the suspension cables in their mouths.

Further up the Nevsky, on the left-hand side, is the luxurious **Grand Hotel Europe**, which has undergone the same fate as the Astoria Hotel. The street on which it stands, Ulitsa Mikhailovskovo/Brodskovo, leads into **Ploschad Iskusstvo** (Square of the Arts), home of the **Russian Museum**. The yellow classical building of the Russian Museum was built by Rossi between 1819 and 1825 for Grand Duke Mikhail, Alexander I and Nicholas I's younger brother. Unlike the Hermitage it houses only Russian art and is a smaller, more manageable museum. The exhibits span almost 1,000 years of the history of Russian art, from a magnificent icon collection through works by avant-garde artists such as Malevich and Kandinsky to the art of the present day.

Also in Ploschad Iskusstvo stands the **St Petersburg Philharmonia** building and the **Maly Theatre of Opera and Ballet**. In the middle of the square is a statue of Pushkin by one of the city's leading sculptors, Michail Annikuchin. (Alexander Pushkin, Russia's Shakespeare, is something of a cult figure in this city and those interested should visit the **Pushkin Flat-Museum**, No 12, Moika Embankment, perhaps before a concert at the **Capella Music Hall**, No 20 Moika Embankment.)

Back on the Nevsky Prospekt, with Ploschad Isskustvo behind you, notice the long yellow and white facade of **Gostiny Dvor** on the right-hand side. This is one of St Petersburg's largest department stores. Further up the Nevsky, at No 58, is a food shop with a highly extravagant art nouveau interior, built for the rich merchant **Elyseev** and once the grandest delicatessen in St Petersburg. Where Sadovaya Ulitsa crosses the Nevsky look out for the famous Metropole Restaurant. It used to sell the best eclairs in the city. If you continue down this street you come to **Ploschad Mira** (Peace), now called **Sennaya** (Hay) **Ploschad**, a traditionally seedy area. Raskolnikov, in Dostoevsky's *Crime and Punishment*, wandered here, where "types so various were to be seen that no figure, however queer, would have caused surprise."

To the right just after the junction of Sadovaya Ulitsa and Nevsky is a huge square with a statue of Catherine the Great surrounded by her many lovers. This square is named after the play-wright Ostrovsky: **Ploschad Ostrovskovo.** Its buildings include the **Saltykov-Schedrin library** and, at the other end, the **Pushkin Theatre of Drama**, with its white columns. Behind the theatre, leading away from the right-hand corner of the square, is **Ulitsa Zodchevo Rossi** (Street of the Master-Builder Rossi). This street has perfect proportions with the width of the street equalling the height of the buildings. Among its buildings is the **Vaganova Ballet School**, the training ground for some of the greatest names in ballet, including Pavlova, Nijinsky, Nureyev, Makarova and Baryshnikov.

Back on the Nevsky Prospekt, the next canal is the **Fontanka** with its impressive **Anichkov Bridge.** The horses which decorate the bridge are the work of the sculptor Pyotr Clodt. During the war the horses were buried underground in the nearby gardens of the Palace of Young Pioneers, as were many of the cities' famous statues. Crowds stood on the bridge and cheered when they were restored to their former posi-

Beloselsky-Belozersky Palace.

tion. Behind the Anichkov Bridge stands the dark-red **Beloselsky-Belozersky Palace**, built by Stakenschneider between 1884 and 1848 for Prince Beloselsky-Belozersky.

To the left, on the banks of the Fontanka, is the yellow **Sheremetev Palace** built by Chevakinsky between 1750 and 1755. One of its outbuildings, the **Fontanny Dom**, houses the literary museum of Anna Akhmatova, one of Russia's greatest poets who was writing at the height of Stalinist terror.

At the next junction, **Liteiny Prospekt**, is the famous second-hand bookstore called Bukinist (No59). Vladimirskiy Prospekt, to the right, leads to the best farmers' market in town, **Kuznechny Rinok**. Just by the market is the **Dostoevsky House**, where the writer lived and died. It now operates as a museum. Nearby is the working **Vladimir church.**

At the very end of the Nevsky Prospekt (the section in the middle is not described here in detail as it is not nearly so interesting as the first half) is **Ploschad**

Alexander Nevskovo, where the Hotel Moscow stands. Here is the **Alexander Nevsky Lavra**, the oldest and most beautiful monastery complex in the city. Alexander Nevsky defeated the Swedes on this spot in the 13th century and was canonised after his death. His remains can still be found in a silver coffin inside the Hermitage.

"Lavra" is a title bestowed upon a monastery of the highest order: a seat of Metropolitans. Before the Revolution there were only four in Russia. This one became a lavra in 1797 although it was founded by Peter the Great in 1713. The monastery was enlarged under Peter's successors, and the **Holy Trinity Cathedral** was built under Catherine the Great by the architect Vasily Stasov.

There are several cemeteries inside the complex and many interesting headstones outside the Cathedral, among them the propellors of an aeroplane marking the grave of a pilot killed in World War II. The most interesting cemeteries are the **Tikvin** and **Lazarus** cemeteries, where Russia's most famous

The study where Dostoevsky wrote *The Brothers Karamazov*.

countrymen lie buried. In the **Lazarus Cemetery**, where Peter the Great's sister, Natalya Alexeyevna, lies, you will find the graves of famous architects, including Rossi and Voronikhin. The composers Mikhail Glinka, Pyotr Tchaikovsky, Modest Mussorgsky and Nikolai Rimsky-Korsakov are buried in the **Tikvin Cemetery** opposite, together with Fyodr Dostoevsky. Famous people from the arts world continue to be buried here. **The Church of the Annunciation**, built by the same architect as the Peter and Paul Fortress, Domenico Trezzini, also stands in the monastery complex. The Nevsky Prospekt ends at this point.

Another religious building not to be missed is the beautiful **Smolny Cathedral**. The Smolny was designed by Rastrelli. Painted pale blue and white and standing in the shape of a Greek Cross, it seems to float rather than stand on the horizon.

Smolny means "tar" and the site of the cathedral was a tar yard until 1723. The building was not completed until the time of Catherine the Great, when it became an institute "for the education of well-born young Ladies", the first of its kind in Russia. At the beginning of the next century, **the Smolny Institute** moved to the yellow, classical building next door, designed by Quarenghi. This was to become the headquarters of the Bolshevik Central Committee, and it was from here that Lenin led the uprising in October 1917.

Nearby are the **Kikin** and **Tauride** palaces. Kikin was an associate of Peter the Great and although the palace has been rebuilt the basic structure dates back to 1714. The Tauride Palace was built between 1783 and 1789 for Gregory Potemkin. Potemkin was one of Catherine the Great's greatest favourites, arguably no less than co-regent in view of his influence over her. Potemkin is remembered in history for annexing the Crimea in 1783.

Out-of-town palaces: A visit to St Petersburg is not complete without a trip outside the city to one or more of the five palaces now open to the public.

Monplaisir at Petrodvoretz.

Petrodvoretz, the Catherine Palace at Pushkin (Tsarskoe Selo), and Pavlovsk attract the most people as they are more geared for tourism. They have been fully restored after the devastation of German occupation. Fewer people visit the palaces at Oranienbaum and Gatchino, which are undergoing major restoration work.

Petrodvoretz, Peter's summer palace, is situated on the Gulf of Finland, 29 km (18 miles) west of the city. One of its most striking features is its fountains, which are turned off in the winter. The original palace was built by Peter the Great in 1720 to the design of the French architect, LeBlond. It was much simpler than the version that now stands, which was embellished and enlarged by Empress Elizabeth. But traces of Peter the Great and LeBlond show through the baroque glitz. They chose the magnificent site on a natural slope – a Versailles by the sea – and were responsible for the intricate fountains, a major feat on land consisting of marshy clay.

Looking at pictures of Petrodvoretz after the World War II, one wonders how they ever rebuilt it. Some, but by no means all, of its treasures were smuggled out in time to escape bomb damage. The **Grand Cascade** is the focal point of the water gardens in front of the palace, with the famous **statue of Samson** rending apart the jaws of a lion. The gardens contain three pavilions. The first, **the Hermitage**, was where Peter entertained, helped by a "dumb waiter" device – a section of the round table was lowered below ground to be cleared and replenished. The **Marly** is built in a simple, Dutch style and **Monplaisir**, built by the water's edge, became Peter's favourite retreat; he could see the sea from his bed.

Inside, Peter the Great's taste is reflected in the **oak staircase, oak study** and the **throne room**, where his original throne sits. Catherine the Great introduced such rooms as the **Portrait Gallery**, with its portraits of 368 women in different costumes.

Twelve km (7 miles) down the coast is **Oranienbaum**, built by Alexander Menshikov. It was the construction of Oranienbaum that inspired Peter the Great to build Petrodvoretz. The main palace is closed to the public and about to undergo restoration. In the summer the **Chinese Palace**, built by Catherine, is open to the public, along with the **Coasting Pavilion**, though its roller coaster with wooden toboggans no longer stands. Also in summer you can hire a pedalo or boat on the lake.

Pushkin or **Tsarskoe Selo** (Tsar's Village) can be reached by train from St Petersburg's Vitebsk Station. This station is well worth seeing for its splendid Russian art nouveau interior. It was the first Russian railway station and the line between here and Tsarskoe Selo was the first experimental railway (1837).

Peter the Great's wife, Catherine, chose the site for a stone country house, intended as a surprise for her husband while he was away for two years in Poland. It seems to be the fate of each royal palace to be altered by successive monarchs and Peter's daughter, the Empress Elizabeth, decided to build a new and more opulent palace here in

Flute-player in front of the Catherine Palace.

1741. She asked Rastrelli to model it on Versailles. She named it the **Catherine Palace** in honour of her mother. Although it was enlarged by subsequent rulers, particularly by Catherine the Great, whose architect, the Scotsman Charles Cameron, gave the palace a more stately feel, it is above all Elizabeth's creation. Although it was not finished in her lifetime, the extravagant, baroque design is symbolic of the mood which dominated during her reign.

The town expanded rapidly in the late 19th and 20th centuries and it is said that Tsarskoe Selo was the first city with electric street lighting in Europe. It developed as a popular summer resort, for the climate is much better here than in St Petersburg. In 1918 it was renamed Detskoe Selo (Children's village) on account of the many sanitoria and holiday homes for children. In 1937 the name changed again to Pushkin on account of the famous poet having studied at the Lycée in 1811. In 1941 Tsarskoe Selo was occupied by the German army, which left the city and palace in ruins.

One of the mysteries of this palace is the disappearance of the amber panels given to Peter the Great by Friedrich Wilhelm, King of Prussia, in exchange for 248 soldiers, a lathe and a wine cup made by Peter himself. They disappeared after the German occupation. There are rumours that they have been found, but so far only rumours.

The interior, like the exterior of the palace, is a mixture of styles by different architects: for example, the baroque of Rastrelli and the classicism of Cameron. **The Great Hall**, with its massive mirrors, wood carvings, glistening gold and sense of space, is perhaps the most sumptuous of all.

There is a great deal to see in the park, including the **Upper and Lower Baths**, the **Hermitage**, the great pond, the **fountain of the milkmaid with the broken pitcher**, inspired by one of La Fontaine's fables, and the **Caprice**. When visiting a palace that has been so highly restored, it is important to see the ruins – so a visit to the **Chinese Village** is also recommended. In the grounds stand the **Alexander Park** and **Palace**. This smaller, more classical palace, which is not open to the public, was presented to Alexander I by his grandmother, Catherine the Great, on his marriage.

The next stop on the Electric Railway, some 4 km (2 miles) further, is **Pavlovsk**. The palace at Pavlovsk, much smaller than the others, was built by Catherine the Great for her son Paul and his wife Maria Feodorovna. The architect, who was also commissioned to redesign the gardens in accordance with the then fashionable English style, was Charles Cameron. Later on an Italian architect, Vincenzo Brenna, was brought in. The land was originally chosen for the royal hunt, on account of all the elk and wild fowl. Unlike the other palaces, Pavlovsk is surrounded by small hills, which channel the Slavyanka river.

The rooms inside the palace (the finest are upstairs) reflect the personalities of Paul and his wife. Paul's militaristic interests can be seen in the **Hall of War** as well as in the **Throne Room** and the **Hall of the Maltese Knights of St John**. His wife's **Hall of Peace** forms a pleasant and intended contrast. The tapestries in the **Carpet Room** represent motifs from Cervantes' *Don Quixote*. There is a lot of French furniture, embroidered French curtains in the Greek Hall, and in the Hall of Peace a tripod-vase of crystal and red-gold made in the St Petersburg glass factory in 1811. In Maria Feodorovna's boudoir stands a piano from London. There is also a large amount of Sèvres porcelain and a clock in Paul's study given to him by Pope Pius VI.

The gardens are very large indeed (600 hectares/1,480 acres), their most important features being the **Temple of Friendship** (the friendship between Maria and her mother-in-law), the **Centaur Bridge**, the **Cold Baths**, the **Apollo Colonnade** and the **Pavilion of the Three Graces**.

In time Paul transferred his affections to the palace at **Gatchino**, a stone-built palace which changes colour with the movement of the sun. When restoration work there has been completed, a visit is recommended, but until then, it should not be a priority.

Right, the Church of the Resurrection of Christ, known as Spas na Krovi (the spilt blood).

THE EUROPEAN NORTH

The north begins with Vologda, or so they say. In fact it stretches to the Urals in the east, up to the White Sea and the Sea of Barents, and across to Finland and the northwest of Russia. It has many romantic associations for the average Russian: a land of great natural beauty, of hard winters, and of real Russian peasants – strong, rugged, honest, hardworking. Here you find summer "white nights", when the sun never sets, and polar nights when it never rises.

The importance of the north dates from medieval times. When Kiev came under the Mongol yoke many Russians fled north, taking their skills with them. Monks settled in the region and founded monasteries which grew into major cultural centres. With the formation of a single Russian state under Moscovite rule, the northern border needed defending and a series of fortresses were constructed, sometimes from scratch,

Preceding pages: you know what sailors are… Left, cub confrontation

sometimes on the site of an existing monastery, such as at Solovetsky.

In 1553 Richard Chancellor, an Englishman, opened up the northern waterways and foreign merchants sailed along the rivers Sukhona and Dvina en route to Moscow. Archangel was founded as a trading port and soon flourished, along with other towns such as Veliky Ustiug. Huge fairs attracted goods and traders from both East and West, from England, Holland, Greece, Armenia, China and Persia. There was a large community of English merchants in Archangel and an English wharf in the port. Local crafts – nielloed metalwork from Ustiug, carved ivory from Kholmogory – were valued all over Russia.

The area is rich in wooden churches, reflecting the wealth of the area between the 16th and 18th centuries, when the church was the centre of social and administrative life in a community. Indeed, the social significance of churches was so great that the galilee (covered "porch") was often larger than the church itself – in the case of the church of St Nicholas in the monastery of Muyezero, four times its size.

Peter the Great was responsible for the decline of the area. With the foundation of St Petersburg in 1703, the glorious days of the Russian North were suddenly over. Peter Westernised his backward country by looking south rather than north. For 150 years the region was isolated from the mainstream of Russian life and the fairs and markets died for lack of goods. As merchants turned to other routes, towns and villages dependent on trade declined to provincial status.

But what may have seemed to be a tragedy was, in ethnographical terms, the area's salvation. When the North was rediscovered in the late 19th century by ethnographers, then by artists, they found a society which was living in the past. Not only were there hundreds of stone churches and monasteries set in magnificent landscapes, but there was a wealth of wooden buildings, religious and secular. What's more, the population had maintained age-old traditions, preserving fairytales, folk songs and

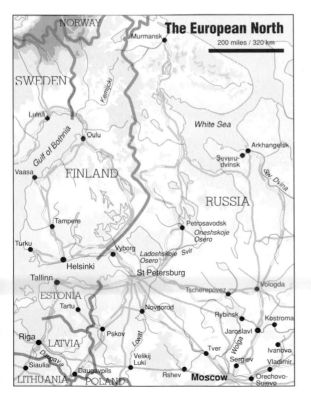

The European North

200 miles / 320 km

customs which had already disappeared from much of Russia.

Artists flocked to the North. Vasily Vereshchagin, whose paintings hang in the Tretyakov Gallery and the Russian Museum, was one of the first. He was followed by Konstantin Korovin and Ivan Bilibin. Nationalist composers like Balakirev and Rimsky-Korsakov collected folk songs, incorporating the melodies in numerous compositions. The works of these men in turn opened up the North to the rest of the world. For today's traveller who wants to get close to traditional Russian life and architecture, to understand how people lived in the past, even to hear real folk songs sung by the people and not by a concert performer, this is the only place to go.

Favoured City: Ivan the Terrible loved **Vologda** and built a strong **Kremlin** (fortress) here, in case he ever needed a place of refuge. He received Chancellor here on his memorable voyage, and from here a Russian envoy was sent to England. The chronicles record how Ivan personally oversaw the building of the **Cathedral of St Sophia** (1568–70) though, according to legend, when a "red tile" fell on his head as he walked round his new church the irate tsar set off for Moscow leaving the Cathedral unconsecrated for 17 years.

The Cathedral stands on the high bank of the River Vologda, in the centre of what was once the Kremlin. Its late 17th-century frescoes combine medieval monumentality and the contemporary decorative manner. The Archbishop's residence, an attractive huddle of buildings by the Cathedral, includes the baroque **Palace of Joseph the Golden** (1764–69).

Vologda itself, a charming if Sovietised city, is best seen from the river, with its 18th-century churches and secular buildings running along the embankment. Of particular note are the **church of SS Constantine and Helen** (1690), with its typical tent-shaped, free-standing belfry, and, among the secular buildings, the **Barsh Mansion**, the neoclassical **Skuliabin Almshouse** and the wooden **Levashov House**, as well as

Ecologists ring an elder at the Barents.

the enchanting wooden **Zasetsky House** (1790–95).

Monasteries: North of Vologda on the road to Beloye Ozero is the **Spaso-Prilutsky Monastery**, the Monastery of the Saviour on the Bend. In medieval times most churches in the north were built along waterways, particularly at bends in a river or stream. The best view is obtained by climbing the steep wooden staircase under the roof of the Water Tower. From here you can see the oldest and most typical northern building in the complex: the stone **Cathedral of the Saviour** (1542), the jumble of buildings around it and, over the walls, the St Sophia Cathedral in Vologda. During Napoleon's invasion of Russia, treasures from the Kremlin and many Moscow monasteries were stored here.

Rather than go by road, take a boat from Vologda to the **Kirillov-Belozersky Monastery**, which stands on the edge of Lake Siverskoye. The boat wends past wooden windmills and churches before arriving at Kirillov, where the monastery emerges from be-

hind the trees, its white stone buildings and domes reflected in the water.

The monastery was founded in 1397 and by the beginning of the 17th century was one of the richest foundations in Russia, largely due to the sale of salt. Vasily III, first tsar of Russia, came here to pray for a child by his apparently barren wife, Elena, and the following year the miracle happened. They were blessed with a son, who went on to become Ivan the Terrible.

The 17th-century fortifications are so wide that two cars could drive along the inner galleries side by side. There are a number of 15th- and 16th-century churches, but the star is the **Cathedral of the Assumption** with its superb frescoes and 17th-century iconostasis.

Twenty km (12 miles) from the Kirillov-Belozersky Monastery is the **Ferapontov Monastery** (St Therapont) on the bank of Lake Borodava. Its main claim to fame lies in the frescoes in the **Cathedral of the Nativity of the Virgin**, painted in the first few years of the 16th century by the famous Dionysius

River fish drying in the wind.

and his sons. The superb cycle, devoted to the life of the Virgin, is regarded as Dionysius's swan song. A romantic local legend attributes his appearance this far north to the death of his beloved wife and his subsequent desire to find peace in the monastery.

The town of **Belozersk** retains much of its wooden 19th-century appearance, plus the symbols of its wealthy past: the massive **church of the Dormition** (1553), void of ornament; the heavy **Cathedral of the Transfiguration** (1670s) and the jolly **church of the Most Gracious Saviour** (1723). Most impressive of all are the remains of the ancient fortress, the high earthen ramparts which run around the old town.

East of Vologda is the attractive small town of **Totma**, with its few but superb 18th-century churches displaying fine monumental brickwork. In the 16th century the town had only 4,000 inhabitants but was rich enough to support 16 religious buildings. Lunacharsky, the first Soviet Commissar for Enlightenment and friend of numerous avant-garde art-

ists, was exiled here by the tsarist government between 1902 and 1904.

Veliky Ustiug, now a sleepy provincial centre, was once one of the great market towns of the North – hence the "Veliky" (Great) – and its tiered churches, monasteries and mansions are strung out along the meandering river. The 17th-century **Cathedral of the Assumption** is the eighth building on the site. Of particular note are the **church of the Holy Women** (1714–22), the baroque **church of Simeon the Stylite** (1725–65) and the **Monastery of the Archangel Michael**, not to mention the wealth of 18th- and 19th-century mansions such as the **Shilov House** on the embankment. It is an easy walk across the old town.

One of the richest periods in the history of Russian art is linked with the so-called Stroganov masters, artists employed by the wealthy Stroganov family, who made their fortune from the salt mines along the Northern Dvina. The Stroganovs settled in **Solvychegodsk** and founded many churches, such as the fortress-like **Annunciation Cathedral** (1560–79), which was not only the Stroganovs' own church but also their treasury and citadel, standing adjacent to their grounds. It is still rich in icons and frescoes. They also founded the **Monastery of the Presentation of the Virgin** (1689–93), its carved white stone details set off against the red brick and coloured tiles. The local museum contains many more icons and pieces of applied art linked with the Stroganovs and the town still has plenty of picturesque wooden buildings. Solvychegodsk is a well-known health resort, with salt and mud baths, particularly good for the relief of rheumatism.

The Archangelsk region: North in the Archangelsk region is the small town of **Kargopol**, yet another point on the important trading waterways of the North. Its key position on the River Onega led to a boom between the 16th and 17th centuries, manifested in the highly decorative white stone **church of the Annunciation**.

The opening up of the northern trade route created the need for a port near the **Country life.**

mouth of the Dvina on the White Sea. In 1584 the town of Novye Kholmogory was founded; it later became know as Arkhangelsk or **Archangel**. By the beginning of the 18th century this was the centre of Russian shipbuilding. Now it is a big timber-logging and fishing area, known to the West through centuries of foreign trading links and the area's occupation by anti-Soviet White troops immediately after the Revolution (1918–19). The great Russian scientist and poet Mikhail Lomonosov was born close to the town.

Thirty km (18 miles) outside the town itself is the **Open Air Wooden Architecture Museum Reserve** at **Lyavlya**. The whole area is rich in wooden buildings but for those without the time or inclination to go trotting around hundreds of small villages a visit to the reserve is a must. The forests make an effective backdrop for wooden churches, *izbas* (cottages) and outhouses, many of them superbly decorated with carved window surrounds, eaves and crests running along the roof. The museum also

Russian matriarch.

holds concerts of folk music and dancing and provides a home to craftsmen producing traditional folk art.

Grim reminder: Archangel is a departure point for those taking off to the **Solovetsky Islands** in the White Sea, familiarly known as Solovki. This name has a particular ring to those whose relatives were imprisoned or died in the Solovetsky Special Purpose Camp, one of the camps in what Solzhenitsyn called the Gulag Archipelago. There were several camps here in different monasteries scattered around the islands. The Russian acronym for the camp was SLON, a word meaning elephant, and thus the symbol of the camp was an elephant.

Solovetsky Monastery was a medieval fortress and major border post, and this can be seen in its grim, grey aspect, defensive walls and towers rising above the White Sea. The high windows recall embrasures, and the two 16th-century cathedrals were once linked by secret underground passages containing huge vaults for food and a hidden water supply in case of siege. The fortress was "annulled" in 1814, although the monastery was attacked one last time by the British during the Crimean War. Whatever we think of the Soviet camps, the Communists were not the first to use the Solovetsky Islands as a place of exile and imprisonment. Political and religious opponents were despatched here from the Middle Ages onwards. They were held in cells in the walls and towers and beneath the cathedrals.

The whole area is of outstanding natural beauty and this particular part of the White Sea has a comparatively moderate, sheltered climate. Nowadays you can take a boat around the islands and examine the system of lakes and connecting canals on the islands themselves. The church on **Golgotha Hill** on Anzersky Island is a good place from which to look over the whole archipelago. The labyrinths to be found on several islands are of unknown purpose.

Karelia and Murmansk: Head northeast from St Petersburg for **Karelia**, with its rich flat landscape and lakes. The southern reaches of Karelia are for those who like to combine a bit of church-spotting with their travelling while the northern reaches are really only for explorers.

To see what the area has to offer most comfortably, take a five-day trip on a river boat. The tours start from St Petersburg (much longer cruises from Moscow) and take in the Valaam Islands in the north of Lake Ladoga, Petrozavodsk (capital of the Karelian Autonomous Republic) and the island of Kizhi, passing through beautiful countryside . The cruise also saves the agony of a hotel. Shorter trips cover only Kizhi (3 days) or Valaam (1 day). Kizhi can also be reached by hydrofoil from Petrozavodsk.

For those on the five-day cruise, the **Valaam islands** come into view early on the second morning. Energetic passengers are advised to skip the organised boat tour and lecture and walk the 5 km (3 miles) or so through the woods to **Valaam Monastery**. Returned to the Church in 1990, the monastery is an active religious community, with a farm and workshops, and tourism is now big business. The buildings on the main island, as well as the more outlying cells and chapels, are currently being restored: major damage to the frescoes in the Cathedral of the Transfiguration was caused not by years of neglect but by over-officious guardians covering them with perspex over a decade ago, thus trapping moisture and causing the paint and plaster to flake off.

The port of **Petrozavodsk** runs 25 km (15 miles) along the banks of Lake Onega. It was founded in 1703 to serve a cannon foundry nearby. Despite the destruction wrought during World War II, Petrozavodsk is an attractive town, built on a series of plateaux rising from the water. The neoclassical **Kruglaya (Lenin) Square** survived the Nazis. About 70 km (43 miles) from the town is the **Kivach waterfall**, the best of many on the River Suna, set in the midst of a vast nature reserve.

Petrozavodsk is a good springboard for exploring the northern reaches of Lake Onega and the island of **Kizhi**, a unique museum of wooden architecture. The 22 domes of the **church of the**

Northern seascape.

Transfiguration (1714) are made entirely of wood and without the use of nails. The iconostasis inside the church is also of interest, not least because it is curved rather than straight. The interiors of some houses look much as they did when they were still home to local peasants. The houses look vast from the outside, but only part of their structure comprises the living area. Northern *izbas* incorporated the barn and livestock area all under one roof to reduce the need to go out in the depths of winter.

Heading north, you come to **Belomorsk**, from where it is also possible to take a trip to the Solovetsky Islands. If you have come this far by train and are intending to go on to Murmansk, the journey north takes in some stunning scenery at any time of the year.

To members of the older generation, **Murmansk** is equated with the Allied Forces who defended the town and port during World War II. It was through here that supplies reached the rest of Russia. British veterans still make annual trips in the summer to visit the graves of the fallen. The town is very new. The port was founded in 1916 – with British assistance (even the first houses were brought over from England) – out on the Barents Sea, which does not freeze even in the depths of winter thanks to the North Cape Stream. Small and pleasant, Murmansk rests between two low hills by the mouth of the River Kola and it is here, 68.5° north, that you really appreciate the meaning of a long winter night: the sun does not rise for 52 days.

The Leningrad Region: Back down south, the Leningrad Region (so-called despite the city itself now being St Petersburg) is well worth exploring if you get the chance. The area northwest of the city between Lake Ladoga and the Gulf of Finland is dominated by country houses (*dachas*) belonging to residents in St Petersburg. Everything from Sestroretsk onwards was part of Finland until 1940, and some of the best houses here were Finnish built. To establish Soviet rights to the land, plots were allocated to workers and former soldiers who where then encouraged to build on them. Now the area is closely packed with sanatoria and wooden houses, often huddled round the picturesque lakes. It is ideal for cross-country skiing in winter and swimming in summer. The houses thin out and the lakes become more numerous the closer you get to the Finnish border. The last, small, Russian town is **Vyborg**.

This area changed hands many times between the 13th and 20th centuries. It may not seem very Russian, for many of its buildings are left over from the Finnish rule. Vyborg Castle dates largely from the 16th century, and there are defensive towers from the 14th, but buildings from all periods survive, and the early 20th-century art nouveau buildings are especially striking. If you like follies, then the early 19th-century castle burial vault will be of interest.

The peace and quiet of Vyborg has been disrupted since the coming of perestroika, as this is the main crossing point for Finns coming to work in joint ventures in northern Russia and St Petersburg and for Russians or foreign-

Wooden church in Kizhi, built without a single nail.

ers making their exit to the West. There has been an upsurge in tourism and massive improvements in the availability of goods and services, but it has also made the city fertile territory for black marketeers and others who pick the pockets of innocent foreign tourists with ease. Keep your valuables out of reach of itchy fingers.

If you go east out of St Petersburg, towards Lake Ladoga, you come to the town of **Petrokrepost**, famous to those familiar with Russian history as Schlüsselberg. The **Assumption Cathedral** (1764) is attractive, but the town's main claim to fame is the fortress, which was used as a prison in pre-Revolutionary times. Peter the Great's sister was imprisoned here (by him), as was his first wife after his death, and in 1887 Lenin's brother, Alexander Ulyanov, was executed in the yard for his role in an attempt on Alexander III's life. Further along the south side of the Lake is **Staraya Ladoga**, with its 12th-century church of St George filled with marvellous frescoes, the remains of the

medieval fortress and other 17th-century buildings. Sixty km (37 miles) to the southeast is Tikhvin, worth a visit for its 16th- and 17th-century monuments and the **Rimsky-Korsakov House Museum**.

Going west along the south bank of the Gulf past Petrodvorets and the imperial summer palaces, you come to **Sosnovy Bor**, best known for its nuclear power station. In fact, the road (full of holes and terrible for any but the most hardy of cars) passes through the pine forest from which the town takes its name. If you are going on to Estonia, this is definitely the long way round, but it is by far the most scenic route. On reaching the border at Narva, jump out on the Russian side, which is called **Ivangorod,** and take a look around the fortress there.

The Northwest: Novgorod and Pskov ruled the roost when the Tartars took over the rest of ancient Rus, building up trading links with the Hanseatic League and protecting themselves against attacks by the Poles and Livonians with

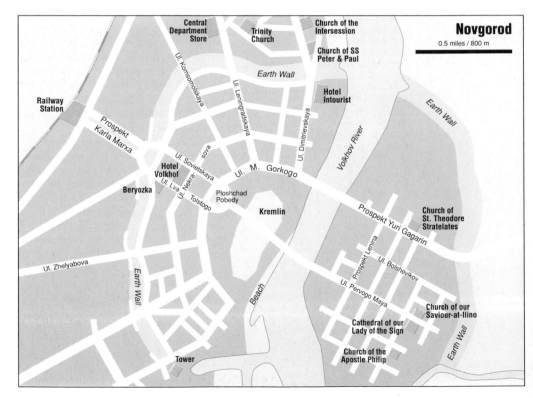

heavy fortifications. Rich merchants built themselves churches galore, and when Russia was united under the rule of the Moscow princes Vasily III invited Pskov master masons to help in the building of the churches in the Moscow Kremlin. The local monasteries were centres of learning, and Novgorod's historical chronicles and texts, scratched on pieces of birch bark, are known to historians all over the world.

The area suffered appallingly from the Nazi occupation. Despite stout resistance from the partisans, whole villages were burned, complete with all their inhabitants. Buildings of interest that have survived or have been restored are generally concentrated in the two main towns.

Novgorod has a rich past. At its height, the principality ruled from here spread all the way up to the White Sea and west to present day Poland. Its power did not always work to the city's good, however: in 1570, for example, Ivan the Terrible is supposed to have put down a plot to kill him by butchering some 60,000 of Novgorod's citizens. Nowadays the town itself lacks great beauty, but is redeemed by its monuments: the magnificent fortress, the churches round Yaroslav's Court, and the churches scattered all around.

The fortress built on the bank of the River Volkhov is at the heart of the old city. It is dominated, within its heavy red brick walls, by the magnificent 11th-century **Cathedral of St Sophia**, only moderately altered by later additions. Inside are 12th-century frescoes, including a portrait of Constantine and Helen, and the remains of 11th-century mosaics. One of the most surprising things to be found here is the east portal, with 12th-century bronze doors made at Magdeburg, taken – according to legend – from the fortress of Sigtunain in 1187. They are a superb example of Western European Romanesque metalwork (similar examples can be found in Pisa) tucked away in the heart of Russia.

The **Novgorod Museum** is also housed here. It has a wealth of icons and what is misleadingly described as "ap-

Peasants in Novgorod (1880).

plied" art: church utensils including censers, candelabra and icon covers of the finest work. The monument outside the building, erected to commemorate the millennium of Russia in 1862, is by the sculptor Mikhail Mikeshin.

On the opposite bank of the river is **Yaroslav's Court**, a pretty ensemble of 12th- to 16th-century churches. It was thought to have been the residence of the princes of Yaroslav until the end of the 14th century. There are plenty of other churches in town, some in the most unexpected places. If you count less than 30 as you wander round you have missed more than a few.

Outside the town itself, only a short bus trip away, are two more sights. The **Yuriev (St George) Monastery** is still being restored and can be pretty bleak on a grey day, but work is coming along nicely. There is an excellent open-air museum of wooden architecture just across the road – especially recommended for those who are unable to make it north to the museum reserve near Archangel.

South of Novgorod, on the other side of Lake Ilmen at the confluence of two rivers, is **Staraya Russa**. More intimate than Novgorod, the town is also rich in churches, for this was the centre of salt production. In times of war, Novgorod withheld supplies of salt from its enemies, and used it as a powerful bargaining tool.

Fyodor Dostoevsky and his family spent their summers in Staraya Russa from 1872, and *The Brothers Karamazov* is set here. There is now a **Dostoevsky Museum** and a picture gallery with plenty of Soviet Realism.

For many people outside Russia, all they know about **Pskov** is that it was here, in the royal train – delayed at the station – that Nicholas II signed his abdication. Like Novgorod the town is dominated by its fortress and churches, but being much closer to the western border of the Russian lands Pskov was more open to attack. Lake Chudovo, where the hero of Eisenstein's film *Alexander Nevsky* defeated the Livonians in the famous battle on the ice in 1242, is not far from Pskov.

Because of the ever-present danger from across the border, Pskov's churches played a bigger defensive role than those in Novgorod, their basements being used as bunkers in times of siege. Pskov's **Kremlin** is more fairytale in appearance than that of Novgorod. Instead of square red-brick towers, here we have heavy, round, squat towers with wooden roofs. The **Trinity Cathedral**, built in 1669, still dominates any view of the town. This white structure was not only a church, but also the place where the state council sat in session and where important state documents were kept. The **Kutekrom Tower** in the corner of the Kremlin walls was where Pushkin liked to look down over the river.

South of the Kremlin, excavations have revealed the remains of numerous churches, and outside the old town are yet more religious buildings, too numerous to mention individually. However, the magnificent **Cathedral of the Transfiguration** in the Mirozhsky Monastery, decorated in the 12th century by Greek masters and their Russian

St Sophia's Cathedral in Novgorod.

apprentices, is a world in itself. The frescoes definitely merit a visit.

There are several trips to be made outside Pskov, each of them requiring a whole day including travelling time. About 30 km (18 miles) along the main road to the west of Pskov, you find **Old Izborsk**. The village is build around the remains of a medieval fortress. Another 20 km (12 miles) further on, nestling in a deep ravine, is the 16th-century **Monastery of the Caves** at **Pechory**, its picturesque beauty matched only by the strangeness of its underground caves, used as burial vaults for monks. There are nearly 10,000 bodies here, with coffins bricked into the walls or just lying in niches. The oldest burial dates back to 1530. The numerous churches were built between the 16th and 18th centuries, but of particular note is the **Cathedral of the Dormition**, erected on the site of an ancient cave church. The monastery is still a religious institution, and it is possible to come here for a retreat.

Even Russians indifferent to the medieval history of the Pskov area do not remain unaffected by its connection with the poet Pushkin. The **Mikhailovskoye Estate** at **Pushkinskiye Gory** (the Pushkin Hills) belongs to an ensemble of three estates and the nearby Svyatogorsky Monastery. The estates were restored after the war and the parks were returned to their former glory. They are not to be seen in a rush, but savoured. Amble round the grounds and across the bridge over the Lower Ponds, and drop into Pushkin's study, where he worked during his exile, then take a peek into the small cottage where his old nanny (mentioned frequently in his works) lived out her old age.

The other estates here, Petrovskoye and Trigorskoye, and the monastery, are all reflected in Pushkin's poetry and prose. Mikhailovskoye and Trigorskoye form the background to *Eugene Onegin*, Petrovskoye to the stories *Dubrovsky* and *The Blackamoor of Peter the Great*, and the monastery features in *Boris Godunov*. The area is a favourite for romantic couples, honeymooning or just enjoying a weekend away.

The Gulf of Finland.

ALONG THE VOLGA

The Volga is the longest river (3,530km/ 2,195 miles) in Europe. It rises in the Valdai Hills (Valdaiskaya Vozvyshennost), not far from the picturesque Lake Seliger, and discharges its waters into the Caspian Sea. For many centuries the Volga has been like a mother feeding the Russian nation. It has witnessed numerous battles and wars, and has always stirred strong feelings in Russian hearts. From time immemorial, people have gravitated to the river, as the ancient settlements along its banks testify. One of the best preserved of these is Great Bulgar, the former capital city of the Volga Bulgars, near the Bulgar Village in Tataria. Other great sites are the remnants of Itil and Sarai, former capital cities of the Golden Horde, not far from Volgograd and Astrakhan.

The Povolzhye (Volga Region) comprises the middle and lower parts of the river from Kazan to Astrakhan. **Kazan** is the capital city of Tataria, a sovereign republic in the Russian Federation. It was founded in the second half of the 13th century, and in the mid-15th century became the capital city of the Kazan khanate. Kazan has witnessed numerous wars, sieges and revolts. In the second half of the 15th and in the early 16th centuries Moscow princes besieged the city repeatedly. In 1552 it was incorporated into the Russian state and in the 18th century developed into a major administrative, trade, industrial and cultural centre.

The **Kazan kremlin** is a marvellous ensemble of 16th-century architecture. Particularly handsome are the towers. They include the **Spasskaya Tower** (45 metres/147ft high), begun in 1555, the seven-tier **Suyumbiki Tower** (55 metres/180ft) with its stone dome and gate leading to the Sovereign's yard, and the **Tainitskaya Tower**.

Kazan is famous for its university, which is one of the oldest and most respected in Russia. Its students have included illustrious scholars, writers and politicians, notably Bekhterev, Butlerov,

Lenin, Lobachevsky and Leo Tolstoy. Kazan is also the native town of Tartar poet Musa Jalil and Russian singer Fyodor Chaliapin.

Around 74 km (46 miles) downstream from Kazan, the Volga joins the Kama, its largest tributary. Just south of here is the town of **Ulyanovsk** (formerly Simbirsk), occupying both banks. It was founded in 1648 to protect the southeastern outskirts of the Russian state from incursions. It is perhaps most famous for being Lenin's birthplace.

Another 125 km (78 miles) downstream of Ulyanovsk, a truncated cone of the Karaulny (guard) mound and the Kabatskaya hill rise on its right bank. This is where the **Zhiguli Hills** begin, the most beautiful part of the Volga. Occupying the northern part of the Samara bend, they form the only real mountain range on the Russian lowland. On the left bank of the Volga (opposite the Usolye Village) stands **Tolyatti** at the bottom of the Zhiguli Hills. A modern city, it is well known for its Volzhsky Car Factory, which

Preceding pages: whooper swans. <u>Left</u>, a fisherman grapples with a sturgeon. <u>Right</u>, flooded willows.

manufactures Zhigulis, Ladas, Sputniks and Samaras.

Further downstream, approximately half-way down the Volga's entire length, stands the town of **Samara** (Kuibyshev from 1935 to 1991), extending for dozens of kilometres along the bank. A broad staircase leads from the bank to the city centre, and a cast-iron grille adorns a riverside park. Named after the Samara River which flows into the Volga at this point, the town was built in 1586 as a fortress on the Volga's left bank. The easternmost town on the Samara protected trade routes along the Samara bend. The town was an important crossing point, and used for monitoring the nomads' movements around the Trans-Volga's steppes. By the early 19th century Samara had grown considerably, and only its centre was confined by the disintegrating fortress. Though known as an industrial town throughout its history, Samara is especially proud of its theatre, which is one of the best local theatres in Russia.

After Samara the Volga turns sharply to the west, rounding the Samara bend and then flowing to the south. The landscape here is stunningly beautiful. The right bank with its steep and high cliffs is mountainous while the left bank is a lowland of emerald-green meadows. Behind Samara you can feel the breath of the steppes.

Trading centre: After Samara comes **Saratov**, an industrial, modern town, founded on the left bank of the Volga in 1590. In 1674 the town was moved to the right bank, to a sloping hollow surrounded by the Lysaya, Altynnaya and Uvekskaya Mountains. In the first 100 years of its existence it was little more than a small fortress designed to protect river trade routes from the raids of nomads. During the reign of Peter the Great, the city's central square was called Gostinaya, on account of the Gostiny Dvor (rows of shops) built for merchants. The **Trinity Cathedral** was built in Gostinaya Square in 1695. In the 18th century Saratov emerged as a major trading centre and a trans-shipping point. The production of salt on Lake Elton

Laying a pipeline.

234

boosted the city's development. The first industrial enterprises date from that time. In the late 18th century agriculture progressed rapidly in the Saratov region and grain became a key commodity, along with salt and fish.

In 1798 Saratov was made the centre of a *guberniya* (a pre-Revolution province) and awarded a coat of arms. Like many other Russian towns, Saratov was a wooden town and as a result, it often suffered from fires. There was a particularly devastating fire in 1810, which prompted new city planning. In 1865 a new theatre was built of stone; this has survived as the **Opera and Ballet Theatre** on Teatralnaya Square.

Also here is the **Art Museum**, named after Radishchev, which opened in 1885. It boasts rich collections of paintings, graphic works, sculptures, porcelain and furniture. The city's main street, Moscovskaya, leads to Muzeinaya (museum) Square, a remnant of old Saratov. Its major feature is the **Stary** (old) **Cathedral** and, nearby, the former theological seminary, with arcades and col-

umns. The **Museum of Local Lore** is worth a visit.

Some 394km (244 miles) downstream from Saratov stands the town of Volgograd (originally Tsaritsyn and later Stalingrad). In the 13th century the whole area hereabouts was occupied by Tartars from the Golden Horde. When the Kazan and Astrakhan khanates eventually collapsed in the second half of the 16th century, a new town called Tsaritsyn was built on the island where the Tsaritsyn river flows into the Volga. It was designed to protect the country's southeastern borders.

The town suffered numerous raids by nomads, and the Don Cossacks, who rose in rebellion against the ruling regime, entered the town more than once. Peter the Great attached great importance to the town and built a barrage more than 60km (38 miles) long and a rampart about 12 metres (40ft) high. In 1765, Catherine the Great issued a decree allowing foreigners to settle in Russia. Among Tsaritsyn's newcomers from Western Europe was a sizeable

Amateur folk-singers.

colony of Germans, whose neighbourhood became known as Sarepta.

By the 19th century the town had lost its function as a fortress and become a trading and industrial centre. With the introduction of railways, industry developed rapidly, and soon saw-mills and cast-iron foundries were put into operation. The town grew with each passing day. The main building material was red brick.

In the winter of 1942–43 the town (then called Stalingrad) was the focus of a major battle of World War II: the devastating Stalingrad Battle. It changed the course of both the Great Patriotic War and World War II. The fierce fighting lasted for 200 days and nights – on land, in the air and on water. Some 300,000 of Hitler's crack troops were destroyed in Stalingrad, where each house and even each stone was an obstacle for the enemy. After the battle the whole town, factories and houses included, lay in ruins.

After the war, the town was literally built anew. It extended along the Volga for nearly 100km (60 miles). New factories and houses were built and parks set out. The memorial on Mamyev Mound by sculptor Vuchetich and architect Belopolsky was raised to commemorate the battle. It depicts a group of grieving citizens carrying wreaths to put on the heroes' graves. Behind the sculpture is a ramp paved with granite slabs and on both sides of the ramp are granite blocks resembling anti-tank teeth; they are engraved with the dates of all the major battles that took place near the town. The ramp ends with an 11-metre (36-ft) high sculpture of a warrior with a submachine-gun and a grenade in his hand ready to fight. The warrior symbolises the defender of his native country standing firm. Behind him, near the terrace with red flowers, rises a wide staircase with high walls on both sides showing the town's ruins. The staircase leads to a sculpture of a female figure symbolising the Mother Country, a sword high in her hand.

The memorial is in harmony with the landscape. There are extensive views of **Water lily on the Delta.**

the city and the river from the bottom of the main monument and from the top of the mound.

Cultural crossroads: Downstream from Volgograd, the river turns to the southeast, flowing along the sandy-clay steppe of the lower Volga area. The right bank of the river near **Astrakhan** (the last town on the Volga) is 12 metres (40ft) high. Astrakhan lies in the Volga's delta, straddling 11 islands separated by channels and rivulets. In the 18th century Astrakhan was on the Caspian Sea; today the sea falls short by some 200 metres (218 yards).

In the 8th century, 10–12km (6–7 miles) upstream on the Volga's right bank stood Itil, the capital city of the Khazar (Turkic-speaking nomadic tribes). The name "Astrakhan" wasn't used until the 13th century. In 1558 Ivan IV's troops captured Astrakhan without a fight and annexed it to Moscovy (Moscow state). Another turning point in the town's history was 1558, when New Astrakhan was founded on the opposite, left bank. The first wooden fortifica-

tions were built here, though between 1582 and 1589 they were replaced by a stone fortress: **the Astrakhan Kremlin**. This has seven towers, three of them with gates. **Krasniye Gate** and **Nikol–skiye Gate**, located in the Kremlin's northwestern part, led to the Volga. The third tower, **Prechistenskiye Gate**, with a bell tower incorporated in the eastern wall, led to the suburb called Bely Gorod (White Town).

Close to the Prechistenskiye Gate is the **Cathedral of the Assumption**, built in 1698. The cathedral is a marvellous architectural monument built by the serf master, Dorofei Myakishev. From all sides, the church is surrounded by a two-tier gallery decorated with filigree carved stone, creating an impression of light and air. The upper church with five graceful domes rises from this unusual, seemingly weightless pedestal. The Cathedral of the Assumption together with the place of execution and a high bell tower, built in the 19th century, make up a majestic architectural ensemble. The pseudo-Russian details over-

Astrakhan.

load the facades of the structure, but its tiers, evenly diminishing as they rise, make the bell tower look austere.

The Cathedral of the Trinity Monastery, built between the late 16th and 18th century on the opposite side of the kremlin territory, looks rather modest compared with the Cathedral of the Assumption. But from the point of view of craftsmanship, it is a large and intricate complex.

Many of the kremlin's architectural structures date from the 19th century. Of particular interest and importance are the **Guard House** (1807) and the **Kirillovskaya Chapel.** In the early 19th century, the chapel's original 17th-century structure was enclosed in a classical shell. The main portal (17th-century) is hidden behind the short massive Doric columns.

Another architectural structure that has survived on the territory of the former Bely Gorod is the **Tower of the Spasso-Transfiguration Monastery** in the northeastern part of Bely Gorod territory. Its snow-white octahedron, adorned with multi-coloured belts and insets and crowned with a dome, is magnificent. Not far from the Spasso-Transfiguration Monastery there is the **Demidov Homestead,** another architectural legacy of the 17th and 18th centuries. It was the largest and the most important home in the town. The Demidovs were an ancient merchant family in Russia. The size of the building was truly immense and even today it occupies half the block.

Among the churches that survived outside the kremlin's boundaries is the **Ioann Zlatoust church.** It was built in 1763, and its octahedron-on-tetrahedron composition was common in Central Russia. The church was reconstructed more than once, the final version in the form of a cross and incorporating the decor associated with classicism. The entrance to the church is adorned with the figure of Christ. The bent figures of angels on the western facade of the belfry express grief.

Buildings in classical style became a regular feature in towns after 1769. The **Volga boatman.**

238

early 19th century gave rise to such imposing and outstanding buildings as the City Technical School and the Department for the Supervision of the Kalmyk People. Stone structures were built not only in the centre of Astrakhan but in the outskirts, too. A striking example of this trend is the surviving building of the hospital for the charity department on Parobichev Hill.

Eastern merchants, who enjoyed extensive privileges, settled in Astrakhan. They built their trade rows and lived in tight-knit communities in the centre of Bely Gorod. The surviving structures of the **Indian and Persian homesteads** were built in the 19th century.

Foreign merchants also built their own religious institutes, hence the **Persian mosque** (1859) and the **white and black mosques**, erected by Strakhan Tartars in the mid-19th century. In the eastern part of town, at the confluence of the Kutum river and the canal stands a Roman Catholic church dating from the 18th century.

Such architectural imports form a magnificent contrast to Astrakhan's other buildings. Equally impressive are the commercial buildings that served the merchants. Huge expense was lavished on their construction, witness the **Azovsko-Donskoi Bank** and the **Exchange**. The latter combines elements of modernism and early constructivism. The merchants' estates on the Kutum's northern bank also illustrate the luxury of the times. One of the most interesting features of the Astrakhan's architecture of the 19th century is the elaborate metalwork. A strong Oriental influence is evident in the fancy grilles, balconies, arches and gates.

Astrakhan boasts a **picture gallery** named after its most famous native resident – Boris Kustodiyev, a Russian graphic artist and colourist. It contains works by artists from the 18th and 19th centuries and modern masters.

The city is still expanding. New buildings are constantly appearing, both in the centre and on the outskirts. The best of these complement the ensemble of the old town.

Reed-burning.

THE URALS

To picture the Urals, imagine smoke-stacks, factories and heavy industry. That is how leaders of the old USSR envisaged this mountain chain, and they proceeded to transform it into a succession of massive industrial enterprises.

The region has never attracted many tourists, partly because Soviet leaders declared most of the Urals off-limits to foreigners – bans that have only recently been lifted. Today, the few foreigners in the area are generally businessmen sifting through the tattered remains of Soviet industry in search of investment opportunities.

There are still some areas of outstanding natural beauty where lakes and hiking paths dot the landscape, but the lack of tourist facilities make them inaccessible for everyone except the experienced traveller in Russia. One enthusiast of the great outdoors, Boris Yeltsin, records in his memoirs that: "The Urals forest is very fertile; one can survive there for a considerable time."

The 2,000-km (1,250-mile) long Ural Mountains – stretching between the Karskoye Sea in the north and Kazakhstan in the south – have long been an important geographical landmark in Russia, marking the divide between Europe and Asian Siberia.

In comparison with many of the world's mountain chains, the Urals are not particularly high, reaching only 1,894 metres (6,213 ft) at their highpoint with a width of 40–200 km (25–125 miles). That's barely enough to merit brown on a topographical map of the region. The lack of a major geographical barrier (the main highway crosses the Urals at a height of just 420 metres/1,380 ft) left Russia open to attack during its early history.

Russia's Ural Mountain region dates back 250 million years, but before the 15th century it was sparsely inhabited by a variety of local tribes. The Urals' rich mineral wealth of iron ore, coal, precious minerals and ferrous and non-ferrous metals eventually attracted large-scale European migration in the 18th century. Between 1752 and 1762 alone, 55 factories were built in the region, and industrial centres sprouted up in Yekaterinburg, Perm, Orenburg, and other areas.

Industry moves in: Russia's devastation during World War II brought a boom to the Urals. After the German Army roared across much of the European part of the USSR, Stalin moved 1,360 factories and thousands of his people behind the Urals for protection – not only from ground troops, but also from German air bombing. The new Ural industrial base tripled capacity and was able to supply 40 per cent of the Soviet Union's military output for the war. The German armies never came close to the Urals, and historians cite Stalin's relocation of industry as a decisive factor in the Soviet defeat of the Nazi war machine.

After the war, Soviet authorities continued to expand heavy industry and weapons manufacture. Stalin adopted Lenin's slogan: "We must catch up with

and overtake the most advanced capitalist countries, or die." Traditional rural life in the region changed permanently as people flocked to the cities to work. Between 1940 and 1979, the Urals' urban population more than doubled, whereas the number of rural villagers fell slightly. Even though the Ural Mountains still has one of the lowest population densities in Russia, it claims one of the highest outputs in heavy industry and defence.

By the final years of Soviet power, the Urals accounted for a third of the country's steel production and a quarter of its cast iron. "The Ural economic region plays an important role in building the material technical base of Communism," the country's main encyclopedia enthused. The intense industrialisation has also made the Urals one of the most polluted regions in the world. The assault on the air, land, and water has created a staggering series of health problems for local inhabitants. Only recently has the government acknowledged the dangerous side-effects.

Yekaterinburg, a city omitted from many tourist maps until 1990, is the Urals' most important urban centre. It's the first major Russian city in Asia; 40 km (25 miles) to the west along the highway, a 4-metre (13-ft) high memorial marks the Asian-European border. Like most major cities in the Urals, Yekaterinburg's history has been closely associated with industry. The city was founded in 1723, and within five years the area had set up an ironworks, the first of many industrial enterprises attracted to the abundant raw materials of the region.

It remained modestly populated for many decades – just 10,000 people at the start of the 19th century – but the population exploded under socialism, climbing from 100,000 in 1917 to four times that number by the end of World War II.

The death of a tsar: Yekaterinburg is most famous in the history books not for its industry, but for its role in the execution of Tsar Nicholas II following the Bolshevik Revolution. After seizing

Far left, site of Tsar Nicholas II's execution at Yekaterinburg. **Left**, 200-year-old door handle.

power, the Communists imprisoned Tsar Nicholas II and his family, moving them to several locations before bringing them to Yekaterinburg in April, 1918. The family was confined to a brick home formerly belonging to a businessman called Ipatyev.

Accounts of the royal family's end were wrapped in secrecy throughout the Soviet period, but historians believe that guards treated the family cruelly during their final days. In July the Bolsheviks decided to dispose of the tsar once and for all, in case he was recaptured by counter-Revolutionaries. He was moved into the basement of the house and informed that he was about to die. As historian William Henry Chamberlin wrote: "The tsar did not understand and began to say 'What?' whereupon Yurovsky shot him down with his revolver. This was the signal for the general massacre. The other executioners, seven Letts and two agents from the Cheka, emptied their revolvers into the bodies of the victims. The Tsar fell first, followed by his son. The room was filled with shrieks and groans, blood poured into streams on the floor."

The man said to have helped arrange the executions, Bolshevik leader Yakov Sverdlov (1885–1919), was rewarded posthumously with a new name for Yekaterinburg, a city originally dedicated to Empress Catherine the First. After 1924, the city became Sverdlovsk, a name it retained until 1991. Even today, local legislators voted to cling to the name Sverdlovsk to describe the province around Yekaterinburg.

World War II triggered an industrial boom in the city, and 437 factories were transferred here, making the area one of the Soviet Union's most important manufacturing centres for years afterwards. Heavy industry remains the town's main economic base. Recently, as Communist subsidies to inefficient industry have dried up, many enterprises have suffered sharp cutbacks in production and employment. Thousands of workers have lost their jobs and been forced to seek new employment. Crime, often instigated by local mafia clans, has soared.

Boris Yeltsin's roots: Modern Yekaterinburg is best known for its political sons, Russian President Boris Yeltsin and Nikolai Ryzhkov, the prime minister under Mikhail Gorbachev. Yeltsin was born in near-poverty 150 km (93 miles) away in a village called **Butka**. He spent most of his life in Yekaterinburg however, first studying at Urals Polytechnic (now called the Urals State Technical University), then building his career in the construction industry and rising up the ranks of the Communist Party here. Many remember Yeltsin as a tough but popular leader, and locals still recall the day that a big Party official came to visit in 1985. "Don't take Yeltsin away from us, we need him here," one citizen yelled out. Yet a few months later, Yeltsin was called to Moscow, where he was eventually elected Russia's first president.

In August 1991, Yeltsin's demonstrated his enduring attachment to Yekaterinburg by drawing up contingency plans to take refuge in a bunker outside town if the right wing attempted

On the production line.

coup succeeded in holding on to power. As the coup failed within three days, Yeltsin stayed in the Kremlin.

Exploring Yekaterinburg: Town planners have thankfully kept most of the industry outside the town centre, creating instead pleasant wide avenues lined with trees and modern apartment blocks and offices. Perhaps the biggest surprise about the town is the number of wooden houses, complete with carved window frames and other details on the facades, which are a vestige from the past and a remarkable sight in this firmly modern city. Many of these houses are still used as homes and offices.

Start your sightseeing by walking north from Lenin Prospekt, the city's main street, on Ulitsa Karl Liebknecht. The first major sight a few minutes to the right is the **Regional History Museum**, Ulitsa Malisheva 46. Here you'll find an interesting historical collection starting with late tsarist rule and continuing through to the present. Highlights include pre-Revolutionary photographs and objects from Yekaterin-burg, a photographic record of the men who killed the Tsar Nicholas II and his family, and objects connected with the original inhabitants of the Ural region, including tents, hunting implements, and fur garments.

A little further down the street is the **Youth Museum**, Ulitsa Liebknecht 32. Once belonging to the Komsomol Communist youth organisation, the museum now takes an imaginative and unusual look at Soviet history. In 1988 the museum opened a radically different exhibition on Soviet life. Displays include a maze of mirrors, said to illustrate the futility of Soviet bureaucracy, and a man walking through a glass wall, showing how Russians are looking forward and backward at the same time. Another room gives an artist's rendition of the world after nuclear war, with tubas flying to heaven, useless in a world without people. The museum is currently compiling an archive of documents and videos about Boris Yeltsin, and they plan one day to open an exhibition on the first Russian president.

Folk display in Yekaterin-burg's History Museum.

A five-minute walk northward on Ulitsa Liebknecht is the site of the former Dom Ipatyev, the house where Russia's last tsar was killed. In the decades after the execution, many Russians came to the house to peer quietly into the last link with former times. But in 1977 the Kremlin, increasingly worried that the house could become a place of worship, ordered local party boss Boris Yeltsin to remove it. "It was impossible to disobey a secret decree from the Politburo," he wrote in his memoirs. "A few days later the bulldozers were driven up to the Ipatyev house in the middle of the night. By the next morning, nothing was left of the building."

Since the fall of Communism, locals have commemorated the tragic event by erecting a cross and wooden chapel on the site of the assassination. Efforts are now underway to raise $100 million to build a church on the site.

There are several other museums a few blocks west of Lenin Prospekt. In an area that is the site of the city's original settlement is the **Art Museum**, ul. Voyevodina 5, home to mostly second-rate Russian paintings. The large building's centrepiece is a 4.5-metre (15-ft) high iron pavilion crafted in an intricate Oriental style for display in Paris in 1900. Other highlights include local applied art in metals.

A few blocks away is the **Geological Museum**, Ulitsa Kyibisheva 39, a collection of 600 minerals from the Ural region including malachite, topaz, a 748-kg (1,650-lb) crystal, and a collection of meteorites.

If you return to Lenin Prospekt and turn one block to the east, you'll come to **1905 Square**, Yekaterinburg's main square and the home to **City Hall**, which was built between 1947 to 1954 by German prisoners captured in World War II; a large statue of Lenin was erected in 1957.

On the east side of town where Lenin Prospekt starts is the **Urals State Technical University**, the largest university in the Asian half of Russia, boasting 20,000 students and 7,000 teachers and employees. Known for its strong science departments in particular, the school has produced a series of prominent Soviet and Russian officials, including Boris Yeltsin and his wife, Naya, who met and fell in love while students here. At one time the school boasted 12 graduates on the Central Committee of the Communist Party. More recently the university has experienced rather harder times, since local industry has cut back its need for university-level engineers.

Although hardly worthy of a tourist visit, the **Ural Factory of Heavy Machine Construction** on the north part of town is famous in Russia. A machine tool factory, Uralmash once employed a staggering 50,000 people over 352 acres (142 hectares). As a Soviet pamphlet published in 1991 states: "For many decades, this name was the symbol of the newest, most powerful, most progressive technology in the country." The introduction of market economics to Russia gave this factory, as well as many of its sister operations, a harsh slap in the face. Output fell dramatically, and Uralmash management re-

Urals State Technical University.

duced the number of workers to 29,000 by 1993. Further declines in jobs and output are expected.

Steel city: A name virtually synonymous with Soviet industrialisation, **Magnitogorsk** (population: 450,000) is also one of the world's most polluted cities. Ironically, this most Soviet of places 113 km (70 miles) into Asia from the European divide was designed by an American firm. When the Soviet government decided to increase exploitation of the Urals' rich iron ore deposits, which had already been mined for hundreds of years, they turned to the McKee Corporation of Cleveland, Ohio (at the time selected US businesses were free to cooperate with the new but underdeveloped Soviet state). McKee was called upon to help in the design of Magnitogorsk, and it drew its inspiration from the US Steel plant in Gary, Indiana, which was at the time the largest iron and steel plant in the world. The American firm was paid $2.5 million worth of gold for its services.

The building of Magnitogorsk was begun in 1929; pig iron was already under production by 1932, and steel was being manufactured by the following year. The initial name of the plant launched during the USSR's first Five-Year Plan was the Stalin Magnitogorsk Metallurgy Kombinat.

Workers in this model industrial project settled in an area called Sotsgorod, a Russian language abbreviation for "The Socialist City". The city's population exploded to 146,000 people by 1939, and it soon become one of the country's major industrial centres. The area still stamps out huge quantities of steel: in 1990 Magnitogorsk produced 25 per cent of all Soviet goods containing metal.

Founded in 1736 as a defensive fortress, **Chelyabinsk** (population: 1.2 million) is the southern Urals' administrative centre. It grew rapidly in the 19th century as an important trading centre along the Great Siberian Magistral, transporting goods and travellers between Europe and Asia. Located 200 km (125 miles) from Yekaterinburg, the city is

Central Market, Yekaterinburg.

an important industrial centre for cast-iron products such as tanks, and other ferrous and non-ferrous metal products are common.

Accidents and experiments: The Chelyabinsk area is also the site of two of the worst nuclear accidents in the postwar period. In September 1957, a mechanism designed to cool nuclear waste failed in nearby Kyshtym, and contaminated the area with 70 or 80 tons of radioactive material. For many years the incident was shrouded in secrecy. And for a 10-year period starting in 1951, the Mayak (or Lighthouse) nuclear bomb plant 100 km (80 miles) northwest of Chelyabinsk dumped huge quantities of radioactive waste into a local lake. The lake has since evaporated, but the radioactive dust remains a lethal threat. "They have been concealing the truth about this radioactive pollution from the people for 30 years," Boris Yeltsin said during a 1991 visit to the region.

Intourist arranges a tour called "For Nuclear Safety". It includes a visit to a biophysics centre specialising in treating radiation victims, and meetings with local scientists specialising in nuclear and energy problems. Within the city of Chelyabinsk, the main sights are the **Geology Museum**, highlighting Ural minerals, on Ulitsa Truda 98; the Picture Gallery of 15th–20th century Russian and foreign artists, on Ulitsa Truda 92; and the **Applied Art Museum**, on Ulitsa Revolutsii 1, showing off the best of local masters.

An industrial centre founded in 1735 that today boasts over 90 manufacturing enterprises, **Orenburg** (population: 500,000) is located near the site of one of the most grotesque experiments of the Cold War. According to recent press accounts, in 1954 the Red Army exploded an atomic bomb near the city during military exercises, the only time any nation has used the bomb in such a way. World War II hero Georgy Zhukov, Defence Minister Nikolai Bulganin and other top Soviet leaders watched the exercise from a distance of 15 km (9 miles). In subsequent years, local villages suffered a 50 per cent increase in cancer, and of the 44,000 soldiers who participated only 1,000 are still alive.

Orenburg is also home to a military aviation academy where Yury Gagarin, the first man in space, studied. A jet which he used is located at the entrance to the academy.

On the European side of the Ural Mountain range, **Perm** is another large industrial centre (population over 1 million). It was founded in 1723 as a village around a factory, and other businesses soon sprouted up in the area. From 1940 to 1957, Perm was renamed Molotov, in honour of the Soviet foreign minister best remembered for signing the non-aggression pact with Nazi Germany in 1939. Perm's highlight is the **State Picture Gallery**, Komsomolsky Prospekt 4, with its fine display of 16th to 19th-century icons, 17th to 19th-century sculptures, and Russian and foreign paintings. The **Khokhlovka Ethnographic Architecture Museum** 45 km (28 miles) away preserves examples of rural life before the beginning of the 20th century.

Long lines for public transport.

THE EUROPEAN SOUTH

The European South, or northern Caucasus as it is also called, is bounded by the Black and Azov seas to the west, the Caspian Sea to the east, the Donskoi steppe to the north, and the central Caucasus to the south. The landscapes are diverse: from the fertile black-earth steppes to the snow-capped Caucasian mountains; from the subtropical Black Sea coast to the semi-deserts by the Caspian; from alpine grasslands to mountain rivers which flood the steppes in spring. The vegetation is equally varied: coniferous forests at the foot of the mountains, subtropical vegetation along the shores, and rush-filled river valleys. The Caucasus has been home to dozens of different peoples over time, resulting in the ethnic diversity which characterises the region to the day.

The Kuban Cossacks (named after the river) and their descendants live on the plains. Their capital is **Krasnodar** (population: 500,000). Before the Revolution, Krasnodar was called Yekaterinodar – from *Yekaterina* (Catherine) and *dar* (gift). Catherine the Great gave this city to the Kuban Cossacks in return for conquering southern lands for the Russian crown. Today the city is the capital of the Krasnodarsky krai, an area rich in minerals, especially oil, and famous for its wheat. In addition to Cossacks, the region is home to Ukrainians, Russians, and various Caucasian peoples (Circassians, Adygeis, Kabardians, Balkars, Ossets). They have their autonomous republics. Greeks, Abkhazians, Georgians, and Armenians also live here.

The northern part of the Caucasus Mountains is known for its vineyards. In the small town of **Abrau-Dyurso**, near the Black Sea port of Novorossiisk, vintners have been producing one of Russia's best champagnes for over 150 years. However, during Mikhail Gorbachev's anti-alcohol campaign, nearly one-sixth of the Soviet Union's vineyards were destroyed, and many kinds of grapes disappeared altogether.

Both the climate and the soil in the Caucasus favour a wide variety of fruits and vegetables: apples, pears, peaches, plums, tangerines and lemons; tomatoes, cucumbers, eggplant, summer squash, and peppers. Plantations just north of Sochi produce Krasnodarsky tea, considered the best of those grown in Russia, Transcaucasia, and Central Asia. A large percentage of the tea goes for export. Tobacco, including rare oily kinds, is another important resource.

The **Black Sea** is an internal and virtually isolated body of water, which is why even 200 metres (650 ft) below the surface areas are contaminated with hydrogen sulphide. It is also why there are few fish. Fish are found, however, along the coast, in artificial reservoirs and irrigation canals, and abundantly in the Caspian and Azov seas. The Caspian is home to the sturgeon, source of the sought-after black caviar.

Novorossiisk, southern Russia's principal port, is especially important now that Ukraine has become independent of Russia. Russia's military base in the Crimean port of Sevastopol is moving

Preceding pages: the Caucasus. **Left**, a wild iris blooms. **Right**, raising lambs.

to Novorossiisk, which also receives most freight and passenger traffic. Another vital Black Sea port is **Tuapse** where most of the Russian oil tankers berth. Black Sea ports are set to play an even greater role now that Russia wants to expand its trade with Turkey, Greece, and other Mediterranean countries.

The northern Caucasus has a solid infrastructure: good roads and railroads by Russian standards, plus the navigable Kuban river. The Black Sea ports are all connected by regular ferries. Air routes link the main Black Sea cities and resorts with Moscow, St Petersburg, etc. Foreign tourists arrive by plane or on cruise ships from Marseilles, Istanbul, Genoa, and Athens.

Balmy weather: Russia's most popular beaches stretch from Georgia in the south to the port of Tuapse in the north, 164 km (102 miles) along the Black Sea coast. The best known resort is **Sochi**, which, like the rest of this coast, is protected from the cold northerly winds by mountains. Here, winters are short and very mild, with only the occasional snowfall, though winter storms can cause the sea to flood the coastal railway track. Summers are very warm and sunny. The average annual temperature is 14°C (57°F). In winter the mean temperature is 6°C (42°F). The swimming season lasts from May to October with a mean water temperature of 24°C (75°F). The town has long been a favoured venue for Soviet and Russian leaders' meetings with foreign heads of state.

Cypresses, palms, and magnolias are just a few of the nearly 3,000 types of trees and shrubs to be found in Sochi. Some 1,600 of these can be seen at arboretum (**Dendrary park**). Only in Sochi will you find Japanese tangerines, Italian lemons, American oranges, Indian grapefruits and other exotic fruits all grafted onto the same tree. This unique tree was cultivated in Sochi's Mountain Horticulture and Flower-growing Research Institute.

Sochi boasts over 250 medical and therapeutic establishments: a result of Lenin's 1919 decree "On National Health Centres". By the end of 1920, **Water from the well.**

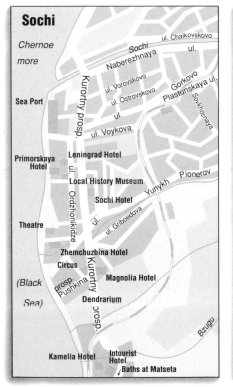

Sochi had its first sanatorium. Since then Soviet leaders – Stalin, Khrushchev, Brezhnev, Gorbachev – have considered it their duty to build themselves a *dacha* (country house) here. Indeed Khrushchev was on holiday at his Black Sea *dacha* when he was removed from power in October 1964 and Gorbachev was arrested at his *dacha* in Foros during the 1991 attempted coup. Autumn (known as the "velvet" season) is the best season in Sochi.

The resort enjoyed a building boom in the mid-1980s. One of the best known hotels from that era is the Intourist-run **Dagomys**. This world-class complex can accommodate 2,500 guests and includes several buildings reminiscent of resort hotels in Acapulco. The cuisine, entertainment and seaside walks are all first-rate. Lifts take you down to a beach lined with restaurants, bars and cafés.

More hotels line the main avenue, Kurortny Prospekt, including the **Zhemchuzhina** (Pearl), **Kameliya**, **Svetlana** (named after Stalin's daughter), **Leningrad**, **Intourist**, and **Aktyor** (Actor).

Here you may stroll through the wood created in honour of the 1975 US-Soviet space link-up (Apollo-Soyuz). The Prospekt begins at Riviera park, crosses several small rivers, and is crossed by the funicular running between the beach and hotels and sanatoria up in the hills and glens. Kurortny is the favourite avenue for leisurely walks; in the evening life shifts to its main restaurants and cafés, where merry diners can dance to the tunes of orchestras. The best eating establishments feature gypsy ensembles.

Sochi also has several casinos, video saloons, a theatre featuring acting troupes from all over Russia, an excellent circus, and cinemas. It has the added distinction of being the first Russian city to sell Pepsi-Cola produced by Russia's first Pepsi plant, built in Novorossiisk in the 1970s. Other foreign beverages available in Sochi include Czech beer.

Country pursuits: Most compelling of all, though, is the countryside around Sochi. Take the bus up to **Krasnaya Polyana**, just 50 km (30 miles) away

An abundant crop of tomatoes, but how many will reach the market?

and 600 metres (1,970 ft) above sea level. The ride is a pleasure in itself. Scientists believe people lived here as far back as the Stone Age. More recently (at the turn of the 20th century century), the area was a hunting preserve for the tsar and his family. Today, it's the **Caucasian State Preserve**, famous for its herd of bison.

Krasnaya Polyana is surrounded by snowy mountain peaks, at the foot of which are dense forests containing dozens of different kinds of coniferous and deciduous trees. You'll also find subalpine and alpine meadows, rushing rivers and waterfalls. The road up to Krasnaya Polyana snakes along ledges cut into the crags. Views are breathtaking if a bit hair-raising. Along the way, look out for two crowbars sticking out of the rock, a memorial to the workers who died while building this treacherous road between 1897 and 1899.

A fork in the road takes you to a place called **Medvezhy Ygol** (Bears' Corner), an allusion to the brown bears that roam these parts, alongside wild boar and deer. There is also a Narzan mineral water spring. The village of **Krasnaya Polyana** (Red Glade) was founded in 1878 by settlers who were struck by a huge clearing overgrown with ferns that turned red in the autumn.

Today Krasnaya Polyana has two large tourist hotels (1,500 beds each). Footpaths lead to an arboretum and the remains of the tsar's hunting lodge, and to river valleys and waterfalls. From the edge of the swimming reservoir you can see the snowy peaks of the central Caucasus. Also available to guests are gyms, a swimming pool, cinemas, a library, a billiard room, and hiking equipment. Krasnaya Polyana also hosts rock-climbing competitions. Anglers can fish for trout in the rivers and lakes.

Twelve km (7 miles) from Sochi is the region's main spa, **Matsesta**. In the language of the local Circassians, *matsesta* means "fire water". These sulphur waters turn bathers' skins bright red. They also cure systemic disorders, trophic ulcers, and skin diseases. The marble baths date back to tsarist times.

A riding lesson.

Twenty-five km (15 miles) from Sochi is **Khosta**, another spa with hot mineral springs. It can be reached by train, bus, or boat. The beaches are less populous than those in the centre of Sochi. Three km (1½ miles) inland is a forest preserve. Some of the mossier trees are as much as 800 years old. Here, too, are the ruins of an 11th-century fortress believed to have been built by Genoans. Nearby is a unique collection of cork oaks brought from Portugal, France, Spain, and Algeria.

Twenty km (12 miles) from Sochi is **Mt Bolshoi Akhun** with a 660-metre (2,165-ft) observation tower. Because of an optical illusion and the crystal clear air, the snowy Caucasus look almost close enough to touch (in reality they are over 40 km/25 miles away). You can also see Sochi from the tower and even the Abkhazian resort of Pitsunda. A little way from the tower are **Agurskie vodopady** (Agur waterfalls). Nearby restaurants feature the local Caucasian cuisine – so spicy you'll need lots of wine to wash it down.

Spa towns: Kavkazskie Mineralnie Vody (Caucasian Mineral Waters), an extremely popular resort region with access by plane, rail, bus, or car, has four main towns: **Kislovodsk**, **Pyatigorsk**, **Zheleznovodsk**, and **Yessentuki**, all connected by non-polluting trolleybuses. The area is located on the northern spur of the central Caucasus. Summers are warm (20°–25°C/68°–77°F) and long. Winters are mild, the sun shines nearly 300 days a year. Autumn is considered the best season. The marvellous climate, the dozen different curative waters, the lush vegetation and lovely mountain scenery have lured the health-conscious for nearly two centuries. Tsars, aristocrats, Soviet officials, and Russian actors, film directors and musicians have all come here. Today there are a few Intourist hotels as well as the sanatoria.

The region is also known for its abundant fruits and vegetables, dry and sweet wines, cognacs and, of course, drinking waters. Some of the waters are for bathing, others for drinking. There are over

A mountain wedding.

130 mineral springs, 80 of which are curative. They are reputed to improve the heart and vascular systems and the nervous system and to cure stomach ailments, gynaecological problems and skin diseases.

Pyatigorsk (Five Peaks), the region's oldest spa, was founded some 200 years ago on the southern slopes of **Mt Mashuk** (993 metres/3,257 ft). Most of Pyatigorsk's 110,000 residents are connected in some way with the spa, which has 43 mineral springs. Eleven km (6 miles) away is **Lake Tambukanskoye**, famous for the mud which slathers its bottom. This mud supposedly improves muscle tone and blood vessels. Users swear by it. Pyatigorsk has its own Balneological Research Institute where new cures are being developed.

Pyatigorsk is connected with the Russian poet Mikhail Lermontov (1814–41). It was the place of his exile for publishing a revolutionary poem on the death of Pushkin and where he fought his fatal duel. The people on which he based the characters in his celebrated

novel *A Hero of Our Time* all came from Pyatigorsk. There are several memorials to Lermontov, one at the place where he died. The **Lermontov Gallery** is located in the city's picturesque central park, which boasts grottoes, flowerbeds, and mineral springs. The gallery is a wooden building of original construction with four spires and a sloping roof.

The local museum has exhibits of flora and fauna but these are better viewed *au naturel* on the outskirts of Pyatigorsk, reached by bus or car. If you're feeling more ambitious, drive to the foot of **Mt Elbrus**, Europe's highest peak, 168 km (104 miles) away. The region is famous for its horse farms. Racing fans may wish to visit the local hippodrome (open May-September).

Kislovodsk (Sour Waters), located 40 km (25 miles) southwest of Pyatigorsk and 850 metres (2,790 ft) above sea level, is supposed to have the best climate in the region. Founded in 1803, Kislovodsk is renowned for its Narzan mineral water. In the local language, Narzan means "drink of the gods" or "drink of warriors"; it is used in medicinal baths. The town is surrounded by beautiful landscapes, including a 12-hectare (30-acre) artificial lake. Nearby is a strange rock formation known as the "Castle of Perfidy and Love". Here you'll also find the Caucasian restaurant **Zamok** (Castle). Order the delicious fresh trout.

Halfway between Pyatigorsk and Kislovodsk is **Yessentuki**, named for a local mineral water that is prescribed for stomach, intestinal, and urological disorders. Built in the early 19th century, the spa is known for its original Gothic- and Greek-style architecture and for its mud baths.

Zhleznovodsk (Iron Waters), the smallest of the four spa towns, dates from 1819 and is perched 630 metres (2,066 ft) above sea level. This spa was built at the recommendation of the famous Russian infantry general Aleksei Yermolov who fought in the Caucasian war. Visit the Mauritanian-style **Ostrovsky Baths** (1893), the Emir of Bukhara's turn-of-the-century palace, and the permafrost caves.

Left, a white-knuckle ride. **Right**, distinguished gents.

SIBERIA AND THE FAR EAST

In 1982, Russian geologists exploring a remote region of the Siberian taiga near Gorniya Khasiya, found a family of Raskolniki (Old Believers) who had been living in hiding since tsarist times and knew nothing of the fall of the tsar and the rise of Soviet rule. Such is the vastness of the great Siberian plain.

Exploring **Siberia** is a lifetime's ambition, not a vacation. But for a determined and hardy traveller, much of the flavour of this remote part of the world can still be savoured in the Russian and Soviet-era outpost towns that dot the vast Siberian taiga from the Urals to the Pacific, the Arctic Ocean to Mongolia.

Presently, there are no restrictions to prevent a foreign traveller from reaching almost any point in Siberia. And it is far more likely that a foreigner would be invited into a home than hassled about his or her camera, but both events occur. For this reason, it is important in Siberia to have all of your documents in order, including a visa that has been validated for all destinations. But be warned, even armed with the proper documents, a suspicious policeman who wants to cause problems is capable of doing so.

Travel in Siberia tends to take two forms: stop offs along the Trans-Siberian Railway and city jumping on Aeroflot jets and helicopters. Logistically, the first is far easier (as well as cheaper) while the second affords more freedom and greater access to the vastness of Siberia. But with the easing of travel restrictions, even more exotic excursions are also possible: deep tundra snow-mobiling, boat cruises up the Yenisey and Lena rivers with helicopter shuttle in between, and hunting and fishing expeditions.

Adventurous travelling requires careful planning, with the help of private Russian travel agencies. Such agencies – some good, some bad, many simply incompetent – are a new phenomenon to a tourism industry that was until recently rigidly controlled by the KGB-managed Intourist. In Siberia, the best of the new agencies are located in Irkutsk where a steady stream of tourists to Lake Baikal has spawned a more sophisticated type of travel agent.

Finally, be warned. Where amenities are concerned Siberia makes Moscow seem like Paris. Many towns have no restaurants or hotel rooms. Russia is gradually trying to improve its services for tourists, but change is slow, and even slower in Siberia. A dose of patience is as important to a traveller as bottled water.

The region's geography: Covering 12.5 million sq. km (4.8 million sq. miles), Siberia is a geo-political invention rather than a physical, geographical identity. The name Siberia comes from the Mongolian word *sibi*, which means sleeping land. It encompasses a wide range of terrain, related by little more than the remoteness of European Russia to the west and China and Mongolia to the south. The Buryats in desert-like Ulan Ude consider themselves residents of Siberia just as much as the Yakuts living near the Bering Strait.

Preceding pages: an effective way to travel. **Left,** Nentsy mother and child. **Right,** Siberian tiger.

A journey from west to east Siberia starts at the rolling Urals and passes immediately on to the great primeval forests of the taiga. The taiga is almost equal in size to the whole of Western Europe. It stands pretty much as it has for millions of years, since logging is economically impractical in the remote forests. Only along the riverbanks have trees been felled. Further east is the Ob River, Russia's longest river (5,410 km/ 3,362 miles), and the first of a network of rivers flowing north to the Arctic Sea. The other key rivers of Siberia are, in the order west to east, the Yenisey, the Angara and the Lena.

To the south of the taiga is the world's biggest bog, the Urmany. The region has some of the richest oil reserves in the world, which, together with oil rigs in the North Sea, once accounted for 95 percent of the Soviet Union's hard currency earnings. Foreign oil workers are beginning to explore the region, but for the most part the work is being done by outdated Soviet-era equipment and Russian workers. Roads cannot be built over the soft ground, nor can railroad tracks be laid.

Further east is Lake Baikal, "the Pearl of Siberia", and the boundary between Siberia and the Russian Far East. To the north, Siberia hugs the Arctic Circle, passing over the diamond-rich region of Yakutia on to the Bering Strait. Technically, Siberia peters out on the island of Big Diomede, within sight of the US island of Little Diomede, seven time zones away from where it starts

A little history: Though sporadic fur-trading was underway by the 11th century, the process of "opening" Siberia to Russia did not really begin until 1552 – the year Ivan the Terrible liberated Kazan from the Tartars and created a gateway for Russian expansion.

Siberia has endured two great waves of exploration and settlement. The first occurred during the expansion of tsarist Russia, when Russian explorers reached the coast of California. Expansion was characterised by brutal suppression of native peoples followed by waves of exiles and serfs seeking freedom. The

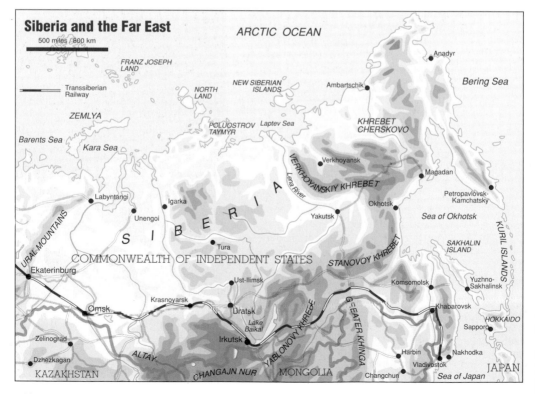

explorer credited with doing most to open up Siberia is the Cossack Yermak, an outlaw who travelled with a band of mercenaries in the hope of winning the tsar's favour and pardon. Yermak was killed in 1564, but not before founding the fortress of Tomolosk on the river Ob. Successive explorers and settlers continued to arrive right up to the Bolshevik Revolution of 1917.

But the greatest wave of Siberian settlement came with Josef Stalin's first Five-Year Plan in 1929, which called for the rapid transformation of Russia from an agrarian to an industrial society. This daring, ultimately brutal, programme led to the founding of thousands of small and medium-sized industrial towns across Siberia and the Urals.

Industrial expansion led to ecological disasters for many regions, as improper care was taken to guard the delicate environment. Today, Siberia is littered with leaky oil pipelines, ill-conceived reservoirs, nuclear waste disposal sites, and blighted by short sighted logging and thousands of smoke-spewing facto-

On the Trans-Siberian Railway.

ries. The only thing that has protected Siberia from ruin is its vastness. Even Soviet-era recklessness could not destroy something as large as Siberia.

During this period of settlement, enthusiastic young Communists (*Komsomol*) were encouraged to go to Siberia to work on one of the hundreds of large industrial projects designed to transform Russia into a modern, industrial power. To this day, the most disillusioned ex-Communist will speak fondly of those heady days of building the great society in Siberia.

The Trans-Siberian Railway: The world's longest continuous train journey, the Trans-Siberian Railway (in Russian "The Great Siberian"), crosses seven times zones and 9,299 km (5,778 miles) from Moscow to Vladivostok, passing from a stretch across the north Gobi Desert to a 4,000-metre (13,125-ft) high mountain pass in the remote Amur Mountains. It actually comprises three routes: the Trans-Siberian, the Trans-Mongolian and the Trans-Manchurian railways, the last two making

the connection to Beijing (for details of routes and facilities, see *Travel Tips*).

The railway was built as Russia's answer to Western Europe's commercial shipping fleets and to break their monopoly on trade with the Orient. Tsar Alexander III dreamed of creating a faster route to the Orient, which could also transport more goods. Due to political upheavals at home and abroad, this aim was never achieved, but the Trans-Siberian railway did support Russia's expansion into Central Asia and allowed it to keep a grip on its Far East holding as far south as Vladivostok. The ability of Russia to transport troops and weapons quickly to these remote regions allowed the country to become the world's largest empire.

Construction began in 1891 with Tsar Nicholas II laying the first stone. At the time, it was the world's most ambitious engineering project. Dozens of tunnels and hundreds of bridges were built. The entire stretch from St Petersburg to Vladivostok was finished in 1903.

Natural advantages: A trip to Siberia is not complete without seeing the "Pearl of Siberia," Lake Baikal, 66 km (41 miles) from the town of Irkutsk (on the Trans-Siberian Railway). One of the world's great lakes, Baikal is more than simply Siberia's top tourist attraction – it is a force of nature. For once, Russian statistics are not gratuitous. The lake's area is roughly the size of Belgium. It holds 20 percent of the world's fresh water and its maximum depth plunges to 1,637 metres (5,370 ft). More than 300 rivers feed the lake, but just one empties it, the Angara River. Its age, 20 million years, means it was already ancient when humans were living in trees.

Lake Baikal offers so many endemic species (1,500) and so much geological diversity that the study of the lake has created a new scientific discipline: Baikology. Fifty-two species of fish inhabit the waters, plus 250 different species of shrimp. Among the more interesting fish species is the golomyanka, which lives 1 to 1.5 km (up to a mile) below the surface and gives birth to living young.

On the shore of Lake Baikal.

But perhaps the most popular of Baikal's indigenous species is the nerpa, or Baikal seal. The world's only fresh water seal, it lives only in Lake Baikal. Its nearest living relative is the Arctic Ringed Seal, which inhabits waters over 4,830 km (3,000 miles) away to the north. How the nerpa came to live in Lake Baikal is one of Baikology's great mysteries. The prevailing theory is that the seal became trapped in the lake following the retreat of the last Ice Age. The seal then adapted to the fresh water environment of its new home. Today, the grey-coloured seal is a protected species, but Russian authorities still allow 6,000 to be killed each year for their fur and blubber.

The Baikal climate is ideal for mink and sable, and fur farms dot the area around the lake. Live trapping of mink, sable, fox and beaver is also common in the area. The first snow appears in early October, with the lake freezing over by the New Year. The ice can be up to 10 metres (30ft) in depth – so thick that during the 1904 Russo-Japanese War the Russians were able to lay railroad track across the lake and transport locomotives to the front. The ice begins to break up in May and is totally gone by June. In the summer, Baikal is warm enough for swimming, and several fine beaches attract bathers. The best beaches are located near the entrance to Olkhon Island on the lake's west shore, about 1½ hours by car from Irkutsk.

No matter what season, weather on Baikal is unpredictable. The lake is ruled by a micro-climate in which storms may rise and fall without passing over the shoreline. Weather often bears little relation to that in Ulan-Ude or Irkutsk. Even on the lake, it may change drastically in minutes.

The best time to visit Lake Baikal is August. Tourist facilities on the lake continue to improve, with helicopter rides, ferry boat crossings, shoreside restaurants, horseback riding, troika rides and ski and skate rental all on offer. Arrangements can be made from Ulan-Ude and Listvyanka, though Irkutsk is the best launching point for

Winter weather.

trips to Lake Baikal (it has the best hotel – the Intourist – and restaurants in the region, well-trained tourism personnel and a large supply of translators, guides, mini-vans and travel packages for exploration of the lake). Some people prefer to stay on the lake's shores in Listvyanka, but this isolated location leaves little to do once the sun sets. (For options on accommodation on and around Lake Baikal, see *Travel Tips*.)

Port Baikal is a charming Baikal village, a former crossroads on a now-dead end line of the Trans-Siberian. Timber, coal and sand from around the lake is ferried to the port where it is loaded onto rail cars which leave once a day. There are no tourist facilities to speak of, but a stroll through the town gives a delightful sense of what life on Baikal is like for the locals.

Irkutsk is arguably the most appealing Siberian city and the one best developed to accommodate tourists, mainly as a result of being the main launching point for excursions to Lake Baikal. It is located along the Angara River, 66 km (41 miles) from the lake, about 30 minutes by car.

It was founded in 1662 as a place of exile on the crossroads to Mongolia and China. Its most famous residents were the Decembrists, who were exiled there following an unsuccessful coup against the tsar in December 1825. A museum dedicated to the Decembrists is located on Ulitsa Dzherzhinskaya in the centre.

For many years a centre of the defence industry, the city is undergoing enormous change as it retools itself in the post-Cold War period. Tourism is seen as a possible saviour for the depressed region. The fur trade, the timeless Siberian standby, is also growing in importance. Irkutsk's largest factories are a tannery, shoe and fur factory. Other industries include heavy machinery, timber and building materials. The population is a comfortable mixture of Russians and assorted tribes, including about 20 per cent Buryats, the Mongolian Buddhist descendants who settled Lake Baikal's southern shore.

The city has expanded to cover both

Local History Museum, Irkutsk.

banks of the Angara River, but the historical and commercial centres are located on the west bank. The layout is easy to grasp, with two main cross streets: Ulitsa Lenina and Ulitsa Karla Marksa. Though the central districts are characterised by the usual Soviet-era concrete ghetto blocks and monuments to the Great Patriotic War, the older outer districts still feature wood frame homes – even Russian log *izbas*.

A beautiful riverside park has been constructed along Ulitsa Gagarina, directly across from the Intourist Hotel, and this is the best starting point for a tour of the city. Begin at Ulitsa Karla Marksa and proceed to the bridge at the city's promenade. Looping back, take Ulitsa Lenina, making sure you stop by at the city's central market. This four-storey indoor bazaar of clothing, electronics and other soft goods draws Siberians from hundreds of miles away.

A coal miner takes a break.

What little shopping exists in Irkutsk can be found between the central market and Ulitsa Karla Marksa. From Ulitsa Karla Marksa, proceed back to the river,

passing the delightful Local History Museum, across from the large concrete obelisk.

All tourist assistance can be found at the Intourist office located in the Intourist Hotel, on the first floor to the right of the reception desk. Here you can arrange tours to Lake Baikal, as well as make dinner reservations and purchase tickets for train and plane.

Rich pickings: At the centre of the Kuzbass (Kuznetsk Basin) coal-mining region, **Kemerova** is politically and economically critical to Russia. It is the prime supplier of the country's coal. Founded in 1918, the modern Soviet-era city is now ringed by seven large coal mines, which in one way or another employ nearly every inhabitant in the town. Large wage concessions won first from Mikhail Gorbachev and later from Boris Yeltsin have made the city relatively prosperous.

The only reason to come to Kemerovo is to see a genuine Russian coal mine (the mines are working mines, not tourist attractions, but a day trip can be

arranged privately with a taxi driver outside the Kuzbass hotel and should cost no more than about $25), but the city has a fine museum of the nature, history, architecture and ethnology of the region and it is possible to arrange a train trip from here across the taiga to the nature preserve 50 km (31 miles) outside of Tomsk. (In 1992 a Moscow firm began to expand the preserve into an open-air museum dedicated to the life, culture and nature of south Siberia. No completion date for the project has yet been set.)

Siberia's second largest city, **Omsk**, is also one of its oldest. It was founded in 1716 as a fort city and later became a place of exile. Among those banished here was Dostoyevsky, who spent four years in Omsk. Until the 18th century, Omsk traders also supplied Asian markets with slaves, which were kept on Katonsky Ostrov (Katon Island) until they could be sold.

Two forts can still be visited: the **Stary Krepost** (old fort), which was built in 1716, and **Novy Krepost** (new fort), which was built by the Russians near the end of the 18th century. The 19th-century **Nikolsky Kazachy Cathedral** is also worth a visit.

Today, Omsk is the administrative centre of Western Siberia with a population of 1.2 million. It has one of the best museums of fine art in Siberia, featuring a collection of 7,000 works.

Intourist in Omsk offers day tours to **Tara**, a Siberian fort town founded in 1594 lying 300 km (186 miles) away. It is also possible to travel to **Krutinskiye Ozera** (Steep Seas), three beautiful natural lakes (Ik, Saltaima and the Tenisa), 200 km (125 miles) away. During the summer months, these lakes are popular among the locals as a getaway for hiking and swimming.

Wood and water: Founded in the late 1600s by Cossacks, **Bratsk** has been overtaken by progress – literally. The old city is now under the reservoir of the **Bratsk Hydroelectric Station**, once the largest in the world (Intourist can arrange a tour at a hefty price). New Bratsk, founded in 1955 as the logging

Homes built of local wood.

and wood processing centre of Central Siberia, is an ecological nightmare where production targets have taken precedence over all other concerns.

The world's largest paper mill is located in Bratsk and the billowing fumes from its stacks leave a smelly haze that can, on bad days, make your eyes burn. Logging is done on the surrounding taiga and then transported to the city for production. The extent of the ecological disaster is clearly evident on a drive out to the taiga. Winds whip over vast, denuded expanses of land: no replanting has taken place.

However, Bratsk is not without attractions. Before the basin that held Old Bratsk was flooded, workers transported all the historic buildings to a nearby hillside. The result is a wonderful **open-air museum** devoted to the woodworking skill of Bratsk's first residents. Several *izbas*, barns, towers and black-smoke *banyas* have been constructed here. The highlight is a beautiful church composed entirely of wood – including the cupola. Take special notice of the wood farming instruments. As a final testament to the settlers' mastery of wood, everything was built without a single nail.

Novosibirsk, Siberia's largest city, is the quintessential dull Soviet city. It was built predominantly as an industrial centre. Planners gave little thought to appearance, entertainment and general quality of life for residents. Indeed, the city is a virtual monument to Stalin's single-minded drive to industrialise Russia. The city's airport is Siberia's hub, and nearly all flights between Moscow and the Far East refuel here.

Attached to the city is the research centre of **Akademgorodok** (Academic Town), a once prestigious Soviet-scale think-tank that has been emptied by the brain-drain of the early 1990s.

Novosibirsk has the usual array of theatres and worthy museums, but one museum does stand out: the **Local History Museum**, which does an excellent job of documenting the history, geography and ethnic makeup of Siberia. It even includes the requisite woolly mammoth display.

Krasnoyarsk is one of the latest Russian cities to open its arms to foreign tourists, though it's hard to imagine there will be much of a rush. Founded in 1628 along the River Yenisey, Krasnoyarsk became a place of political exile. Today, Krasnoyarsk is choking in industry: iron, aluminium, heavy machinery and agricultural equipment are all manufactured here. The city scarcely knows what to do with foreign tourists: the pride of the town is the 18th-century **Pokrovskaya Tserkov** (Pokrov Church), located on Ulitsa Mira and Ulitsa Surikova. However, the city does have several museums, including a museum of shipping which includes the *Saint Nikolai*, the ship on which Lenin is supposed to have sailed into exile in Sekhushenskoye.

The new tourist office is also offering trips along the Yenisey River; outings to the Krasnoyarskiye Stolby (Krasnoyarsk Pillars), a striking rock formation; as well as hunting packages.

The capital of the Republic of Buryatia, and closed to foreigners until

Carved lintel.

1988, **Ulan-Ude** is beginning to discover its identity. Perhaps no city in Russia today shows the diversity of the Russian empire better than Ulan-Ude. Buryat culture and language, which bear a close resemblance to those of Mongolia, were nearly extinguished under Soviet rule. Today, though 50 percent of the population has the appearance of Buryats, few except the old people can speak Buryat. However, more young people are beginning to show an interest in Buddhism. In 1991, the nearby Ivolginsk Datsan opened a school for lamas. Thirty young Buryats promptly signed up. The Dalai Lama himself made three trips to Ulan-Ude from 1989 to 1993 to encourage the re-education of the Buryat people.

Ulan-Ude is located on the badly polluted Selenga River, which winds its way through Mongolia and eventually empties into Lake Baikal. To the south, a desert stretches to the Mongolian border. To the north a range of mountains frames the southern shore of Lake Baikal, about three hours away by car.

Architecturally, Ulan-Ude is laid out like the archetypal Soviet city. The central square, an enormous stretch of empty asphalt, is overlooked by what is surely the biggest head of Lenin in the world. On the outskirts, wooden homes are common, reminders of the city's status as a Cossack frontier town.

Seat of Buddhism: The greatest attraction of Ulan-Ude is the Ivolginsk Datsan, the seat of Buddhism in Russia. The temple was opened in the 1960s ostensibly to show the world that religious tolerance existed in the Soviet Union.

In reality, it was all a charade. The KGB had secretly sent a dozen agents to Ulan Bator, Mongolia, to become sufficiently familiar with the rituals of Buddhism to open the *datsan*. The KGB agents enjoyed large *dachas* in the mountains and were driven to the temple each day in Zil limousines. In the late 1980s, however, the pretence became reality as more and more curious Buryats attended the temple.

The temple, modest by the standards of Tibet or other Buddhist centres, is about 30 minutes' drive from Ulan-Ude. The setting is splendid, with snow-capped peaks towering over the scrubby plain, and with a small mountain stream running nearby. Today, the temple may be visited by tourists without supervision. Follow the path running along the *datsan's* inside walls: the prayer wheel (spin it as you pass) is said to write a prayer 1,000 times for each spin. You may visit a service at the main temple, but keep to the rear of the building as the main part is reserved for the lamas.

Intourist arranges half-day tours to the *datsan* for $80 or more, but a taxi driver could take you there and back for a fraction of this price.

Vladivostok is sometimes called the San Francisco of Russia, a reference to its Pacific-side location and its steep streets. But that's as far as the comparison goes with this Soviet naval city, which was completely closed to foreign shipping between 1958 and 1991.

It was first grabbed from the Chinese in 1860 as the Russians pushed across the Amur River, and has since become the country's main port in the Far East.

A Buryat Lamaist monk.

Today, it is possible to stroll along the docks and freely shoot pictures of the naval fleet anchored here – a stark contrast to the days when a careless photo could trigger an international incident – but don't be surprised if a citizen begins to scold you for your presumption.

It is one of the few Russian cities interesting enough to take a stroll through. The twists and turns over the steep streets offer many beautiful views of the city and the Pacific Ocean. The climate is pleasant with summer temperatures reaching 20°C (68°F) and winter lows rarely dipping under –15°C (5°F). Entertainment is still lacking, but the night club, Zyolyony Lantern (Green Lantern), on the waterfront, is a raucous exception. If you want to go, make reservations early in the day.

Old Believers' gate: Siberia still has enclaves of Old Believers.

Volcanic isles: The **Kurile Islands**, a chain of volcanic islands extending from Kamchatka to the northern Japanese island of Hokkaido, would probably be unheard of outside Sakhalin if they were not the subject of a territorial dispute between Russia and Japan. The dispute centres on the south Kuriles – Kunashir, Shikotan, Iturup and a cluster of uninhabited islands – which Japan claims and calls its Northern Territories, but which Russia took in the final hours of World War II.

The islands are stunningly beautiful, with towering volcanoes sloping into violent seas. The Russians have done very little to develop the islands, save for creating a number of fishing villages and a naval base on Shikotan. As the only civilian airport was closed for repairs in 1991, there remains no way of getting to the islands except by ship. The trip takes 1½ days from the closest port, Korsakov on the island of Sakhalin, south of Yuzhno-Sakhalinsk. Ships also leave daily from Vladivostok, but take three days. Departure schedules depend on season, weather and passenger interest. Cashiers will not sell foreigners a ticket on a ship without a special visa. These must be obtained from the OVIR office in Vladivostok or Yuzhno-Sakhalinsk.

With a population of 6,000, **Yuzhno-**

Kurilsk, a fishing village on the island of Kunashir, is the capital of the Kurile chain, and the most accessible destination in the group. At its southern tip, the island is within 12 km (7 miles) of Japan, whose hills are clearly visible from most points on the island. The village itself is little more than a maze of rickety huts and a fishing plant. Mud streets snake up and down the steep slopes on which the village was built. Overall, there is a strong sense of residents simply camping out, though many of them have been Kurilchani for more than 25 years.

The island has a small museum of natural history, located near the mayor's office in the town square. At the entrance a Japanese face is carved into a stone, a compelling reminder of the island's former landlords.

From Yuzhno-Kurilsk it is possible to arrange boat trips to nearby **Shikotan**. The most beautiful island in the chain and with a sunny micro-climate, this is where residents of the Kuriles go to enjoy themselves.

Russia's Alaska: The island of **Sakhalin** has long held an exotic allure for Russians as a remote land of possibilities. With an area of 74,000 sq. km (28,570 sq. miles) and rich in natural resources like oil, natural gas and non-ferrous metals, it is Russia's Alaska. Passed back and forth between Japan and Russia during the 19th and 20th centuries, Russia finally occupied all of Sakhalin in the final days of World War II.

Currently, Sakhalin is one of the few free trade zones that is actually working. This injection of entrepreneurism is evident at the airport in Yuzhno-Sakhalinsk, which is modern by Russian standards, as well as in the city's many well-stocked commercial stores. A great many of the cars are right-hand drive, indicative of the growing trade with Japan.

The capital of **Yuzhno-Sakhalinsk** was founded in 1881 at the base of what is now known as Mount Bolshevik. Surrounding the city are virgin forests blanketing mountainous terrain, which provide a spectacular backdrop. Unfortunately, the appearance of the city does not live up to its setting. Typical Soviet concrete apartment blocks dominate the city, making it possible to believe you are eight time zones to the west in a Moscow suburb.

It is difficult to imagine what would draw a foreign tourist to **Magadan**, a remote gulag centre in northeast Siberia: winter temperatures can plummet to –65°C (–85°F) and even in July temperatures rarely exceed 12°C (53°F) and can drop rapidly at night. It was first named on maps in 1939 – its history before that is scant – and it relies on building materials manufacture and a small fishing industry.

Hardy swimmers looking for something exotic might take a dip at **Arctic Beach**, where water temperatures reach 3–6 °C (37–42°F) during the summer.

Settlement in **Yakutsk** dates from the first wave of Russian exploration, in this case 1632. Like most outposts of its kind it was founded by Cossacks, working to please the tsar, who permitted them freedom in an empire of serfs. Later, it became one of the most cruel

Prisoner in Sakhalin, 1894.

places of exile, notorious for its brutal cold (winter temperatures can plunge to –70°C or –94°F). The city might have remained a simple outpost had it not been for the discovery of enormous mineral riches in the region – including diamonds. Today Yakutsk (population 150,000) is capital of the Yakutia Republic, a swatch of Far Northern Siberia covering over 2.6 million sq. km (1 million sq. miles).

For the tourist, Yakutsk offers an excellent base for exploring the native Yakut and Evenki villages on the tundra. Intourist offers bus trips and helicopter trips to the villages. Because of the cold climate, the best time to visit is between June and August. Try to be in Yakutsk on 25 June, when the city hosts the Ysykh festival, a colourful celebration of native Yakut culture.

Otherwise, Yakutsk is a dull Soviet city, but it has a fine museum of "North Peoples", providing a glimpse of how Yakutia's native peoples lived before the Soviet era. Included is a display of mammoths. The museum is near Ordz-

Natural gas plant.

honikidze Square at Prospekt Lenina, 5/2, in the city centre.

Intourist offers several expensive package tours from Yakutsk. You can take a hydrofoil to Lenskiye Stolby (Lena Pillars), giant rock formations about an hour upstream from Yakutsk. The price (approximately $100) includes a picnic. City tours, cruises on the river Lena and a trip to "Derevnaya Yakutsk", the old village of Yakutsk, are also offered. A tour of the city's Permafrost Research Institute provides an offbeat but interesting Intourist excursion.

Nakhodka was a Soviet-era solution to the problem of closing Vladivostok to foreign shipping in the 1950s. Until the opening of Vladivostok, Nakhodka was the commercial port, while Vladivostok was the naval port. As Vladivostok re-emerges as the dominant Far Eastern port in both sectors, Nakhodka will have to fall back on its fishing industry. Before Vladivostok opened, Nakhodka was the end of the Trans-Siberian railway line. From here foreigners caught ships to Japan and elsewhere.

Belorussia and The Ukraine

125 miles / 200 km

Simbirsk

Volga

Engels

Saratov

Volgo-gradskoje Wdchr.

Kamyschin

Volga

Volgograd

Pjatigorsk

Saransk

Pensa

Zimljanskoje Wdchr.

Stavropol

Arsamas

RUSSIA

Don

Manytsch

Don

Maikop

Murom

MORDOVIA

Tambov

Schacht

Rostov-on-Don

Krasnodar

Mitschurinsk

Lugansk

Taganrog

Lipezk

Voronesh

Lutsch

Novorossijsk

Rjasan

Oka

Severodonezk

Donez

Kertsch

Orechovo-Sujevo

Kolomna

Novo-Moskovsk

Jelez

Kommu-narsk

Donetsk

Mariupol

Elektrostal

Nog-insk

Serpu-chov

SREDNERUSSKAY

Slavjansk

Berdyansk

Moskva (Moscow)

Podolsk

Tula

Belgorod

Kursk

Kharkov

Zaporozhye

Melitopol

Kaluga

Orjol

Sumy

Poltava

Dnepro-Petrovsk

Crimea

Brjansk

Simferopol

Yalta

SMOLENSKO-MOSKOVSKAYA

UKRAINE

Krementschug

Krivoy Rog

Sebastopol

Yevpatoriya

Smolensk

Krementschugskoje Vdchr.

Cherkassy

Kirovo-grad

Kherson

Dnepr

Nikolayev

Vitebsk

Mogiljov

Gomel

Chernigov

Dnepr

Kiev

Black Sea

Orscha

PRIDNEPROVSKAYA VOS

Bobruisk

Kievskoje Wdchr.

Belaja Zerkov

Odessa

Beresina

Borissov

BELO-RUSSIA

Zhitomir

Daugavpils

Minsk

Vinnitsa

Dnestr

Chisinau

Constanta

MOLDAVIA

Khmelnitskiy

Prut

Danube

Vilnius

Baranovitschi

Rovno

Ternopol

Chernovtsy

Buzău

Bucharest

Panerezys

Lutsk

Ploiesti

LITHUANIA

Brest

Iwano-Frankovsk

Kolomyya

Brasov

Bialystok

Lvov

ROMANIA

Craiova

RUSSIA

Ushgorod

Cluj-Napoca

Kaliningrad

Warsaw

Radom

Rzeszov

Wisla

Debrecen

Timisoara

Baltic Sea

POLAND

Tisza

Gdansk

Torun

Lódź

Kraków

SLOVAKIA

HUNGARY

278

Ukraine and Belarus (formerly Byelorussia) were once commonly known as White Russia and Little Russia, a hint of the kinship which by inference made them integral to the Russian core of the Soviet Union. If only with hindsight, the collapse of the Berlin Wall in November 1989 was bound to galvanise independence movements in the Soviet Union's satellite states, but even so no-one – least of all the men in the Kremlin – expected the fragmentation process to extend to declarations of independence by Ukrainian and Belarussian Soviet Socialist Republics. Only then were skeletons heard rattling in their cupboards, and the truth dawned that the implicit solidarity of the three Russias took altogether too much for granted.

The defection of the two lesser Russias from their senior partner, "Great Russia", underscored differences which had previously been expeditiously overlooked. In the case of Ukraine, the disposal of joint assets in the divorce proceedings of 1991 proved to be extremely sticky. To begin with, there was the Crimea, a strategic peninsula on the Black Sea and coincidentally the Russian riviera. It became part of the Russian Empire in the 18th century, but in 1954 Russia made a symbolic gift of it to Ukraine to celebrate the 300th anniversary of Russian-Ukrainian "re-unification". The Russians were celebrating, but there were Ukrainians present who secretly regarded 1654 as the darkest year in their country's history.

In any case, newly independent Ukraine was determined to hold Russia to its word on the question of Crimean sovereignty, and the debate went on to consider the rightful ownership of the Soviet Black Sea fleet which was therefore based in Ukrainian ports. A large part of the Soviet missile arsenal, moreover, was on Ukrainian soil, and a disproportionate number of officers in the Soviet Army were actually Ukrainians, as many as 70 per cent according to some estimates. The argument was still going on two years after Ukrainian independence.

Belarus, it transpired, had a virtual monopoly on the manufacture of all sorts of Soviet domestic appliances, most under the brand-name "Minsk". Belarussian independence threatened to reduce dramatically what little Russia had at the best of times in the way of refrigerators, radios and television sets, agricultural machinery and so on. The parting shot was that the newly independent country would prefer to be called Belarus rather than Byelorussia, the former being the transliteration of its name (in Cyrillic) from what must now be called the Belarussian language rather than Russian proper. The fact that there was a technically distinct Belarussian language, and indeed a Ukrainian one as well, had been all but forgotten outside the nationalist circles which had shored them up in the face of remorseless Russification beginning in tsarist times.

Preceding pages: the trident is the symbol of Ukrainian independence.

Ironically, both Ukraine and Belarus have longer and initially grander histories than the Russian colossus which subsequently overwhelmed them. Both owe their origins to strategic geography, specifically rivers. Very simply, the Vikings (or Varangians) who opened up trade between the Baltic and the Black Sea in the 9th century rowed rather than walked, and the most convenient route was up rivers from the Baltic, the Dvina being the most heavily travelled example, which then put traders within porterage distance of the Dnieper for the long ride downstream to Byzantium.

The Varangians colonised the early Slav settlements along these rivers. Those on the first leg of the outward journey, the most notable being the principality of Polotsk, were the nucleus of the future Belarus. The Dnieper leg was dominated by Kiev, so much so that it was dubbed "the Mother of Russian cities". The early history of "Russia" was therefore written in these places, and it was only under the aegis of the "Mongol Yoke" in the 13th century and for 250 years afterwards – from which Polotsk and Kievan Rus were excluded – that "Great Russia" evolved in the northern forests with Muscovy preeminent.

In its heyday before the Mongol invasion, Kievan Rus had a place in the first rank of European states. Within a remarkably short time after Prince Vladimir's controversial conversion to Christianity in 990, Kiev boasted a cathedral modelled on and named after St Sophia's in Constantinople and 40 other churches of note. Three of Vladimir's daughters married the kings of France, Hungary and Norway and his successor-but-one, Vladimir Monomakh, married the daughter of Harold, the King of England defeated by William the Conqueror in 1066.

All but St Sophia's and a couple of hundred houses in Kiev were destroyed by the Mongols, and those of its citizens who decamped to the northern forests and into the subsequent Mongol Yoke lost all contact

Preceding pages: coloured lithograph of the Battle of Balaklava, Left, Ukrainian musicians, 1880. Right, Tartar women.

with the West. The size and splendour which Muscovy had acquired while hidden from Western eyes astounded visitors when they rolled up at roughly the same time Christopher Columbus went off in search of the New World. Ukraine and Belarus had not been so isolated. They lay in the path of a Lithuanian empire which eventually reached all the way to the Black Sea, while Belarus was also exposed to growing German influence on the Baltic coast, the channel of contact being the same rivers which the Varangians had used

to travel inland.

These foreign contacts were the decisive factors in giving Ukraine and Belarus their special characters. The Lithuanian empire was subsumed by Poland after their dynastic union in the 14th century. Belarus was absorbed into the Polish feudal system, which meant that the land was parcelled out among Polish land barons and worked by serfs according to the rigid pecking order of the system. Ukraine, the more remote and seemingly endless steppes, defied neat administration and remained an almost ungovernable Wild West, the refuge for disenchanted serfs, runaway slaves and outlaws who constituted the original Cossacks, their numbers swollen by fugitives from the outrages of Ivan the Terrible.

Poland, ever the ardent champion of the Roman Church, did its utmost to bring Ukraine within the fold but eventually settled for a compromise which recognised a local hybrid, the "Uniate" Church combining Orthodox and Roman elements. Come the Reformation, religion in Belarus was exposed to the Lutheran influence of the nearby Baltic Germans. Religious differences in Central and Eastern Europe resulted in the horrific Thirty Years' War of the 17th century, a full dress rehearsal for World War I, and they were as keenly felt in the three

Russias as they were elsewhere. The ancient antagonism between the Russian and Ukrainian Churches never quite abated, and even after the uniform religious suppression of the Communist era, the two of them were immediately snapping at one another as soon as they were at liberty to do so.

Russia had not long cast off the Mongol Yoke (in the 15th century) when it began to work for the "recovery" of Ukraine and Belarus, a recipe for conflict with Poland which by then regarded them as its own. It was Belarus's unfortunate lot to be the common battleground, as it would be again when Napoleon and then Hitler invaded Russia.

Therein lies the simple explanation for the singular lack of historical buildings in Belarus; poor Minsk, the capital, has barely had time to draw breath between successive military steamrollers. In any case, there was very little respite in the contest between Poland and Russia until Catherine the Great, acting in concert with Frederick the Great of Prussia and Maria Theresa of Austria, engineered the total vivisection of Poland during the latter half of the 18th century. Russia's share of the spoils was the greater part of Belarus and Ukraine.

The Cossacks: The long course of this struggle had the side-effect of turning disparate bands of Cossacks into something resembling a nation. Although on occasion they fought for or against either Russians or Poles with perfect impartiality, the Cossacks nurtured the idea of their own state, and it was with this goal in mind that an anti-Polish rebellion under Bogdan Khmelnitski in the mid-17th century ended with a nominally independent Cossack Ukraine putting itself in 1654 under the protection of the Russian tsar, the event commemorated by the massive Reunification Monument in Kiev and the occasion, 300 years later, of Russia's "gift" of Crimea to Ukraine. As far as the Kremlin was concerned, the union of Russia and Ukraine was set in stone in 1654 in spite of continuing Polish recalcitrance which resulted in Ukraine being split into eastern (Russian) and western (Polish) sectors along roughly the line of the Dnieper river. In the opinion of Ukrainian nationalists, however, the request for Russian protection in 1654 was the death sentence on the dream of true independence.

The Cossacks surrendered their fierce sense of independence to service under the tsars, although some bands did retain closely-knit identities for some time to come. The Zaporogian Cossacks provide the link with developments in Crimea. They remained largely independent of Moscow and retained with Moscow's approval one of their old habits, their private war with Turkey. With the settling of the Polish problem in the west, however, Catherine the Great felt able to tackle Turkey herself and was indeed able with the help of Alexander Suvorov, Russia's most successful general, to capture Crimea and thus secure Russia's long coveted access to the Black Sea. One of her more famous lovers, Prince Gregory Potemkin, was commissioned to make Crimea fit for Russian habitation.

The Crimean War: In the mid-19th century Ukraine's Crimea became the focus of a bitter war between Russia on the one side and Britain, France, Turkey, Piedmont and Austria on the other. The Crimean War essentially reflected the Western powers' distrust of Russian expansionism and in particular Tsar Nicholas's designs on Turkey.

The Allies expected a swift victory over Russia, but in the event it was protracted and hard won. One of its most famous episodes was the misguided Charge of the Light Brigade during the Battle of Balaklava, immor-

the two biggest asses in the British army, the Lords Cardigan and Lucan. Lord Cardigan misunderstood an order and sent 600 men straight into the barrels of Russian guns which lined three sides of the contested valley. Almost half of them were killed.

Another figure to gain immortality through the war was Florence Nightingale, whose noble nursing in the appalling conditions led to a reappraisal of military affairs throughout Europe and in the United States. A system which had reserved commission and promotions for men who could afford to buy them was abolished in favour of staff colleges and professional officers.

World War I was a severe test of the status

talised by Alfred Tennyson's eponymous poem, whose haunting refrain about the futility of the charge is quoted here :

> *Theirs not to reason why,*
> *Theirs but to do and die:*
> *Into the valley of Death*
> *Rode the six hundred.*

The 600 in question were the most brightly-plumed troopers in the British army – the "cherry-coloured pants" of 11th Hussars looked and fitted like a coat of paint – whose singular misfortune was to be officered by

Left, a 17th-century engraving of a Cossack. **Above**, nursing in the Crimean War.

of Ukraine and Belarus as supposedly integral parts of Russia. Aware of the undercurrent of Ukrainian nationalism, Germany courted favour by promising recognition of some kind of independent state, but of course this came to nothing with Germany's ultimate defeat. Instead, Poland, reconstituted at the Paris peace conference, nipped in under cover of the Russian civil war to stake its old claim to eastern Ukraine. The result was utter confusion, and after three years of civil war and no fewer than 14 changes of government, Ukraine was partitioned in 1922 along the old Dnieper division, the east remaining with Russia while the west was divided among

Poland, Czechoslovakia and Romania. For a while the Russian sector did reasonably well, but this was reversed by Stalin's collectivisation of farming, which resulted in a famine that cost 7 million lives. The ensuing wave of protest prompted Stalin to order his secret police to exterminate the educated classes.

The Eastern Front between the Russian and German forces in World War I split Belarus ideologically and physically in half. Nationalists yearning for an independent state nestled in Vilnius, the present capital of Lithuania then occupied by Germany, while a second group based in St Petersburg was, after 1917, pre-disposed towards the Bolsheviks. The two sides managed to settle their

lin's worst suspicions about Ukrainian treachery. The direct clash between Nazi and Soviet forces on Ukrainian territory was terrible – 6 million Ukrainians were killed amid total material destruction – but there was more to come as Stalin exacted his revenge after 1945. The combined total of war casualties and the victims of post-war famine and purges amounted to half the male population and a quarter of the females.

The Nazi-Soviet pact of 1939 envisaged a reunified Belarus under Russia, but this agreement evaporated with Hitler's invasion of Russia. Brest on the Belarussian-Polish border felt the full weight of the 178 divisions which Hitler committed to the campaign,

differences in order to declare in 1918 the "Byelorussian National Republic", a presumption unacceptable to the Polish and German forces which had continued to fight one another on Belarus soil long after the 1918 Armistice. Russia offered help on condition that the ensuing state came under its wing as the "Byelorussian Soviet Republic". This duly happened, but the soviet republic in question was reduced to little more than Minsk and its environs.

Stalin's heavy hand made significant numbers of Ukrainians and Belarussians ready to regard Hitler as a liberator. Entire Cossack units rallied to the swastika, confirming Sta-

and the resistance put up by a combined force of Russian troops and Belarussian irregulars had no hope of altering the course of events which saw Belarus behind German lines until the last stages of the war. The Red Army then moved in and the Soviet Republic of "Byelorussia", first mooted in 1918, became a reality.

The region's riches: Ukraine's role in the post-war USSR was second in importance only to Russia's. At 232,000 square miles (600,000 sq kms) and with a population of 52 million, it was a large country by European standards. The renowned fertility of its black soil accounted for nearly a quarter of Soviet agriculture, and its industrial contribution was of the same order. While the Cossack bloodstock bred a high proportion of officers for the Soviet armed forces, Ukrainian politicians carved out a niche in the Kremlin, the most notable example being Brezhnev.

Belarus, the poorest part of Russia at the turn of the 20th century, was paraded as the quintessential Soviet success story. Not only were its new industries conspicuously efficient by Soviet standards, but the people had seemingly followed the blueprint for Soviet Man, eschewing atavistic national instincts in favour of a standardised Russian language, atheism and sincere socialism. The fact that in 1990 a population of just 10 20 per cent of the population. In Belarus, the agitation was spearheaded by environmental concerns, and it was actually the Chernobyl disaster in 1986 that gave Ukrainians and Belarussians common cause. The doomed nuclear plant was about 97km (60 miles) from Kiev, and only the vagaries of the prevailing winds saved the Ukrainian capital from lethal deposits. Nevertheless, any number of villages had to be abandoned and vast tracts of agricultural land were made unusable. The radioactive cloud rose from Chernobyl and was blown twice around the globe before dropping the bulk of its deadly contents on Belarus, yet again the unhappy victim of a neighbour's malice or misfor-

million had no less than 13 billion roubles stashed away in private savings accounts was interpreted as evidence of contentment.

Conventional wisdom failed to take adequate stock of undercurrents in both Ukraine and Belarus. While intellectual dissidents made the running in Russia itself, resentment in Ukraine was channelled through the working class, notably miners. They were alarmed at the number of Russian immigrants, a total of some 11 million or roughly tune, as the case may be.

As Mikhail Gorbachev tried to salvage the remains of the Soviet Union under the auspices of the "Commonwealth of Independent States", Belarus dropped its bombshell by announcing that, on reflection, it would not be joining. Boris Yeltsin attempted to reach an accommodation with the independently minded Ukrainian leadership. The borders of an independent Ukraine, he said ominously, would be subject to review. On the other hand, an agreement would be as good as 1654 all over again. That, said the silent stares of the Ukrainians in the audience, was what they were afraid of.

Left, vast numbers were sent to Siberian labour camps after World War I. **Above left**, the ruins of Chernobyl. **Above right**, testing for radiation.

BELARUS

Belarus is, as it ever was, one of the busiest thoroughfares in Eastern Europe. Visitors arriving by road or rail from the West enter the country through **Brest** on the Polish border, the city which gave its name to the Brest-Litovsk Treaty by which Germany and revolutionary Russia reached a separate peace in 1917. Railway passengers get scent of Brest's moment of glory in World War II without leaving the station: a plaque commemorates the partisans who tried to resist the first step of Hitler's invasion of Russia in 1941.

An overpass from the station leads to a park with a war memorial over a mass grave. Another heroic action in 1941 took place in the Brest Fortress on the outskirts of the city, where the Russian garrison managed to hold on for six weeks. Their resistance persuaded the German army commanders that the main body of their forces would have to bypass Brest in order to stick to a timetable whose next objective was Minsk. The tables were turned in 1944 when German defenders were inside the fortress and under attack from the advancing Red Army. The fortress was reduced to rubble, but it has since been partially re-built and contains the Brest Fortress Defence Museum.

On leaving Brest, the road to Moscow passes through the **Belovezhskaya Puscha**, 210,000 preserved acres (85,000 hectares) of the kind of terrain which serves as a backdrop to the migrations from Central Asia. It has a herd of animals said to be the descendants of some ancient mammoth, the East European equivalent of the buffalo which once roamed the North American plain in countless numbers.

Kobrin was a town in the era of Polotsk, but it tends to be remembered now as the place where the Russian army managed to check Napoleon on 15 July 1812. Alexander Suvorov, the Russian general reputed never to have been

Left, **Brest remembers World War II.**

beaten, had an estate in the area which is now a municipal park. His house is the **Suvorov Military History Museum**.

Beryoza, about 60 miles (100 km) out of Brest, had one of the monasteries which served as a beacon of Roman Catholicism in Polish times. It later became a prison and, under the Nazis, part of a concentration camp. The journey continues unremarkably through **Ivatsevichi**, **Kossovo** and **Baranovichi**, the last the junction for roads going to Vilnius and Rovno. Dzerzhinsk was Koydanovo before being renamed after the Soviet secret police chief. Ironically, Koydan was as feared in his time as was Dzerzhinsky. He was the Mongol commander who was checked, if not beaten, in a battle at this site in 1241. At any rate, the Mongols withdrew to the north and Polotsk, left out on its own, began the cultural drift towards Lithuania, Poland and the Roman Church. Dzerzhinsky was born in the nearby village of Petrivolichi in 1877.

The capital, **Minsk**, important enough to feature on Abu Abdallah Muhammed's map in 1154 and once a contender for the title of the European Jerusalem, has been a massive casualty of war. Anything that looks older than World War II has been heavily restored or totally rebuilt, the exceptions being some 17th-century houses in Bakunina and Ostrovoska streets. The ruins of the 12th-century Zamchische Cathedral are the oldest relics, a memento of Varangian times when Minsk was an outpost of Kievan Rus and at the receiving end of Byzantine influence making its way up the Dnieper River. The Svisloch River flowing through the city made up part of the river grid which linked the Baltic with the Black Sea.

The partially restored **Minsk Cathedral** is 17th-century, built in the city during its Polish period when Poland and Russia were at one another's throats. The capital's other monuments are connected with the world wars, the most prominent being the World War II granite obelisk which acts as a landmark. The monument in Ratomskaya Street commemorates the Jewish dead in that

The Brest Fortress.

294

war. Whereas Minsk was once a predominantly Jewish city, the Jewish population of all Belarus is now only 1 per cent of a total of 10 million and dwindling through emigration to Israel.

Reconstructed Minsk has a number of agreeable parks and avenues. All were named after members of the Soviet pantheon – Marx, Lenin, Engels etc. – and at the time of writing the names are under review and almost certain to be changed. Foreign visitors usually put up at the Hotel Minsk which, for the record, is on what used to be Lenin Prospekt, effectively part of the main Brest-Moscow road.

East of Minsk on the Moscow road is **Zhodino**, a museum-in-the-making. It is quintessential Soviet heavy industry, where standing at antiquated assembly lines the work-force heroically churned out the wheels on which the empire ran. Such Dickensian enterprises enabled Byelorussia to achieve a favourable balance of trade with the other republics. A bit further on, about 60 miles (100 km) east of Minsk, is **Borisov**, so-named after Boris, Prince of Polotsk. It is on the **Berezina River**, where nemesis in the form of the Russian army caught up with Napoleon in his retreat from Moscow in 1812. The battle took place on the outskirts of Borisov, near the village of Studenka. Borisov is known today for its tapestries and musical instruments.

Orsha, a total of 350 miles (560 km) from Brest, shares with other Belarussian centres like Vitebsk an ancient history completely masked by an unimposing industrial appearance. There may well be more to such places than meets the eye, but international tourism had no place in Byelorussia's appointed role in the Soviet scheme of things so there was no infrastructure in place when independence was declared. Moreover, the sights which Western visitors might find interesting probably did not correspond with what officialdom thought was worth showing. Left to their own devices, independent Belarussians are bound to produce a different and very much more comprehensive list.

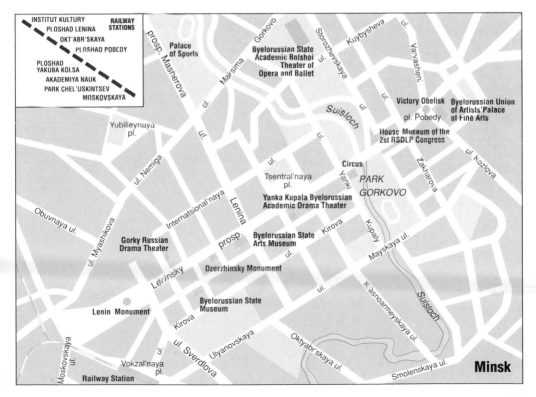

THE UKRAINE

The capital of the Ukraine, Kiev ("Kiy's great city", named after the eldest of the three brothers who, according to legend, founded the city late in the 5th century AD), has seen it all: Christian unification with Byzantium in 988, the Mongol invasion in 1240, Polish and Lithuanian conquerors (1363–1653), unification with Russia in 1654 and the vandalism of the plundering Nazi "priests of the new world" (1941–43).

Later still, the city was put within an inch of its life by the Chernobyl tragedy. The disaster happened in the spring of 1987, the terrible outcome of a policy which lacked both responsibility and principle, even though it was ostensibly oriented towards public welfare.

Chernobyl became a new frame of historical reference for Kiev and, probably, for the entire nation. They say that natural calamities and wars purify a nation's morals. The terrible effects of the tragedy made many people, in Kiev and in other towns, take stock of the past and present. Suddenly, people started paying attention to forgotten spiritual and cultural values, ecology, moral salvation and respect. Kiev is cleaner, and not merely because the streets are now watered twice a day.

Who are the people of Kiev, the inhabitants of the capital of the Ukraine? Most of them are Ukrainians. They are bilingual, but Russian is usually spoken, even in the homes. In terms of outward appearance, the people are similar to the citizens of Moscow or St Petersburg, except that the women tend to be darker and the men wear moustaches.

Ukrainian hospitality is evident to visitors from the moment they arrive. The town is pretty in any season. It has mild winters (it is on the same latitude as Frankfurt and Prague) and warm, sunny summers when the city is a sea of green.

The Golden Gate of Kiev: It is customary to start a tour of the town at its old centre, the **Verkhny** (Upper) **Town**. Unfortunately, the walls of the ancient fortress of the Polyans (an eastern Slav

tribe) did not survive. Of the few remaining fortifications from the times of Yaroslav the Wise (1019–54), the **Golden Gate** is the most remarkable. It has greeted many visitors, invited or otherwise. They say that Batu Khan himself entered the captured city through this gate. Today, its former glory fully restored, the gate once more hails the traveller with the glittering gilded cupolas of the gate church. Today, there is an exhibition of ancient Russian fortification here.

A little further up Vladimirskaya Street is **St Sophia's Cathedral**. The majestic 19-domed cathedral was named after its Constantinople counterpart (Sophia means wisdom in Greek). Its construction was started in 1037 on the site of the decisive battle of the Pecheneg War; for many centuries afterwards, it served Ancient Rus as the centre of religious and political life. It was in this cathedral that great princes were anointed and foreign ambassadors were received.

In the square in front of the cathedral

Preceding pages: interior of Kiev's opera house. Left, St Sophia's Cathedral. Right, gate of the Kievo-Pecherskaya Monastery.

is a monument (1888) to the great Cossack leader, wise politician and military man, Bogdan Khmelnitsky, who stood at the helm of the Ukrainian people's liberation struggle against the Polish overlords in 1648. In 1654, the Ukrainians gave the oath of eternal allegiance to Russia in this square.

Closer to the Dnieper, in the oldest part or the town – "the settlement of Vladimir", the man who baptised pagan Russia with fire and sword in 988 – stand the remains of the 10th-century **Desyatinnaya church**, the first Christian church in Russia to be made of stone. The church was destroyed in 1240, when the armies of Batu Khan conquered the city and burned it to the ground.

Another highlight in the old town is Rastrelli's **Andreevskaya church**. Rastrelli, the accomplished architect of St Petersburg fame, worked in Kiev, too. The single-domed cathedral with its five lesser cupolas seems to hover over the city. This is supposed to be where Kiy founded his settlement.

From the observation platform there is a magnificent view of **Podol**, another old quarter of the city on the left bank. The first chain bridge over the Dnieper was built between 1848 and 1853; at that time, it was the largest in the empire. Today, there are six bridges. New residential areas have appeared on the left bank in Berezniaki, Darnitsa and Rusanovka. **Gidropark**, overflowing with every shade of green, is loved by the locals for its sandy beaches, bars, restaurants and yacht club.

The Montmartre of Kiev: Andreevskaya church stands at the beginning of one of the oldest streets in Kiev – **Andreevsky spusk** (descent). In ancient times, the street linked the administrative part of the Upper City with Podol, the merchant and artisan quarter. Andreevsky descent is young in spirit, a street akin to Moscow's Arbat or Montmartre in Paris. It is a traditional place for outdoor fetes, film festivals and concerts. On holidays, the street is decked out in bunting and filled with dancers (*skomorokhi*), young painters and jewellers keen to sell to the holiday-makers. No 13 was the home of

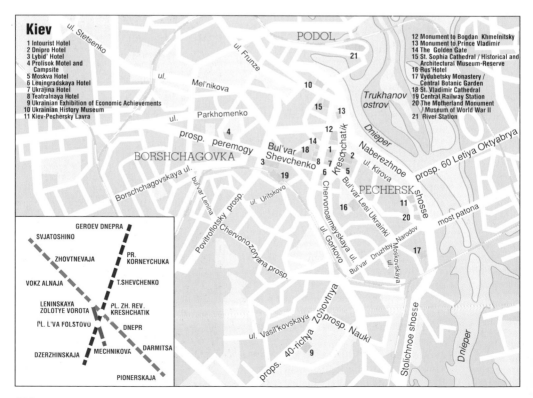

Kiev

1 Intourist Hotel
2 Dnipro Hotel
3 Lybid' Hotel
4 Prolisok Motel and Campsite
5 Moskva Hotel
6 Leningradskaya Hotel
7 Ukrajina Hotel
8 Teatralnaya Hotel
9 Ukrainian Exhibition of Economic Achievements
10 Ukrainian History Museum
11 Kiev-Pechersky Lavra

12 Monument to Bogdan Khmelnitsky
13 Monument to Prince Vladimir
14 The Golden Gate
15 St. Sophia Cathedral / Historical and Architectural Museum-Reserve
16 Rus'Hotel
17 Vydubetsky Monastery / Central Botanic Garden
18 St. Vladimir Cathedral
19 Central Railway Station
20 The Motherland Monument / Museum of World War II
21 River Station

the Russian writer Mikhail Bulgakov (1891–1940).

At the square of the River Terminal boats leave for trips along the Dnieper. Disembark at Kalinin Square, to go down to the Kreschiatik, or stroll along Vladimirskaya Street, with its modern architecture and hustle and bustle. The massive grey structure at the start of Vladimirskaya Street, isolated behind the "triumphal arch", is a symbol of Stalin's "triumphal progress of socialism". Straight ahead, the bulk of St Sophia's Cathedral fills the square, a blend of grandeur and simplicity.

Vladimirskaya Street crosses Sverdlov Street. The Golden Gate is uphill to the right. A little further down that street, is the **kenasa**, formerly a church of the Karaim monks, and now the Actor's House. At the crossroads of Vladimirskaya Street and Lenin Street is the **Opera and Ballet Theatre**, founded in 1863, which bears the name of the great Taras Shevchenko (1814–61). This theatre has hosted Fyodor Chaliapin, Ivan Kozlovsky, Titta Ruffo, and the

great primas – Maya Plisetskaya and Galina Ulanova.

A little further up Shevchenko Boulevard is **St Vladimir Cathedral**. Here, in the midst of a great modern megacity, the cathedral evokes the presence of distant Byzantium. Enter the rounded vaults painted with folklore scenes by the great Russian masters, Viktor Vasnetsov, Mikhail Vrubel and Mikhail Nesterov. Down the street, at the corner of Shevchenko Boulevard, Kiev's younger generation congregrate.

The small square before the university has been known since the 19th century for its student rallies. Demonstrations of the democratic front *Rukh* were held here prior to Ukrainian independence. It was Nicholas II who ordered the university to be painted red.

Directly down Shevchenko Boulevard is the Bessarabskaya Square and its main attraction, the **Bessarabsky Market**, built early in the 20th century in the style of Ukrainian Modern. The markets overflow with produce from the Ukraine. There are souvenirs and folk crafts, too.

Kievan woman in festive spirit.

It is here that the main street of contemporary Kiev starts (or, more accurately, ends).

Kreschiatik (derivative of the Old Russian word for baptism) probably owes its name to the baptisms of the 10th century, when there was a gorge here. The street was much narrower before World War II. After Kiev was almost totally destroyed – it compares with Dresden in terms of damage done – it was completely rebuilt in the 1950s and '60s.

In the early 1960s, the Kreschatik Restaurant, which incorporates a Metro entrance in its ground floor, was built, as was the 16-storey **Moskva Hotel**. The hotel faces the **Oktiabrsky Palace of Culture**, a venue for folk, classical and pop concerts. There's also the Central Post Office next door. When a portal of the post office collapsed in 1989, it killed 11 people.

This tour of Kiev ends at the **Dnipro Hotel**. From the hotel, Kirov Street takes you into **Pechersk**, starting at the old Dynamo Stadium, the home of Kiev's most popular football team. Not far away is the **Mariinsky Palace**, designed by the famed Rastrelli and built by Ivan Michurin in the middle of a park in 1755, originally for Empress Elizabeth, the daughter of Peter the Great. The palace is named after the wife of Alexander II, Maria, who had the palace rebuilt after a fire in 1819.

The caves of the ancients: Another must-see sight is the **Kievo-Pecherskaya Lavra**, perched on the steep bank or the Dnieper. It was founded in 1051 and expanded over the centuries. Yaroslav the Wise spent lavishly on churches. From the utilitarian point of view, the monastery was a valuable fortress, which saved the city during enemy invasions. It was rebuilt in the times of Peter the Great, who added a stone wall and assorted fortifications as defence against the Swedes.

The oldest part of the monastery, the Lower Lavra, comprises a series of caves (the name "Pechersk" derives from *peschera* which means cave). The subterranean galleries of the **Nearer**

Frescoes at the Kievo-Pecherskaya.

Caves stretch for over 1.5 km/4,920 ft, connecting cells, crypts and three underground churches. The monks found it advantageous to serve God without leaving their underground sanctuary. The walls of the caves bear inscriptions in ancient Russian, Polish and Armenian. The **Farther Caves** are linked to the Nearer Caves with a sheltered gallery; their length is 300 metres/985 ft. They say that in the old days, there was a secret passageway, which the monks used for exits.

Next to the Lavra, in the territory of the ancient village of **Berestovo**, there lie, in the 12th-century **Spas Church**, the remains of Yuri Dolgoruky, the son of Kiev's Vladimir Monomakh and the founder of Moscow. The monument was erected by the grateful people of Moscow to commemorate the city's 800th anniversary .

The monastery, naturally, has a steeple 96.5 metres (316 ft) high, with, incredibly, a clock that still ticks. The oldest buildings in the monastery are the **Troitskaya Gate Church** (12th-century) and the **Assumption Cathedral**, now in ruins. Most buildings in the Lavra date from the 18th century. They were built by Stepan Kovnir, a serf architect. To commemorate Russian Christianity's millennium, part of the monastery – the Nearer Caves and the Farther Caves – were returned to the Russian Orthodox Church.

CHERNIGOV: One of the oldest cities of Ancient Rus, Chernigov is about 140 km (87 miles) north of Kiev. It is a river port on the Desna and its tributary, the Strizhen. In 1990 the city marked its 1,300th jubilee. Travel agencies in Kiev offer one-day excusions here, but it is easy enough to get to by car along the main Odessa–St Petersburg highway.

Chronicles from the 9th century describe Chernigov as an important economic, political and cultural centre of Eastern Europe. In the 10th century the Emperor Konstantin Porphyrogenitus ("born in the purple room") included Chernigov on his list of the largest cities of Rus in his treatise *On Governing the Empire*.

The city stood on the historical "water-road from the Varangians to the Greeks", connecting the Baltic Sea with the Black Sea. Advantageously located on a merchant route, it flourished between the 9th and 10th centuries. At that time Chernigov was the economic and political centre of the strong Chernigov principality, famous for its considerable wealth and advanced culture. In the 10th century books were copied and schools and libraries emerged. Crafts, trade, construction and monumental painting were also well-developed. Chernigov's cathedrals and architectural monuments of the 11th and 12th centuries have been preserved to the present day.

The city's era of prosperity was interrupted by the hordes of Batu Khan in 1239. In the 14th century, Chernigov was conquered by the Great Lithuanian Principality, and at the end of the century it was ruined by the Crimean Tartars. The city began to recover only in the 14th century. Today Chernigov has a population of 300,000 and is an administrative centre. It is an industrial

Kievo-Pecherskaya seen from the Dnieper.

centre, too, known for its textile mill, chemical fibre factory and handicrafts.

The lives and creative endeavour of many Ukrainian and Russian writers are associated with the city. Taras Shevchenko, Alexander Pushkin and Nikolai Gogol, and the British novelist Joseph Conrad all spent several years of their lives here.

The approach to the city is dominated by the elegant **St Catherine Church**, built between the late 14th and early 17th centuries in the Ukrainian baroque style. It is built on the site of an ancient cathedral of Kievan Rus. The church commemorates the Cossacks of the Chernigov Regiment who heroically stormed the Turkish fortress of Azov.

In the centre of the city, at the Detinets, is a beautiful park named after Mikhailo Kotsiubinsky, a classic name in Ukrainian literature, who lived in Chernigov between 1898 and 1913. Architectural monuments from the 12th–17th centuries include the house of the Chernigov archbishop, a regiment's office and the Chernigov collegium, one of the oldest schools of higher learning in Ukraine.

The city's **Byzantine Cathedral of the Saviour** was built in the early 11th century. Its walls of brick and sandstone are handsomely ornamented. The interior is decorated with small frescoes of various colours. Ceramic amphorae, inserted in the vaults during the construction work act as resonant cavities and improve the acoustics. The cathedral was restored between the 17th and 18th centuries, but still looks much the way it did in the 11th century.

Towering above the park is the 17th-century **Boris and St Gleb Cathedral**. It was rebuilt several times and restored between 1952 and 1958 in keeping with the traditions of traditional Russian art. Nearby is the Bohdan Chmielnicki Boulevard, containing **St Praskeva Church,** a fine example of 12th to 13th-century architecture.

In ancient Chernigov, on the terraced Boldin Hills, a monk by the name of Antony of the Pecherskaya Lavra founded the monastery of the **Trinity and St Ilya**. The caves dug by Antony and his followers later formed a multi-level underground complex that later still became a monastery itself. In 1239 the monastery was destroyed by Tartars. It was restored in the 17th century and became a centre of book-printing. The **St Ilya Church**, the **Trinity Cathedral** (1679–89) and the 58-metre (190-ft) tall belfry built in front of the entrance to the monastery are well preserved.

Chernigov's **Assumption Cathedral**, the main church of the **Assumption Monastery** in Yelets, is 12th-century. The cathedral was partially destroyed in 1239 but restored between 1445 and 1499. Its interior includes 12th-century murals. The Chernigov **Museum of Fine Arts** has an extensive collection of 17th–19th-century masterpieces by Ukrainian and Russian artists, as well as West European art.

LVOV: Lvov is the most culturally diverse city in the Ukraine. Its architecture ranges through rococo, Renaissance, Gothic and baroque styles. At the apex of several European empires over the centuries, it has absorbed Polish,

Traffic on Lenin Street, Kiev.

Habsburg and Soviet characteristics. Yet, bizarrely, it is also the most Ukrainian of cities. It was here that the movement for independence found its greatest support: within the political movement Rukh and in the resurgent **Uniate Church**. It is the one city of Ukraine where Ukrainian is spoken as a statement of identity. Questions posed in Russian will very frequently be met with feigned incomprehension.

Moscow didn't exercise its control over Lvov until 1939 when it took the Galician region of eastern Poland as part of the Non-Aggression pact signed by Stalin and Hitler. The Soviet yoke never sat easily upon the region, and many Western Ukrainians joined a partisan army under Stepan Bandera which fought the Red Army until 1952 when it was finally subdued.

Background facts: Lvov was founded in the 13th century when a fort was established by Prince Daniel Romanovich of Galicia, an old principality of Kievan Rus. It has remained the chief city of Galicia, a district that retained its name until this century and its seizure by Soviet forces. Galicia was first taken over by Poland in the 14th century and adopted both Polish and Roman Catholicism, though the peasants stayed largely Orthodox. Many left to avoid persecution; the ones that remain established the **Uniate Church** in 1596. This acknowledged the Pope's spiritual authority but allowed Orthodox traditions of worship to continue.

In 1772, Lvov became part of the Austro-Hungarian Empire after the partition of Poland by the great powers and its name was changed to Lemburg. The city's bizarre ethnic mix surfaced when the Habsburg Empire began to collapse. Ruthenian and Ukrainian nationalist movements had emerged before World War I and when the empire fell there was a brief period of independence though no-one could decide whether it should be called Ruthenia, Galicia or Western Ukraine. Bolshevik and then Polish troops soon put an end to the problem and the Soviets found a new solution in 1939.

The band plays on.

The central part of the city follows virtually a medieval pattern, with large squares connected by narrow cobbled streets. It is roughly encased by four large avenues of which **Prospekt Svoboda** (formerly Prospekt Lenina) is the easiest one for orientation.

This has the neoclassical **Opera House** rising at one end and **Minkiewicz Square**, named after the Polish poet Adam Minkiewicz, at the other. Since independence, at the spot where the Ukrainian nationalist rallies were convened by Rukh, a statue of Taras Shevchenko, Ukraine's most famous poet, has been unveiled.

Just a short distance from Taras Shevchenko is the **Roman Catholic Cathedral** in Rosa Luxemburg Square. It was started in the early 14th century, but work was stopped in 1480 and it was never entirely finished. Much of the interior work, including the frescoes, was undertaken in the 17th and 18th centuries. The western Gothic tower, one of the city's landmarks, was finished in this period too.

To the southeast of the cathedral is the **Boim Chapel** built between 1609 and 1617 for Georgi Boim, a wealthy Hungarian merchant, as a mausoleum for his family. It is a beautiful example of early baroque with fine carvings on the west side, particularly of SS Peter and Paul.

Rinok Square, the old market square of Lvov, reflects the city's history. Every style of architecture introduced by its various rulers is found in its facades. Three of the houses – Nos 4, 6 and 24 – form part of the **Historical Museum**, open to visitors 10am–6pm every day except Wednesday.

No. 4, "The Black Stone House", was built for an Italian merchant in 1577 and features St Martin on a horse.

No. 6, "Korniakt", was also built at the end of the 16th century for a well-known Greek merchant who used his influence to build a specially wide house. It was later bought by the Polish King, Jan Sobieski.

No. 10, with the cannon and cannonballs, holds the furniture and **A quiet read.**

porcelain collection of the Lvov Arts and Crafts Museum.

No. 14 displays a winged lion, the symbol of Venice, whose consul lived here in the early 16th century.

No. 18 is one of the earliest houses (1523) and is extravagantly decorated for the period.

The most convoluted building, with influences in its lions and angels from both the Renaissance and German architecture, is No. 23.

No. 24 is the third part of the Historical Museum and has particularly interesting stone heads on the facade.

No. 29, an agreeable classical house, was built by rebel peasants at the end of the 18th century. They were executed as soon as they had completed their task.

The northern side of the square derives almost entirely from the 18th century. There are some wonderful gargoyles, in particular the grinning moustachioed face on the front of No. 41.

Leaving Rinok Square at the northern corner you come to the **Armenian Church**, which was founded in 1363 by Armenian merchants living nearby. Close by is the house where the resident Armenian Archbishop lived.

East from Rinok Square is the **Dominican church**, now the city's **Museum of the History of Religion**, and a fine example of rococo architecture. Further down Podvalnaya Street is the former Royal Arsenal and the City Arsenal, now the **Museum of Old Arms**, and, another monument to the medieval past, the **Gunpowder Tower** across the street. On the next corner is the **church of the Assumption** and the **Three Prelates Chapel** with the Korniakt Belltower rising in between, built with the money from the same Greek merchant who lived in Rinok Square.

At the very southern end of the street is the former **Benedictine Convent** which has the appearance of a fortress though it never was one. The main Uniate church, **St George's**, is a fair distance from the centre (on the way to the train station) but is a pretty, baroque sandstone building worth seeing, especially on a festival day.

Aboard the cruise ship *Taras Shevchenko*.

Lvov's other sights include **Castle Hill** (Samkovaya Gora), where the original fortress of the city was built. It offers good overviews of the city from the top.

The open-air **Museum of Popular Architecture and Life** in Shevchenkovsky Park, a couple of kilometres east of the centre, has over 100 old wooden buildings depicting rural life in Western Ukraine and is an agreeable place to spend a sunny afternoon.

ODESSA AND THE CRIMEA: Imagine the hissing and crackling sound of an old gramophone record, a sweet and tender melody and the soft voice of Leonid Utsov, a variety show and jazz great of the 1940s and '50s, and you may understand what Odessa, his hometown, has been – indeed still is – to generations of its residents:

A beautiful city in my dreams I see,
If only you could know how dear,
I hold its acacias, bright sun and
*   Black Sea,*
My message is loud and clear,
Odessa, I hold you so dear.

Though Odessa owes its name to the ancient Greek settlement called Idissos (wrongly supposed to have been built on its site), the city is much younger than Kiev. On 27 May 1794, the Russian Empress Catherine II issued a decree to found a new city on the site of a village called Khadzhibei: "Bearing in mind the advantageous position of Khadzhibei on the Black Sea and the numerous benefits that result from this, we have found it expedient to have a military harbour there together with a pier for merchant ships… All work shall be held under the supervision of General Suvorov, Count of Rymnik, who has been entrusted with the mission of building fortifications and all other military facilities in that land".

Odessa's youth is reflected in its character. Despite a harsh history – it went though enormous suffering in the 1941–1945 war with Nazi Germany – it is a lively, vibrant city: its people take credit for the country's funniest jokes and most popular songs. But the people of Odessa are also hard-working. The

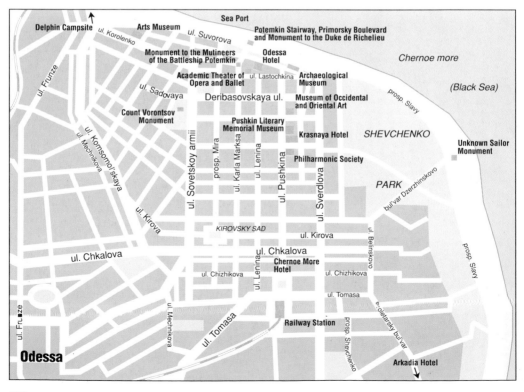

city is an important sea port with all the infrastructure that goes with it, and it is the Ukraine's major centre of industry, culture and science.

However, Odessa is best known as a health resort. Its recreation facilities receive more than 40,000 holiday-makers every year. Sea air, excellent beaches stretching 40km (25 miles) along the Crimean coast, spa waters and the mud baths of the Khadjibei and Kuyalnitsky coastal salt lakes provide excellent conditions for rest, medical treatment and leisure.

A walking tour: Start a city tour at the sea port, crossing Suvorov Street and walking the Potyomkin Stairway (designed by Boffo between 1837 and 1842 and named after Count Potemkin, who did a great deal for Odessa) straight to the monument to Armand Emmanuel, Duke of Richelieu, who was Odessa's first Governor. The monument was designed by Melnikov and Boffo. Local people call it "Our Duke". A walk along Yekaterinskaya – named after Catherine II – reveals more of Melnikov's and Boffo's work, a crescent of handsome houses (1826–33).

A right turn into the square passes the Odessa Opera and Ballet Theatre – home of one of the best companies in the world and an architectural pearl. The theatre – a splendid medley of several architectural styles (the Italian Renaissance, and the Viennese and classical baroque) was built between 1884 and 1887 by two Viennese architects, Gelmer and Felner. The three-storey building is decorated with sculptures of the muses. Its interior is an architectural feast: its five tiers seat 1,664 spectators.

Deribasovskaya, closed to motorised traffic, is Odessa's main street and a tourist must. There are quite a few old buildings, hotels and cafés and tourists from all over the world stroll leisurely back and forth.

The city centre has seven museums, all early 19th-century buildings that are architectural monuments themselves. The **Fine Arts Museum** and the **Museum of Occidental and Oriental Art** have particularly rich collections.

Northern Beach, Odessa.

The central squares all have monuments to outstanding scientists, statesmen and writers, including Pushkin in Primorsky Boulevard, Leo Tolstoy in the square of the same name, Shevchenko in the Shevchenko park and Odessa's Governor-General Count Vorontsov in Cathedral Square. Many buildings have memorial plates honouring important people who lived and worked in Odessa, including Tchaikovsky, Kuprin, Adam Michiewicz and Les Ukrainka.

Not far from Odessa, close to the Nerubaiskoye village, are the labyrinthine **Catacombs**, long galleries left by the quarrying of limestone, which were used by resistance workers between 1941 and 1942.

One of the best ways to see Odessa in summer is to take a pleasure boat to Chernomorka and back. This way you can take in the newly-built high-rise residential areas, the health resort facilities and the beaches of Longeron, Arcadia and the Golden Shore.

YALTA: At the heart of the Crimea is Yalta, the playground hideaway of the former top brass of the Communist Party. Rolling vineyards, roads snaking through mountains overlooking the teal-blue Black Sea, plenty of sunshine and relaxed, smiling faces account for its vaunted reputation. The area is laden with history, too. Sevastopol and Balaklava were central to the Crimean War, and Yalta itself was where Churchill, Stalin and Roosevelt carved up post-World War II Europe.

While political leaders argue over whether the Crimea is independent or belongs to Ukraine or Russia, savvy tourists flock to the palm-lush resort. Water-lovers can splurge and go windsurfing, water skiing and even yachting – all for roubles. Those wanting to stay closer to land can explore the main strip with its palm trees, bookshops, and fully-stocked shops, or sit in a waterfront café sipping either the local wine – which can be quite good – or pints of Heineken.

A trip by taxi or rented car into the surrounding hills is also recommended. Highlights include the perched castle, called **Swallow's Nest**, which was used as a set for the movie *Ten Little Indians* by Agatha Christie, and Tsar Nicholas II's **Marble Palace**, the villa where Churchill, Stalin and Roosevelt convened in 1945.

In Yalta it is almost possible to forget that the former Soviet Union ever existed – unless, that is, you are staying at the concrete monstrosity called the Yalta Hotel. While upscale by Soviet standards – hard currency stores, televisions which get CNN and Super Channel, bars, swimming pools and tennis courts – rooms are modest, at best. The so-called boardwalk by the pebble beach is one huge slab of concrete. Equally unattractive is the strong presence of Russian mafia.

But Yalta remains a great getaway from the hustle and bustle of Moscow. With a little bit of research ahead of time, it's possible to avoid the Yalta Hotel and stay in one of the posh sanatoria – now desperate for tourists. During summer months, it is even possible to return to Moscow with a deep Mediterranean tan.

Left, catching a tan. **Right**, the famous Swallow's Nest.

TRAVEL TIPS

GETTING THERE

RUSSIA

Until recently, foreigners could only penetrate Russia through special entry points whose number could be counted with the fingers of one hand. Although today the number of these "doors" is almost the same, all the procedures, including customs formalities, are now much simpler.

BY AIR

Over 30 international airlines connect Moscow's Sheremetyevo II airport with the rest of the world. Flights take about 9 hours from New York, 4 hours from London, Paris and Rome; from Frankfurt it takes 3 hours, 2 hours from Stockholm, 6 from Delhi and 8 hours from Peking. In addition to Moscow, some international carriers also fly to Pulkovo-2 in St Petersburg.

BY SEA

Several Russian ports accept international passenger liners. St Petersburg on the Baltic Sea is connected with London, Helsinki, Gothenburg, Stockholm and Oslo. Nakhodka on the Japan Sea coast is connected with Yokohama, Hongkong, Singapore and Sydney. Additional information about sea routes, schedules and bookings can be obtained from Intourist or Morflot offices.

BY RAIL

Railways are the most important means of passenger transportation within Russia and the CIS. Railways connect the largest CIS cities (Moscow, St Petersburg, Kiev, Minsk) with Western European capitals. Travellers who have the time can travel in a comfortable first-class sleeping-car, the pride of the Russian railways.

From Western Europe the train takes two to three days to Moscow, with a change of gauge on reaching Russia. The most popular rail routes for international traffic is Helsinki to St Petersburg (departing 1pm and arriving at 9pm) and Helsinki to Moscow (departing 5pm and arriving at 9.30am the next morning).

BY ROAD

During the past few years marked changes have taken place in the quality of services along Russian roads. Moscow now boasts new service and repair stations for non-Russian cars. However, you should still be cautious of travelling through Russia by car. Travelling by car can be dangerous and road borders take hours to cross due to delays at customs. Outside towns petrol stations are, on average, 100 km (60 miles) apart. You can bring your own car by sea through St Petersburg, Tallinn in Estonia, Odessa on the Black Sea and Nakhodka in the far east.

There are no international bus lines to the CIS, but special bus tours operate from the UK, West Germany and Finland.

BELARUS

BY AIR

Lufthansa was first off the mark with flights into Minsk from Frankfurt and Vienna. Polish Airlines also fly to Minsk.

BY RAIL

In addition to the traditional rail connections with Russia, there is an overnight train from Tallinn in Estonia.

UKRAINE

BY AIR

Kiev can now be reached through an increasing number of Western airlines, and these tend to be better value than Aeroflot.

Currently Austrian Airways and Lufthansa are the most regular flyers, although KLM, SAS, Malev, Poland's Lot and a Ukraine-based airline, Ukraine International, also fly into Kiev. The main airport, Borispol, is a 40-minute car journey from the city centre.

BY RAIL

A slower option is to take the train. From Moscow, Kiev is only a night's ride away. There are trains going almost every half-hour from Moscow's Kiev station in the evening.

BY SEA

Odessa on the Black Sea is on the itinerary of liners from Marseilles, Istanbul, Naples, Barcelona, Malta, Piraeus, Varna, Dubrovnik, Alexandria and Constanta.

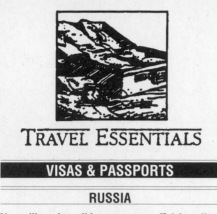

TRAVEL ESSENTIALS

VISAS & PASSPORTS

RUSSIA

You will need a valid passport, an official application form, confirmation of your hotel reservations (for both business travellers and tourists) and three passport photographs, to get your visa from a Russian embassy or consulate. If you apply individually, rather than through a travel agency, you should allow ample time, as it might take a month or so to check your papers.

According to the new regulations, this term can be shortened to 48 hours if an applicant is a business traveller or if he or she has a written invitation (telex and fax are also accepted) from a Russian host (bear in mind that it might take the Russian counterpart some time to have the invitation stamped by the local authority). However, fees for this express service are astronomical.

The visa is not stamped into the passport as is the norm, but onto a separate sheet of paper consisting of three sections. The first part is removed when a person enters the country, and the last is taken out when he or she leaves the country.

There are several types of visas. Transit visas (for not more than 48 hours), tourist, ordinary and multiple entry visas (for two or more visits).

If you go to Russia on the invitation of your relatives or friends, you will get a visa for a private journey which presupposes that no hotel reservation is needed. Independent tourists should have their trip organised through an Intourist accredited agent or their Russian hosts. They need an itinerary, listing in detail, times, places and overnight reservations. You should carry your passport at all times while you are in Russia. Without it you might be prohibited from entering your hotel, the embassy of your country and many other places.

Intourist hotels will give you a special hotel card that serves as a permit to enter the hotel and use its restaurant and currency-exchange office.

BELARUS

Visas are issued by Belarussian embassies abroad or on arrival providing you can provide evidence of an offical invitation or confirmation of booked accommodation through Belintourist (the Belarussian equivalent of Intourist). Currently there is a Belarussian embassy in Paris (tel: 45 74 14 23) and Washington (tel: 986 1606), but not in London. Fees fluctuate wildly. Transit visas are issued on the train to people who have a Russian visa and are travelling to Moscow via Belarus.

UKRAINE

Visas can be purchased at the airport for $50 without all the fuss and delay entailed in getting a Russian visa. This visa is a simple entry-exit visa valid for a month.

For those travelling from Kiev to Moscow, it is now possible to pick up transit visas to Russia from the Russian Embassy in Kiev, but this is a recent development and it is still advisable to arrange all Russian visas before arriving in Kiev. People have been charged over $350 for trying to leave Moscow on a Ukrainian visa.

HEALTH REGULATIONS

Visitors from the US, Canada, European countries and Japan need no health certificate. But for visitors from regions suspected to be infected with yellow fever, especially from some territories in Africa and South America, an international certificate of vaccination against yellow fever is required. If necessary, cholera and tetanus vaccinations may also be required. Visitors from certain AIDS-infected regions who are going to stay in Russia for a longer period of time may be subjected to an AIDS test.

CUSTOMS

When entering Russia you must fill in the customs declaration which must be kept as carefully as your passport during your stay on Russian territory. It must be returned to the customs office, along with another declaration which you fill in on leaving the country.

Russian customs regulations have been revised several times in the last few years. Customs authorities want to find a compromise between conforming to international standards of customs regulations and preventing the export of large batches of cheap goods bought in Russian shops for resale in other countries.

The latest edition of the Russian customs regulations prohibits the import and export of weapons and ammunition (excluding approved hunting tackle), and also drugs and devices for their use. It is prohibited to export antiquities and art objects except for those imported and declared on entry.

It is permitted to import free and without limitation:
1) Gold and the other valuable metals except for gold coins, whose import is prohibited.
2) Materials of historic, scientific, and cultural value.

3) Articles approved by the licensees of V/O Vneshposyltorg.
4) Foreign currency and foreign currency documents.
5) Personal property except for computers and other technical devices (see limited duty-free import).

Limited duty-free import:

1) Gifts with a total value less than about US$770. Gifts, highly appreciated among the Russian people, can be ballpoint pens, elegant business notebooks, calculators, electronic watches and other inexpensive items. You are recommended not to have more than 10 units of an article if you want to escape time-consuming questions from customs officers.
2) Cars and motorcycles approved according to International Traffic Convention, but no more than one unit per family and with the obligation to export the vehicle when you leave.
3) Spare parts of vehicles insured by the Russian international insurance company Ingosstrakh and approved by the documents of Ingosstrakh or Intourist (for other spare parts duty must be paid).
4) Medicines not registered in the list of the Russian Ministry of Health Protection must be approved by the Russian medical institutions.
5) Personal computers, photocopying apparatus, video-recorders, TVSat systems with the obligation to export (if the obligation is broken and the article is sold in Russia, duty must be paid).
6) Alcohol (limited to persons over 21): spirits – 1.5 litres, wines – 2 litres.
7) Tobacco (limited to persons over 16) – 200 cigarettes or 200 grams of tobacco per person.

Duty-free export:

1) Articles imported by the visitor.
2) Articles bought in the Russian hard currency shops or in rouble-shops for legally exchanged Russian currency (with some limitations – see below).
3) Food stuffs to a limited value (because of spiralling inflation, you will need to check current limits locally).
4) Alcohol (over 21): spirits – 1.5 litres, wines – 2 litres per person.
5) Tobacco (over 16): 100 cigarettes or 100 grams tobacco.

It is prohibited to export the following articles bought in rouble-shops: electric cables, instruments, building materials, fur, cloth, carpets, leather clothes, linen, knitted fabric, socks and stockings, umbrellas, plates and dishes, medicines and perfumes, sewing machines, refrigerators, bicycles, cameras, vacuum cleaners, washing machines, children's clothes and boots, all articles produced abroad, valuable metals and jewels.

Some of the customs officers are quite severe in their observation of these regulations. Therefore when you enter or leave the country, expect careful examination of all your luggage. On arrival, you will be asked if any personal items are intended for sale in Russia (if yes, you will have to pay duty).

WHAT TO WEAR

Today Russia is visited by visitors from many different countries and with many different styles of dress. Therefore the old guide-book phrase: "When going to Russia, follow a modest and classic style of clothes," is out-dated. You may dress as you would dress at home.

Coming to Russia in the cold months (November to March), you should not be surprised to meet temperatures of 25° to 30°C below zero (–13°F to –22°F). Waterproof shoes are a necessity in winter, since the legendary Russian frost is often interrupted by periods of thaw. For business meetings, formal dress is obligatory. The dress code is as rigorously enforced as in the West and compliance is an important matter of status.

MONEY MATTERS

RUSSIA

Rouble notes are now issued in denominations up to 10,000 and will soon go higher. New notes are constantly being issued to keep pace with inflation. Kopeck coins (in theory there are 100 kopecks in a rouble) have been withdrawn and replaced by tokens. In July 1993 it was abruptly announced that all old notes would cease to be valid currency.

Roubles can neither be imported nor exported to or from Russia. As a rule, tourists need few roubles as most hotels take only foreign currency. There is no limit to the import of hard currency, but the sum must be declared on entry. The amount exported should not exceed the amount declared when entering the country. Unspent roubles can be reconverted at the airport bank providing you show bank receipts which document the official (rather than black market) exchange you have made. If you intend to do this, count on spending at least half an hour, since there are always long queues at bank counters.

The black market continues to thrive despite the fact that the rates offered by the banks are often similar. The most active dealers on the black market are taxi drivers and waiters.

All Intourist hotels have an official exchange counter where you can buy roubles with hard currency cash, traveller's cheques and credit cards. You will need your customs declaration form, on which all your money transactions must be recorded. You will need this form when leaving the country and you should, as with your passport, guard it with your life. Most major hotels have bars, restaurants and shops where you must pay with hard currency, and these transactions do not need to be recorded on your exchange certificate. On leaving the country, expect customs to check that you have exchanged money officially for the goods you want to export and that you are not exporting more hard currency than you have imported.

Credit cards: Most tourist-related businesses and restaurants accept major credit cards. As new currency facilities for tourists are continually expanding, you should check up-to-date information with your travel company or a travel agent. American dollars are the preferred currency. If in doubt, try to take a credit card, loose dollar notes as well as traveller's cheques.

BELARUS

Belarus still uses roubles, though this will probably change in the near future.

UKRAINE

Ukraine is now outside the rouble zone and has a currency of its own, the Ukrainian coupon. At the moment this is worth a third of a rouble but is subject to inflation of almost 3 percent per day.

Coupons can be purchased at your hotel or on the black market, which consists of men holding little dollar or Deutschemark signs at practically every corner in the centre of towns. If you change your money on the black market, count it carefully.

When bringing foreign currency into the country, dollars are really the only option, though Deutschemarks are also usable. Bring small denomination bills.

GETTING ACQUAINTED

CLIMATE

Russia spans all climatic zones. It covers arctic and subarctic zones, where the average winter temperature is minus 50°C (minus 58°F) and where lowest temperatures reach minus 70°C (minus 94°F).

By contrast, in the Crimea and the Caucasus, summer temperatures of 45°C (113°F) are not uncommon. But then, the short subarctic summer can also be quite hot (around 38°C (100.4°F).

The main tourist routes lead through the European territory of Russia. This has a typical continental climate with hot summers (30°C/86°F) and cold winters (minus 25°C/minus 13°F). Maritime European regions are characterised by smaller temperature extremes, with comparatively mild winters (although not in St Petersburg and Arkhangelsk),

cool summers and hot summers, particularly on the Black Sea coast. The Caucasus has a lot of rain while, at the same time, the Crimean steppe and southern Russia suffers because of low rainfall.

Mountain regions include the Carpathian mountains in the Western Ukraine and the Caucasus, where the climate is similar to that of the Alps.

Mild summers, a rich vegetation and cold winters are typical for the Far East and Kamchatka; that region belongs to the Pacific zone of volcanic activity.

Average Temperatures:
Moscow: minus 13°C to 22°C, St Petersburg: minus 12 C° to 21°C, Irkutsk: –26°C to 22°C, Kiev: minus 10°C to 25°C, Odessa: –4°C to 26°C, Yalta: –1°C to 28°C.

TIME ZONES

Moscow time is GMT plus 3 hours. Officially, Moscow time is adopted nearly everywhere west of the Urals. Moscow time is also shown on the station clocks along the whole Trans-Siberian Railway.

When it is 3pm in Moscow, it is 7pm in Novosibirsk; in Irkutsk it is 8pm, in Chita 9pm, in Vladivostok 10pm. By then, the inhabitants of Petropavlovsk-Kamchatsky have just started a new day and the polar bears on the frozen Chukchi Sea are already a whole hour into the new day.

ELECTRICITY

Electrical current in tourist hotels is normally 220 V AC, but don't count on it. In some remote places you will also find 127 V. Sockets require a continental-type plug, but no Schuko plug. It is best to have a set of adaptors with you. The same is true for batteries. If your appliances depend on batteries, bring plenty with you – they might not be available in Russia, not even for hard currency.

TIPPING

Though the CIS has been Socialist for over 70 years, tipping, one of the capitalist sins, is still an accepted practice. Waiters, porters, taxi drivers, especially in Moscow and St Petersburg, have always appreciated tips. Ten percent is the accepted rule.

Do not tip guides, interpreters or Intourist personnel. If you want to show your gratitude they will appreciate a small souvenir or gift.

OFFICIAL HOLIDAYS

After the collapse of Communism many official holidays, of which there were many, either ceased to exist or were toned down. New Year's Day continues to be a big celebration, together with International Women's day on 8 May.

RELIGION

In Russia and the eastern region of the Ukraine and Belarus, the Russian Orthodox Church is the most influential faith. The western regions of these are under the influence of the Roman Catholic Church. Baptists, Adventists and other Protestant branches are also quite influential. Islam is the main faith in the Caucasus and amongst the Tartar population, mainly from the middle and lower Volga. In a country where anti-Semitism is rife, there are less than 100 synagoues. Many Jews have emigrated. Buddhism is practised by the Buryats near Lake Baikal and the Kalmyks of the lower Volga. Below is a selection of religious establishments in Moscow.

RELIGIOUS SERVICES

RUSSIAN ORTHODOX
Bogoyavlensky (Elokhovsky) Cathedral, ul. Spartakovskaya 15. Tel: 261-6913.
Troitsky Cathedral, Svyato-Danilov Monastery, Danilovsky Val 22.
Uspenskaya Church, Novodevichy Convent, Novodevichy proezd 1. Tel: 245-3168.
Voskresenskaya Church, ul. Nezhdanovoy 15/2. Tel: 229-6616.
Vsekh Svyatykh Church, Leningradsky prosp. 73. Tel: 158-5515. Services: Monday–Saturday 8am and 6pm; Sunday and holidays 7am and 10am.

GREEK ORTHODOX
Church of Archangel Gabriel, Telegrafny per. 15a. Tel: 923-4605. Sunday Mass at 10am.

BULGARIAN ORTHODOX
Uspenskaya Church, ul. Volodarskovo 29. Tel: 271-0124.

CATHOLIC
St Louis, Malaya Lubyanka 12. Sunday 8am, 11am and 6pm; Monday–Friday 8am; Friday and Saturday 6pm.
Chapel of Our Lady of Hope, Kutuzovsky prosp. 7/4, korp. 5, kv. 42. Tel: 243-9621. Monday–Wednesday and Friday 8.30am, Thursday 7pm, Saturday 6pm.

BAPTISTS
Maly Vuzovsky per. 3. Tel: 297-5167. Sunday 10am, 2pm and 6pm, Thursday 6pm.

PROTESTANT AND ANGLICAN
US Embassy. Tel: 252-2451, 143-3562.

EVANGELISCHE GEMEINDE
German Embassy, services twice a month at 10.30am. Tel: 238-1324.

OLD BELIEVERS
Cathedral, Rogozhsky per. 29.

MOSQUE
Vypolzov per. 7. Tel: 281-3866.
SYNAGOGUE
ul. Arkhipova 8. Tel: 923-9697.

COMMUNICATIONS

THE PRESS

Foreign language press: In Moscow, you will find the excellent and informative *Moscow News*, and the more recent *Moscow Times*. Both are translated into English, and are on sale in most major hotels. Other English language publications are distributed free in hotels or sold from kiosks. Unfortunately, St Petersburg does not have an equivalent newspaper, although such publications as *The Neva News* will give you important information on local events. If you are staying in the country for some time, a copy of *The Traveller's Yellow Pages*, which can be bought from hotels in Moscow and St Petersburg, gives invaluable information.

Russian-language press: *Pravda*, the best known Russian newspaper in the West, is no longer the "official paper of the Communist party". Most national and local papers are financed by the State as well as private subsidy. *Argumenty i Facty*, a national newspaper has a circulation of over 25 million and *Komsomolskaya Pravda*, a circulation of over 17 million. Also popular but of smaller circulation are *Izvestia* (4 million) and *Literaturnaya Gazetta*.

The most widely read Moscow newspaper is the *Moscow News* (over 1 million) and in St Petersburg, the *Sankt-Petersburg Vedomosti* (over 3,000).

COURIERS

There are three international courier services now in Moscow: DHL (tel: 203-1641 or 203-7049; TNT Skypack (tel: 578-9030); and UPS (tel: 430-7069). A 250 gram envelope costs approximately US$60 to send. Payment in hard currency only.

POSTAL SERVICES

The opening time of post offices varies, but most of them open 8am–7pm or 8pm during the week, and 9am–6pm on Saturdays. They are closed on Sundays. Some post offices, however, work only one shift a day, 9am–3pm or 2–8pm. The mail service in Russia is badly understaffed.

Not all post offices accept international mail bigger than a standard letter. Postal delivery is quite slow, and it may take some two or three weeks for a letter from Moscow to reach Western Europe and sometimes even a month or more to reach the US.

CABLES & TELEGRAMS

Cables to addresses within the CIS can be sent from any post office. The same applies to international cables. It is simpler, but more expensive to send from a hotel.

TELEPHONE

There are pay phones on the streets which accept tokens for making local calls. To dial further afield, go to a post office. As this whole process can be complicated and time consuming, it is simpler but more expensive to phone from your hotel.

You can now dial the UK and the USA direct from Moscow. To call the UK from a private address in St Petersburg, you will have to book your call in advance through the international operator. A direct call can be made through a hotel service bureau. To dial the CIS from abroad, the country code is 7. The prefix for Moscow is 095, for St Petersburg 812.

EMERGENCIES

HEALTH

During the last few years the CIS has experienced a shortage in the supply of basic medicines. It is quite common for simple aspirin or vitamins to be unavailable in drugstores. If you need special medication it is best to bring it with you. Some medicines are still available, especially in Moscow which is better supplied with most daily necessities. In Moscow, the following three pharmacies in the capital are normally well stocked:

Nikolskaya (Ul. 25 Oktyabrya) 1. Tel: 925-1846.
Mjasuitskaya (Ul. Kirova) 32. Tel: 923-1388.
Kutuzovsky prosp. 14. Tel:. 243-1601.

Tips: Like anywhere else, it is recommended that you wash fruit and raw vegetables before you eat them. Likewise, you should not drink unfamiliar tap water because a different and unfamiliar mineral composition can easily produce intestinal disorders. It is particularly important not to drink St Petersburg's tap water, even in small quantities. Bottled mineral water is available everywhere.

DOCTORS

Your hotel service bureau will find a doctor to come to your hotel room or will refer you to the nearest clinic. Medical standards in Russia are good and in the big cities there are specialists for every kind of illness available. Doctor's visits and first aid treatment is free of charge but medicines and hospital treatment must be paid for (in roubles).

HEALTH SPAS

The healing properties of the mineral waters in the Rayon Kavkazskikh Mineralnykh Vod (Caucasian Spa District) have been known for centuries. This area, and the customs of resort people, were described by Lermontov, who was killed in a duel in the spa town of Pyatigorsk. Now duels are no longer in fashion but Pyatigorsk mineral waters are still used to treat bowel complaints, the neural system, dispepsia, pathological metabolism, and vascular, gynacaeological and skin problems. Other spas in this region – Essentuki, Kislovodsk and Zheleznovodsk – are as famous as Pyatigorsk.

Sochi and Matsesta, are also in the vicinity of the Rayon Kavkazskikh Mineralnykh Vod, on the coast of the Black Sea. Not far away is another spa, Tskhaltubo.

EMERGENCY NUMBERS

All Russian cities have unified emergency telephone numbers. These numbers can be dialled free of charge from public telephones.

Fire Guards (Pozharnaya okhrana)	01
Police (Militsia)	02
Ambulance (Skoraya pomoshch)	03
Gas Emergency (Sluzhba gaza)	04
Information (Spravochnaya)	09

Officials responding to these calls will speak little English, so a knowledge of Russian is needed to make yourself understood.

GETTING AROUND

BY TRAIN

With some 145,000 km (90,050 miles), the railway system of Russia is the longest in the world. It is a means of transport used for 4 billion individual trips per year. The busiest lines in European Russia connect Moscow with St Petersburg and Kiev, where a train leaves almost every hour. In overnight sleeping cars, tea is always served and trains travelling for more than 8 hours have a restaurant car attached during the day.

You should make your reservation several days ahead since, as with everything else in Russia, reserved train seats are in short supply, especially 2nd class tickets, which are cheap but fairly comfortable.

You can reserve your seat through Intourist or at the Intourtrans Office (situated in Moscow, Ul. Petrovka 15). There is also an Intourist booking office in the railway stations of every major city. The ticket must have a cover and a coupon (it is only valid with both these components).

Intourist provides an English language telephone information service in Moscow: tel: 921-4513.

THE TRANS-SIBERIAN RAILWAY

This rail link from Europe to the Orient is one of the most exotic – as well as the longest – train trips in the world. Over a period of nine days the train crosses seven times zones from Moscow to Vladivostok, passing through much of the diversity of Siberian Russia. It makes many scheduled stops along the way, but never lingers longer than 15 minutes. If you want to explore further than a few hundred yards from the tracks, you must disembark and rejoin a later train. As far as possible, stop-offs should be scheduled ahead of time, since you could easily lose your first-class cabin if you choose simply to "wing it".

With the opening, in 1992, of the port of Vladivostok to foreign tourists, it is now possible to begin or end a Trans-Siberian rail trip in Yokohama, Japan. A two day cruise connects Vladivostok with Yokohama. Adding to the network is the Baikal-Amur Mainline (BAM), which connects Tayshet to Komsomolsk. Combined with the lifting of most travel restrictions, this has opened up eastern Siberia considerably.

Located just 66 km (41 miles) from Lake Baikal, Irkutsk is the most popular stopover for Trans-Siberian travellers. A typical Trans-Siberian train trip would include a two-day stop in Irkutsk, from which excursions to Lake Baikal are easily arranged. Other popular stopovers are Novosibirsk, Listvyanka (on Lake Baikal), Bratsk (by jet or train from Irkutsk) and Khabarovsk.

Train accommodation is available in first-class (two-person compartments) and second-class (four-person compartments). Get the conductor to lock your compartment whenever you leave it, as theft is rampant on Russian trains. Most embassies also recommend that foreign travellers speak as little as possible on the train so as not to attract attention.

The train plying the route, the Rossiya train, is of slightly better quality than most Russian trains. The food is also better than normal. The soups are usually good, and tea is always available from the conductor at a nominal charge. The best strategy is to do like the Russians: pack your own food and eat it in your own carriage. Bed linen and towel are provided and there is a toilet and wash basin at the end of each carriage.

If nine days on a train doesn't appeal to you, it is possible to disembark somewhere along the route and fly the rest of the way. Taking the train from east to west as far as Irkutsk and connecting to Moscow by plane would include the most exotic portion of the trip and leave plenty of time to tour the capital.

But there are also trans-Continental rail routes, such as those from Moscow to Peking in China and Ulan Bator in Mongolia. They demand an adventurous spirit and a willingness to spend a week in the train contemplating the endless trans-Siberian landscapes.

BY CAR

CAR RENTAL

Western car companies are opening in the major cities and you will find branches at international airports. Cars can also be hired with a driver. Check up-to-date details before you leave or at hotels, who advertise such companies. Before you hire a car, read the advice printed under "Routes". **Warning**: in view of rising crime against car-travelling tourists, many tour companies discourage tourists from hiring a car.

Downtown address for **Hertz** in Moscow: Gorburiova Ulitsa 14. Tel: 448 8035.

ROUTES

If you intend to visit Russia by car you should first get in contact with Intourist as they have worked out a number of routes which can be easily negotiated with your own vehicle. Road conditions off these routes are very poor.

The ideal route through European Russia means

entering from Finland, driving via St Petersburg and Moscow to the Caucasus and the Black Sea, ferrying the car across to Yalta or Odessa and crossing the Ukraine to the Czech and Slovak republics or Poland.

Sovinterautoservice, Institutski per., 2/1, Moscow, tel: 101-496, are the specialists for car travel in Russia. They solve nearly every problem a foreigner can have on Russian roads.

RULES OF THE ROAD

Russia is a signatory to the International Traffic Convention. Rules of the road and road signs correspond to international standards. The basic rules, however, are worth mentioning.

1) In Russia vehicles are driven on the right side of the road.
2) It is prohibited to drive a car after consuming any, even the smallest amount, of alcohol. If the driver shows a positive alcohol test, the consequences may be very serious. It is also prohibited to drive a car under the effect of drugs or any powerful medicine.
3) The driver must have an international driving licence and documents verifying his or her right to drive the car. These papers must be in Russian and are issued by Intourist.
4) Vehicles, except for those rented from Intourist, must carry the national registration code. All must have a national licence plate.
5) The use of the horn is prohibited within city limits except in emergency situations.
6) The use of seat belts for the driver and front seat passenger is compulsory.
7) The speed limit in populated areas (marked by blue coloured signs indicating "town") is 60 kph (37 mph); on most arterial roads the limit is 90 kph (55.5 mph). On highways the limit can differ, so look out for road signs specifying other speeds.
8) You can insure your car in Russia through Ingosstrakh, the national insurance company.

BY BOAT

Many rivers in the European part of the CIS are open to navigation during the spring and autumn. You can travel along the Dnieper, Volga, Oka, Moskva, Don, Dniester, Neva and other rivers. The cities on the banks of the rivers are connected by passenger ships and hydrofoils. (Raketa and Kometa Class).

If you plan a trip along one of these routes, you can make a reservation through Intourist or directly at the Moscow River Station (Rechnoy Vokzal).

RIVER STATIONS
Moscow: Severny Rechnoy Vokzal, Leningradskoe shosse 51. Tel: 457-4050.
St Petersburg: Rechnoy Vokzal, prosp. Obukhovskoy Oborony 195. Tel: 262-1318 (information), 262-5511 (booking office).
Kiev: Rechnoy Vokzal, Poshtova Pl. Tel: 416-1268.

CRUISES
Intourist offers organised river cruises on comfortable river liners which are relaxing and interesting but quite expensive. These cruises are sold through foreign travel agencies that sell Intourist tour packages. Intourist has started to offer trips along the Lena and soon the Ob and the Yenisei will also be part of their programme.

BY PLANE

Aeroflot, once the world's largest airline, has been broken up, and each republic now runs its own airline. The name Aeroflot is still used by the Russian airline. It flies to many remote and outlying areas, sometimes using helicopters and small hopper planes. Many of its aircraft have been designed primarily for military purposes and lack the comfort of Western carriers, but it has recently bought a fleet of European Airbuses.

As with most airlines, the cheapest fares cannot be bought from Aeroflot direct but from consolidators.

Fares within Russia can be reasonable, though flights have to be booked far in advance since demand exceeds capacity. Check-in at Aeroflot counters starts one and a half hours before departure and ends half an hour beforehand. Foreigners have to pay for their tickets in hard currency.

AEROFLOT OFFICES IN THE CIS
Moscow: 4, Frunzenskaya Naberezhnaya. Tel: 156 8019.
St Petersburg: 7/9 Nevsky Prospekt. Tel: 314 6963.
Kiev: 1 Ulitsa Menzhinskogo. Tel: 274 9921.
Minsk: 38 Ulitsa Chkalova. Tel: 250 259.
Khabarovsk: 5, Amursky Boulevard. Tel: 332 071.
AEROFLOT OFFICES ABROAD
Amsterdam: Weteringsehans 26. Tel: 624 5715, 625 4049.
Athens. Xenofontos 14. Tel: 322 1022.
Bangkok: Kamol Sukosoi Building, 8th Floor, 317 Silom Rd. Tel: 238 1293.
Berlin: Unter den Linden, 51/53. Tel: 229 2833.
Bombay: 241–242 Nirmal Building, Nariman Point. Tel: 221 682, 221 743.
Brussels: Rue des Colonies 58. Tel: 513 6066.
Bucharest: 35, Boulevard Nicolae Balcescu. Tel: 178 972, 150 314.
Budapest: Váci utca 4, 1052 Budapest. Tel: 118 5955, 118 5892.
Copenhagen: 1/3, Vester Farimasgade. Tel: 331 25757, 331 26338.
Delhi: No 1, BMC House, Middle Circle, Connaught Pl. Tel: 331 0426, 331 2843.
Frankfurt: Wilhelm-Leuschner-Strasse 41, 6000 Frankfurt/Main 1. Tel: 273 0060, 690 5315.
Helsinki: Mannerheimintie 5. Tel: 659 655, 666 217.
Lisbon: Av. da Liberdade 36-D. Tel: 346-7776, 347 4906.
London: 70 Piccadilly, London W1. Tel: 071-355 2233, 071-491 1584.

Madrid: C/Jose Oretega y Gasset 2. Tel: 431 3706, 431 4107.

Milan: 19, Via Vittor Pisani. Tel: 986 985/6.

Munich: Ludwig Strasse. 6. Tel: 288 261/2.

New York: 630 Fifth Avenue, Suite 1710. Tel: 332 1050, 332 1041.

Paris: 33, Avenue des Champs Elysées. Tel: 42 25 43 81, 42 56 19 30.

Peking: 2-2-42, Jianguomenwai. Tel: 523 581.

Prague: Parizska 5. Tel: 232 3333, 232 8021.

Rome: 27, Via Leonida Bissolati. Tel: 482 6661, 481 7475.

Singapore: 15 Queen Street, Tang Chong Tower. Tel: 336 1757, 542 5582.

Sofia: 2, Russky Boulevard. Tel: 879 080, 874 253.

Tokyo: Daini Matsuda Building, Toranomon 3-4-8. Tel: 3-434 9671.

Vienna: 10, Parkring. Tel: 512 1501.

Warsaw: 29, Allee Jerozolimskie. Tel: 281 710, 211 611.

Washington: 1620 1 Street NW. Tel: 466 4080, 429 4922.

Zürich: Talacker 41, 8001 Zurich. Tel: 211 4633, 211 4634.

CITY TRANSPORT

In all cities, streets are reverting to their pre-Revolutionary names with a speed rarely matched by the available maps. Particularly recommended for Moscow and St Petersburg are the German Falk plan maps, available from most large bookshops.

MOSCOW

Trolleybuses: Slow, because of traffic conditions, but extremely cheap. Most maps show routes, and bus stop are clearly marked by yellow boards indicating route number and terminus.

Taxis: Always establish a price before setting off, and try to settle on roubles rather than dollars. There is a central taxi service and you can book a cab by calling 927 0000 or 927 2108 day or night. Waiting time is about an hour. Never take unlicensed cabs at night.

Chauffeur-driven cars: This can save time and hassle and need not be that expensive, especially if you use one of the private individuals who advertise in the classified columns of the *Moscow Times*. Residents currently pay about $60 a week for this service. For a more official, and posibly more comfortable arrangement, check out Intourist (tel: 215 6191), InNis (tel: 927 1187) and Autosan (tel: 280 3600).

The Metro: The Moscow Metro system is famous for its fabulous architecture. It is also fast, reliable and cheap and the best way to travel around in Moscow. Buy tokens from the ticket windows in the entry halls or, if you can, buy a monthly pass. Each station, including those which are at the same location but on different lines, has its own name.

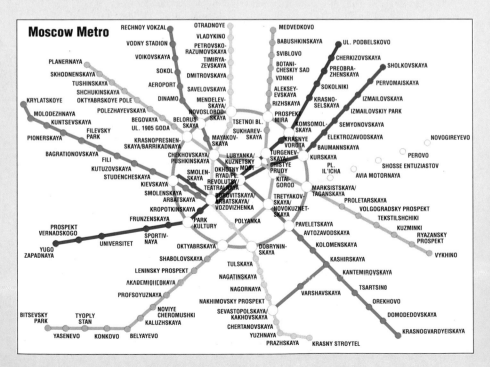

Moscow Metro

ST PETERSBURG

Buses, trams and trolleybuses: These run from 6am–1am the following morning. To make full use of the system, it is essential to buy a special map called Marshruti Gorodskovo Transporta – Tolleibus, Avtobus i Trambai (Town Transport Routes for Trolleybuses, Buses and Trams). Ask your hotel reception where you can buy a copy.

Stops marked by an "A" sign serve buses, while stops marked "T" served trolleybuses. The latter are less crowded than buses during rush-hour. Tram signs hang from wires above the middle of the road.

Taxis: Though taxis are now too expensive for most local people, they remain very cheap for Westerners. St Petersburg taxis are pale yellow with a "T" sign. Those which congregate outside hotels inflate their prices considerably, so it is cheaper to flag down a vehicle in the street. As in Moscow, determine the price of a journey before setting out.

The Metro: Like St Petersburg's buses and trams, the Metro runs from 6am–1am, and like the Moscow Metro it is famous for its architecture and murals. This is the fastest way to get around St Petersburg, and it is well worth trying to get to grips with routes and Cyrillic signs (*see map, page 324*).

TOUR OPERATORS

Intourist cooperates with more than 700 foreign firms who are agents for Intourist in their respective countries. It offers services in more than 200 cities in the CIS and runs numerous hotels, motels, campsites and restaurants. Intourist offers more than 600 different programmes within Russia. These include local sightseeing trips, thematic tours for history, art and nature lovers, as well as sporting and hunting tours and arrangements for medical treatment. A visit to the nearest Intourist office will give you a good overall impression of what is on offer.

Intourist also runs a car rental service, with and without driver in the larger cities. Lada, Chaika and Volga cars as well as Ikarus coaches, LAZ, PAZ and RAF buses for 9 to 42 people can be hired.

In addition, Intourist manages 110 hotels, motels and campsites for 55,000 guests. A variety of hotels are now built and reconstructed in cooperation with foreign partners like Moscow's Savoy Hotel and St Petersburg's Astoria, which are operated jointly with the Finnish INFA Hotel company and Finnair.

Over 5,000 guide-interpreters, speaking more than 30 languages work for Intourist.

Since co-operatives are now permitted, Intourist is no longer a monopoly tourist agency; a few small and independent firms have sprung up during the last few years, now serving special interest groups.

Besides group tours, Intourist also arranges individual journeys to Russia. These trips must be planned on a day by day basis in advance, and Intourist arranges transport, accommodation and food. But such tailor-made itineraries are expensive.

INTOURIST OFFICES

Amsterdam: Honthorststraat 42. Tel: 020-679 8694.
Athens: 2 Plutarhou Street, Kolonaki. Tel: 729 0696.
Berlin: 15 Kurfürstendamm 63. Tel: 30 880 070.
Budapest: 1053 Budapest 5, Ferennciek Tere 2. Tel: 118 0098.
Brussels: Galerie Ravenstein 2. Tel: 02-513 8234.
Copenhagen: Vester Farimagsgade 6. Tel: 112 527.
Delhi: Plot 6/7, block 50-E, Njaja Marg Chanakiapuri. Tel: 67 6336.
Frankfurt: Stephanstr. 1. Tel: 285 776.
Helsinki: Erottajankatu 11 A 12 Tel: 611 802.
London: Intourist House, 219 Marsh Wall, London E14 9FJ. Tel: 071-538 3202.
New York: 630 Fifth Avenue, Suite 868. Tel: 212-757 3884/5.
Paris: 7, Boulevard de Capucines. Tel: 474-24740.
Prague:Praga 6, Bubenech, Ul Volkerova 13. Tel: 341 341.
Quebec: 1801 McGill College Ave. Tel: 849 6394.
Rome: Piazza Buenos Aires 6/7. Tel: 85 53892.
Sydney: Underwood House, 37-49 Pitt Street. Tel: 247 7652.
Tokyo: Roppongi Heights, 1-16, 4-chome Roppongi, Minato-ku. Tel: 3-584 6617.
Toronto: 1013 Bloor Street, West Toronto. Tel: 537 2165.
Vienna: Schwedenplatz 3-4. Tel: 533 9547.
Warsaw: 15 Podwale Street. Tel: 31 6356.
Zurich: Bleicherweg 15A. Tel: 281 1114.

ALTERNATIVE TOUR OPERATORS

It is possible to arrange holidays to Russia without going through Intourist, but it is impossible to list all the other options, particularly as many of the companies open and close rapidly. **Voyages Jules Verne** in London offers cheap package tours as well as cruises (tel: 071-723 5066) and **Serenissima Travel** (part of the same company) organise more expensive, specialist tours. **Cox & Kings** in London (tel: 071-834 7472) and New York (tel: 212-935 3935) arrange luxury train journeys throughout Russia on the Bolshoi Express. **Regent Holidays UK Ltd** (tel: 0272-211 711) can provide cheap flights, bespoke tours and trips on the Trans-Siberian Railway. More specialist companies such as **Kola Salmon Limited** in London (tel: 071-386 9100) organise expensive salmon fishing holidays on the Kola Peninsula.

If you want to arrange an organised tour in Russia itself, try the following companies:

Sputnik, International Centre for Youth Tourism, 15 Kossygin Street, 117946 Moscow. Tel: 139-8665.

International Center MIR, Pr. Nepokoryonnyh 74, 195273 St Petersburg. Tel: 249-9400.

Both specialise in inexpensive group travel, accommodation and international group exchange.

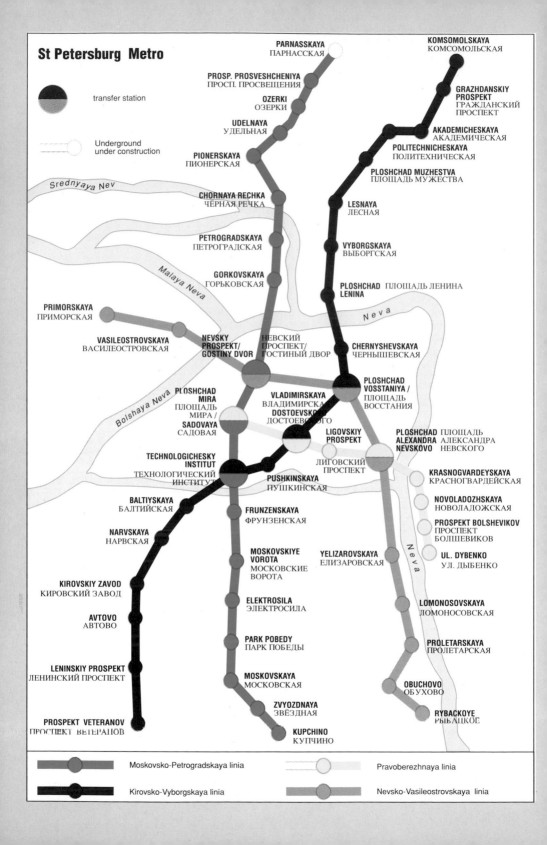

St Petersburg Metro

transfer station

Underground
under construction

PARNASSKAYA
ПАРНАССКАЯ

KOMSOMOLSKAYA
КОМСОМОЛЬСКАЯ

PROSP. PROSVESHCHENIYA
ПРОСП. ПРОСВЕЩЕНИЯ

GRAZHDANSKIY
PROSPEKT
ГРАЖДАНСКИЙ
ПРОСПЕКТ

OZERKI
ОЗЕРКИ

AKADEMICHESKAYA
АКАДЕМИЧЕСКАЯ

UDELNAYA
УДЕЛЬНАЯ

POLITECHNICHESKAYA
ПОЛИТЕХНИЧЕСКАЯ

PIONERSKAYA
ПИОНЕРСКАЯ

PLOSHCHAD MUZHESTVA
ПЛОЩАДЬ МУЖЕСТВА

Srednyaya Nev

CHORNAYA RECHKA
ЧЁРНАЯ РЕЧКА

LESNAYA
ЛЕСНАЯ

PETROGRADSKAYA
ПЕТРОГРАДСКАЯ

VYBORGSKAYA
ВЫБОРГСКАЯ

Malaya Neva

GORKOVSKAYA
ГОРЬКОВСКАЯ

PLOSHCHAD   ПЛОЩАДЬ ЛЕНИНА
LENINA

PRIMORSKAYA
ПРИМОРСКАЯ

Neva

VASILEOSTROVSKAYA
ВАСИЛЕОСТРОВСКАЯ

NEVSKY
PROSPEKT/
GOSTINY DVOR

НЕВСКИЙ
ПРОСПЕКТ/
ГОСТИНЫЙ ДВОР

CHERNYSHEVSKAYA
ЧЕРНЫШЕВСКАЯ

PLOSHCHAD
MIRA
ПЛОЩАДЬ
МИРА /
SADOVAYA
САДОВАЯ

PLOSHCHAD
VOSSTANIYA /
ПЛОЩАДЬ
ВОССТАНИЯ

Bolshaya Neva

VLADIMIRSKAYA
ВЛАДИМИРСКАЯ
DOSTOEVSKO
ДОСТОЕВСКОГО

PLOSHCHAD   ПЛОЩАДЬ
ALEXANDRA   АЛЕКСАНДРА
NEVSKOVO   НЕВСКОГО

LIGOVSKIY
PROSPEKT

TECHNOLOGICHESKY
INSTITUT
ТЕХНОЛОГИЧЕСКИЙ
ИНСТИТУТ

ЛИГОВСКИЙ
ПРОСПЕКТ

KRASNOGVARDEYSKAYA
КРАСНОГВАРДЕЙСКАЯ

PUSHKINSKAYA
ПУШКИНСКАЯ

NOVOLADOZHSKAYA
НОВОЛАДОЖСКАЯ

BALTIYSKAYA
БАЛТИЙСКАЯ

FRUNZENSKAYA
ФРУНЗЕНСКАЯ

PROSPEKT BOLSHEVIKOV
ПРОСПЕКТ
БОЛШЕВИКОВ

NARVSKAYA
НАРВСКАЯ

Neva

UL. DYBENKO
УЛ. ДЫБЕНКО

MOSKOVSKIYE
VOROTA
МОСКОВСКИЕ
ВОРОТА

YELIZAROVSKAYA
ЕЛИЗАРОВСКАЯ

KIROVSKIY ZAVOD
КИРОВСКИЙ ЗАВОД

LOMONOSOVSKAYA
ЛОМОНОСОВСКАЯ

ELEKTROSILA
ЭЛЕКТРОСИЛА

AVTOVO
АВТОВО

PARK POBEDY
ПАРК ПОБЕДЫ

PROLETARSKAYA
ПРОЛЕТАРСКАЯ

LENINSKIY PROSPEKT
ЛЕНИНСКИЙ ПРОСПЕКТ

MOSKOVSKAYA
МОСКОВСКАЯ

OBUCHOVO
ОБУХОВО

ZVYOZDNAYA
ЗВЁЗДНАЯ

RYBACKOYE
РЫБАЦКОЕ

PROSPEKT VETERANOV
ПРОСПЕКТ ВЕТЕРАНОВ

KUPCHINO
КУПЧИНО

Moskovsko-Petrogradskaya linia

Pravoberezhnaya linia

Kirovsko-Vyborgskaya linia

Nevsko-Vasileostrovskaya linia

Russia does not have an extensive system of youth hostels. Only big cities have youth hostels belonging to Sputnik, the Bureau of International Youth Tourism, once a part of Comsomol but now acting independently. During the summer months, when demand exceeds hostel capacity, Sputnik falls back on unused, inexpensive university dormitories.

An inexpensive way to visit Russia is through institutes that run Russian language courses: Lomonosov and Lumumba Universities and the Pushkin Institute of Russian Language in Moscow, the Shevchenko University in Kiev, the University of St Petersburg and other universities and new linguistic co-operatives. They are all able to arrange visas and inexpensive accommodation during the period of studies. To communicate directly with the universities you should contact the cultural attaché of the Russian embassy or consulate. It is rather more difficult to communicate with the co-operatives since they are not represented abroad. When selecting such courses, care should be taken to ensure that the teaching is on a professional level. It is also worth contacting the Russian departments of universities at home. Many are now running short (one or two-week) overseas study tours (including flight to Russia, accommodation and transport within Russia, and tuition fees) for the general public.

WHERE TO STAY

HOTELS

Until the advent of perestroika, by Western standards the hotels on offer were uncomfortable, expensive and usually depressing. Things have now changed and there is a much wider choice, with a number of new foreign-run hotels pushing up standards (and prices) considerably.

MOSCOW

Metropol, Teatralny Proyezd 1 4. Tel: 927 6000. This is the place to stay if you can possibly afford it. It has been beautifully renovated and is elegant, luxurious and expensive.

Savoy, Rozhdestvenka 3. Tel: 929 8500. This was the first Western-Soviet joint venture into the hotel business. First class standards.

Mezhdunarodnaya I and II, Krasnopresnenskaya Nab 12. Tel: 253 2382 (I) and 253 2760 (II). Built in the 1970s but still one of the best hotels. Prices reflect that status.

Aerostar, Korpus 9, 37 Leningradsky Prospekt. Tel: 155 5030. Canadian/Russian hotel with excellent seafood restaurant. Moderately expensive.

Novotel, Sheremetyevo II Airport. Tel: 578 9407. Airport hotel with usual Novotel standards.

Slavyanskaya/Radisson, Berezhkovskaya Bab 2. Tel: 941 8020. Brand-new luxury hotel. Boasts a 24-hour coffee shop.

Pullman/Iris, Korovinskoye Shosse 10. Tel: 488 8080. A comfortable, stylish hotel with good restaurants.

Marco Polo/Presnaya, Spridonyevsky per. 9. Tel: 202 0381. Well-run, quiet and luxurious. Formerly reserved for Soviet VIPs.

Rossiya, Ulitsa Vavarka 6. Tel: 298 5531. Claims to be the biggest hotel in the world (more than 5,000 rooms). Its best feature is its location – on Red Square. Inexpensive compared with joint venture establishments.

Moskva, Okhotny Ryad 7. Tel: 292 1100. Ex-Soviet hotel which was built for People's Deputies and visiting dignitaries. Beautiful rooms, many overlooking the Kremlin. Inexpensive.

Intourist, Ulitsa Tverskaya, 3–5. Tel: 203 4008. Central. Double rooms only. Medium price range.

Ukraina, Kutuzovsky Prospekt 2/1. Tel: 243 3030. A Stalin wedding cake. Centrally located with clean, spacious rooms with wooden floors. Relatively inexpensive.

Akademicheskaya I, Lenisky Prospekt. Tel: 238 0902. Close to Gorky Park, this is where the Academy of Sciences used to put up their visiting foreign academics. Relatively clean and very convenient. So far, still open only to academics.

Akademicheskaya II, Donskaya Ulitsa. Tel: 238 0508. Less conventient and much bigger than its sister establishment.

Cosmos, Prospekt Mira 150. Tel: 217 0785. Large and sleazy, but with adequate rooms and relatively low prices.

ST PETERSBURG

Astoria, 39 Herzen Ulitsa. Tel: 219 1100. Grand and luxurious. Stay here if you can afford it.

Grand Hotel Europe, 1/7 Mikhailovskaya Ulitsa/Ulitsa Brodskovo. Tel: 210 3149. Another upmarket option, with character.

Hotel Olympia (Floating), 1 Ploshchad Morskoy Slavy. Tel: 217 8054. Well-run floating hotel.

Pribaltiskaya, 14 Ulitsa Korablcotroitelcy. Tel: 356 5112. Modern luxury hotel 7 km (4 miles) from the centre.

Pulkovskaya, 1 Ploshchad Pobedy. Tel: 264 5100. Also a long way from the centre, but close to the airport.

St Petersburg (former Leningrad), 5-2 Vyborgskaya Naberezhnaya. Tel: 542 9031. Central and adequate.

Moskva, 2 Ploshchad Alexandra Nevskovo. Tel: 272 2051. Central, medium-range hotel.
Sovietskaya, 43 Prospekt Lermontovo. Tel: 216 0032. Also central in the mid-price range.
Karelia, 27/2 Ulitsa Tukhachevskaya. Tel: 226 5701. Inexpensive hotel used by Intourist, but 10 km (6 miles) from the centre.

Cheap options, where the standard will be pretty basic, include: **Hotel Druzhba**, 4 Ultisa Chapygina, tel: 234 1844; **Dvoretz Molodyozhy**, 47 Ulitsa Professor Popov, tel: 234 3278; **Vyborgskaya**, Ulitsa Torzhkovskaya, tel: 246 9141; **Hotel Sputnik**, 34 Prospekt Morisa Toreza, tel: 552 5632; **Hotel Gavan**, 88 Sredny Prospekt, tel: 356 8504; and **Hotel Morskaya**, 1 Morskoy Slavy Ploshchad, tel: 355 1416.

THE GOLDEN RING

Best places to stay on the Golden Ring route are Yaroslavl, Vladimir and Suzdal.

YAROSLAVL
Hotel Yaroslavl, tel: 21275.

VLADIMIR
Hotel Vladimir, tel: 3042.

SUZDAL
Suzdal Hotel and Motel, tel: 21137. An **Intourist** hotel in the town centre, set in a suburban leisure complex which also includes the **Pokrovskaya Hotel** (tel: 20131) inside a former monastery.

Other possibilities in the Golden Ring include the eponymous **Pereslavl-Zalessky** and **Rostov-Veliky** hotels.

THE EUROPEAN NORTH

If you are on a cruise around the north you will not require a hotel or a restaurant. The Western-run tour boats have excellent facilities, while the Russian ones are very pleasant, if limited on the choice of food. Both provide evening entertainment, whether a dance in the café or a dubbed American film.

For those travelling under their own steam, finding Western standard hotels is not going to be possible, so you have to take what is on offer. The best option is to stay in one of the larger urban centres and journey out from there or, if possible, to stay in one of the monasteries, such as the Solovetsky.

MURMANSK
The best hotel is **Arctica**, Ploschad Pyat Uglov. Tel: 57293.

VOLOGDA
The **Severnaya**, on Sennaya (Revolution) Square, enjoys a good location right in the heart of the town. But you might prefer the **Volgda** at 92 Ulitsa Mira (tel: 23079) or the **Oktyabr** at 7 Ulitsa Karla Marksa (tel:20569).

VYBORG
The old **Vyborg Hotel** is pleasant but the very modern **Druzhba** (built by the Finns), at 5 Zheleznodorozhnaya Ulitsa (tel: 21654), has better service. Not far away is the ship hotel **Korolenko** (tel: 94478).

NOVGOROD
Facilities are getting better with the arrival of more businessmen. The best are at the new **Rossia** on Nab Alexandra Nevskogo, tel: 94849. You can also stay at the Yurino camp site outside town.

PSKOV
The **Oktaybrskaya** at 36 Oktyabrsky Prospekt, tel: 39912; the **Rizhskaya** at 25 Rizhsky Prospekt, tel: 62223; and the **Turist** at 4 Krasnoznamenskaya Ulitsa, tel: 25151 are modest but adequate.

THE EUROPEAN SOUTH
SOCHI
Kamelia (Intourist), Kurortny prosp. 91. Tel: 990-292.
Zhemchuzhina (Intourist), ul. Chernomorskaya 3. Tel: 934-335.
Dagomys Intourist Complex (Dagomys Hotel & Campsite, Olimpiyskaya Hotel, Meridian Motel), ul. Leningradskaya 7, Dagomys. Tel: 322-994, 321-994, 322-987.
Khosta, ul. Yaltinskaya 14, Khosta.
Magnolia, Kurortny prosp. 50.
Moskva, Kurortny prosp. 18.
Sochi, Kurortny prosp. 50.
Svetlana Guest House, Kurortny prosp. 75.

THE URALS
YEKATERINBURG
Hotel Oktyabrskaya, ul. S. Kovalevskoi 17. Tel: 445146; fax: 443193. The former Communist Party hotel. A Finnish-built brick building, it is easily the best hotel in town, with 69 clean rooms with well-kept bathrooms and a quiet environment. It's located slightly outside the centre, a few blocks from the Urals State Technical University.

Hotel Sverdlovsk, Chelyuskintsev 106. Tel: 536261. Located across from the train station. Its 561 rooms accommodate large numbers of merchants from across the former Soviet Union. Heavy traffic here over the years has resulted in grim decay. Best left as a second choice.

SIBERIA
LAKE BAIKAL
The Baikal Hotel, Listvyanka. 120 rooms. The only hotel on the lake, the Baikal Hotel offers splendid

For the fastest weekend refunds anywhere in the world.

Ensure your holiday is worry free even if
your travellers cheques are lost or stolen by buying
American Express Travellers Cheques from;

Lloyds Bank	Leeds Permanent Building Society*
Royal Bank of Scotland	Woolwich Building Society*
Abbey National*	National & Provincial Building Society
Bank of Ireland	Britannia Building Society*
Halifax Building Society*	American Express Travel Offices.

As well as many regional building societies and travel agents.

*Investors only.

Not all travellers cheques are the same.

views and a good restaurant. The local perch is delicious. Even if you stay in Irkutsk, stop by the restaurant for lunch. Many of the Intourist packages include a lunch stop at the restaurant.

IRKUTSK

Stay at the **Intourist Hotel**, Bulvar Gagarina, 44. Though it is overpriced and a magnet for hustlers hoping to change money and offer private tours of Lake Baikal, it is well located with views of the Angara River. It also has several restaurants in the hotel and the best Intourist Service bureau in the city. Staff are relatively experienced at handling tourists and offer mini-van trips to Lake Baikal, English-speaking guides and advice on the city.

Other hotels are:
Angara, Ulitsa Sushebatora, 7.
Siberia, Ulitsa Lenina, 18.
Gorniak, Ulitsa Lenina, 21.

KEMEROVA

The only decent hotel in town is the **Kuzbass**. Tel: 250 254.

ORMSK

The **Taiga Hotel** (tel: 44000) is the best hotel in town. Otherwise try **Tourist Moskva**, Prospect Marksa, 9. (tel: 316 419).

NOVOSIBIRSK

The best hotel is the new Intourist offering, the **Sibir**, located on Ulitsa Lenina, 21. Tel: 231 215, 233 381.
Other hotels are:
Hotel Tsentralnaya, tel: 221 366.
Hotel Novosibirsk, tel: 201 120.
Hotel Severnaya, Ulitsa Dzherzhinskaya, 32.
Hotel Vostok, Ulitsa Khmelnitskogo, 42.
Hotel Zolotaya Dolina, Ulitsa Ilyicha, 11.

KRASNOYARSK

Presently all foreign guests are housed in the **Oktyabrskaya Hotel**, the former hotel of Party guests. The high price of the rooms reflects the naiveté of tourism in its present state. A single costs $40 per night, a double $60 and a so-called "lux" costs $120. Tel: 221 916.

ULAN-UDE

The best hotel in town is the red-brick **Hotel Oktyabrskaya**, located off the main square of Ploshad Sovietov. Technically it is off-limits to tourists, but walk-in traffic is sometimes accommodated. The extra effort is worth it given the sorry condition of the next best hotel, the Baikal.

The **Hotel Baikal** is a noisy and decrepit reminder of how poorly developed this once-closed city is in terms of tourism It is located on Ulitsa Yerbanova 12, in the city centre. Other hotels are:
Hotel Barguzin, Sovietskaya, 28.
Hotel Selenga, Lenina, 21.

VLADIVOSTOK

The best hotel in Vladivostok is the **Hotel Vladivostok**, located on Ulitsa Naberezhnaya, 10. Tel: 222 246. The next best hotel is the maze-like **Amursky Zaliv**, a huge, depressing, Soviet-style hotel with a great location on Amur Bay. It lies directly across the street from the Hotel Vladivostok. Both are overrun with prostitutes who may call or knock on your door at any time of the night.

THE KURILE ISLANDS

Hotel Magnolia, with its 19 rooms, is the only hotel in the Kurile Island chain. You do not need to call ahead; if you succeed in arriving to Kunashir, you will be immediately whisked to the hotel.

MAGADAN

The only hotel is the **Hotel Magadan** on Proletarskaya 30-A. Tel: 205 989.

YAKUTSK

The best hotel in Yakutsk is the **Ontario**, a new joint venture hotel which has opened outside the city centre. At $50 per night, it is rather pricey for Siberia. Tel: 65058.
Other hotels are:
Hotel Yakutsk, Ulitsa Oktyabrskaya, 20/21. Tel: 50700.
Hotel Yakut-Zoloto, Prospect Lenina, 11. Tel: 24351.
Hotel Taiga, Ulitsa Ordzhonikidze, 23. Tel: 24555.

BELARUS

MINSK

Yubileinaya Hotel, 19 Masherov Prospekt. Tel: 298 835, 298 024.
Minsk Hotel, 11 Lenina Prospekt. Tel: 292 363.
Planeta Hotel, 31 Masherov Prospekt. Tel: 238 416.

UKRAINE

KIEV

Unlike in Moscow and St Petersburg, there is still no Western owned and run hotel in Kiev, and Intourist offers the only option for a comfortable stay.
The better hotels are:
The Intourist Hotel, on Gospitalnaya 12. Tel: 2227 9555.
Dnipro, Kreshchatik 1/2. Tel: 229 8387.
The Ukraine, Taras Shevchenko 5. Tel: 274 6132.

LVOV

Intourist, 1 Mickiewicz Square. Tel: 726 752. A rather grand though slightly faded European style hotel. Fun to stay in.
Dnestr, 6 Ulitsa Mateyka. Tel: 797 037. Newer and the plumbing is probably better, but it lacks atmosphere.

ODESSA

Foreigners used to be billeted in the three hotels mentioned below, but there are numerous others which will soon drop their discrimination clauses, if they have not done so already.

Chernoye More Hotel, 59 Lenin Street. Tel: 242-025.

Odessa Hotel, 11 Primorsky Boulevard. Tel: 225-019

Krasnaya Hotel, 15 Pushkin Street. Tel: 227-220.

THE CRIMEA

Dozens of hotels catered for the Russians who used to throng here. With the Russians less welcome than before, foreigners with hard currency can expect open arms. Sevastopol and Balaklava, Crimean War drawcards, were virtually closed to foreigners because of arms shipments en route to the Middle East, among other sensitive activities. They are still tricky but no longer impossible.

Oreanda Hotel, 35/2 Lenin Embankmnet, Yalta. Tel: 325-794. A 19th-century hotel effectively taken over by Virgin Airlines and a revelation.

Yalta Hotel, 50 Drazhinsky Street, Yalta. Tel: 350-150. A huge place with windsurfing, etc.

Tavrida Hotel, 13/2 Lenin Embankment, Yalta. Tel: 327-784.

FOOD DIGEST

Most of the different ethnic groups populating the CIS pretend to have their own national cuisine, and some of them genuinely have one. Within this diversity, Georgian, Ukrainian and Russian cuisines are said to be the best.

Georgian: With perestroika, Georgian food was introduced to the rest of the CIS (for example, to the traditional Aragvi restaurant in Moscow and the Tbilisi in St Petersburg). Numerous co-operatives run by people from the Caucasus opened restaurants serving Georgian food. The Georgian cuisine is famous for its *shashlyk*, *tsyplyata tabaka* (chicken fried under pressure), *basturma* (specially fried meat), *suluguni* (salted cheese) and *satsyvi* (chicken). It can be served with *lavash* (a special kind of bread) or with *khachapuri* (a roll stuffed with cheese) flavoured by various spices like *tkemali* or with a delicious *bazha* sauce.

Ukrainian: Ukrainians have traditionally been known to eat a lot – but also tastily. Specialities include *borscht* (beetroot soup with cabbage, meat,

mushrooms and other ingredients), *galushky* (small boiled dumplings) and *varenyky zvyshneyu* (curd dumplings with red cherries served with sugar and sour cream). Known and served around the world is Chicken Kiev (or Kiev cutlet), prepared with different spices and garlic. Loved by everyone in the Ukraine is *salo* (salted raw lard spiced with garlic) served with black bread. Also very popular is *kolbasa* (assorted smoked sausages).

Russian: Famous are beef Stroganov and Beluga caviar. Russian cuisine includes less refined but no less popular dishes like *bliny* (pancakes served with butter and sour cream, caviar, meat, jam etc), *shchi* (sour cabbage soup with meat pepped up with mustard), *pelmeni* (boiled dumplings with meat) and *kasha* (gruel or porridge of different grains).

RESTAURANTS

Inevitably the following list of restaurants concentrates on Moscow and St Petersburg where choice is continually expanding. In other cities and towns, it is often best to ask around when you arrive. In the current climate, restaurants often open and close within the space of weeks. At some restaurants, you should take your own alcoholic drinks as these may not be available, or you may not like the overwhelmingly sweet champagnes and wines.

MOSCOW

At most of the better restaurants in Moscow, it is important to reserve a table in advance – usually on the morning of the day you want to visit. If you don't want to arrive to a table laden with hors d'oeuvres, specify a *chisti stol* (a "clean table") when booking.

Aist, 1/8 Malaya Bronnaya. Tel: 291 6692. Popular co-op restaurant which specialises in Georgian cuisine. No reservations needed at lunch time. Roubles.

Aragvi, 6 Ulitsa Tverskaya. Tel: 229 8506. Excellent state-owned restaurant. Try the chicken *satsivi* (chicken in a walnut and coriander sauce). Roubles.

Arkadia, 3 Teatralny Proyezd. Tel: 926 9008. Bags of Russian atmosphere. Good Georgian wines. Roubles, but expensive.

Arlecchino, 15 Druzhinnikoskaya Ulitsa. Tel: 205 7088. Italian. Expensive. Major credit cards only.

Atrium, 44 Leninsky Prospekt. Tel: 137 3008. Stylish establishment serving Russian nouvelle cuisine in attractive atrium. Moderate prices, but major credit cards only.

Boyarksy, Metropol Hotel (fourth floor), 1/4 Teatralny Proyezd. Tel: 927 6089. Traditional Russian cuisine at expensive prices. Try the caviar-stuffed trout.

Champs Elysées, Pullman Hotel, 10 Korovinskoye Chausse. Tel: 488 8000. Expensive but superb French food. Hard currency.

Danilovsky, 5 Bolshoi Starodanilovsky Pereulok. Tel: 954 0566. Excellent but pricey Russian restau-

Our history could fill this book, but we prefer to fill glasses.

When you make a great beer, you don't have to make a great fuss.

rant next to the Danilov Monastery. Roubles and hard currency.

Druzhba, Expocentre, 12 Krasnopresnenskaya Nab. Tel: 255 2970. Lavish co-op restaurant that doubles as an art gallery. The suckling pig is recommended. Roubles and major credit cards.

Farkhad, Bolshaya Marfinskaya 4. Tel: 218 4136. Recommended Azerbaijani restaurant. Roubles and hard currency. Take your own wine.

Karina, 1-3 Solyansky Proyezd. Tel: 924 0369. Traditional Russian cuisine. Highly recommended. Roubles.

Kolkhida, 2 Stroyenie, 6 Sadovo-Samotechnaya. Tel: 299 6757. First-rate Georgian food. Roubles.

Kropotkinskaya 36, 36 Ulitsa Prechistenka. Tel: 201 7500. The first and best co-op restaurant. Try stuffed carp followed by home-made ice cream. Hard currency and credit cards.

Mei-Hua, 1 Stroyenie, 2/1 Ulitsa Rusakovskaya. Tel: 264 9574. Excellent Chinese restaurant. Roubles and hard currency.

Razgulyai, 11 Ulitsa Spartakovskaya. Tel: 267 7613. Cellar restaurant serving simple Russian food. Gypsy musicians at weekends.

Rusalochka, 12 Smolensky Buvar. Tel: 248 4438. Danish venture. Excellent seafood.

Stanislavskogo 2, 2 Ulitsa Stanislavskogo. Tel: 291 8689. Great food and ambience. Classical music. Bookings only taken on the day, and only after 6pm. Roubles.

THE GOLDEN RING

YAROSLAVL

Moskva Restaurant, 1 Ulitsa Komosomolskaya.
Chaika, Ultisa Lenina.
Rossiaya, Ulitsa Chkalov.

VLADIMIR

Traktir Restaurant, 2 Ulitsa Stolyarova.
Golden Gates Restaurant, 17 Ulitsa Tretyego Interntsionala.

SUZDAL

Pokrovskaya Hotel in the Motel Suzdal complex.
Trapeznaya, in the town kremlin.

ST PETERSBURG

Brasserie (Grand Hotel Europe), 1–7 Mikhailovskaya Ulitsa/Ulitsa Brodskovo. Tel: 113 8066/312 0072. Mainly French, but also serves hamburgers and spaghetti. Hard currency.

Cafe Literaturnoye, 18 Nevsky Prospekt. Tel: 312 8543. Offers stylish interior and chamber music. Moderate prices. Separate rouble menu available. Moderate prices.

Café 01, 5 Ulitsa Karavannaya/Tolmachova. Good food with French influence. English spoken. Roubles.

Café Baghdad, 35 Furshtadskaya Ulitsa/Petra Lavrova. Unpretentious café serving Middle-Eastern cuisine. Roubles.

Cafe Iveria, 35 Ulitsa Marata. Georgian food for roubles. Recommended.

Demyanova Ukha, 53 Prospekt Maxim Gorky. Tel: 232 9090. Excellent fresh fish from Lake Ladoga. Roubles.

Dom Architecturi – House of Architects, 52 Ulitsa Gertzena. Intended for architects, but general public is admitted. Food is only average but interior is stunning. Roubles.

Dom Uchernikh (House of Scholars), 26 Dvorsovaya Naberezhnaya. Turkish coffee, cakes, tea, alcohol. Elegant interior and view over the Neva. Great for afternoon tea.

Hotelship Peterhof, Naberezhnaya Makarova (by Tuchkov Bridge). Restaurant, coffee shop, piano bar and night club. Hard currency, but prices moderate.

Imperial, Kamenoostrovsky Prospekt/Ulitsa Professora Popova. Expensive prices warranted by elegant Tsarist-style decor. Hard currency preferred but roubles accepted.

Restaurant St Petersburg, 5 Griboedov/Ekaterinsky Canal. Tel: 314 4947. Candlelight, live entertainment and elegant decor. Hard currency. Expensive.

Sadkos (Grand Hotel Europe), 1–7 Mikhailovskovo Ulitsa/Ulitsa Broskovo. Tel: 113 8066/312 0072. Rouble bar and restaurant with fixed menu. Book for the evening.

Schwabsky Domik, 28/19 Krasnogvardeisky Prospekt. Tel: 528 2211. German food. Separate rouble restaurant.

Téte à Téte, 65 Bolshoi Prospekt (Petrograd side). Tel: 232 7548. Good food and romantic ambience. Book well in advance for evening. Roubles.

The Metropole, 22 Sadovaya Ulitsa. Tel: 310 1845/310 1181. Flamboyant old restaurant, with live music. Roubles.

Tbilisi, Sytninskaya Ulitsa, 10. Tel: 232 9391. Delicious Georgian food, again for roubles.

Venice, 21 Korablestoiteley Ulitsa. Tel: 352 1432. Good Italian food and floor show. Separate rouble menu available.

THE EUROPEAN NORTH

MURMANSK

Thanks to the large number of foreign sailors in town, restaurants are better here than might be expected. The **Darya Morya** at 26/9 Prospekt Lenina is for those who love seafood, while lovers of a good view should try the **Panorama** near the monument to the city's wartime defenders.

VYBORG

Even though this is a small town, you can eat your heart out in a variety of grill bars and restaurants. The rouble restaurant in the **Hotel Druzhba** and the café **Pogrebok** two doors down are very good. You can also eat well at the **Sever Restaurant** at 11

Prospect Lenina (tel: 21837) or the cafés **Brigantina**, 16 Yuzhny Val (tel: 25317) or **Pantseriaks**, 1 Luzhskaya Ulitsa (tel: 26301).

NOVGOROD

The best place to eat, particularly if you are here only for the day, is in the **fortress** itself (roubles and dollars), which provides warming sustenance in winter and has an open veranda for the hot summers. It has got the best location. Otherwise, you can try **Lakomka Café** at 11 Leningradskaya, tel: 36108 or **Posad** at 14 Ulitsa Bolshevikov, tel: 94849. There is also a restaurant in the **Intourist Hotel** which stays open until midnight and can sometimes come up with a passable meal, tel: 94288.

PSKOV

You could try the **Gera** on Ulitsa Jan Fabricus, but you are better off sticking to the restaurants in two of the hotels, the **Rizhsky** (tel: 67634) and the **Tourist** (tel: 33521), both open until midnight.

THE URALS

YAKATERINBURG

Among the hotels, **Hotel Oktyabrskaya**, Ulitsa S. Kovalevskoi 17 (tel: 445 146) is the best option for eating. The restaurant at **Hotel Sverdlovsk**, Chelyuskintzev 106, offers sporadic choice and as well as quality.

Restaurant Kharbin, Ulitsa Kyibisheva 40D. Tel: 226 325. A Chinese palace rising up from the urban landscape, this is an unusually appealing Chinese restaurant for Russia, with authentic chefs from China. Hanging lanterns and elaborately decorated rooms add to the atmosphere. Reservations in advance are essential.

SIBERIA & THE FAR EAST

IRKUTSK

The **Intourist Hotel** has a choice of restaurants. Its second-floor restaurant is the best in town, though the music is too loud and the menu irregular. As in most state restaurants, the menu diminishes as the night goes on, so arrive early. Its Peking restaurant costs hard currency and serves a dreadful imitation of Chinese food (Ketchup over shashlik tries to pass for sweet and sour pork). However, on the fourth floor of the hotel there is a delightful little tea shop that serves tea and caviar blinis.

Other restaurants are:
Baikal, Ulitsa Khmelnitskogo, 1. Russian cuisine
Arktika, Ulitsa Marksa, 26 Russian cuisine. Good seafood, especially the perch, fresh from Lake Baikal.
Tsentralny, Ulitsa Timirjazeva. Russian cuisine.

ORMSK

The **Taiga Hotel** (tel: 44000) has two restaurants: a noisy dining room on the second floor and a cosy café on the first floor.

YAKUTSK

The **Ontario** restaurant, a joint venture, is Yakutsk's best restaurant. Prices run about $20 per person. Tel: 65058. Other restaurants include **Sever**, Prospect Lenina, 38 (tel: 24486) and **Volna**, Prospect Lenina, 1 (tel: 28628).

UKRAINE

Ukraine is famous for several dishes: chicken Kiev and *borscht* being best known. The first – the white meat of chicken stuffed with garlic and butter – is almost invisible on the menus of the cities' restaurants. The second, a cabbage, beetroot and potato soup, is available everywhere and often the best thing to be had on the menu. Also commonly found and good are *vereniki*, small dumplings filled with curd cheese.

KIEV

Stories abound about the impending starvation of the populace of the former Soviet Union. These are not true, but at present it is nonetheless difficult to find good food in Kiev.

The food in hotel restaurants tends to be bland and the best chance for getting good food is in one of the co-operative restaurants starting to appear around the city. **Maxim's** (*see below*) and **Lestnitsa**, just off Independence Square, are the best.

Vitriak, 11 Prosp. Akedemika Glushkova Tel 266 7138. Ukrainian national cuisine: *vareniki* (dumplings filled with curd cheese), *bortschs pampushkami*. Ukrainian wine. The restaurant overlooks an old windmill.

Dinamo, 81 Boulv. M. Grushevskovo. Tel: 228 0939. European cooking, large choice of hard liquor.

Dybki, 1 Boulv. Stetsenko. Tel 440 5188. European cooking, spirits.

Zolotoye Vorota, 8 Lvivenka Pl. Tel 212 5504. European cooking. A big choice of Ukrainian wine and spirits.

Kiev, 26/1 Boulv. M. Grushevskovo. Tel: 293 1310. Ukrainian dishes, a large selection of vodkas, cognacs, liqueurs, Crimean wines. Speciality: *Kotleti po Kievskiy* (cutlets Kiev-style).

Krakov, 23 Prosp. Peremogi. Tel: 274 1908. European food.

Kureni, 19 Parkovaya doroga. Tel: 293 4062. Ukrainian national cuisine. Specialities: *vareniki s kartoshkoi i gribami* (vareniki with potatoes and mushrooms), *ushki s gribami* (patties filled with mushrooms). Ukrainian wine. The restaurant is situated on the beautiful slopes by the Dniepr. Open from May to November.

Lisova Pisnya, 1 Minskiy Prosp. Tel: 432 1887. European cooking.

Maxim's, 21 Boulv. Bogdana Khmelnitskovo. Tel: 224 7021. Restaurant-bistro. European and Ukrainian food. Strong spirits, Crimean wine. Can order any Ukrainian national dish 24 hours in advance.

Delivers prepared dishes to all the hotels in the town.

Melodiya, 36 Boulv Volodimirska. Tel: 228 7683. European food. Ukrainian wine.

Mlin, Gidropark. Tel: 517 0833. Ukrainian national cooking. Noted for its dumpling dishes, in particular *Vareniki s tvorogom v smetane* (dumplings with curd cheese and sour cream). Ukrainian wine. The restaurant is designed like a windmill and the noise of the rotating wheels and the trees of the Gidropark (hydropark) creates a wonderful atmosphere.

Moskva, 4 Boulv. Institutska. Tel: 229 1967. Russian cooking, Russian vodka and Crimean wine. Specialities: *Rastegai* (small fish pies in yeast dough); *Griby po Tolstovskiy* (mushrooms Tolstovskiy).

Rus, 4 Boulv. Gospitalna. Tel: 220 40557. European cooking. Large selection of spirits and wine. The restaurant has three big dining halls and a bar.

Salute, 11a Boulv. Sichnevovo Povstaniya. Tel: 290 5119. European cooking, spirits, Crimean wine, champagne.

Stolichniy, 5 Boulv. Kreshchatik. Tel: 229 8188. European cooking, and vodka, cognac, champagne and Ukrainian wines.

ODESSA

Krasniy, 15 Pushkinskaya. Tel: 252 246. European dishes. Specialities: chicken *tabaka* (boned chicken cooked flat in a shallow pan.) Spirits, Crimean wine.

Kiev, 1 Grecheskaya Pl. Tel: 229 731. Ukrainian cooking. Vodka, cognac, champagne. Crimean wine.

Londonskiy, 11 Primorskiy Boulv. Tel: 228 488. European dishes. Vodka, liqueurs, cognac, champagne.

Restoran Pecheskovo, 12 Ul. Khalturina. Tel: 250 395. Russian cooking, Turkish and Greek dishes. Strong spirits.

Chernoye Moriye, 55 Ul. Rishelevskaya. Tel: 240 125. European cooking. Spirits and wine.

Ukraina, 12 Ekaterinskaya Ul. Ukrainian national dishes: *bortschs pampushkami* (bortsch with dumplings), *zharkoe v gorshechkakh* (pot roast), Ukrainian wine.

At the end of Kreshchatik, you'll find the Besserabsky Market, where fresh produce can be bought. There is also an increasing number of Western-run hard currency stores where luxury foodstuffs can be purchased.

LVOV

Bristol, 19 Pr. Svobodiy. Tel: 742 081. European cooking. Vodka, whisky, cognac, liqueurs, champagne, Ukrainian wine.

Dnistr, 6 Boulv. Mateika. Tel: 727 008. European dishes. Strong spirits. Cognac. Specialities: salad Dnister.

Intourist, 1 Pl. Mitskevicha. Tel: 799 011. The restaurant has three halls: Chinese, Caucasian and Carpathian cooking.

Lviv, Boulv 700-richa Lvova. Tel: 782 590. Ukrainian cooking. Transcarpathian-Ukrainian wine.

Pid Levom, 20 Pl. Mitna. Tel: 741 004. European cooking. Strong spirits. Transcarpathian-Ukrainian wine.

Tourist, 103 Boulv. Konovaltsya. Tel: 345 032. Ukrainian cooking, strong spirits, Transcarpathian-Ukrainian wines.

Visokiy Zamok, Park Viskokiy Zamok. Tel: 799 011. Ukrainian national dishes. Transcarpathian-Ukrainian wines. Specialities: *bortsch s pampushkami*. The restaurant is situated in a picturesque park, on the hill overlooking Lvov.

Zolotoy Koloss, 18 Boulv. Kuaketsovo. Tel: 230 489. Beer-drinkers' restaurant. Original cooking: meat dishes include lamb cooked in beer. The restaurant is situated in the grounds of a famous Lvov brewery and the beer is delivered straight from the vats.

CHERNIGOV

Druzhba, 45 Boulv. Lenin. Tel: 135 739. European cooking. Hard liquor, Ukrainian wine, champagne.

Desna, 20 Boulv. Lenin. Tel: 733 50. Ukrainian and Belarussian dishes. Specialities: *Roulet Lakomka* (roulade) and *Lakomka blinchiki Polesskoye* – crêpes "Polesskoye".

Gradetskiy, 68 Boulv. Lenin. Tel: 167 450. Ukrainian and Belarussian cooking. Hard liquor, Ukrainian wine, champagne. Specialities: "*Myaso po Gradetskiy*" (meat cooked Gradetskiy-style).

Siberskiy, 15 Boulv. Rokossovskovo. Tel 320 21. Belarussian cookery: *kolbaski Siberskiye* – sausages "Siberskiye", *kotleti Desna* – cutlets "Desna".

Stariy Chernigov, 137 Prospekt Oktyabrskoy Revolutsiy. Tel: 721 77. Ukrainian cooking. Ukrainian vodka and wine. Specialities *bitki Chernigovskiy* (meatball/hamburger *Chernigovskiy*).

Ukraina, 38 Ul. Lenina. Tel: 748 32. Ukrainian and Belarussian cooking. Vodka, cognac, Ukrainian wine, champagne.

DRINKING NOTES

Everyone knows what they drink in Russia: vodka, and tea from the samovar. This is only half the truth. There are numerous other drinks within different national cuisines.

The Ukrainian traditional alcoholic drink is *gorilka* which resembles vodka. But more popular, and more refined, is *gorilka z pertsem*, i.e. gorilka with a small red pepper. The traditional non-alcoholic drink is *uzvar* (made of stewed fruit).

Georgians drink different dry and semi-dry wines. *Tsinandali, Mukuzani, Kinzmarauli, Alazan Valley*, and *Tvishi* (reported to have been the favourite wine of Stalin). Non-alcoholic drinks from Georgia are represented by the best in Russian mineral water such as *Borzhomi* and the so-called *vody Lagidze* (mineral water with various syrup mixtures).

In summer Russians prefer to drink *kvas*, a refreshing drink prepared from bread fermented with water and yeast.

SHOPPING

The regular absence of a variety of goods, and sometimes the absence of even the most basic goods, often affects the opening hours of shops. If there are no goods, the shop need not open! At least in the small towns.

Many small shops have a one-hour lunchbreak sometime between noon and 5pm. Larger shops are open all day, even on Saturdays. On Sundays, all shops, with the exception of some food stores, are closed. In big cities, shops open up between 7am and 9am and close sometime between 8pm and 9pm. In Moscow and St Petersburg and some capitals of the republics certain food stores might be open until 10pm. Bookshops and other specialist shops open around 10 or 11am and close around 7 or 8 in the evening, with a break usually between 2 and 3pm.

Hard currency shops: There is an increasing number of special shops where you can buy almost anything for hard currency. There are now different chains of such shops in hotels, international airports and at certain points in the big cities called Beriozka (the birch tree), Sadko, etc. The sales personnel in these shops usually speak English, French or German. They offer Russian goods of comparatively good quality. Furs, glass, ceramics, vodka, caviar, Crimean and Georgian wines. Many goods that are hard to come by in other city shops are available for hard currency.

Beriozka prices generally correspond with prices in Western European countries, though they tend to be lower for Russian goods than for imported ones.

Souvenirs: Inexpensive souvenirs, toys and other knick-knacks abound on Russian streets. Many co-operatives prefer not to wrestle with such difficult matters as food production or the maintenance of computers and instead produce souvenirs, hair combs and belts. They also produce famous Western jeans labels which Russian youngsters can sew onto their own jeans. All this cheap stuff is sold on the streets, in the vicinity of department stores and in co-operative markets.

The "must see" street in Moscow is Arbat, where Moscow painters and wood carvers sell their works. Prices are quite high, so don't be in a hurry to buy a set of Russian Matryoshkas (the wooden dolls which fit inside one another). The same set may be found much cheaper somewhere else.

There are places similar to Arbat in St Petersburg (Ostrovsky Ploschad), in Kiev (on October Revolution Square) and in other big cities. More upmarket souvenirs can be bought in special shops for foreigners, art-salons and curio shops. But beware of the problems waiting at customs: according to new Russian regulations, antiquities and art works may not be exported. The danger of confiscation is real. For all goods bought in a Russian shop, including those you bought at Beriozka, keep the receipts to show that you paid in hard currency and that the goods are not antique.

Outside Moscow and St Petersburg, look out for lace, nielloed jewellery (Veliky Ustiug), painted wooden objects (Archangel) and carved ivory (especially in the village of Lomonsovo, near Archangel). Ukraine does not have such a rich art and crafts tradition as Russia, and items such as lacquer boxes tend to be better and more easily purchased in Russia.

But items common to both countries, such as fur hats, can be just as easily bought in Kiev. A particularly good place to buy is the huge weekend market at the central Republican stadium. Ukraine's crafts are the more simple ones, such as painted wooden boxes, plates and spoons, earthenware pottery, embroidered cloths and linen and woollen rugs. Though souvenir shops are quite common in Kiev, the best selection is at Andryivsky Uzviz.

SHOPPING AREAS

MOSCOW

DEPARTMENT STORES

GUM (State Department Store), Krasnaya Ploshchad 3 (Red Square). This famous arcade has been commandeered by branches of foreign stores, and you won't find many Russian goods here. However, it is worth visiting, if only for the fabulous decor.

Detsky Mir (Children's World), Okhotny Ryad 2. Everything from toys and clothing to buggies.

TsUM (Central Department Store), Ulitsa Petrovka 2. Plenty of kitsch, but also Russia's traditional specialities, such as amber and coral jewellery, samovars, rugs and furs. Stock changes according to what the small co-operative boutiques that now inhabit the store can lay their hands on.

Voentork (Military Goods Store), Noivy Arbat. Eclectic mixture of goods, as well as Red Army surplus.

FUR SHOPS

Fur Kommissioni, Pushkinskaya Ulitsa 30. Coats, hats, muffs, gloves, stoles, etc. Expensive.

SPECIALITY SHOPS

Izmaylovsky Park, a good place for traditional Russian crafts (not antiques, which should only be bought from registered shops), with a weekend market.

Unisat, Ulitsa Vakhtangova. The place for antique silver and porcelain. Purchases intended for export must be supported by the necessary paperwork.
Yantar, Gruzinsky Val 14. Amber imported from Lithuania.
Russkiye Souventiry, Kutuzovsky Prospect 9. The place for upmarket souvenirs, such as lacquer boxes, silverware and ethnic costumes.
Kommissioni, Ulitsa Tverskaya Yamskaya. Ignore the chothes and porcelain and head for the good quality and reasonably priced crystal.

FOOD SHOPS
Gastronoom No. 20, Ulitsa Bolshaya Lubyanka 14. Good for chocolates and champagne.

ST PETERSBURG

One of the best places to buy souvenirs is **Klenovaya Alleya** (Maple Alley). To find it, walk towards Manege from the Engineers' Castle.

DEPARTMENT STORES
Gostinny Dvor, 35 Nevsky Prospekt. Most famous of St Petersburg's department stores.
Passage, 48 Nevksy Prospekt. Another big department store. Specialises in women's clothing.

BOOKS, MAPS, RECORDS
Isskust, 16 Nevsky Prospekt. Art books, posters and postcards.
Dom Knigi, 28 Nevsky Prospekt. Posters, postcards and maps.
Antikarnaya Kniga, 18 Nevsky Prospekt. Secondhand books.
Melody, 32/34 Nevsky Prospekt. Records.
Rapsody, 13 Ulitsa Bolshaya Konnushennaya (Zhelyabova). Sheet music and records.
Bukinist, 59 Liteiny Prospekt. Secondhand books.
10-10 Gallery, 10 Pushinskaya (Room 10). Art Gallery. Closed at weekends.

JEWELLERY
Yahont (Amber), 24 Ulitsa Gertsena. Jewellery shop occupying former Fabergé building.

PHOTOGRAPHY

The diplomat services agency (UPDK) and some new co-operative laboratories develop Agfa, Kodak and Fuji films (E6 process). But these services are only available in a few large cities. Hard currency shops usually sell Ektachrome and Fuji films. Kodachrome, which needs a special development process, is officially unavailable.

At the following addresses you can buy slide and print film and have your films developed.
Mezhdunarodnaya Hotel (hard currency). Tel: 253-1643.
Vozdvishenka, prosp. Kalinina, 25 (Kodak, Fuji – a rouble shop). Tel: 203-7307.
Tverskaya, ul. Gorkovo, 1. Tel: 203-5462.
Universitetskaya Hotel, 1st Floor (Kodak).
Salyut Hotel, 1st Floor (Kodak).
National Hotel, 1st Floor (Kodak).

LANGUAGE

Modern Russian has no established and universally used forms of addressing. The old revolutionary form "*tavárishch*" (comrade), still used amongst some party members, lacks popularity among the rest of the population.

One way is to say: "*Izviníte, skazhíte pozhálsta…*" (Excuse me, tell me, please…) or "*Izvinite, mózhna sprasít'…*" (Excuse me, can I ask you…).

If you want to look original and to show your penetration into the depths of history of courteous forms, you can address the man as *súda* (sir), and the woman as *sudárynya* (madam). Many people want to restore these pre-Revolutionary forms of address in modern Russian society. If you know the name of the father of the person you are talking to, the best and the most neutral way is to use both these when addressing him (her). In business circles you can use forms *gaspadín* to a man and *gaspazhá* to a woman.

The English forms of address Mister or Sir will also be accepted quite well.

You can hear common parlance forms *Maladói chilavék!* (Young man!) and *Dévushka!* (Girl!) to a person of any age and also *Zhénshchina!* (Woman!) to women in the bus, in the shop or at the market. These forms should be avoided in conversation.

TRANSLITERATION

There are four systems of transliteration of Russian words into English (see: *The Transliteration of Modern Russian for English Language Publications* by J.T. Shaw, the University of Wisconsin Press, 1967). If necessary, the systems can be combined so that one letter or a group of letters is transliterated according to one system and the other according to another.

To transliterate some Russian letters, English letter combinations are used:

ж = zh, x = kh, ц = ts, ч = ch, ш =sh, щ = shch, ю = yu, я = ya, ё = yo. The Russian letter combination кс is transliterated both as *ks* and as *x*. Russian letters are transliterated (with a few exceptions) in a similar way: й, ы = y, е, ё = e.

To transliterate Russian soft sign between the consonants and before no-vowel, the apostrophe is used, or the soft sign is ignored, as before vowels.

The transliteration of nominal inflections has some peculiarities: ый, ий = y, ие, ье = ie, ия = ia.

If the traditional English spelling in names differs from their letter-by-letter transliteration they are mostly translated in their English shape: Moscow (city), but river Moskva.

The Genetive inflections in the names of the streets and the other objects are translated according to their pronunciation, and not their spelling: площадь Горького, (*ploshchad' Gór'kogo*) = pl. Gorkovo in this book.The transliteration in this section shows the way to pronounce Russian words and therefore does not correspond exactly with their spelling.

The city maps and their captions use Russian words and abbreviations: ul. (*úlitsa*), means street; per. (*pereúlok*) – lane; prosp. (*prospékt*) – avenue; pl. (*plóshchad'*) – square; *alléya* – alley; *bul'vár* – boulevard; *magistrál* – main line; *proézd* – passage; *shossé* – highway; *spusk* – slope.

The Russian system of mentioning house numbers is as follows *prosp. Kalinina 28* (28 Kalinin Avenue).

ENGLISH/RUSSIAN

From a linguistic point of view, Russian belongs to the Slavonic branch of the Indo-European family of languages English, German, French, Spanish and Hindi are its relatives.

It is important when speaking Russian that you reproduce the accent (marked here before each stressed vowel with the sign ') correctly to be understood well.

Historically Russian can be called a comparatively young language. The evolution of the language to its present shape on the basis of the spoken language of Eastern Slavs and the Church-Slavonic written language is thought to have occurred between the 11th and 14th centuries.

Modern Russian has absorbed a considerable number of foreign words. Very few tourists will be puzzled by Russian words like *telefon, televizor, teatr, otel, restoran, kafe, taxi, metro, aeroport.*

The thing that intimidates people making their first aquaintance with Russian is the Russian alphabet. In fact the alphabet can be remembered easily after a few repetitions and the difference with the Latin alphabet is only minimal. An understanding of the Russian alphabet permits one to make out the names of the streets and the shop signs.

The Russian (or Cyrillic) alphabet was created by two brothers, philosophers and public figures Constantine (St Cyril) and Methodius, both born in Solun (now Thessaloniki in Greece). Their purpose was to facilitate the spread of Greek liturgical books in Slavonic speaking countries. Today the Cyrillic alphabet with different modifications is used in the Ukrainian, Belarussian, Bulgarian and Serbian languages, as well as a few others.

THE ALPHABET

printed letter	sounds, as in	Russian name of a letter
А а	a, archaeology	a
Б б	b, buddy	be
В в	v, vow	v
Г г	g, glad	ge
Д д	d, dot (the tip of the tongue close to the teeth, not the alveoli)	de
Е е	e, get	ye
Ё ё	yo, yoke	yo
Ж ж	zh, composure	zhe
З з	z, zest	ze
И и	i, ink	i
Й й	j, yes	jot
К к	k, kind	ka
Л л	l, life (but a bit harder)	el'
М м	m, memory	em
Н н	n, nut	en
О о	o, optimum	o
П п	p, party	pe
Р р	r (rumbling – as in Italian, the tip of the tongue is vibrating)	er
С с	s, sound	es
Т т	t, title (the tip of the tongue close to the teeth)	te
У у	u, nook	u
Ф ф	f, flower	ef
Х х	kh, hawk	ha

THE COLOUR OF LIFE.

A holiday may last just a week or so, but the memories of those happy, colourful days will last forever, because together you and Kodak Ektachrome films will capture, as large as life, the wondrous sights, the breathtaking scenery and the magical moments. For you to relive over and over again.

The Kodak Ektachrome range of slide films offers a choice of light source, speed and colour rendition and features extremely fine grain, very high sharpness and high resolving power.

Take home the real colour of life with Kodak Ektachrome films.

LIKE THIS?

OR LIKE THIS?

A KODAK FUN PANORAMIC CAMERA BROADENS YOUR VIEW

The holiday you and your camera have been looking forward to all year; and a stunning panoramic view appears. "Fabulous", you think to yourself, "must take that one".

Unfortunately, your lens is just not wide enough. And three-in-a-row is a poor substitute.

That's when you take out your pocket-size, 'single use' Kodak Fun Panoramic Camera. A film and a camera, all in one, and it works miracles. You won't need to focus, you don't need special lenses. Just aim, click and... it's all yours. The total picture.

You take twelve panoramic pictures with one Kodak Fun Panoramic Camera. Then put the camera in for developing and printing.

Each print is 25 by 9 centimetres. Excellent depth of field. True Kodak Gold colours.

The Kodak Fun Panoramic Camera itself goes back to the factory, to be recycled. So that others too can capture one of those spectacular phooooooooootoooooooooooos.

Ц ц	ts (pronounced conjointly)	tse
Ч ч	ch, charter	che
Ш ш	sh, shy	sha
Щ щ	shch (pronounced conjointly)	shcha
ъ	(the hard sign)	
Ы ы	y (pronounced with the same position of a tongue as when pronouncing G,K)	y
ь	(the soft sign)	
Э э	e, ensign	e
Ю ю	yu, you	yu
Я я	ya, yard	ya

NUMBERS

1	adín	один
2	dva	два
3	tri	три
4	chityri	четыре
5	pyat'	пят́
6	shes't'	шесть
7	sem	семь
8	vósim	восемь
9	d'évit'	девять
10	d'ésit'	десять
11	adínatsat'	одиннадцать
12	dvinátsat'	двенадцать
13	trinátsat'	тринадцать
14	chityrnatsat'	четырнадцать
15	pitnátsat'	пятнадцат́
16	shysnátsat'	шестнадцать
17	simnátsat'	семнадцать
18	vasimnátsat'	восемнадцать
19	divitnátsat'	девятнадцать
20	dvátsat'	двадцать
21	dvatsat' adin	двадцать один
30	trítsat'	тридцать
40	sórak	сорок
50	pidisyat	пятьдесят
60	shyz'disyat	шестьдесят
70	s'émdisyat	семьдесят
80	vósimdisyat	восемьдесят
90	divinósta	девяносто
100	sto	сто
200	dv'és'ti	двести
300	trísta	триста
400	chityrista	четыреста
500	pitsót	пятьсот
600	shyssót	шестьсот
700	simsót	семьсот
800	vasimsót	восемьсот
900	divitsót	девятьсот
1,000	tysicha	тысяча
2,000	dve tysichi	две тысяч и
10,000	d'ésit' tysich	десятьтысяч
100,000	sto tysich	сто тысяч
1,000,000	milión	миллион
1,000,000,000	miliárd	миллиард

PRONOUNS

I/we
ya/my
я/мы

You
ty (singular, informal)/
vy (plural, or formal singular)
ты /вы

He/she/they
on/aná/aní
он/она/они

My/mine
moj (object masculine)/
mayá (object feminine)/
mayó (neutral or without marking the gender)/
maí (plural)
мой/моя/моё/мои

Our/ours
nash/násha/náshe/náshy (resp.)
наш/наша/наше/наши

Your/yours
tvoj etc. (see My)
vash etc. (see Our)
твой/ваш

His/her, hers/their, theirs
jivó/jiyó/ikh
его/её/их

Who?
khto?
Кто?

What?
shto?
Что?

GREETINGS & ACQUAINTANCE

Hello!
zdrástvuti (neutral, often accompanied by shaking hands, but it is not necessary)
Здравствуйте!

zdrástvuj (to one person, informal)
Здравствуй!

alo! (by telephone only)
Алло!

priv'ét! (informal)
Привет!

Good afternoon/Good evening
dóbry den'/dobry véchir
Добрый день/Добрый вечер

Good morning/Good night
dobrae útra/dobraj nóchi (= Sleep well)
Доброе утро/Доброй ночи

Good bye
dasvidán'ye (neutral)
До свиданья

ciao! (informal)
Чао!

paká! (informal, literally means "until")
Пока!

Good luck to you!
shchislíva!
Счастливо!

What is your name?
kak vas (tibya) zavút?/kak váshe ímya ótchistva?
(the second is formal)
Как вас (тебя) зовут?/Как ваше имя и
отчество?

My name is…/I am…
minya zavut…/ya…
Меня зовут…/Я…

It's a pleasure
óchin' priyatna
Очень приятно

Good/excellent
kharashó/privaskhódna
хорошо/отлично

Do you speak English?
vy gavaríti pa anglíski?
Вы говорите по-английски?

I don't understand/I didn't understand
ya ni panimáyu/ya ni pónyal
Я не понимаю/Я не понял

Repeat, please
pavtaríti pazhálsta
Повторите, пожалуйста

What do you call this?
kak vy éta nazyváiti?
Как вы это называете?

How do you say…?
kak vy gavaríti…?
Как вы говорите…?

Please/Thank you (very much)
pazhálsta/(bal'shóe) spasíba
Пожалуйста/(бальшоэ) спасибо

Excuse me
izviníti
Извините

Where is the…?
gd'e (nakhóditsa)…?
Где находится…?

beach
plyazh
…пляж

bathroom
vánnaya
…ванная

bus station
aftóbusnaya stántsyja/aftavakzál
…автобусная станция/автовокзал

bus stop
astanófka aftóbusa
…остановка автобуса

airport
airapórt
…аэропорт

railway station
vakzál/stántsyja (in small towns)
…вокзал/станция

post office
póchta
…почта

police station
…milítsyja
…милиция

ticket office
bil'étnaya kássa
…билетная касса

marketplace
rynak/bazár
…рынок/базар

embassy/consulate
pasól'stva/kónsul'stva
…посольство/консульство

Where is there a…?
gd'e z'd'es'…?
Где здесь…?

currency exchange
abm'én val'úty
…обмен валюты

pharmacy apt'éka …аптека	Do you have…? u vas jes't'…? У вас есть…?
(good) hotel (kharóshyj) atél'/(kharoshaya) gastínitsa …(хороший)отель(хорошая)гостиница	I (don't) want… ya (ni) khachyu… Я (не) хочу…
restaurant ristarán …ресторан	I want to buy… ya khachyu kupít'… Я хочу купить…
bar bar …бар	Where can I buy… gd'e ya magú kupít'… Где я могу купить…
taxi stand stayanka taxí …стоянка такси	cigarettes sigaréty …сигареты
subway station mitró …метро	wine vinó …вино
service station aftazaprávachnaya stantsyja/aftasárvis …автозаправочная станция	film fotoplyonku …фотоплёнку
newsstand gaz'étnyj kiósk …газетный киоск	a ticket for… bilét na… …билет на…
public telephone tilifón …телефон	this éta …это
hard currency shop val'útnyj magazín …валютный магазин	postcards/envelopes atkrytki/kanv'érty …открытки/конверты
supermarket univirsám …универсам	a pen/a pencil rúchku/karandásh …ручку/карандаш
department store univirmák …универмаг	soap/shampoo myla/shampún' …мыло/шампунь
hairdresser parikmákhirskaya …парикмахерская	aspirin aspirn …аспирин
jeweller yuvilírnyj magazin …ювелирный магазин	I need… mn'e núzhna… Мне нужно…
hospital bal'nítsa …больница	I need a doctor/a mechanic mn'e núzhyn dóktar/aftamikhánik Мне нужен доктор/автомеханик

I need help
mn'e nuzhná pómashch'
Мне нужна помощ́

Car/plane/trains/ship
mashyna/samal'yot/póist/karábl'
машина/самолёт/поезд/корабль

A ticket to…
bil'ét do…
билет до…

How can I get to…
kak ya magu dabrátsa do…
Как я могу добраться до…

Please, take me to…
pazhalsta atvizíti minya…
Пожалуйста, отвезите меня…

What is this place called?
kak nazyváitsa eta m'ésta?
Как называется это место?

Where are we?
gd'e my?
Где мы?

Stop here
astanavíti z'd'es'
Остановите здесь

Please wait
padazhdíti pazhalsta
Подождите, пожалуйста

When does the train [plane] leave?
kagdá atpravl'yaitsa poist [samalyot]?
Когда отправляется поезд (самолёт)?

I want to check my luggage
ya khachyu prav'érit' bagázh
Я хочу проверить багаж

Where does this bus go?
kudá id'yot état aftóbus?
Куда идёт этот автобус?

How much does it cost?
skól'ka eta stóit?
Сколько это стоит?

That's very expensive
eta óchin' dóraga
Это очень дорого

A lot, many/A little, few
mnóga/mála
много/мало

It (doesn't) fits me
eta mn'e (ni) padkhódit
Это мне (не) подходит

I have a reservation
u minya zakázana m'esta
У меня заказана комната

I want to make a reservation
ya khachyu zakazát' m'esta
Я хочу заказать место

A single (double) room
adnam'éstnuyu (dvukhmestnuyu) kómnatu
одноместную (двухместную) комнату

I want to see the room
ya khachyu pasmatrét' nómer
Я хочу посмотреть номер

Key/suitcase/bag
klyuch/chimadán/súmka
ключ/чемодан/сумка

Waiter/menu
afitsyánt/minyu
официант/меню

I want to order…
ya khachyu zakazat'…
Я хочу заказать

Breakfast/lunch/supper
záftrak/ab'ét/úzhyn
завтрак/обед/ужин

the house speciality
fírminnaya blyuda
фирменное блюдо

Mineral water/juice
minirál'naya vadá/sok
минерал'ьная вода/сок

Coffee/tea/beer
kófe/chai/píva
кофе/ чай/пиво

What do you have to drink (alcoholic)?
shto u vas jes't' vypit'?
Что у вас есть выпить?

Ice/fruit/dessert
marózhynaya/frúkty/disért
мороженое/фрукты/дессерт

THE KODAK GOLD GUIDE TO BETTER PICTURES.

Good photography is not difficult. Use these practical hints and Kodak Gold II Film: then notice the improvement.

Move in close. Get close enough to capture only the important elements.

Frame your Pictures. Look out for natural frames such as archways or tree branches to add an interesting foreground. Frames help create a sensation of depth and direct attention into the picture.

One centre of interest. Ensure you have one focus of interest and avoid distracting features that can confuse the viewer.

Use leading lines. Leading lines direct attention to your subject i.e. – a stream, a fence, a pathway; or the less obvious such as light beams or shadows.

Maintain activity. Pictures are more appealing if the subject is involved in some natural action.

Keep within the flash range. Ensure subject is within flash range for your camera (generally 4 metres). With groups make sure everyone is the same distance from the camera to receive the same amount of light.

Check the light direction. People tend to squint in bright direct light. Light from the side creates highlights and shadows that reveal texture and help to show the shapes of the subject. If shooting into direct sunlight fill-in flash can be effective to light the subject from the front.

CHOOSING YOUR KODAK GOLD II FILM.

Choosing the correct speed of colour print film for the type of photographs you will be taking is essential to achieve the best colourful results.

Basically the more intricate your needs in terms of capturing speed or low-light situations the higher speed film you require.

Kodak Gold II 100. Use in bright outdoor light or indoors with electronic flash. Fine grain, ideal for enlargements and close-ups. Ideal for beaches, snow scenes and posed shots.

Kodak Gold II 200 A multipurpose film for general lighting conditions and slow to moderate action. Recommended for automatic 35mm cameras. Ideal for walks, bike rides and parties.

Kodak Gold II 400. Provides the best colour accuracy as well as the richest, most saturated colours of any 400 speed film. Outstanding flash-taking capabilities for low-light and fast-action situations; excellent exposure latitude. Ideal for outdoor or well-lit indoor sports, stage shows or sunsets.

INSIGHT GUIDES

COLORSET NUMBERS

160 **A**laska
155 Alsace
150 Amazon Wildlife
116 America, South
173 American Southwest
158A Amsterdam
260 Argentina
287 Asia, East
207 Asia, South
262 Asia, South East
194 Asian Wildlife, Southeast
167A Athens
272 Australia
263 Austria
188 **B**ahamas
206 Bali Baru
107 Baltic States
246A Bangkok
292 Barbados
219B Barcelona
187 Bay of Naples
234A Beijing
109 Belgium
135A Berlin
217 Bermuda
100A Boston
127 Brazil
178 Brittany
109A Brussels
144A Budapest
260A Buenos Aires
213 Burgundy
268A **C**airo
247B Calcutta
275 California
180 California, Northern
161 California, Southern
237 Canada
162 Caribbean The Lesser Antilles
122 Catalonia (Costa Brava)
141 Channel Islands
184C Chicago
151 Chile
234 China
135E Cologne
119 Continental Europe
189 Corsica
281 Costa Rica
291 Cote d'Azur
165 Crete
184 Crossing America
226 Cyprus
114 Czechoslovakia
247A **D**elhi, Jaipur, Agra
238 Denmark
135B Dresden
142B Dublin

135F Düsseldorf
204 **E**ast African Wildlife,
149 Eastern Europe,
118 Ecuador
148A Edinburgh
268 Egypt
123 Finland
209B Florence
243 Florida
154 France
135C Frankfurt
208 **G**ambia & Senegal
135 Germany
148B Glasgow
279 Gran Canaria
169 Great Barrier Reef
124 Great Britain
167 Greece
166 Greek Islands
135G **H**amburg
240 Hawaii
193 Himalaya, Western
196 Hong Kong
144 Hungary
256 **I**celand
247 India
212 India, South
128 Indian Wildlife
143 Indonesia
142 Ireland
252 Israel
236A Istanbul
209 Italy
213 **J**amaica
278 Japan
266 Java
252A Jerusalem-Tel Aviv
203A **K**athmandu
270 Kenya
300 Korea
202A **L**isbon
258 Loire Valley
124A London
275A Los Angeles
201 **M**adeira
219A Madrid
145 Malaysia
157 Mallorca & Ibiza
117 Malta
272B Melbourne
285 Mexico
285A Mexico City
243A Miami
237B Montreal
235 Morocco
101A Moscow
135D Munich
211 Myanmar (Burma)
259 **N**amibia
269 Native America
203 Nepal

158 Netherlands
100 New England
184E New Orleans
184F New York City
133 New York State
293 New Zealand
265 Nile, The
120 Norway
124B **O**xford
147 **P**acific Northwest
205 Pakistan
154A Paris
249 Peru
184B Philadelphia
222 Philippines
115 Poland
202 Portugal
114A Prague
153 Provence
156 Puerto Rico
250 **R**ajasthan
177 Rhine
127A Rio de Janeiro
172 Rockies
209A Rome
101 Russia
275B **S**an Francisco
130 Sardinia
148 Scotland
184D Seattle
261 Sicily
159 Singapore
257 South Africa
264 South Tyrol
219 Spain
220 Spain, Southern
105 Sri Lanka
101B St Petersburg
170 Sweden
232 Switzerland
272 Sydney
175 **T**aiwan
112 Tenerife
186 Texas
246 Thailand
278A Tokyo
139 Trinidad & Tobago
113 Tunisia
236 Turkey
171 Turkish Coast
210 Tuscany
174 **U**mbria
237A **V**ancouver
198 Venezuela
209C Venice
263A Vienna
255 Vietnam
267 **W**ales
184C Washington DC
183 Waterways of Europe
215 **Y**emen

You'll find the colorset number on the spine of each Insight Guide.

Salt/pepper/sugar
sol'/périts/sákhar
соль/перец/сахар

Beef/pork/chicken/fish/shrimp
gavyadina/svinína/kúritsa/ryba/kriv'étki
говядина/свинина/курица/рыба/креветки

Vegetables/rice/potatoes
óvashchi/ris/kartófil'
овощи/рис/картофель

Bread/butter/eggs
khleb/másla/yajtsa
хлеб/масло/яйца

Soup/salad/sandwich/pizza
sup/salát/butyrbrót/pitsa
суп/салат/бутерброд/пицца

A plate/a glass/a cup/a napkin
tar'élka/stakán/cháshka/salf'étka
тарелка/стакан/чашка/салфетка

The bill, please
shchyot pazhalsta
Счёт, пожалуйста

Delicious/Not so good
fkúsna/ták sibe
вкусно/так себе

I want my change, please
zdáchu pazhalsta
Сдачу, пожалуйста

MONEY

I want to exchange currency (money)
ya khachyu abmin'át' val'yutu (d'én'gi)
Я хочу обменять валюту (деньги)

Do you accept credit cards?
vy prinimáiti kridítnyi kártachki?
Вы принимаете кредитные карточки ?

Can you cash a traveller's cheque?
vy mózhyti razminyat' darózhnyj chek?
Вы можете разменять дорожный чек?

What is the exchange rate?
kakój kurs?
Какой курс?

TIME

What time is it?
katóryj chas?
Который час?

Just a moment, please
adnú minútachku
Одну минуточку

How long docs it take?
skól'ka vrémini eta zanimáit?
Сколько времени это занимает?

Hour/day/week/month
chas/den'/nid'élya/m'ésits
час/день/неделя/месяц

At what time?
f kakóe vrémya?
В какое время?

This (last, next) week
eta (próshlaya, sl'édujshchiya) nid'elya
эта (прошлая, следующая) неделя

Yesterday/today/tomorrow
fchirá/sivód'nya/záftra
вчера/сегодня/завтра

Sunday
vaskris'én'je
воскресенье

Monday
panid'él'nik
понедельник

Tuesday
ftórnik
вторник

Wednesday
sridá
среда

Thursday
chitv'érk
четверг

Friday
pyatnitsa
пятница

Saturday
subóta
суббота

The weekend
vykhadnyi dni
выходные дни

SIGNS & INSCRIPTIONS

вход/выход/входа нет
fkhot/vykhat/fkhóda n'et
Entrance/exit/no entrance

туалет/уборная
tual'ét/ubórnaya
Lavatory

Ж (З)/М (М)
dlya zhén'shchin/dlya mushchín
Ladies/gentlemen

зал ожидания
zal azhidán'ya
Waiting hall

занято/свободно
zánita/svabódna
Occupied/free

касса
kassa
booking office/cash desk

медпункт
mitpúnt
Medical services

справочное бюро
správachnae bzuro
Information

вода для питья
vadá dlya pit'ya
Drinking water

вокзал
vakzál
Terminal/railway station

открыто/закрыто
atkryta/zakryta
Open/Closed

запрещается/опасно
zaprishchyaitsa/apásna
Prohibited/danger

продукты/гастроном
pradúkty/gastranóm
Grocery

булочная/кондитерская
búlachnaya/kan'dítirskaya
Bakery/confectionery

закусочная/столовая
zakúsachnaya/stalóvaya
Refreshment room/canteen

самообслуживание
samaapslúzhivan'je
Self-service

баня/прачечная/химчистка
bánya/práchichnaya/khimchístka
Bath-house/laundry/chemical cleaning

книги/культтовары
knígi/kul'taváry
Books/stationery

мясо/птица
m'ása/ptítsa
Meat/poultry

обувь
óbuf'
Shoe-store

овощи/фрукты
óvashchi/frúkty
Green-grocery/fruits

универмаг/универсам
univirmák/univirsám
Department store/supermarket

USEFUL ADDRESSES

RUSSIAN MISSIONS ABROAD

Argentina, 1741 Rodriges Penya, Buenos Aires. Tel: 42-1552.
Australia, Griffis, 70 Canberra Avenue, Canberra. Tel: 062-956 6408.
Austria, 45-47 Reisnerstr., Vienna. Tel: 721 229.
Belgium, 66 Avenue de Fre, 1180 Bruxelles. Tel: 373 3569, 374 3406.
Canada, 285 Sharlotta Street, Ottawa. Tel: 613-235 4341.
Denmark, 3-5 Christianiagade, Copenhagen. Tel: 314 25585.
Estonia, Pikk 19, Tallinn. Tel: 443 014.
Finland, 6 Tehtaankatu, Helsinki. Tel: 661 876.
France, 16 Boulevard Lann 40/50, Paris. Tel: 1-45 01 05 50.
Germany, Embassy: 2 Waldstr. 42, 5300 Bonn. Tel: 0228-312-086.
   Consulate: 76 Am Feenteich, 2000 Hamburg. Tel: 040-229 5301.
Greece, 28 Nikiforu Litra Street, Paleo Psyhico, Athens. Tel: 672 6130, 672 5235.
India, Shantipath Street, Chanakiapury, Delhi. Tel: 606 026.

Ireland, 186 Orwell Road, Dublin. Tel: 975 748.
Italy, 5 Via Gaeta, Rome. Tel: 494 1681.
Japan, Minato-ku, Adzabu-dai 2-1-1 T-106, Tokyo. Tel: 583 4224.
Lithuania, c/o Draugyste Hotel (Rooms 807, 705), Vilnius. Tel: 26 16 37.
Netherlands, 2 Andries Bickerweh, The Hague. Tel: 07-045 130.
New Zealand, Carory, 57 Messines Road, Wellington. Tel: 766 113.
Norway, 2 Dramensveien 74, Oslo. Tel: 553 278.
Singapore, 51 Nassim Road 1025. Tel: 235 1834.
Spain, 6 & 14 Maestro Ripol, Madrid. Tel: 411 0706, 262 2264.
Sweden, 31 Ervelsgatan, Stockholm. Tcl: 08-13 044 044.
Switzerland, 37 Brunnadenrein 3006, Bern. Tel: 031-440 566.
Thailand, 108 Sotorn Nua, Bangkok. Tel: 258 0628.
Turkey, Caryagdy, Soc. 5, Ankara. Tel: 139 2122.
United Kingdom, 5, 13 & 18 Kensington Palace Gardens, London. Tel: 071-229 3828.
United States, Embassy, 1125 16th Street, Washington DC 20036. Tel: 628 7551, 628 8548, 628 6412. Consulate, 2790 Green Street, San Francisco, California. Tel: 415- 922 6644.

UKRAINIAN MISSIONS ABROAD

France, 1 Miollis, 75015 Paris. Tel: 40 72 86 04.
Germany, Wald Str. 42, 5300 Bonn 2. Tel: 311 995.
United Kingdom, 78 Kensington Park Road, London W11 2PL. Tel: 071-727 6312.
United States, 335 O Street NW, Washington DC. Tel: 333 0606.

EMBASSIES IN MOSCOW

Argentina, Sadovaya-Triumfal'naya ul. 4/10. Tel: 299 0367.
Australia, Prechistenka (Kropotkinsky) per. 13. Tel: 246 5012.
Austria, Starokonyushenny per. 1. Tel: 201 7317.
Canada, Starokonyushenny per. 23. Tel: 241 5070.
China, Leninskie Gory, ul. Druzhby 6. Tel: 143 1543.
Czechoslovakia, ul. Fuchika 12/14. Tel: 250 2225.
Denmark, per. Ostrovskovo 9. Tel: 201 7868.
Finland, Prechistenka (Kropotkinsky) per. 15/17.
France, Kazansky per. 10. Tel: 236 0003.
Germany, B.Gruzinskaya ul. 17. Tel: 252 5521.
Greece, ul. Stanislavskovo 4. Tel: 290 2274.
Hungary, Mosfilmovskaya ul. 62. Tel: 143 8955.
India, ul. Obukha 6-8. Tel: 297 1841.
Ireland, Grokhol'sky per. 5. Tel: 288 4101.
Italy, ul. Vesnina 5. Tel: 241 1533.
Japan, Sobinovsky per. 5a. Tel: 202 0061.
Luxemburg, Khrushchevsky per. 3. Tel: 202 2171.
Malaysia, Mosfilmovskaya ul. 50. Tel: 147 1415.
Netherlands, Kalashny per. 7. Tel: 291 2999.

New Zealand, ul. Vorovskovo 44. Tel: 290 3485.
Norway, ul. Vorovskovo 7. Tel: 290 3872.
Poland, ul. Klimashkina 4. Tel: 254 3612.
Portugal, Grokholsky per. 3/1. Tel: 230 2435.
Romania, Mosfilmovskaya ul. 64. Tel: 143 0424.
Singapore, per. Voevodina 5. Tel: 241 3702.
Spain, ul. Gertsena 50/8. Tel: 291 9004.
Sweden, Mosfilmovskaya ul. 60. Tel: 147 9009.
Switzerland, per. Stopani 2/5. Tel: 925 5322.
Thailand, Eropkinsky per. 3. Tel: 201 4893.
Turkey, Vadkovsky per. 7/37. Tel: 972 6900.
Ukraine, 18 Stanislavskogo ul. Tel: 229 3422.
United Kingdom, nab. Morisa Toreza 14. Tel: 231 8511.
United States, ul. Chaikovskovo 19/23. Tel: 252 2451.

CONSULATES IN OTHER CITIES

IRKUTSK

Mongolia, ul. Lapina 11. Tel: 242 370.

KIEV

Bulgaria, ul. Hospitalnaya 1. Tel: 225 5119.
Cuba, Bethersky per. 5. Tel: 216 2930.
Czechoslovakia, Yaroslavov Val 34. Tel: 229 7269.
Germany: ul. Chkalova 84. Tel: 216 1477, 216 6794, 216 7854, 216 7498.
Hungary, ul. Reiterskaya 33. Tel: 212 4094, 212 4134.
Mongolia, ul. Kotsyubinskovo 3. Tel: 216 8891.
Poland, Yaroslavov Val 12. Tel: 224 8040, 225 7090.
Romania, ul. Kotsyubinskovo 8. Tel: 224-5261.
United Kingdom, 252025 Kiev, Desyatinna 9 252025. Tel: 228 0504.

ST PETERSBURG

Bulgaria, ul. Ryleeva 27. Tel: 273 7347.
China, 3-Linia 12. Tel: 218 1721, 218 3492, 218 7953.
Cuba, ul. Ryleeva 37. Tel: 279 0492.
Finland, ul. Chaikovskovo 71. Tel: 273 7321.
France, nab. Moiki 15. Tel: 314 1443, 312 1130.
Germany, ul. Petra Lavrova 39. Tel: 273 5598, 273 5731, 273 5937.
Hungary, ul. Marata 15. Tel: 312 6458, 312 6753.
Italy, Teatral'naya pl. 10. Tel: 312 2896.
Japan, nab. Moiki 29. Tel: 314 1434/18.
Mongolia, Saperny per. 11. Tel: 243 4522.
Poland, ul. Sovetskaya 12. Tel: 274 4331, 274 4170.
Sweden, 10th line (VO). Tel: 218 3526/27/28.
United States, ul. Petra Lavrova 15. Tel: 274 8235.

LVOV

Poland, ul. Ivana Franko 10. Tel: 723 949.

MINSK

Bulgaria: Bronevoy per. 3. Tel: 225 500.
Germany: ul. Sakharova 26. Tel: 330 752.
Poland: Omsky per. 6. Tel: 331 313, 331 3601, 331 1114, 331 5109, 331 0260.
United Kingdom: ul Sacharova 26. Tel: 330 752.

NAKHODKA

Japan: ul. Lunacharskovo 9. Tel: 56 371.
Korea: ul. Vladivostokskaya 1. Tel: 55 310.

ODESSA

Bulgaria: ul. Posmitnovo 9. Tel: 662 015.
Cuba: ul. Tomasa 7/9. Tel: 251 469.
India: ul. Kirova 31. Tel: 224 333.

AIRLINE OFFICES

MOSCOW

Air France: Korovy Val. Tel: 237 2325, 237 3344. Monday–Friday 9am–1pm, 2–6pm.
Air India: ul. Korovy Val 7. Tel: 237 7494, 236 4440. Monday–Friday 9.30am–1pm, 2–5.15pm, Saturday 10am–3pm.
Alitalia: ul. Pushechnaya 7. Tel: 928 2166,928 1704. Monday–Friday 9.30am–1.30pm, 2–6pm, Saturday 9.30am–1pm.
Austrian Airlines: Sovincenter, Suite 2005, Krasnopresnenskaya nab. 12, floor 18, Office 1805. Tel: 253 8988. Monday–Friday 9am–6pm, Saturday 9am–1pm.
British Airways: Sovincenter, Suite 1905, Krasnopresnenskaya nab. 12, floor 19, Office 1905. Tel: 253 2492. Monday–Friday 9am–6pm.
Finnair: Kamergersky per. 6. Tel: 292 8788. Monday–Friday 9am–5pm.
Japan Airlines: ul. Kuznetsky Most 3. Tel: 921 6448, 921 6648. Monday–Friday 9am–6pm.
KLM: (Royal Dutch Airlines), Krasnopresnenskaya nab. 12, floor 13, Office 1307. Tel: 253 2150, 230 2304. Monday–Friday 9am–5pm.
Lufthansa: Hotel Olympic Penta, ul. Olimpski. Tel: 975 2501. Monday–Friday 9am–5.30pm.
LOT: (Polish Airlines), Korovyva Val 7. Tel: 238 0003, 238 0313. Monday–Friday 9am–6pm, Saturday 9am–5pm.
Sabena: (Belgian World Airlines), Sheremetyevo II Airport, Room 615, C/O Aeroflot. Tel: 578 5614, 578 5634. Monday–Friday 9am–1pm, 2–6pm.
SAS: (Scandinavian Airlines), ul. Kuznetsky Most 3. Tel: 925 4447, 925 4747. Monday–Friday 9am–6pm, Saturday 9am–noon.
Swissair: Krasnopresnenskaya nab. 12, floor 20, Office 2005. Tel: 253 8988, 253 1859, Monday–Friday 9am–6pm.

Those with downtown addresses in this list also have offices in Sheremetevo-II Airport.

ST PETERSBURG

Finnair: ul. Gogolya 19. Tel: 315 9736, 312 8987. These airlines and Air France, British Airways, KLM, Lufthansa and LOT also have their offices in Pulkovo-2 Airport.

CHAMBERS OF COMMERCE

Russia Chamber of Commerce and Industry: 6 Ilyinka (Kuybyshev) St, Moscow 101000. Tel: 923 4323.
US-Russia Trade and Economic Council: 805 3rd Ave, New York, NY 10022. Tel: 644 4550. Moscow office: 3 Shevchenko Embankment, Moscow 121248. Tel: 243 5470.
British-Russian Chamber of Commerce: 2 Lowndes St, London SW1X 9ET. Tel: 235 2423. Moscow office: 1904, 19th Floor, World Trade Centre, 12 Krasnopresnenskaya Embankment, Moscow 123610. Tel: 253 2554.
French-Russian Chamber of Commerce: 22 Ave Franklin D. Roosevelt, 75008 Paris. Tel: 422 59710. Moscow office: Apt. 3, 4 Pokrovsky Blvd, Moscow 101000. Tel: 207 3009.
Italian-Russian Chamber of Commerce: 5 Via San Tomaso, Milan. Tel: 481 6725. Moscow office: 7 Vesnina St, Moscow 121002. Tel: 241 5729.

INTERNATIONAL TRAVEL AGENTS

UNITED STATES

Four Winds Travel: 175 Fifth Ave, New York, NY 10010.
Russian Travel Bureau Inc.: 245 E 44th St, New York, NY10017. Tel: 986 1500.

UNITED KINGDOM

American Express Co. Inc.: 6 Haymarket, London SW1. Tel: 071-930 4411.
Drifters: 22 Craven Terrace, Lancaster Gate, London W2. Tel: 071-402 9171.
Regent Holdiays UK Ltd: 15 John Street, Bristol BS1 2HR. Tel: 0272- 211 711.
Swan Hellenic Art Treasures Tours:77 New Oxford St, London WC1. Tel: 071-831 1616.

GERMANY

Lindex Reisen: Rauchstr. 5, 8000 München
Intratours, Eiserne Hand 19, 6000 Frankfurt.
Morgenstern Resisen: Alt Sossenhelm 47, 6000 Frankfurt. Tel: 346010.

SINGAPORE

Folke von Knobloch: 126 Telok Ayer, #02-01 Gat House, Singapore (specialist for Siberia trips).

FURTHER READING

HISTORY

The Blackwell Encyclopaedia of the Russian Revolution, edited by H. Shukman. Blackwell, 1989.

Catherine the Great, by J.T. Alexander. Oxford University Press, 1989.

Comrades 1917 – Russia in Revolution, by Brian Moynihan. Hutchinson, 1992.

History of Soviet Russia, by E.H. Carr. Pelican. In three volumes, first published 1953.

A History of the Soviet Union, by G.A. Hosking. Fontana/Collins, 1990.

The Icon and the Axe, by James Billington. Vintage US.

The Last Tsar, by Edvard Razdinsky. Hodder and Stoughton, 1992.

The Making of Modern Russia, by L. Kochan and R. Abraham. Penguin, 1983.

Nicholas II: Emperor of all the Russians, by Dominic Lieven. John Murray, 1993.

Paul I of Russia, by Roderick E. McGrew. Oxford, 1993.

Peter the Great: His Life and Work, by Robert K.. Massie. Abacus.

Soviet Colossus: History of the USSR, by Michael Kort. M.E. Sharp, 1993.

Stalin, Man of Contradiction, by K.N. Cameron. Strong Oak Press, 1989.

Stalinism and After: Road to Gorbachev, by Alec Nove. Routledge, 1993

POLITICS

Against the Grain, by Boris Yeltsin. Jonathan Cape, 1990.

Glasnost in Action, by A. Nove. Unwin Hyman, 1989.

Lenin's Tomb, by David Remnick. Viking, 1993.

The Other Russia, by Michael Glenny and Norman Stone. Faber and Faber, 1990.

Perestroika, by M.S. Gorbachev. Fontana, 1987.

Soviet Union: Politics, Economics and Society, by R.J. Hill. Pinter Publishers, 1989.

Towards a Better World, by M.S. Gorbachev. Richardson and Steirman, 1987.

Voices of Glasnost, by S. Cohen and K. van den Heuvel. Norton, 1989.

BIOGRAPHY/MEMOIRS

Alone Together, by Elena Bonner. Collins Harvill, 1986.

An English Lady at the Court of Catherine the Great, edited by A.G. Gross. Crest Publications, 1989.

The Gulag Archipelago, by Alexander Solzhenitsyn. Collins Harvill, 1988.

The House by the Dvina, by Eugenie Fraser. Corgi, 1986.

In the Beginning, by Irina Ratushinskaya. Hodder & Stoughton, 1990.

Into the Whirlwind. Within the Whirlwind, by Eugenia Ginzburg. Collins Harvill, 1989.

The Making of Andrei Sakharov, by G. Bailey. Penguin, 1990.

On the Estate: Memoirs of Russia Before the Revolution, edited by Olga Davydoff Bax. Thames & Hudson, 1986.

Russia: Despatches from the Guardian Correspondent in Moscow, by Martin Walker. Abacus, 1989.

Ten Days that Shook the World, by John Reed. Penguin, first published 1919.

ART

Folk Art in the Soviet Union. Abrams/Aurora, 1990.

The Hermitage. Aurora, 1987.

History of Russian Painting, by A. Bird. Phaidon, 1987.

The Irony Tower, by Andrew Solomon. Knopf.

The Kremlin and its Treasures, by Rodimzeva, Rachmanov and Raimann. Phaidon, 1989.

Masterworks of Russian Painting in Soviet Museums. Aurora, 1989.

New Worlds: Russian Art and Society 1900-3, by D. Elliott. Thames & Hudson, 1986.

Russian Art of the Avant Garde, by J.E. Bowlt. Thames & Hudson, 1988.

Russian Art from Neoclassicism to the Avant Garde, by D. V. Sarabianov. Thames & Hudson, 1990.

Street Art of the Revolution, Tolstoy, V. I. Bibikova and C. Cooke. Thames & Hudson, 1990.

TRAVEL & NATURAL HISTORY

Among the Russians, by Colin Thubron. Penguin, first published 1983.

Atlas of Russia and the Soviet Union, by R. Millner-Gulland, with N. Dejevsky. Phaidon, 1989.

The Big Red Train Ride, by Eric Newby. Picador, 1989.

Caucasian Journey, by Negley Farson. Penguin, first published 1951.

Epics of Everyday Life, by Susan Richards. Penguin, 1991.

First Russia, Then Tibet, by Robert Byron. Penguin, first published 1933.

The Food and Cooking of Russia, by Lesley Chamberlain. Penguin, 1982.

Imperial Splendour, by George Galitzine. Viking 1991.

Journey into Russia, by Laurens van der Post. Penguin, first published 1964.

The Natural History of the USSR, by Algirdas Kynstautas. Century Hutchinson, 1987.

The Nature of the Russia, by John Massey Stewart. Boxtree, 1992.

The New Russians, by Hedrick Smith. Vintage 1990.

Portrait of the Soviet Union, by Fitzroy Mclean. Weidenfeld and Nicolson, 1988.

Russia. Bracken Books, 1989.

Russia, with Tehran, Port Arthur and Peking, by Karl Baedeker, 1914.

Sailing to Leningrad, by Roger Foxall. Grafton, 1990.

The Taming of the Eagles: Exploring the New Russia, by Imogen Edwards-Jones. Photographs by Joth Shakerley. Weidenfeld & Nicolson, 1993.

The Trans-Siberian Rail Guide, by Robert Strauss. Compass, 1993.

The USSR: From an Original Idea by Karl Marx, by Marc Polansky and Russell Taylor. Faber and Faber, 1983.

Ustinov in Russia, by Peter Ustinov. Michael O Mara Books, 1987.

LITERATURE & FICTION

A Hero of Our Time, by Mikhail Lermontov. Penguin.

And Quiet Flows the Don and *The Don Flows Home to the Sea*, by Mikhail Sholokov.

Children of the Arbat, by Anatoli Rybakov. Hutchinson, 1988.

Crime and Punishmentt, The Brothers Karamazov and *The Idiot*, by Fyodr Dostoevsky. Penguin.

Dead Soul, by Nikolai Gogol

Doctor Zhivago, by Boris Pasternak. Penguin.

Eugene Onegin, by Alexander Pushkin. Penguin.

Fathers and Sons, by Ivan Turgenev. Penguin.

Lady with Lapdog and other Stories, by Anton Chekhov. Penguin.

The Master and Margarita, by Mikhail Bulgakov.

The Penguin Book of Russian Short stories, edited by David Richards. Penguin, 1981.

The Russia House, by John le Carré. Coronet, 1990.

War and Peace and *Anna Karenina*, by Leo Tolstoy. Penguin.

We, by Evgeny Zamyatin. Penguin.

OTHER INSIGHT GUIDES

Other *Insight Guides* which highlight destinations in this region are:

Insight Guides to the *Baltic State*s, *Eastern Europe*, *Moscow* and *St Petersbur*g provide exhaustive coverage and stunning photography of these increasingly popular destinations.

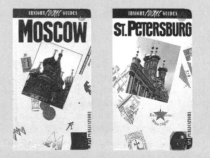

Insight Pocket Guides to *Moscow* and *St Petersburg*, designed for visitors keen to make the most of a short stay, provide carefully timed itineraries to these stars in Russia's crown.

ART/PHOTO CREDITS

INDEX